Child Decoded

Child Decoded

Unlocking
complex issues in
your child's
learning, behavior
or attention

Edited by:

Robin E. McEvoy, PhD, Kim Gangwish
& Marijke Jones

Child Decoded: Unlocking Complex Issues in Your Child's Behavior, Learning and Attention
Published by L.E.A.R.N., LLC
Louisville, CO

Library of Congress Control Number: 2016946558

Authors:
McEvoy, PhD, Robin E.
Gangwish, Kim
Jones, Marijke

Child Decoded: Unlocking Complex Issues in Your Child's Behavior, Learning and Attention

ISBN: 978-0-9976165-0-7

PSYCHOLOGY / Developmental / Child
EDUCATION / Behavioral Management

QUANTITY PURCHASES: Schools, companies, professional groups, clubs, and other organizations may qualify for special terms when ordering quantities of this title. For information, contact authors through www.ChildDecoded.com.

For all the families who wouldn't give up

Contents

Acknowledgments

This book was such a labor of love, and so much more work than we ever envisioned! Huge thanks to everyone who helped our ambitious idea grow up to become a real book.

We especially wish to express our gratitude to: each and every author who contributed his or her time, expertise, and patience to this project – this would not exist without you; Debby Hamilton and Mark Baker, for their insight into the challenges and pitfalls of self-publishing; Dick Fischer, for his advice and support; Linda Halvorsen, for her support, publishing expertise, and willingness to take our calls at all hours; Lori de Boer, for keeping Marijke sane and helping her relocate her muse when necessary; our friends, families, colleagues, and clients for reading endless versions of chapters and for their honest feedback; Rachel Moran and Polly Letofsky for their assistance in getting this across the finish line; every client or friend who was generous enough to share their child's story; and finally, every stranger that we waylaid for feedback on airplanes, at parties, and random other confined spaces where you were stuck with us!

An Interview with Kim Gangwish and Robin McEvoy

Why did you decide to write this book?

Robin: For me, it was the phone time. I have countless conversations with parents who don't know what to do. However, over the years I have seen that I am often not the most effective starting point. Rather than waste families' time and money, I like to talk to parents for a bit before going ahead and scheduling an appointment. Sometimes there are foundational issues that need to be addressed before it's productive to figure out the cognitive, learning, or attention issues. At other times, it is a much more specific problem that does not need the comprehensive exploration that I do. I wanted to empower families to find their own starting point without having to wait for me to catch up on my phone calls.

Kim: I have a lot of those conversations too. Basically, we started this book because we wanted it to exist and no one else had done it! I tried to find an existing resource I could recommend to parents, but was frustrated by the lack of scope. Robin and I spent many hours, on many Saturdays, searching bookstores and Amazon.com for books that might help, but didn't find anything suitable. People only write about their particular area of expertise. It's good info, but not complete; they're only looking through their own lens. I see so many parents who are at their wits' end trying to find answers, and no one was looking at the overall picture. Way too many kids were coming through my door demoralized after multiple therapies that didn't work, or that didn't do enough. If you catch them earlier in the process with the right therapies, it's so much kinder to children's self-esteem, parents' checkbooks, and everyone's stress levels.

What kinds of things were you seeing in your clients that you didn't think were being addressed elsewhere?

Kim: Patterns. I felt that no one was looking at the larger patterns in a child's profile. Because my work is alternative and not well known, I am often the last-ditch thing they'll try. I get to see what worked and what didn't, what kinds of things other practitioners tried, where kids seemed to be getting stuck. Also, because my work is broad by nature, addressing how the neurology as a whole is working and where it isn't, I started to see patterns in where kids' progress got hung up. For instance, I can't tell you how many children I've seen who just couldn't seem to get past a certain point in vision therapy. Well, if the vestibular and proprioceptive parts of their sensory systems are off, vision is not going to fall into line easily. But there doesn't seem to be a lot of understanding between the specialties.

I also see correlations between biomedical issues, like food reactions, and lack of response or wildly inconsistent response to therapies. One day it all seems to work, or at least be improving, and the next day that same child can't do the same task to save his life. It's the same for sensory processing issues. I see a lot of practitioners give up because they are not trained to spot these kinds of issues and don't know what else to try. It's not that their work won't help, but the child's system might not be ready to respond to those therapies yet. Those deeper issues need to be addressed first. I've seen hundreds of parents finally feel like they're getting somewhere when they target the right problems first.

Robin: I've had so many parents call me about children with complex needs. These parents had thoroughly pursued every avenue of Western standard of care approaches – psychiatry (often more than one psychiatrist), psychology (often multiple evaluators and therapists), Individual Education Plan at school. And still their child was struggling mightily and no one had a next step. Initially, neither did I. So I started looking past standard of care into diet, sleep, sensory processing, and other areas that were not the traditional avenues in which I had been trained. I could not bear to tell a parent there was nothing else to be done when I was not sure that was true. I became well versed in certain questions. If a parent was lamenting that the Ritalin (or any of the four other medications they had tried) was not effective enough for her child's attention problems, I would ask, "Does he have eczema? Are you cutting tags out of his clothes? How is his sleep?" These questions might lead us to some avenues of treatment that might each be worth 10-15 percent of the problem. Now they were moving forward again. I started becoming less interested in finding a diagnosis and more interested in unraveling the larger picture, even if some of what I find doesn't have a convenient label.

Kim: Once you start to see those kinds of patterns, they show up everywhere. I now ask a stock set of questions that clue me into what's going on for the child overall. They might not look related to his symptoms, but they are the key to finding answers. The two most common things parents say to me now are "How did you know?" and "I wish I'd known this five years ago!"

What's the main takeaway you want parents to have?

Kim: Even with a child who has a hard-to-resolve issue or a confusing blend of issues, there's hope. But you might have to look beyond the comfort of clear diagnoses or going with the recommended therapies or drugs. You might have to dig deeper. I know it makes things seem more overwhelming at first, when the picture gets bigger and messier and less easily classifiable. But sometimes that's where the true answers are.

I also want parents to appreciate the complexity of what they're trying to do. I hear a lot of people say, "We've been doing this for six months!" like they can't believe how long it's taking. But looking beneath the symptoms and rebuilding the way your child functions from a deeper level takes time. It's not a quick fix. It can be done, which is actually very exciting. It's amazing what's possible with modern resources and our current understanding of neuro-plasticity. However, I feel like a lot of people give up or get really stressed and discouraged, and I want them to have a more realistic grasp of the process so that they can stay hopeful and positive.

Robin: And also, consider what is possible for your particular child. We may never shift a very active child into sitting quietly for six hours a day. Academics, or a particular area of it, may never be his primary strength. But with changes in the child, as well as in the classroom approach, we can likely help him to be more successful and confident. Our society has a lot of different jobs, so we need lots of different types of minds. Even if a child is not a great fit for the classroom, it does not mean he will not find a great career that suits him just fine.

Section One

GETTING STARTED

———◆———

THIS SECTION GIVES AN IMPORTANT OVERVIEW of what this book offers and how you can get the most out of it. Chapter 2, in particular, will help you create the profile that most closely fits your unique child. Please take the time to do the Master Checklist in that chapter. Don't be surprised if your checklist results suggest that you read about topics that you had not previously considered. The whole point is to discover how to decode your unique child and the overall picture might not be what you have come to believe. New insights may reveal unforeseen perspectives about what's going on, which in turn may point you towards unexplored – and hopefully more helpful – avenues of support!

———◆———

ONE

CJ's Story

I. Forebodings and Fiascos

My son was an enigma from the start. CJ was noticeably late for every possible developmental milestone: sitting up, walking, talking. He never crawled on all fours, preferring a sort of arms-only commando crawl instead. But he seemed to understand what was happening around him astoundingly early, displayed an impish sense of humor before he could speak, and often unnerved people by looking deeply and knowingly into their eyes.

"Whoa, is he an alien?" a friend asked once. "Your baby just probed my soul!"

Once he hit school age, a dozen red flags lit up for me, but I couldn't seem to get anyone else to take them seriously. It was like a nightmare where you're screaming at everyone about the meteor that's about to hit, but they can't hear you above the party music.

His behavior was inexplicable, never seeming to fit a pattern. He always appeared to understand the material, but couldn't finish an assignment to save his life. At recess, he either made up elaborate games that others could barely follow, or watched the other children, looking confused. In the classroom, he had trouble following the simplest instructions. Connection with others was wildly inconsistent: Teachers swooned over his killer smile and bubbly humor, but he seemed mystified by his peers (and vice versa). He was enthusiastic (if unproductive) all day in school, always bidding his teachers goodbye by saying, "I had a great, great, *great* day!" Then he came home and collapsed. Homework was torture for all of us.

Whenever I expressed concern, teachers always reassured me. "Oh, he's fine," they'd say. "We can tell he's smart. Boys develop at a different rate than girls, you know." (If I never hear that line again, it will be too soon.) One master teacher that we sought as a consultant patted my hand, gave me a knowing smile and said, "I think the problem is that his mother worries too much."

I tried to believe them, but my gut told me otherwise.

From kindergarten through third grade, we tried different school models, including a brief stint homeschooling, but it never really changed anything. We both had high hopes for third grade, when he began at a school that used a lot of hands-on manipulatives and encouraged children to go at their own pace. Both he and I may still be recovering from that year.

The usual problems of unfinished work and never knowing the instructions plagued CJ, but he was now so constantly overwhelmed and spaced out that the bullying began. *Why don't you use your brain, CJ! You can't be in our group; you're too stupid. Yeah, you can play with us – it's all of us against you, OK?* It goes without saying that he wasn't invited to a single birthday party, and I went on every field trip I could so that he would have someone to hang out with.

It was the social struggles that finally got my husband on board. Doug had had a bit of a "life's rough sometimes, he'll be fine" attitude, but I convinced him to go observe CJ in the classroom. He returned looking devastated.

"He was being bullied by this kid who was almost a foot shorter than he was," Doug said in amazement. "He just couldn't track anything that was happening around him. This kid started teasing him and CJ knew it felt bad, but it looked like he didn't have a clue what was going on or how to respond. It was so painful to watch!" *Yep. Welcome to my nightmare.*

The constant academic and social stress wore CJ down to an alarming degree. My sweet, bubbly boy with the impish sense of humor became glassy-eyed and unresponsive, slumped in a defeated heap against the car door on the way home from school.

"He always understands the material," his teacher told me in one of our all-too-frequent meetings. "In fact, when I talk to him, he's obviously quite bright. There's no learning disorder that I can see. He just needs to learn to work faster and pay attention better. He'll get there. You know, boys develop at a slower rate…" *Oh, spare me.* Our meetings continued, but never seemed to lead to new insights or strategies. I had no idea what other questions to ask, but the "answers" I was getting seemed in no way adequate to explain the pain, struggle, and shutdown I was seeing in my son.

My heart contracted as I watched him withdraw a bit further into his own personal little fog zone every day. Sleep became a regular battle; we were up at night with him more than when he was an infant. He had exactly one friend, but was too tired to play with her outside of school. I made sure we did fun family activities whenever possible, but inside I was dying. My gut developed a permanent clench. My beautiful child seemed to be withering in front of my eyes and I felt helpless to stop it.

II. Answers…But Few Solutions

Finally, in the spring of that endless, miserable third-grade year, someone told me about a special education expert who could reportedly decode any kid. She was reputed to excel in complicated kids like my son. Good enough for me! We made the appointment and CJ showed up gamely, ready for a new adventure, making his favorite stuffed dog answer the questions. She proceeded to put him through a few hours of testing that wiped him out for the rest of the day.

The results gave us an overwhelming amount of information. For what felt like hours, the tester explained the significance of all the test results. I had no idea brain function was so complicated or that there were so many potential glitches. By the end, I could practically hear my own neurons sizzling as I tried to cope with the ocean of new information.

But at least we finally had some clear data. First of all, she explained, CJ was twice exceptional (gifted but with learning disabilities – who knew?). In an IQ test, people's subtest results will usually fall within the same range, even if they are, say, good at math but bad at English. Having one subtest that is significantly out of range of the others may indicate a learning disorder. Serious discrepancy *throughout* the test indicates 1) a brain that is not working in harmony and 2) a very frustrated and confused child.

CJ's results were either all the way at the top (particularly abstract thinking and 3D spatial skills) or all the way at the bottom (such as coding, which relates to handwriting, and rote memory – both of which apparently live in parts of the brain that never got plugged in because he ranked at a dismal first percentile).

"He's one of the five most twice exceptional children I have ever seen," said the tester, an expert on twice exceptional children. "He's highly intelligent, possibly brilliant, and understands things completely and quickly. But his deficits make output very difficult and exhausting for him. He's demonstrating a tiny fraction of what he understands. It's like having both the accelerator and the brake on all the time."

"I won't lie," she continued. "It'll be a tough road. But with proper support, these kids really come into their own in college." *College?!* My brain froze. *As in, the thing that comes after high school? But I don't even know how to get him through fourth grade!*

Some of the most revealing specifics about him were the following:

🖐 Severe dysgraphia meant that trying to write by hand brought his whole brain to a screeching halt. This explained why he rarely finished a writing assignment (but his handwriting – before he hit the wall – was beautiful, if labored, so no one thought of a writing disorder).

- His rote memory weakness ensured that he would struggle forever with basic math facts (among other things), which is what most of elementary math education is all about.
- Although he had quite a high verbal understanding, even testing at a college level for reading comprehension, he had tremendous trouble finding words himself. "He orients to the world visually and has a deep *sense* of things, but translating his understanding into words may always be difficult for him." That, right there, explained a great deal, confirming my sense since early on, that words were somehow not his first language.
- He displayed slow, but steady, processing speed overall. "That's not one that's going to change, I'm afraid," she informed me. "Processing speed tends to stay steady throughout life." And with all the other problems slowing him down even more… well, it was a wonder he had ever gotten *anything* done in school. (By the way: that was, thankfully, one thing she turned out to be wrong about.)
- On the plus side, his 3D spatial skills – tested by having him solve three-dimensional puzzles – blew even the tester away. "He got them all," she said, adding apologetically, "But I had to take off points because he did some of them upside down. I asked him about those, just to see if he knew they were upside down and he said he wanted the hard ones to be the right way up so I could see them." *Whoa.*
- A separate test with another practitioner revealed Auditory Processing Disorder, which impaired his ability to register verbal input properly, and which had made most of the school day into a confusing, disjointed wall of sound. It also explained why he never knew what the instructions were, or sometimes, that they had even been delivered.
- Yet another evaluation revealed severe Sensory Processing Disorder, which explained a great deal about why he always seemed so exhausted and spaced out. The occupational therapist who tested him recommended some classroom supports, which made no noticeable difference besides increasing the teasing. Although she would have been happy to work with CJ, it was a very long drive and I hoped the classroom supports would be enough. They weren't, but it wasn't until years later that I understood why.

Both kinds of processing disorders (the last two in the previous list) explained his constant overwhelm, which would tip over into complete meltdown in the face of something as stimulating as a birthday party or even a particularly lively day in the classroom.

No wonder CJ was so wiped out! But even armed with so much new data, our meetings with the school were frustrating. Everyone was very sympathetic, but with his high scores canceling out his abysmally low ones, CJ had actually not tested badly enough to qualify for any services from the district.

He needed much more support than it looked like we could possibly get from the school (I found out, much later, that this was not entirely true), so we made the first of many decisions to abandon the usual route of schooling. At first I found myself panicking about "ditching normal," but clarity finally dawned on me: *He's not like everyone else. Stop trying to make this fish climb trees; he's not designed for it.* Education isn't supposed to wear your soul down. It's supposed to teach you how to learn, how to think, and that learning is exciting. So far, all it seemed to be teaching CJ was that he was stupid and weird.

Fortunately, fate had handed us the perfect place for our unique little fish. The woman who had done CJ's evaluation had started a school specifically for twice exceptional (or 2e) children. The tuition was way out of our range, but we took a deep breath, went into debt and signed up anyway. We just couldn't watch our son suffer any more. He was once known for his joy; more and more, he walked around in a spaced-out fog, slouching against walls and collapsing into chairs whenever he got the chance. So when the school opened in a lovely new space the following fall, CJ began his fourth-grade year there.

In so many ways, the new school was a welcome reprieve. Support started where a child was, not where he was *supposed* to be. CJ could read a book three grades above his age level and write a book report worthy of a second grader; that was normal for this demographic. Science class was all hands-on and college level; lab reports were both written (for the practice writing) and verbal (which was how they actually determined whether a student had understood). If CJ was too exhausted from the day to get through his homework, I wrote a note explaining this and we would catch up on the weekend.

Just as importantly, CJ no longer felt like the weirdest kid in the room all the time. Everyone had something they struggled with; issues showed up in different ways; when someone was having a tough time or even a meltdown, everyone understood. This alone helped shift a dangerous trend in his self-identity that had deeply concerned me. It also planted a seed of compassion in him that I still cherish. *Be nice. Everyone has his own hell.*

Overall, CJ seemed quite relieved not to be under such a constant crush of pressure. But during his fifth grade year – his second at that school – I slowly realized that he was not actually much happier or less wiped out, just less actively stressed. He was treading water instead of drowning, which was an improvement for sure – everything is relative – but he was still a long way from learning with enthusiasm or actually being, you know . . . *happy.*

I started seeing more signs that maybe it was time for Plan J, whatever that might turn out to be.

One morning, after I had let him sleep late, he went bounding into the classroom with what I considered to be his usual joie de vivre and beaming smile. His homeroom teacher was shocked.

"Wow, what happened to him?" she asked, bemused. "I don't think I've ever seen him in such a good mood!" *Really?* I thought. *Because that's who he's been since he was born.* If he was never like that at school, that was worrisome to say the least.

Another day soon after, I found myself chatting with a new mother at the school. Her daughter Emily had autism, but was high-functioning.

"CJ's autistic too, right?" she asked knowingly. "He and Emily have that same look, like they're really on Pluto or something. I'm so glad she found someone else from the same planet!" she laughed.

"Uh, no," I stammered, shocked. '"He's not on the autism spectrum."

The Importance of Community

That school, which sadly no longer exists, brought surprising bonuses for me as well as for CJ. Aside from not at all missing the weekly "what's wrong with my kid" meetings, I suddenly found myself in a community of parents that knew what it meant to wander through this strange, mapless territory. "So, what are *you* in for?" we'd ask each other, sounding like prison inmates. But there was sweetness in the shared dark humor, compassion as we listened to each other's universal tales of exhaustion and confusion and school disasters and uncomprehending family members and "fun" excursions that had gone horribly wrong. We understood each other's worlds and daily battles, and the sheer relief of knowing we weren't alone lightened our hearts.

We were the parents who didn't even consider taking our kids to the Chuck E. Cheese birthday parties because we knew that in five minutes, our kids would be either catatonic or crazed. We were the ones who explained to camp counselors what little Sarah or Patrick might need, making the counselors roll their eyes and mutter about "helicopter parents" – only to find little Sarah or Patrick sobbing in a corner when we went to pick them up. Ours were the kids other parents would describe as *too sensitive*, as if there was a thing in the world we could do about it. You could spot our children on the soccer field in a second, watching caterpillars and looking up in great surprise when the ball came by. It had been cute in first grade, but that was long ago. The phone rang and our stomachs tightened, knowing that it might be the school saying we had to come pick up our child early.

We worked overtime to hang onto the one or two friendships our children still had, others having fallen away because our kids just didn't seem able to sync with others their age. All of us had 101 tales of gritting our teeth when well-meaning but ignorant teachers, coaches, friends, and family members hinted, with various degrees of kindness, that we just needed to discipline our children better. Or teach them to "man up." Or whatever utterly useless advice might occur to them. When I took an informal poll of the other parents, I found that the average number of schools these families had tried was about one new school every two years. Some families had moved across the country for this program.

I started to realize just how isolated I had become. My friends had been caring, but no one had fully appreciated the extent of what we were dealing with and I had had no energy to press the point. I got tired of trying to explain the depth of the crisis to blank, uncomprehending faces and averted eyes. Often, I avoided contact because I was such a wreck and didn't want people to start avoiding me and my constant drama. After we left that school, I maintained a few essential friendships with those in the same boat, and even sporadic contact proved crucial to my morale and spirit.

I hope that you do better than I did, especially now that social media makes online community so much easier. It makes an enormous difference, and you will be a happier, more relaxed person if you seek it out. For many of us, the first things we drop in a crisis are the things we need most: self care and reaching out to community. We just don't think we have the time or energy, and we're too caught up in getting through each day to consider our own needs. But that school showed me what a lifeline it is to be surrounded by people who have been down the same weird, hard-to-describe rabbit hole you have. I hope, both for your sake and your child's, that you will find a way to give yourself that.

"Oh, really?" chimed in another mom, who had known CJ since he started at the school. "Huh. I always assumed that too. He's always so in his own world."

This small exchange shook me. Had I gotten so used to CJ's shutdown that it had become the new normal? Or was part of me just so tired of fighting and researching and stressing, that I was hoping it would...what, just work itself out? Were we doing *anything* right?

One afternoon, CJ came home upset that he had bombed a math test.

"What happened?" I asked. He had known that unit cold.

"This stupid fly was buzzing around the room the whole time. I couldn't concentrate."

The situation just didn't seem sustainable. The sensory supports and specialized atmosphere were great, but we couldn't keep CJ in a bubble for the rest of his life lest the presence of a mere fly disrupt his ability to think straight.

I felt overwhelmed and defeated. What was it going to take to get this child through? My file of evaluation results and notes was as thick as a New York City phone book, but somehow even that had not given us enough answers. I started having dreams that CJ was being sucked under giant waves, over and over, looking at me with anguished eyes that seemed to say, "Why aren't you helping me?" I stood by, stricken and helpless, holding the answer no parent wants to admit: *I don't know how.*

Numb from the constant desperation, we went into regroup mode once again. We let ourselves be guided by two questions: Was this the best we could do? And, was it working for CJ? The answer to the second question was definitely *no*. That had to mean that the answer to the first was no as well. But now what?

III. Trusting Myself, Trusting My Child

Making the decision to homeschool involved taking a lot of very deep breaths. If a specialized school with trained personnel had had limited success, who was I to think I could do better?

I'm his mother, dammit, I told myself. *And at this point I have a freaking ton of information from experts. But more importantly, I know my son. I know who he is under all the issues. And what he needs right now – more than the right school or to be on track with math or to learn how to write a book report – is to become that kid again.* I just didn't see how he was going to get anywhere at all without that.

CJ was 11 years old and had yet to experience school in a positive way. We were all in desperate need of a little recovery time. In order to help myself through the occasional anxiety attacks about abandoning any kind of normal path, I kept a card at my desk that read, "What is the priority *right now?*"

We threw away all the thoughts of where he "should" be and focused on two things: getting the intensive therapeutic support he apparently needed, and helping him find the joy in life again. It seemed strange to use joy as a barometer for progress, but I felt I had to trust in CJ's innate desire to participate in life. By *joy*, I do not mean "having fun." It was more about letting his natural curiosity emerge, trusting that his inherent human desire for expression, exploration, and success would guide us both to the paths *he* needed.

Slowly, a plan took shape; an unorthodox one, to be sure, but one that seemed to fit CJ.

First, since CJ's sensory processing issues seemed so severe, we found a clinic that did extensive sensory integration therapy and discovered several things we hadn't known. While the specialized school had always acknowledged CJ's SPD (Sensory Processing Disorder) and provided wonderful allowances and supports for it, no one had ever spelled out three very important points.

1. SPD is very treatable. Some kids seem destined never to be completely free of it, but with appropriate treatment you should see significant improvement at least.
2. *However*, if you don't aggressively treat it, it doesn't ever resolve on its own. Kids don't grow out of it and in-class supports are not, by themselves, enough to make actual progress.
3. If you don't address SPD, higher learning functions are not likely to improve much either.

"SPD happens on the foundational level of the nervous system," explained the occupational therapist who ran the clinic. "You can't build a house, let alone make renovations, until you have a strong foundation." After an in-depth crash course in "SPD and Our Son," Doug and I left the assessment meeting with dazed looks and pages of therapy protocols that needed to be done every day. Several times a day. This was a whole lifestyle change!

We sat in stunned silence on the long drive home. "You'd think someone could have mentioned that before," Doug finally said.

We discovered other significant things, too. The main one was food allergies. On a hunch, our doctor had run a panel on CJ that revealed egg and dairy allergies. He had never shown digestive symptoms, but those foods had apparently been derailing his brain chemistry for years. After a few egg- and dairy-free weeks, a portion of the fog CJ had been perpetually living in cleared dramatically and his energy improved. (He calls it "brain snot" – "It's thicker than fog, Mom" – and, after proving to himself several times that it actually does make a major difference, he stopped trying to cheat on his new diet.)

So began our new life. For the SPD, we brushed CJ's skin and did heavy physical activity five times a day. CJ used a home listening program daily to address the auditory processing issues. I carted him around to a lot of appointments, including vision therapy and speech therapy and craniosacral therapy to support his nervous system through all the changes. (Not all of that should have been done at the same time, however; when you read this book, you'll see why). We found CJ a mentor, an amazing guy who taught martial arts and ancient wisdom and was a wizard at helping kids celebrate their uniqueness.

We spent a lot of time outdoors and found wonderful homeschool groups that did projects together. We also watched and discussed educational videos that CJ chose. I think he can still quote the one on quantum physics. Gradually, after several months, we incorporated more *school* into the homeschool scenario. His portfolio was unusual, but thorough – he and

I took turns choosing topics, so mythical beasts and weird deep-sea creatures sat alongside the Revolutionary War and human physiology on the list. CJ also learned to type on a keyboard, and the world of writing and independent work began to open up to him.

And slowly, the boy I knew came back to life. He laughed more, revealed the full extent of his imagination and goofy sense of humor, showed more initiative and interest in the world. He learned magic tricks and performed them to anyone he could corner. During the many transit hours we logged, he made menageries of brightly colored creatures out of pipe cleaners and constructed elaborate worlds for them. We had never been able to play board games because he would fall apart when he lost, but he learned to deal with his emotions and discovered that he enjoyed them after all. He even started beating me regularly at spelling-related games, which was shocking because he had always had so much trouble with spelling. But because of the way he could turn things inside out mentally, he could see possibilities for rearranging the letters that I could not. I began to breathe deeply for what felt like the first time in years. My gut, where I hold most of my stress, began to think about relaxing.

When he was 12, CJ discovered the sport of fencing at a summer camp. I can barely describe how huge this was. Fencing was his very own activity, something he did for no other reasons than he was startlingly good at it and loved it. It wasn't therapy or an activity designed to "fix" him. The fencing community admired his skill and potential, but knew nothing of his struggles. He was just CJ there. It was an unexpected miracle, something I hadn't known to look for and am grateful for still.

National fencing competitions have continued to be a major part of his life to this day, and I think they have played a central role in building his confidence and independence (not to mention his ability to concentrate in a crowded, noisy room – something that would have been unthinkable a few short years earlier). I have come to believe that finding something like this – something a child really loves, no matter what oddball, un-academic thing it may be – is every bit as important as all the academic supports in the world. Passion for something can be the most therapeutic, motivating, healing thing you can find. It's a way to reach out to life. Ultimately, isn't that what we really want our children to do?

After two years, CJ wanted to return to school. He was 13. Time to see if the transformation would hold.

IV. The Light at the End of the Tunnel

Occupational therapists have a concept they call the *just-right challenge*. When a person is trying to rehabilitate, too little challenge will not do anything and too much will only cause overwhelm and collapse. You want to find that *just right* quality, where the task feels just a teeny bit past what you can do, but then you find you can do it. So you keep pushing, and you keep getting a little bit better, and one day you realize you've gotten pretty darn strong.

CJ had too often experienced collapsing under too much challenge. Finding a place that would represent his just-right challenge felt crucial. As Doug put it, "I don't think he has another school disaster in him." This made the stakes a little higher.

Unexpectedly, we found a relatively new middle/high school in the area that had a very high teacher-to-student ratio, that focused on building community and learning in an engaged way in the real world, and that emphasized quality, meaningful work over quantity. Moreover, this would be the first year they had a middle school, so all the eighth graders would be new, not just CJ.

Overall, it seemed just right. Finally.

Not that it was always pretty. For much of the first year, CJ got in the car at the end of the day looking hammered, but he was always able to rally. He took six months off from his beloved fencing while he tried to decide if he wanted it badly enough to make it work with the new demands on his time and energy. Dealing with social conflicts or misunderstandings was sometimes rough.

But my biggest concern was the trips. The school went on a lot of trips, including a 10-day backpacking expedition for the whole school in the beginning of every year. I was already concerned about CJ having the stamina to get through an entire school day without all of his usual breaks. How would he survive TEN days without a break? Would he be sentenced to being The Weird Kid forever if he had a huge meltdown, or just shut down? Would he lose every single thing he brought? We had fought long and hard to get to this precarious place. Would he come back defeated by an experience that other kids his age could handle? Would this be the final school disaster that he just couldn't get back up from?

You know that crouch you develop when a child is in that wobbly, almost-walking phase, where they constantly look like they're about to topple over, and you're always ready to catch them? I spent most of CJ's eighth grade year in the emotional equivalent of that crouch, always ready to advocate on his behalf, to give him a pep talk, or to give him a mental health day if he felt he needed it. (He never took me up on that offer.) I felt tentatively relieved whenever he cleared some hurdle or other, but flared into full "dread mode" when things weren't going well. *Please don't let him withdraw, don't let him shut down, help him hang in there*, I prayed to whomever might be the patron saint of overwhelmed children. It took a while for me to trust that we were really out on the other side. Frankly, it took a while before we were.

But I had briefed the teachers on his issues and, although I'm sure they saw me as hugely overprotective, they listened patiently and did a wonderful job of supporting him. One, in particular, noticed something about CJ's circular, sometimes random-seeming way of talking about things: If you gave him enough time and persistent gentle questioning, you would start to see where he was really going and how it related to the subject. His insights, once you figured out what they were, often brought the discussion to a whole new level. Once that teacher understood more about how CJ's mind worked, the rest of the class started to see it too. They began to show a level of patience and respect that he had never experienced, which boosted his confidence and allowed him to speak up more, which in turn gave him more practice, so that his thoughts came out in increasingly coherent ways. It was the first truly positive cycle I had ever seen in his school career.

More importantly, no matter how difficult an experience was, he always came out of it with enough victories to make him want to try again. He liked the other students, the teachers, the philosophy of the school. He had an understanding of his issues and had learned tools to take care of himself. He *wanted* to make it work. So – clumsily, doggedly, gradually – he did.

There were many welcome surprises.

First of all, those trips I had worried about so much changed his life. The backpacking trips were a just-right challenge that required lots of heavy physical work, perfect for his sensory needs. They also taught him a resilience and responsibility for self (both his stuff and his internal state) that all the OT in the world couldn't have created. By senior year, he had gotten a scholarship for a month-long NOLS (National Outdoor Leadership School) expedition in the Yukon. He still backpacks with friends for fun.

Other journeys opened the world for him. The school studied urban planning in the city and marine biology in California. CJ spent time with the Navajo in Wyoming and the Tarahumara Indians in Mexico, experiencing a kinship with both that he often didn't feel with his own peers. Service projects introduced them to communities all over the area. CJ learned that there are millions of communities that make up this world, millions of ways to express and experience and connect. To a child whose main experience in life had been of feeling like he was on the wrong planet, this came as eye-opening, heart-lifting news.

Second, he showed a remarkable gift for complex synthesis and public speaking. We were fortunate that his school made an extra effort to build on a student's strengths, whatever they may be; but one part of the curriculum, in particular, turned out to be perfect for bringing out CJ's talents. Final term projects involved both written work and a lengthy presentation, where students were expected to synthesize information from the semester under the umbrella of their own perspective. The presentation rubric was a mile long and required visual components as well as verbal. It was a big deal. Students spent weeks preparing. An adult would have found it challenging.

To everybody's astonishment, CJ produced compelling, sophisticated talks with a rapid-fire collage of digital visuals accompanying him. He was riveting and never once looked at his notes. By his senior year, he had developed a distinctive style that people compared to TEDtalks. Doug and I sat in the audience, clutched each other's hands thought, *Where did that come from?*

But the thing that touched my heart most was his profound sense of compassion. CJ had been through a lot and knew what it felt like to be mocked, misunderstood, ostracized. Somewhere along the way, he made some internal commitment to make the world a kinder place than the one he had experienced. Teachers often commented on his kindness and inclusiveness. Struggling kids knew they had a friend in him.

At graduation, the head of school gave CJ a special prize for outstanding academic work and for being such a leader in the community. Doug squeezed my hand, and I knew we were both thinking the same thing: *My God, that was a long road. And every step was worth it.*

V. Epilogue, or How This Story Illustrates Why This Book Exists

So I have this son that I love to pieces, of whom I am inordinately proud, and who took more sweat equity and emotional investment than anything I have ever taken on in my life. And it worked. He made it. He's even in college across the country, where he manages classes, fencing, social life, and domestic skills all by himself (OK, I'm not actually sure how often he does his laundry, and I'm pretty sure he uses the floor as his closet, but he's hardly alone in that). And, although there will always be challenging aspects to his life, I do believe he's going to be OK. There were many times when I honestly did not believe I would ever speak or write that sentence.

But here's the thing. The number of brick walls and "if only I had knowns" in this story is heartbreaking. We wrote this book hoping to cut down on yours.

This is the book I wish I'd had and Robin and Kim are the guides I wish I'd found.

There are numerous resources out there for every need. Too many. Parents are busy being parents, trying to juggle other children and our own lives. We trust teachers, doctors, administrators, and therapists to give us the information we need, or at least to tell us what we need to research further.

As you can see, that doesn't always work out.

- Why did all of CJ's early teachers dismiss the warning signs? Why is it so hard to find other resources when you hit a dead end like that?
- Why didn't the school tell us we had other options for how to work within the system? (As you will see in the Advocacy Chapter, we did, although ultimately I think the route we took was the best for us.)

- Why did it take so long for anyone to mention the impact that food allergies could have?
- Why, even when people pointed out CJ's sensory processing issues, did they make it sound like a few classroom supports were all he needed?
- Why is there so little information on dysgraphia? Increasing numbers of children, especially boys, have tremendous trouble writing, yet no teacher suggested it because none had even heard of it before. (That's not a criticism of teachers, but of the woeful lack of information on formerly obscure conditions that are now showing up more and more.)
- The answers and supports CJ needed were always out there. Why was it such a long road to find out what he really needed, and a whole different long road to connect us to the right resources?

It's hard enough parenting kids with learning challenges, without adding the bizarre lack of coherent support and guidance that seems to exist.

Some children have more straightforward challenges – they are "just" dyslexic or have speech deficits or mild attention issues. I would never under-rate those challenges, and this book can still help you find the resources you need. But by and large, this book came about because of children who have a confusing mixture of issues that are hard to identify, sort out, and address. CJ had Auditory Processing Disorder, severe Sensory Processing Disorder, visual tracking problems, food sensitivities that affected his brain function, and dysgraphia, all muddled in with several cognitive and athletic gifts that further confused the picture. Kids like this are complicated, sensitive, intense, confounding. And they don't show up with handy little printouts coming out their ears that give you the code for what they need. It can be a very confusing process trying to figure it out, especially when so many things do such a great job of masquerading as Attention Deficit Disorder.

The world of learning and behavior disorders covers extensive territory. Expecting pediatricians and teachers to recognize and understand the full range of possibilities is often not realistic. They aren't specialists. And even when they do have useful information, they are rarely able to see the whole picture. There are simply too many possibilities involved. Even learning and behavior experts often see only their piece of the puzzle, like the blind men in the proverbial story who can only describe their own little piece of the elephant. This is fine and understandable, but more and more often, with the rise of complicated layers of dysfunctions, it can be very unhelpful.

The final profile for so many of these children is complex, with much of the truth beneath the surface. Ultimately, the specific "code" that makes your child who he is resides only in him. It often falls to the parent to hold the whole, unique overview and decide where the priorities are, what pieces still haven't been addressed, what course of action would be best.

We can't make you an expert on all of your child's issues in one book. That's not our goal. But we have put together a comprehensive resource that can help you identify the most likely issues that *your* child is facing, including a few you probably hadn't thought of, and point you in the right direction.

And most importantly, there is a sequence you can follow that is most likely to get results. This is a crucial piece that often gets overlooked. We could have saved ourselves a great deal of money, time, and anguish if we had understood that. We started at the top, as most parents and teachers do, working harder on homework and even changing schools. We then slowly moved down to finding and accommodating his auditory processing and sensory processing issues. We did not get guidance on actually *treating* the sensory issues until CJ was in middle school. We did not find the food sensitivities until after that. But his treatment should have started with those issues, down at the root of it all. The times CJ suffered because we didn't know what questions to ask or who could help, the times we exhausted ourselves and him trying to address too many issues at once, the sheer amount of CJ's childhood that was defined by frustration and unhappiness…it just didn't need to be that hard.

There's a way to do it better. Answers exist. You're going to have to make your own map, though, and this book can help.

And when you find the answers, you get this amazing bonus - that is, besides saving your family money, sanity, and time, and getting your child back. You see, once these kids *get* how they work, they are inevitably amazing and funny, insightful, and delightfully unconventional. They see things in a new way. Sometimes you have to give up on having them go through life like most of their peers. But if you can manage that mindset switch, and support them in their own uncharted course, they will rock your world.

CJ, with a great deal of help, found his way through the worst of his struggles. He is now confident, happy, and eager to find his way through life. From the bottom of my heart, I wish you and your family the same success. May this book help you get there!

About the Author

Marijke Jones is a freelance writer and editor, and one of the editors of this book. You can find her complete bio at the back.

TWO

How to Use This Book

and the Master Checklist

This book is designed to help you in a unique way. It doesn't just describe symptoms; it is solutions-oriented and also helps you figure out an overall game plan. You will get much more out of this book if you take the time to approach it methodically. Completing the Master Checklist before you dive into chapters will help you create a more meaningful overview of where you need to go. Then, as you accumulate information, you have a framework into which it fits.

Please keep in mind that this book is not a diagnostic guide. We created this distinctive format in order to help connect you to the resources that are *most likely* to be relevant to your child's issues. It is still necessary to find the right professionals who can assess and guide you.

In order to make the most out of this book, we suggest you follow these steps and keep this information in mind:

1. Go through the Master Checklist in this chapter carefully. You may not be sure of some of the answers, such as how your child reacts to various foods or how certain activities affect his behavior. It is hard to notice everything, and causal relationships can be difficult to spot if they aren't particularly dramatic. Food reactions, in particular, can be difficult to delineate from regular behavior. If necessary, take a few days to monitor your child's reactions more closely. Even then, it may be impossible to determine what stimulus leads to what behavior. Just do your best and keep an open mind when going through the checklists.

2. Occasionally, symptoms refer to another section as well, which is noted in italics after the symptom. Symptoms do not always represent only one category. If the symptom also pertains to another area, add it to your final tally in that other category as well. The final scoring section will tell you which categories your child probably needs to address.

3. After completing the Master Checklist, read the chapters to which you were directed. Chapters about disorders open with a more detailed list of symptoms, in order to help you determine whether that is indeed where you should be. Checklist formats vary because each disorder has different considerations to take into account. Each chapter includes information about the disorders themselves – what causes them (if that is known), what they look like, how they affect learning, and which practitioners can help. Because we have seen such success with many alternative treatment approaches, we have included both Western standard of care approaches and complementary and alternative medicine (CAM) for your consideration.

   Don't be discouraged if the checklists direct you to chapters that you never expected to be relevant. That's the point. For example, we expect many parents to end up reading Chapter 7: Sensory Processing Disorder, which should ultimately be empowering and revelatory. Learning and behavior disorders act like layers of color that combine to form one final color, but to treat them effectively you will need to identify all of the original contributing colors.

4. **We urge everyone to read Chapter 14: Biomedical Approaches and Chapter 15: Nutritional Approaches.** The media is increasingly awash with stories of relevant research about how probiotics can help stabilize brain chemistry, how gut health affects emotional stability and brain function, and so on. We have seen evidence of this for many years and think it is in everyone's best interest to better understand these issues.

5. So many children with learning or behavior issues struggle with social skills as well. This may or may not be directly related to their area of difficulty. Sometimes, getting through the day is so overwhelming that decoding the mysteries of social dynamics is just too much. If your child seems to have trouble interpreting social cues, responding to others appropriately, or making or keeping friends in general, you might be well served by reading Chapter 12: Social Skills Issues.

6. **Sequence matters.** Read the last part of this chapter, after the Master Checklist. This will help you understand the order that is most likely to be most effective, and why. This is probably the single most important thing to know when trying to help a complicated child. Trying to address everything at once will be ineffective and frustrating for all. You should probably discuss this with your physician or other qualified professional, in order to determine the best sequence and approach for your particular child's profile.

7. Read Chapter 18: Care Management, to help you start breathing again and create a plan of action!

Master Checklist

This checklist covers eight areas of developmental concern (with a few more specific concerns thrown in), as well as some of the more significant nutrition and biomedical markers. Go through each section of the checklist and mark any items that pertain to your child. Once completed, count up the number of checks per domain and put that number in the key code at the bottom of the checklist. If you have checked off at least five items in a given category, you should read the chapter that corresponds to that category. If you have marked more than three items in a section, you may still find the chapter helpful. This is particularly true for *Section 6*, which covers a range of less common issues. Every chapter has additional checklists to further refine your thinking.

Just like kids themselves, child development can get messy. Symptoms do not always divide up neatly into exclusive domains. There are a number of symptoms that might indicate different issues. Therefore, some symptoms in the checklist refer to another section in parentheses. If this occurs, count that symptom for each section indicated.

Two subcategories, Auditory Processing Disorder (APD) and Visual Processing Disorder (VPD), appear in acronym form after some symptoms. If you end up marking those symptoms, you may want to check those chapters as well. APD and VPD are lesser known, but increasingly common, issues. Both are often misdiagnosed as AD/HD, reading disorders, and other more well-known problems.

What should you do if your child's results do not have three to five checkmarks in any one category? This doesn't often happen when there is a true problem, but it can happen occasionally. Here are some ideas for you:

- If you see that your child clearly has a specific problem, (e.g., she fails all her major tests, but otherwise manages class demands), try looking at Chapter 10: Other Learning Disabilities, for less common issues, such as Executive Function Disorder. Some kids have a lot of good foundational skills like reading, paying attention, and socializing, but still struggle in ambiguous situations (which could include test taking).
- Try the checklist again; but this time, include behaviors your child used to exhibit, but has grown out of. There are usually some lingering effects in kids who had noticeable problems earlier in their development. You can also ask other caregivers such as teachers, coaches, or other parents to weigh in.
- If your child finds some part of his daily life very stressful or hard to manage (e.g., the normal school day or being part of a soccer team) but does not have many marks on the checklist, take a closer look at the stressful situation. Highly aggressive schools are not a good fit for some kids who are very sensitive or simply need to grow up at a slower rate. The same is true for highly competitive sports teams.

Section 1

- ☐ Easily distracted (APD)
- ☐ Chronic daydreaming/mind seems to wander elsewhere
- ☐ Does not follow through on tasks/chores/homework
- ☐ Careless mistakes in schoolwork
- ☐ Often off task
- ☐ Disorganized with tasks, loses track of steps (VPD)
- ☐ Loses things/disorganized with things
- ☐ Blurts answers out
- ☐ Talks excessively
- ☐ Impulsive, interrupts others, intrudes on others
- ☐ Typically fidgety and restless, squirmy, does not stay seated
- ☐ Active, on the go, seems to be driven by a motor
- ☐ Forgets to do homework, loses it, or fails to turn it in
- ☐ Loses track of conversation (Section 2, APD)
- ☐ Loses attention while reading (Section 3, VPD)
- ☐ Disruptive at school or group events (Section 8, Section 7)
- ☐ Has trouble concentrating (Section 9)

Total: _____

Section 2

- ☐ Late talker –first words after 20 months (Section 4)
- ☐ Articulation problem (e.g., only parent can understand child)
- ☐ Weak articulation (cannot make all speech sounds by age seven)
- ☐ Doesn't follow directions (or more than one step of the directions)
- ☐ Misunderstands verbal directions (APD)
- ☐ Uses words incorrectly or can't find the right word –"why come" instead of "how come" (after age three)
- ☐ Words out of order in sentence – ("Long time I've not been here")
- ☐ Uses the wrong tense in sentences
- ☐ Can't express him/herself in everyday situations (can't tell a story or explain a situation when he wants to)
- ☐ Dysfluent speech – stutters, starts over

Total: _____

Section 3

- ☐ Poor sense of rhyme (thinks *car* rhymes with *cat*)
- ☐ Trouble matching letters and the sounds they make (VPD)
- ☐ Can sing ABC song, but does not say the alphabet (Section 2)
- ☐ Confuses visually similar letters (e.g., b and d) (VPD, APD)
- ☐ Slow to learn to read
- ☐ Reading weaker than expected for intelligence or educational level
- ☐ Dislikes reading
- ☐ Slow choppy reading, frequently guesses at words
- ☐ Has difficulty sounding out words
- ☐ Slow reading speed (VPD)
- ☐ Poor comprehension of what is read
- ☐ Poor spelling (Section 6)

Total: _____

Section 4

- ☐ Rigid about sticking with routines or schedules
- ☐ Does not make eye contact when being spoken to
- ☐ Has no or very limited friendships (Section 7)
- ☐ Prefers solitary play or activities
- ☐ Play is repetitive (lines up cars, sorts toys, or only has one pretend play theme they will play)
- ☐ Has obscure obsessive interests (e.g., water towers)
- ☐ Regresses in language skills (stops using the words they have) or loses social interests (these changes often occur when the child is a toddler)
- ☐ Limited language skills
- ☐ Has good vocabulary, but poor communication skills (e.g., monologues instead of converses)
- ☐ Does not read nonverbal cues such as facial expressions or gestures
- ☐ Misreads social cues, can't take a hint, misses the joke
- ☐ Concrete linear thinker, very black and white
- ☐ Sleep disturbances, does not sleep well from infancy on

Total: _____

Section 5

- ☐ History of concussion
- ☐ Loss of consciousness
- ☐ Skull fracture
- ☐ Sudden decrease in school performance (Section 7, Section 9)
- ☐ Sudden increase in irritability, anger, or anxiety

Total: _____

Section 6

- ☐ Poor spelling (Section 3)
- ☐ Writing is labored and difficult to produce (VPD)
- ☐ Forgets punctuation, has grammar errors
- ☐ Dislikes writing
- ☐ Poor penmanship (Section 7, VPD)
- ☐ Poor coordination, clumsy, awkward
- ☐ Poor fine motor (can't tie shoes, immature drawing)
- ☐ Very verbal, but can't write or draw well
- ☐ Weak math concepts (can't tell which is bigger, 68 or 86)
- ☐ Poor memory for math facts
- ☐ Specific academic skills are weaker than expected for intelligence or other areas of learning
- ☐ Can't organize thoughts when writing, lack of clarity
- ☐ Poor sense of math sequencing – can't remember how to carry or re-group
- ☐ Appears gifted, but is underperforming at school (Section 1, Section 7)
- ☐ Socially awkward, talks too much, says the wrong thing (APD)

Total: _____

Section 7

- ☐ Early emotional disruption - adoption, loss of caregiver or sibling, experienced violence, other significant stress
- ☐ Traumatic medical history – child had surgery, severe illness or injury, chronic illness
- ☐ Daily tantrums past toddlerhood (Section 4)
- ☐ Intense; prone to meltdowns or tantrums (Section 9)
- ☐ Fearful of typical childhood events (sleepovers, first day of school)
- ☐ Takes little interest or pleasure in typical activities or friendships
- ☐ Has tantrums or meltdowns that disrupt the classroom or household

- ☐ Cries often and without good reason
- ☐ Cannot control worries
- ☐ Complains of being sick or in pain when faced with certain events (e.g., tests, projects, field trips)
- ☐ Extremely short fuse
- ☐ Lacks motivation or energy for most tasks
- ☐ Has panic reactions
- ☐ Worries constantly or commonly seems anxious

Total: _____

Section 8

- ☐ Over- or under-sensitive to clothing tags and textures (hates clothing tags or getting goo on fingers, or doesn't notice when covered with goo)
- ☐ Upset by unexpected light touch
- ☐ High tolerance for pain
- ☐ Chews on fingernails, shirt, pencil, or other objects
- ☐ Clumsy – falls or trips often, seems unaware of body in space
- ☐ Poor balance – fearful on bike or when climbing
- ☐ Gets dizzy or car sick easily or, conversely, never gets dizzy
- ☐ Poor motor planning – can't pump a swing, mount a bike, climb at playground in comparison to peers
- ☐ Sensitive to noise – easily distracted or melts down in crowds, upset by smoke alarms, sirens, fireworks (APD)
- ☐ Can't listen or concentrate with background noise (APD)
- ☐ Over- or under-sensitive to smell – either easily bothered or doesn't notice smells,
- ☐ Sensitive to oral textures – very fussy eater, refusing many foods
- ☐ Sensitive to taste or craves strong tastes
- ☐ Seeker of body input – rough play, crashes into things, hugs hard and often, jumps off of things, "bull in a china shop"
- ☐ Seeks vestibular input – swinging, spinning, being upside down
- ☐ Sensitive to bright lights, sunshine
- ☐ Avoids playing with puzzles
- ☐ Can't catch a ball; does not have good hand/eye coordination

Total: _____

Section 9

- ☐ Premature by at least three weeks
- ☐ Chronic diarrhea or chronic constipation
- ☐ Infantile spasms (Section 6)
- ☐ Diagnosed as Failure to Thrive (Section 1, Section 7)
- ☐ Frequent stomach upset or stomachache (Section 7)
- ☐ Migraines or frequent headaches
- ☐ Craves sugar/carbohydrates
- ☐ Low energy/Lethargy
- ☐ Bloated or gassy
- ☐ Eczema
- ☐ Dark circles under eyes
- ☐ History of frequent antibiotics use

Total: _____

Section 10

- ☐ Only eats white food (pasta, bread, cereal)
- ☐ Skips breakfast
- ☐ Eats a limited number of foods, skips entire food groups (no vegetables or no meats)
- ☐ Eczema
- ☐ Chicken skin on backs of arms
- ☐ Pediatrician is concerned about child's weight
- ☐ Low energy
- ☐ Gets hyperactive or lethargic after eating

Total: _____

Key Code

Tally the scores from each section and enter those scores below. Additionally, tally the scores of all indicators marked as VPD or APD.

Section 1 _____   See Chapter 4: Attention Problems and AD/HD

Section 2 _____   See Chapter 5: Speech and Language Issues

Section 3 _____   See Chapter 6: Dyslexia and Other Reading Disabilities

Section 4 _____   See Chapter 8: Autism Spectrum Disorders

Section 5 _____   See Chapter 9: Concussions

Section 6 _____   See Chapter 10: Other Learning Disabilities

Section 7 _____   See Chapter 11: Emotional and Behavioral Issues
Section 8 _____   See Chapter 7: Sensory Processing Disorder
Section 9 _____   See Chapter 14: Biomedical Approaches
Section 10 _____   See Chapter 15: Nutritional Approaches

_____ APD - See Chapter 5.1: Auditory Processing Disorder
_____ VPD - See Chapter 7.1: Visual Disorder Issues

Creating an Action Plan: Why Sequence Matters

You've completed the checklist. Perhaps you've checked off more items, in more categories, than you expected. So many areas to address! What now – roll up your sleeves, take a deep breath and find practitioners for everything on the list?

As tempting as it is to try to fix it all at once, that might not be your best choice. A child's system can only integrate so much change at a time, even in its best state. There is still a lot to consider before you decide what steps to take, and in what order to take them.

This diagram will help you understand what is a foundational issue and what is probably more of a symptom. The guiding question here is: which end are you looking at, the symptom or the root issue?

Sometimes, a reading disorder is just a reading disorder. All you need to do is find a good specialist to help your child get up to speed. Sometimes, however, it is not that simple. Learning and behavior disorders can be like icebergs: The symptom that everyone notices is often just an indication of how skewed things are in the 90 percent of the system that you don't really see. If you want issues to resolve all the way, without feeling like you are swimming upstream the whole way, you may have to have to dive deeper. One of the purposes of this book is to help you understand what that means.

The following diagram shows that development is a hierarchy, with important foundations underlying many of the more complex skills on the surface. It can be short-sighted and unproductive to try to address only the skills. (Please keep in mind that this diagram represents an attempt to streamline and organize a very un-streamlined, complex process. The idea was to give you broad principles.)

Diagram of Developmental Progression

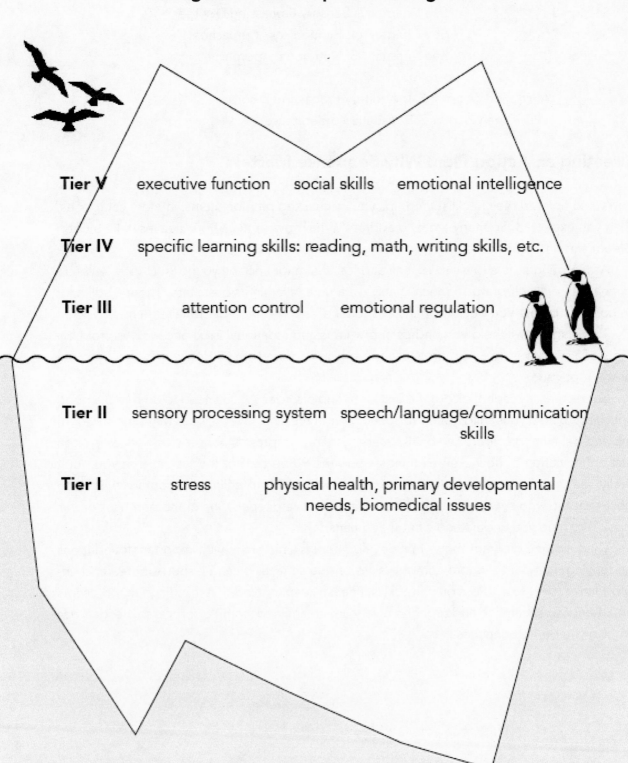

Tier V   executive function   social skills   emotional intelligence

Tier IV   specific learning skills: reading, math, writing skills, etc.

Tier III   attention control   emotional regulation

Tier II   sensory processing system   speech/language/communication
                                                                skills

Tier I   stress   physical health, primary developmental
                                          needs, biomedical issues

Diagram Key Terms and Definitions

- **Stress**, in this context, means extreme and/or prolonged forms of nervous system overwhelm that can undermine proper nervous system development and function. Examples include:
  - Abuse or neglect
  - Divorce, death, or chronic illness in the family
  - Bullying or ostracism
  - Specific traumas such as a car accident, a fall, or sports-related head injury
- **Physical health** involves the following elements, among others:
  - Nutrition
  - Hydration
  - Sleep
  - Exercise
- **Primary developmental needs** include:
  - Consistent physical safety
  - Emotional connection and mirroring
  - Facial expressions and gestures
  - Loving physical contact
  - Adequate stimulation
- **Biomedical concerns** (please see Chapter 14 for more information) include:
  - Ability to process all necessary nutrients
  - Food allergies/sensitivities
  - Genetic variables
- **Sensory processing** refers to the nervous system's ability to process all input at the most basic level, including visual, auditory, gustatory, tactile, and olfactory data. This is not a complete list. Please see Chapter 7 for more information.
- **Speech/language communication skills** encompass everything from instinctual nonverbal forms of connection (such as making eye contact, turning towards a voice, or reaching out to someone), to conversing, to making a complex presentation.
- **Attention control** indicates the ability to pay attention when one chooses, for a reasonable length of time according to one's developmental stage.
- **Emotional regulation** refers to the ability (commensurate with one's developmental stage) to regulate one's emotional intensity and expression, and to calm oneself after emotional arousal (basically, how far "out" you go and how long it takes you to come back).
- **Executive function** acts like the CEO of the brain. It involves the synthesis of several mental skills that enable a person to pay attention, remember things in a way that informs future decisions, organize incoming information, and plan and initiate cohesive responses.
- **Social skills** include the ability to read complex, ever-changing verbal and non-verbal social cues from others, and to then organize and carry out appropriate responses.
- **Emotional intelligence** is the ability, not only to identify and manage one's own emotions, but also to impact the emotions of others.

Tier I

On the bottom are the primary needs for proper development: physical health and fundamental developmental needs, such as safety, emotional connection, and having basic physical needs met. Lack of any of these results in stress – which, in this context, means any input which is more than the nervous system can handle. Chronic nervous system overload can become traumatic, which will actually shift brain chemistry over time. Also, biomedical issues can create chronic imbalance and/or inflammation in the brain, which can undermine normal development. Any of these factors can skew skills that rely on good foundations to develop properly. The higher skills will still develop or emerge, but not optimally.

Tier II

Just above the basic layer is sensory processing development, the building blocks that lay the foundation for how we process all input. (See Chapter 7 to understand more about this essential aspect of development.) Speech and language skills are also crucial as we learn to interact with our world. Impairments in the speech/language domain could actually be placed almost anywhere in this model, depending on severity. But communication is such a fundamental part of expression and connection that severe difficulties can be devastating.

Tier III

Problems in either Tier I or Tier II can impair the ability to control either attention and behavior, the next tier up on our model. Granted, problems with attention or behavior can occur without problems at the lower levels, but any problems below will exacerbate problems above. For example, emotional regulation issues can result from many different kinds of underlying issues. Perhaps a sensory processing problem makes the world more overwhelming than your child can deal with all day long. Perhaps nutrients he is not getting, or not processing, are rendering his brain chemistry unstable. Maybe a constant stomachache or poor sleep is wearing down your child's patience and attitude. You'd be amazed at how many children don't mention these things if they've become used to them – for example, some don't know what a good night's sleep really feels like because they so rarely get one. If you ask them how their sleep is, however, most would probably just shrug and say, "Fine."

Tier IV

Above these lies the realm of specific academic skills: reading, math, relatively minor speech and language issues, and so on. As you can see, a lot of construction has to happen in the brain and nervous system before you even get to this point.

Tier V

Skills that require sophisticated levels of synthesis, such as executive function, social skills, and emotional intelligence continue to develop and mature well into a person's twenties, and even for the rest of his life. They therefore come above the level of individual academic skills. However, although these skills won't be fully developed until adulthood, there are effective ways of addressing problems that arise at any age.

In Conclusion

If your child has a number of different learning difficulties, addressing the underlying factors may help them to resolve. Sometimes, organizing the brain and nervous system can improve processing at the higher levels. At the very least, it should make them easier to rectify. A calm, organized brain responds to therapy much more readily than a brain that is still compromised by foundational issues.

It's important to remember that children can rarely tell you what's really going on. The way they experience the world is just the way they experience the world; it has always been that way for them. So you (and teachers, coaches, and other caregivers) may see a child who doesn't pay attention to directions, and everyone immediately says, "He needs help with attention control!" But this is, so often, just the beginning of your inquiry.

A Note From Our Resident Neuropsychologist

One of the most important aspects of our book is the emphasis on exploring underlying and contributing factors to your child's learning or behavioral concerns. However, not all evaluators take this approach. Many psychologists, neuropsychologists, or psychiatrists, tasked with evaluating a child, converge on finding a diagnosis. They label and treat at the "tip of the iceberg." Their main guide in this process is the DSM-5, the diagnostic resource most practitioners use. While this is helpful, it will not help your situation if there is a lot going on in the more foundational layers of your child's system.

Many of these underlying conditions are not listed in the DSM because the focus there is on cognitive, mental health, and developmental diagnoses. Because of this and the need for efficiency in our insurance system, many practitioners focus specifically on cognitive and mental health symptoms and do not bother to look for or discuss other factors. But issues such as sensory integration, digestive issues, or poor sleep can wreak havoc with a child's ability to learn easily or control her behavior. Sensory Processing Disorder, though growing in acceptance, is still considered a controversial concept by some, precisely because the DSM does not include it. But we believe sensory processing impacts a child's behavior. We believe that nutrition and digestion can influence a child's abilities. We believe in the importance of sleep. And there is sound research to support these beliefs.

When I evaluate a child, I am less concerned about figuring out the diagnosis (though I do give a diagnosis from the DSM-5 when it fits). I am more interested in painting a complete picture, one that has considered a range of underlying contributing factors if possible. I want you to have a broad understanding of how to help your child's overall physical, cognitive, and emotional health, not just give a name to the tip-of-the-iceberg learning or behavior issues you are seeing. If the evaluator you see does not do this, you will have to fill in the blanks yourself. The checklists and chapters in this book will help you with this process.
~ Robin McEvoy, developmental neuropsychologist

THREE

Evaluations: Who Does What?

by Robin McEvoy, PhD

Who You Gonna Call?

You're concerned. Maybe your child has started school and is clearly struggling. Maybe, in social situations, he is too easily upset, unusually uncoordinated, behind in language skills, misses most social cues, or is otherwise not blending in. Perhaps teachers, coaches, or other caregivers have expressed concerns and you want to check it out. Or maybe – and this can be just as critical as other, more measurable factors – you just have a feeling that something is off with your child.

Now What?

Your family pediatrician is the typical place to start. It is important to rule out a medical or health need first, and a pediatrician can do the initial medical screening. Bear in mind that the doctor needs to be told as much as possible about the concerns, even if you are not sure what information is relevant. Pediatricians can do some areas of broad screening:

- A general medical screening should be done to ensure good physical health, particularly if the concerns emerged recently and do not have a long history.
- Most can do a screening to ensure a good foundation for vision and hearing. It is critical to rule out basic problems with any senses before considering another learning, language, attention, or

What if my pediatrician says my child is fine, but I am still concerned?

Trust your gut. If you feel something is off, keep looking for answers. Get a second opinion, talk to friends, research on the internet, check out blogs, read this book. From there, you will find the professionals that can give you more direction.

🔓

Even if the problem is correctable, early hearing or visual problems can affect later development. For example, early hearing impairment can have a significant impact on the ability to discriminate between speech sounds later in life, even if the child's hearing is considered perfectly normal by that time. SO, be pleased if glasses have improved vision or fluid is no longer in the inner ear, but keep monitoring down the road for learning issues.

behavior issue.

Most can do a general developmental screening to ensure that the child is reaching broad developmental milestones for motor development, speech/language, and thinking skills.

If concerns about vision or hearing emerge, a more thorough visual or audiology exam should be scheduled with a specialist. Strabismus (crossed eyes), amblyopia ("lazy eye"), and other visual issues can affect the development of visual skills. Serial or serious ear infections can significantly affect hearing.

A pediatrician can help parents determine if further evaluation is warranted. However, it must be said that many pediatricians have a fairly wide margin for what they consider normal development. For example, if parents mention that their two-year-old son seems behind in language skills, the pediatrician may say (and rightly so) that there is a wide range of normal language development, that many boys develop more slowly in this area, and that everyone should just watch it a little longer. Some parents may let it go at that, particularly if the child seems on track in other areas. (For example, he enjoys other children, enjoys a range of activities, and communicates in other ways such as using gestures or facial expressions.)

However, if the parents notice that their child is often throwing tantrums because he cannot say what he wants, and has other potentially worrisome symptoms such as unusually poor coordination for his age and a lack of interest in other children, then a more in-depth evaluation may be warranted. If your pediatrician does not agree or is not sure whom to recommend, there are many resources available to parents. A broad developmental screening (ask your pediatrician for a referral) will also check language skills, motor skills, problem solving, and other developmental markers.

Assessment vs. Diagnosis: What's the difference?

- Assessment: Collecting data to identify strengths and weaknesses in a particular area.
- Diagnosis: Collecting data to identify a disorder as recognized in a diagnostic manual or classification system.

> Some professionals, such as learning specialists, will do an assessment to evaluate strengths and weaknesses the child is exhibiting. However, they cannot make a diagnosis.

Resources Within the School District

The public school system provides free evaluation resources for families (including non-school aged children or children who are not in public school). Because of legal mandates to provide services for all children who may have special needs, the public school system is often the first point of service for these evaluations. The benefits of this evaluation process are as follows:

- It is free.
- It provides a team evaluation with professionals from several disciplines.
- If your child qualifies, services and funding for those services will be provided.

Depending on district guidelines, the team will give a select number of tests in several domains (e.g., academics, speech/language skills, cognitive skills, mental health, etc). A recommendation is then made about what kinds of services the child needs, *within the scope of the services provided by the district.*

However, the school district does not typically offer a *diagnostic* evaluation. The services provided by the school district are geared toward helping the child make academic progress. This is not the same thing as thoroughly identifying his issues and working towards full remediation. Lack of funding also limits the scope of the evaluation and treatment (funding varies from state to state). Delays are identified according to scores on the tests administered and treatment is planned from there, typically without making a *medical* diagnosis (though an *educational* diagnosis is made in some districts).

Food for Thought

From my experiences working with numerous school districts, I know that some evaluation teams will do an excellent job of integrating background data and test scores to determine if a child will benefit from therapy support. The state guidelines allow for clinical judgment and the team will use this. Parents will get a good explanation of their child's abilities and needs even if the team does not think the child qualifies for district-based services. Other evaluation teams (even in the same district) may not do as thorough a job. Some teams are overwhelmingly busy and simply assess quickly, score quickly, and give a yes or no about receiving services. Parents must rely on their intuition as to whether the reported results make sense. Parents can always then seek opinions from resources outside of the school system.

Without a medical, mental health, or developmental diagnosis, the emphasis in the school-based evaluation is on whether the child qualifies to receive services at his school. State guidelines (and the school team's understanding of the guidelines) drive this process. If the child does not meet the state guidelines for delay or impairment, the parents may be told that the child is doing well or that they do not need services. This may not be true. A child may simply not qualify for *school-based services*. For example, if a state guideline is that a child needs to score below the 7th percentile to receive services and the child scores at the 8th percentile, the parents may not be told of this. They may simply be told that their child does not need services from the school system. Some parents walk away trying to convince themselves that their child is fine and just needs more time to mature, even if their intuition tells them that something is wrong. If your intuition is insisting that something is wrong, you need to look beyond the school-based evaluation for a diagnostic evaluation.

Finally, it is important to note that school personnel cannot recommend you seek outside evaluation or therapy for school-related problems. The school is required to provide a free and appropriate education to each child. If they say any non-medical service or therapy is needed for your child's education, they can be held financially responsible.

The limitations of the school district's offerings are particularly apparent with children whose needs are complex, such as bright children whose sensory issues interfere with performance in the classroom. These children can perform quite well on tests and therefore not qualify for services, although everyone can clearly see that they are struggling.

Beyond the Pediatrician, After the School District: University and Medical Clinics

Many university medical schools, children's hospitals, and general universities have child development units that focus on evaluation and treatment of developmental problems in children. Units are often directed by a developmental pediatrician who has training in developmental-behavioral pediatrics. Sometimes, a child psychiatrist or pediatrician will head up the clinic. The evaluation team will include psychologists, speech/language pathologists, and occupational and/or physical therapists. Many clinics have areas of specialization, such as autism, Fragile X Syndrome, or other medically-oriented diagnoses. **If your child does not have a clear medical diagnosis, it is helpful to inquire whether the clinic deals with non-medical developmental disabilities (such as reading disability, math disability,**

The key question parents need to ask is, "How much experience does this staff have with children like mine?"

inattentive-type attention deficit disorder, Sensory Processing Disorder, or gifted with a learning disability).

There are also private clinics (unaffiliated with a university or medical center) that have a range of specialists in the field of child development and learning. These clinics are often focused on non-medical disabilities, such as reading disabilities and various types of attention problems. They will also treat the learning and developmental needs of children with medical diagnoses such as cerebral palsy or autism.

This type of multi-disciplinary clinic is an excellent resource if your child has complex symptoms that you and your pediatrician are having trouble pinpointing. The group approach brings in different perspectives so that if your child has a number of issues going on, they will all be seen and addressed in a cohesive way.

Individual Specialists

Many individual practitioners address developmental issues, from the broad to the specific. The following three types of practitioners can be excellent alternatives to clinics (if there is not one in your area or you do not feel the local clinic is appropriate for whatever reason). If you are at the beginning of the "figuring out what the heck is going on" phase, or feel that your child is likely to have multiple issues that interact in a complex way, these professionals can help you as they can provide a broad overview.

- **Developmental Pediatricians.** These physicians specialize in developmental delays and learning disabilities. Their post-graduate training focuses on developmental and behavioral pediatrics. These professionals are usually linked with university settings, but some practice individually. They typically have a wide breadth of experience and are able to identify delays and whether a child meets criteria for a specific diagnosis. They will then assist with treatment planning and medication management, but do not typically provide therapy of any sort. They can prescribe medications for certain disabilities or significant behavioral concerns.

- **Developmental Neuropsychologists.** These are licensed psychologists who assess and diagnose children with delays or deviations

> When looking for a specialist, it is best to ask around: Your pediatrician, school counselor, support groups, and other parents can all be valuable sources of information. Other parents, in particular, may have been down some wrong paths and can spare you time, money, and frustration by helping you find the right path more quickly.

in development. They typically have a doctoral degree in clinical psychology, with a specialty in the relationship between the brain and behavior. Psychologists are generally not able to make certain medical diagnoses (such as cerebral palsy or Fragile X Syndrome), but they are qualified to suggest exploration for these conditions if they suspect such a problem.

- **Child Psychologists.** Many of these professionals have evaluation experience in addition to therapeutic skills. Child psychologists typically have a doctorate in clinical psychology with a focus on emotional and behavioral needs of children. Those with evaluation experience can do a good basic cognitive assessment and a more comprehensive assessment of emotional status. Some have training in the diagnosis of learning and developmental disabilities.

Practitioners for Specific Symptoms

If your child has a weakness that seems to be in a specific developmental domain, one of these professionals may be the best place to start.

- **Occupational Therapy.** For the child who is exhibiting delays in motor skills or atypical sensory processing (see Chapter 7: Sensory Processing Disorder), evaluation by a pediatric OT may be the best place to start.
- **Speech and Language Therapy.** Professionals here are known as either speech/language pathologists or speech therapists. The speech therapist will often request an audiology exam to ensure good hearing. Speech/language needs are addressed in greater detail in Chapter 5: Speech and Language Issues.
- **Special Education Teacher (Learning Specialist).** These are teachers with a Master's degree in Special Education. They are trained in a variety of learning and developmental disabilities. Although they primarily work in schools, some practice privately and evaluate academic skills. Learning specialists focus their assessment on academic ability. They can assess reading, writing, and math skills in great detail, but cannot administer intelligence tests, speech/language assessments, or gross and fine motor skills assessment. An experienced learning specialist can give their opinion to parents about concerns in these domains and can often refer to other professionals if they see a need. A learning specialist can identify many learning disabilities based on their experience, but cannot make the formal diagnosis (this is typically the domain of a psychologist or physician). Parents are usually referred to a learning specialist through word of mouth when their child is struggling in school. They typi-

cally do academic remediation or tutoring after assessing the problems.

- **Child Psychiatry.** Child psychiatrists have a medical degree and specialized training in children's mental health. (See Chapter 13: Psychiatry and Functional Medicine Psychiatry.) They can:
  - evaluate behavioral problems that are thought to be emotional in nature (e.g., anxiety, depression);
  - evaluate attention control issues;
  - prescribe medication (within many managed care situations, this is the primary treatment they provide).
- **Pediatric Neurologist.** These physicians have specialty training in the central and peripheral nervous system. They can assess for the possibility of neurological injury or illness. When a child has a developmental delay, they will explore for a genetic abnormality (e.g., Fragile X Syndrome), birth trauma or other trauma (e.g., stroke), or illness (e.g., brain tumor, seizure disorder). Your physician will typically refer you to a neurologist if they suspect a medical origin to your child's problems.

Food for Thought

It is a common occupational hazard that many specialists only think within their domain. They may not know when to draw in professionals from other areas. Some specialists do consider developmental areas other than the one they are trained in, referring to other practitioners readily, but this is not always true. Educate yourself and be prepared to be your child's main advocate. It is always up to the parents to determine if they feel that a professional is the right one at that point in their child's treatment, and it is also up to them to determine when to seek help from other experts. Parents are almost always the case managers in their children's care, monitoring a child's needs in many areas and determining if they are working with the right people. Chapter 18: Care Management, will provide more guidance for this.

What Happens in an Evaluation

Professionals with medical degrees (pediatricians, psychiatrists, neurologists) often collect medical data through physical examination, lab tests, and interview.

Professionals with backgrounds in psychology, child development, and learning are more likely to use *standardized tests* along with interviews with the child and her family, observation, and questionnaires. Standardized tests given in individualized evaluations include such things as intelligence tests, academic achievement tests, and tests of specific skills (e.g., fine motor speed).

There are different standardized tests for the different developmental domains, and there are hundreds of tests from which to choose. A psychologist would typically not give the same tests as a speech/language specialist or an occupational therapist, though they may overlap on some tests.

For a broad developmental check-up, a psychologist who focuses on learning and development may be the best place to start if a parent is unsure of what may be going on. There should be an initial interview (by phone or in person) to decide whether there is a broad developmental assessment need or whether the needs seem to be in a very specific developmental domain. For example, if the child's development is reported to be fine in every way with the exception of reading and writing, then a learning or reading evaluation may be the only thing needed. However, if the parents report that reading therapy was already done with little benefit, and that their child is also socially immature with behavior problems in the classroom, then a broader assessment is warranted. Once the broader assessment is done, then the evaluator can refer to specific areas of specialty for treatment.

If the child is reported to have clear delays across several areas of development, then a team evaluation may be the approach to take. In this situation, a child sees several professionals over several days to have a thorough evaluation in each developmental area. The team then meets to share their findings and develop conclusions and diagnoses where warranted. The findings are then presented to the parents, along with treatment recommendations.

There are many possible areas within a comprehensive evaluation of development, including:

- **Cognitive assessment:** It is good to establish a broad cognitive baseline assessment of a child's abilities. Is his thinking and reasoning above average, below average, or highly uneven across the subtests? Cognition is typically screened with what is traditionally known as an IQ test. Psychologists (including child psychologists, school psychologists, and neuropsychologists) administer these tests.
- **Mental Health:** Psychologists and psychiatrists will also typically screen emotional and behavioral functioning to determine if this is an area to consider in treatment planning.
- **Speech/language assessment:** The speech/language therapist can administer standardized tests to assess speech skills, such as articulation and fluency of speech

(stuttering is a form of speech fluency disorder), and language skills, such as the ability to understand language and use language to express ideas. There are also tests of *pragmatics*, which refers to the practical use of language. Some children may have a sophisticated vocabulary, but cannot clearly communicate what they mean.

- **Sensory motor assessment:** The occupational therapist has standardized tests to evaluate gross and fine motor skills. There are also standardized tests and questionnaires to assess sensory processing. A screen of visual processing and auditory processing should also be considered to determine the need for further assessment in these areas.

- **Academic learning evaluation.** For school age children, there needs to be an evaluation of core academic skills in reading, writing, and math. Psychologists and learning specialists administer these. Some speech/language therapists are also trained in reading and writing assessment. Many occupational therapists can assess writing skills.

Regardless of what kind of practitioner or evaluation you choose, someone should do a broad enough intake interview to ensure that the following factors are taken into account right from the beginning. Even if you think you know what your child needs help with, therapy could be slow or ineffective if something important is missed in these areas.

- ☐ **Medical history.** Is there a history of birth trauma, concussion, or other illness or injury that can have developmental consequences? Are there medical symptoms (sometimes vague) that indicate the child may not always be available for learning, such as when a child is prone to frequent headaches, stomachaches, or allergies/excema?
- ☐ **Developmental history.** Was early development typical? Is there more than one area of developmental concern? Was there any trauma early in development?
- ☐ **Nutrition.** See Chapter 15: Nutritional Approaches, for more information about how profoundly this can affect learning, mood, attention and behavior control, and other issues.
- ☐ **Attention control.** See Chapter 4: Attention Problems and AD/HD.
- ☐ **Emotional and behavioral style.** See Chapter 11: Emotional and Behavioral Issues.

Questions for a Prospective Evaluator

- Do you have experience with children similar to my child?
- Do my child's symptoms or areas of difficulty suggest a need for a medical evalua-

tion (such as with a pediatric neurologist or developmental pediatrician), or would a non-medical provider be more appropriate?

- Do you just do assessment and remediation, or can you also provide a formal diagnosis of a disability?
- Based on what I have told you, is there reason to pursue a formal diagnosis, or is treatment the more efficient option? Why?
- Do you see a reason to do a broad developmental or psychological assessment, or do my child's issues seem specific to a particular developmental area such as speech and language or occupational therapy?
- What are the costs of your evaluation? Does that include a written report?
- Do you provide treatment or would you refer us to appropriate providers after your evaluation?
- Does insurance cover this evaluation?
- If I am confused or have additional questions, what are the charges for additional follow-up after the evaluation?

Resources for More Information

Websites

www.ncld.org/ The National Center for Learning Disabilities

ldaamerica.org/ The Learning Disabilities Association of America. This site will direct you to local or state chapters, which will have more information about local resources for evaluation.

www.robinmcevoy.com/CommonQuestions.en.html This is Dr. McEvoy's website, where she discusses her approach to evaluation.

About the Author

Robin McEvoy, PhD, is a developmental neuropsychologist and one of the authors of this book. You can find her complete bio at the back.

Section Two

DISORDERS AND CHALLENGES

———◆———

THIS SECTION COVERS THE MAJOR CATEGORIES of learning and behavior challenges. Each chapter has another short checklist, to help you determine whether that chapter is truly relevant to your child. Keep in mind that dividing children up into learning disability categories is like dividing people up by hair color. You can do it; there are blondes, brunettes, redheads, and black-haired people. But in reality, there are seemingly endless variations on actual hair color. It is the same with trying to put a child in a category according to a learning disability or challenge. Keep in mind that disorders are broad areas and the difference between *neurotypical* and *neurodiverse* isn't always as clear cut as we would like. However, it is an important and empowering starting point to know what general category describes your child's challenges.

———◆———

Before you dive in and start collecting data, keep these concepts in mind.

NEUROPLASTICITY: REASON FOR HOPE

No matter how many items you checked off or how many chapters you were directed to, take heart. Research increasingly proves the ability of the brain to be *plastic* – meaning that it has more flexibility than we originally thought. The brain can create new neuronal connections and change its response patterns. This ability is called *neuroplasticity*. The appropriate interventions, given in the right order, can often help your child to make enormous shifts. Of course, there are two things to keep in mind here: First, if your child's brain works in a particular overall way, you will probably not be able to make it work in a whole different way (for example, a very artistic, creative person might never be linear or organized; a child with autism may make significant gains but will probably always have some degree of autism). This brings us to the subject of *neurodiversity*, discussed next, and how that may be a completely normal part of the human spectrum. And second, you have to figure what the appropriate interventions are! We hope that this book will help.

NEURODIVERSE AND NEUROTYPICAL: HONORING DIVERSITY

Keep in mind that there are many different kinds of "normal." And, sometimes, living out on the edge of normal is a great place to be. A quote widely attributed to Dr. Suess claims, "You have to be odd to be number one." Of course, we want to support our children, help them with their struggles, and give them the best chance for fulfillment and happiness. But success need not be defined as being like everyone else. We need to remember to value uniqueness.

In the last few years, new buzzwords have emerged in the field of child development. Years ago, child development specialists edged away from describing a child's behavior as *normal* or *abnormal* and moved to using the words *typical* and *atypical*. A child's behavior or learning may not be typical for children, but when do we call it abnormal? Perspectives started to shift.

Then in the late 90s and into the new millennium, people with Asperger Syndrome began to shift things a bit more. Frustrated with being labeled as people with a disability or disorder, even when they had good educations, good jobs, and a comfortable social life, they began to describe themselves as *neurodiverse*. There was nothing wrong with the way they were – they actually liked themselves and their strengths – they just weren't exactly like most other people. Online forums emerged where the neurodiverse could discuss the often mystifying social rules of the NTs (*neurotypicals*). The concept of *neurological pluralism* was introduced by Harvey Blume, a writer and forum participant. Simply put, there is a lot of natural variability that is normal. The scope of neurodiversity was expanded to include people with dyslexia, Attention Deficit Disorder, and other conditions (referred to as Cousins). Slowly, people who did not learn like everyone else could start seeing themselves as part of a natural and necessary diversity in the culture, not as a handicapped member of the community.

And it makes sense. If one in five people have a reading disability and one in fifty has autism, can we say that these conditions are simply natural variations in humans? When does a learning style become a learning disorder or problem? We design schools (and most other settings) for the neurotypicals, so if your child is more neurodiverse, a more mainstream setting may not work. He may need a different educational situation altogether. And if that is not an option, that's when accommodations, modifications, and different interventions or therapies need to be considered. You can respect neurodiversity and still try to ensure that your child can learn, have a rewarding job, and develop the friendships and relationships they want.

For some children, the identification of a disorder or disability will be necessary. A child with severe limitations in cognition, judgment, or communication will need significant supports in childhood and into adulthood. But those who have initiated and nurtured the concept of neurodiversity are role models for the concept of "different but equal" – even for those with more profound challenges.

A Story About AD/HD

The McIntosh Family's Journey

For super-organized Melinda McIntosh, the early days of her relationship with Dan were fun and spontaneous. She'd come home from a busy work week as an occupational therapist delighted to find that he'd booked last-minute tickets to Las Vegas and had their bags packed. "Off we would go. It was great!" she recalls with a smile.

Unfortunately, over time it became clear that problems lay beneath Dan's joyful spontaneity. Melinda became confused and frustrated as it became clear that he had trouble focusing or paying attention to details. A foundational factor in their relationship transmuted into a source of marital strain. When children came along, the issues evolved into a genuine family problem. Dan would forget to drop their son at preschool or he might neglect to organize things needed for the children, despite the fact that his wife had given him lists, with each thing prepared and positioned in plain sight. His inability to manage details cost him many jobs as well, and ultimately resulted in Dan having more than 15 different employers over the course of 23 years.

Family strain increased when their son, Mike, was born. Melinda realized soon after the birth that their new baby had sensory issues. He was extremely afraid of almost any kind of movement, and a simple jiggle or a bump in the car caused him to startle and cry out in fear. He also had a hard time moving around as a baby and toddler, and was late for many key developmental milestones like crawling and walking.

A quiet child, Mike was shy and introverted. He didn't participate in activities or make friends easily. By the time he reached middle school, with its inherent demands for self-organization and increased social pressures, many of Mike's issues came to a head. He began losing ground; was not able to stay on track academically, and became increasingly isolated from other students. Finally, the results of testing came in and the family got an important key to Mike's struggles. He was diagnosed with Attention Deficit Disorder (ADD). When Dan saw the results, he decided to go for testing as well, and was not too surprised to receive the same diagnosis. The family suddenly had the missing link between Dan and Mike's many "like father, like son" traits. Together they started the journey to find medical and therapeutic support for the disorder.

Father and son began trials with different medications. Eventually, treatment improved both of their levels of concentration dramatically, but it was far from a quick and final fix. For Mike in particular, one of the exciting positive results of treatment was a dramatic reduction in social anxiety, and he delighted in finding new friends and participating in athletics. An avid skier, basketball, and soccer player, he was tall and lanky. The ADD medication, while helpful in other ways, caused extreme appetite suppression. Mike was often unable to eat, and the ensuing weight loss put him at risk for malnutrition and passing out during athletic events. The family and their doctors decided to employ a sort of yo-yo approach to treatment, with Mike going on and off his meds depending on whether his weight loss or inability to focus was the more pressing issue.

Over the years, the family also experimented with various complementary and alternative treatments – from the Learning Enhanced Acupressure Program (LEAP) to gluten-free diets to orthomolecular medicine. At one point, high levels of essential fatty acid (EFA) supplementation helped Mike to stay organized, but the regime ultimately failed because it was simply too hard for him to take the large number of pills required throughout the day (and even when he remembered, they often upset his stomach).

With all this unfolding in the family, Mike's little sister, Angela, was growing up. A high-spirited child, she had earned the nick-name "Tigger" for her non-stop, high-energy persona. For many years, the family thought her behavior was simply an endearing personality trait. But by the time she was eight, it became clear that her behavior stemmed from underlying challenges. She clearly had sensory issues, but they were opposite to Mike's. While he sought to minimize sensory input, Angela craved input and created excess. A strong sensory seeker, she attempted to maximize the energy level of every life event. Instead of wanting a simple back rub, she asked for her back to be pounded. Instead of talking, she would yell. "Angela always sought strong sensory experiences and could pitch a tantrum at the drop of a hat," says Melinda.

Sensory therapy helped calm Angela's behavior, but did nothing to help her growing inability to focus. As she grew and encountered the increasing demands of middle school, she also began to exhibit signs of ADD. She understood the academic material, but was not able to organize herself or get work turned in on time. ADD medications had limited success for her, and caused severe side effects including appetite suppression and mood destabilization. On ADD medication, she became irritable and aggressive. She would throw things and react to almost everything with anger.

Then another layer of complexity arose during her freshman year in high school when Angela began to experience severe anxiety issues unrelated to the ADD treatment. The family tried compensatory therapies and treatments, but they were not adequate to meet Angela's escalating anxiety and mood issues. She suffered panic attacks, constantly texted from school begging to come home, experienced major social anxiety, and became intensely anti-social. She would ditch school and stay home curled up in a ball. She also stopped caring for herself, often going days without a shower. The family felt that they had tried everything, and that a dynamic new approach would be needed. They began moving toward re-balancing her mood and attention with medication, as well as potentially changing her school environment.

Through many years of dealing with ADD, this family learned that dealing with Attention Deficit Disorder is a lifelong journey of seeking different treatments and strategies that work for each individual. They know from first hand experiences that ADD requires constant monitoring and adjustments when things get out of balance. At the time of this writing, Mike is a successful college student, pursuing a sports physiology degree. He manages his ADD by taking a four-hour Ritalin after breakfast to help him focus during classes. The medicine wears off before dinner, so he can eat enough to maintain his health and stamina. In addition, he uses a number of other strategies to further his college success, such as sitting in the front row of class, asking for clarification when he is in information overload, and taking more Ritalin after dinner on nights when he has to stay up late to study for exams. Far from being hindered by the social awkwardness of his childhood, Mike surprised the family by choosing to live in a fraternity.

Angela has decided to transfer to a new high school. Despite the challenge of having to meet new friends, the move has been positive and she feels comfortable in her new environment. She continues to work with a number of tools to keep both the ADD and anxiety disorder under control. She and her doctor are collaborating with the goal of finding a good combination of low-dose anxiety medication and ADD medication that will best support Angela into the future.

Dan weaned himself off medication and found a steady job in sales that suits his need for new challenges every day. He still struggles to manage details at home, which continues to frustrate Melinda. "I've asked my husband to get carrots three times this week," she says. "He's been at the store several times, and guess what? Still no carrots!" She's practicing what she considers the best advice she's received in the 23 years that ADD has been such a big part of the family's life. "My pastor told me, 'You're making yourself sick by taking on everyone else's issues. If you take them on, the other people won't get to own them.'" For the past six months, Melinda has been following this advice and taking a deep breath whenever ADD disrupts the flow of the household … even if it means no carrots.

FOUR

Attention Problems and AD/HD
by Robin McEvoy, PhD

Look through the following list to see if your child's symptoms do, indeed, seem to indicate the presence of AD/HD. This checklist will direct you to other chapters that may also be relevant to your child's attention control issues.

Cross-reference guide:
SPD = Sensory Processing Disorder, Chapter 7
Biomed = Biomedical Approaches, Chapter 14
E/B = Emotional and Behavioral Issues, Chapter 11

BEHAVIOR	ADD	SPD	Bio-Med	E/B
Cannot focus on many tasks or chores for the amount of time needed	*			
Ability to focus depends on type of task: repetitive tasks of low personal interest are torturous to stay with, but can hyper-focus for long periods on very challenging tasks, or those of high personal interest	*			
Is easily distracted by noise or movement in the environment	*	*		
Is often lost in his own thoughts or daydreams	*			
Loses things: toys, books, shoes, jacket, glasses, homework	*			
Loses track of tasks or conversations while in the middle of them	*	*		
Gets frustrated with tasks easily	*	*		
Rushes through tasks without attending to quality	*			
Needs supervision to complete age-appropriate tasks or chores	*			
Often kneels in a chair when working	*	*		
Changes position in the chair every few minutes	*	*		
Often gets in trouble for playing too roughly	*	*		

BEHAVIOR	ADD	SPD	Bio-Med	E/B
Gets hurt frequently	*	*		
Blurts out answers	*			
There are safety issues due to impulsive responses (e.g., darts into street)	*			
Likes to take risks or appears fearless	*			
Cannot stay seated for meals, or eats and rushes off quickly	*	*		
Makes many small "careless" mistakes in schoolwork (e.g., forgets to read math sign, forgets punctuation and capitalization when writing, moves on to a new thought in writing or a new math problem before finishing the first)	*			
Symptoms are apparent across home, school, and other settings, not just in one setting or situation. If symptoms seem to be setting-specific, you should probably explore further	*			
Frequently reacts irritably or angrily to minor stresses	*	*	*	*
Prone to eczema			*	
Prone to stomach aches, constipation, diarrhea, or bloating			*	
Craves sugar			*	
Has trouble falling asleep or staying asleep or simply sleeps poorly		*	*	
Has chronic congestion or chronic runny nose			*	

Becky, in first grade, has a heck of a time sitting still for the full day. Twice in the first month of school, she got up, left the class, walked the five blocks home, and greeted her surprised mom at home.

Carl never eats his meals at the table. He is on it, under it or, most often, away from it altogether. Breakfast time isn't so bad when he's rested, but evening meals are a nightmare of scolding and begging.

Grace seems like a model student in some ways. She sits quietly for the most part and, if she loves the topic, contributes enthusiastically to class discussions. However, she rarely finishes her work when the rest of the class does. Her teacher isn't worried because Grace simply volunteers to stay in at recess to finish. Her mother does worry, though, because Grace frequently gets in the car in tears whenever she has missed recess yet again.

Brian loves to ski, but getting him up the hill with his skis, poles, gloves, helmet etc requires his own support team. Other kids make fun of him because he is also prone to frustration and meltdowns. However, once Brian gets going down the hill, his strengths are obvious. He looks like an Olympian.

Georgie is very smart – gifted, actually. But he is also very hyperactive and very distractible. It took four hours to give him a one-hour IQ test because he kept wandering off, but also kept coming back to give the correct answers. Keeping him focused through the school day is a constant challenge for everyone involved. But trials with two different medications for attention had the same effects: Attention was better, but Georgie did not eat for three days after a single dose of either one.

The Basics

Welcome to Attention Deficit Disorder: the most frequently diagnosed, commonly studied behavioral disorder there is. It has become so much a part of our culture that a percentage of any class is likely to have been diagnosed with it, and I often hear people joke about "having an ADD moment."

In fact, joking about ADD has become so prevalent that it is sometimes easy to overlook how serious it can be. Some kids don't just have a little trouble concentrating; their nonstop impulsive behavior can create constant turmoil in classrooms, friendships, and home life. Non-hyperactive kids may cause less mayhem, but have terrible trouble keeping track of themselves and staying motivated. I have seen both disrupt lives to an equal degree.

Medications can be a lifesaver, except when they aren't. Children sometimes feel depressed, jittery, or emotionally flat. Some lose their appetites to an alarming degree and have difficulty gaining weight as they grow. It's no wonder that parents tear their hair out.

So what is it, exactly? ADD refers to Attention Deficit Disorder; ADHD adds the component of Hyperactivity. A diagnosis of either reflects that a person cannot control his attention to the extent that it causes problems in daily living.

Diagnosing Attention Deficit Disorder

The current diagnostic manual (DSM-5) lists three subtypes of diagnoses for attention deficit disorder:

- *Attention Deficit Disorder - Predominantly Inattentive Presentation,* with symptoms such as:

☐ Inability to get necessary work done
☐ Forgetting what one was supposed to do
☐ Responding or reacting before thinking through the consequences
☐ Losing track of the steps necessary to complete a task

- *Attention Deficit Disorder - Predominantly Hyperactive/Impulsive Presentation,* with symptoms such as:
  ☐ Child cannot sit still even for short periods, such as for meals.
  ☐ He is out of his desk at school frequently and for no (or no good) identifiable reason.
  ☐ He is so physically active that he takes risks or hurts himself or others frequently – not in a malicious way, he just doesn't seem to pay enough attention to predict the consequences of his actions.
- *Attention Deficit/Hyperactivity Disorder, Combined Type,* indicating a person has features of both inattention and hyperactivity.

As you can see in the previous box, the choices seem straightforward: A child with attention problems has one of the three subtypes. However, anyone who has met more than three people diagnosed with attention problems may question this. Attention problems can be varied and defy simple descriptions or categorization. So the diagnosis can be ambiguous and lead to confusion. In the U.S., diagnosis rates range from 2 percent up to 16 percent (!!) of elementary-age children. And still there is controversy, with some experts insisting it is over-diagnosed and some insisting (yes, really) that it is under-diagnosed.

To complicate matters more, there are a number of conditions that often co-exist with, or look just like, Attention Deficit Disorder. Each child has his own configuration of issues that make him "act AD/HD." I rarely get the sense that it is as simple as solely having AD/HD. Addressing various issues individually can ease the symptoms and make life more manageable. This knowledge, however, can be both empowering and frustrating for a parent – how are you supposed to sort through the tangle of possibilities and address the right culprits? I won't suggest that this process will be easy, but you should discover some new possibilities to explore here.

Keep in mind that AD/HD has inherent strengths, as well. Many accomplished people have it – Leonardo da Vinci and Mozart, for example, are famously speculated to have had it. To find current examples of people who have actually been diagnosed, you have only to Google "famous people + ADD" to find a long list of public figures who have not only figured out how to manage this disorder, but also to harness its creativity and energy. As with anything, there is trial and error involved in the process of learning how to navigate these waters. You might also need to employ some "out of the box" thinking in terms of how to make your child's world more supportive and suited to him.

Like other learning challenges, Attention Deficit Disorder symptoms can range from mild to severe. One parent's minor inconvenience is another parent's nightmare. Additionally, there can be a number of underlying factors that can contribute to a child's symptoms, which we will discuss in this chapter.

A Closer Look

Parents often ask me, "How can he have Attention Deficit Disorder when he can play with Legos for eight straight hours?" I tell parents that I think of Attention Deficit Disorder as "Attention *Control* Deficit Disorder" (other specialists have dubbed it Attention Disregulation Disorder). Kids with ADD do not control their attention; their attention controls them. When they are highly interested in a task (such as a video game or a Lego model), the house could be burning down and they would not move. However, if they are not interested in a task (especially repetitive, mundane tasks like math problems), they cannot apply their attention just at your request. The fact that your child can focus so deeply on some activities does not mean that she could do better if she tried, on others.

Social Issues and Attention Problems

Kids with attention problems can have a wide range of social issues. Some impulsively interrupt everyone (not just friends, but teachers, coaches, and parents). Others are in trouble for playing too rough (again). Still others are prone to wandering off (either mentally or physically) in the middle of the conversation. There are many ways that poor attention control or hyperactivity will affect a child's friendships, social relationships, and self-esteem; these may require as much intervention as the academic problems. (See Chapter 12: Social Skills Issues, for more information.)

There is a lot of natural variation in attention spans. Let's think anthropology for a second. It was adaptive in some societies or groups to have a lot of energy, be willing to take risks, and to act quickly (like early hunters). Complex societies need people with different skill sets and temperaments to hold different roles. It is not surprising that a high activity level is now a problem in a society that wants all children to sit quietly in a classroom for several hours a day.

However, AD/HD is not just a cultural or social problem related to changes in what we expect of children. True AD/HD is a physiological issue with neurological underpinnings. The neurological profiles vary from person to person and can be complicated by other factors (discussed later in this chapter). Basically, AD/HD (or ADD) is just the way that some brains work, while for others, it is due to injury or illness. There is a huge range of the types of attention problems that are out there. It can be hard to see where to draw the line between normal and abnormal – and often it is not a line, but a broad, gray area.

Whether you consider it a disorder or just a style of learning and being, AD/HD can be a real problem. Children can struggle socially and academically, leading to complicating issues of chronic anxiety and low self-esteem. For children with moderate to severe attention problems, challenges continue through teen years and into adulthood. Finishing school does not necessarily solve these problems; adults can continue having trouble focusing at work or keeping their lives on track. If attention problems or hyperactivity are disrupting your child's life, then intervention may truly be necessary.

AD/HD and The Gender Gap

AD/HD in girls can be a whole different ball of wax. Girls, by and large, are more aware of the social agenda and try hard to meet classroom expectations. They are also less likely to have the hyperactive component, so they tend to be the dreamy ones who doodle in class instead of paying attention. A girl will try harder to maintain the appearance of normalcy all day – but when she gets in the car, exhausted from the effort of pretending, she may melt down completely. Most girls will eventually get their homework done because they don't want to fail, but that doesn't mean it isn't a nightly torture for both her and her parents.

Girls' struggles differ in the social arena too. While boys are known for poking and pushing and being silly, girls lose track of the conversation, of the game that is being played, of their cell phones and everything else they own. They then laugh it off with their friends – "I am SUCH a space cadet!" – but silently suffer from low self-esteem. Girls with attention problems are often identified much later than boys with comparable issues, but they are actually much more at risk for depression and anxiety.

AD/HD "Styles" That Run (and Skip, and Hop, and Climb) in the Family

"My thoughts are like arrows flying through my head. Sometimes I can grab them, sometimes I can't." ~ 18-year old girl, describing her attention problems and worrying about her ability to succeed in college. Her father is an emergency room physician who runs another company in his spare time.

"I had a terrible time in school and I do not want my son to struggle like I did."~ Successful musician, worrying about his middle-school-aged son who has a similar inattentive style in the classroom.

"We adore him. We never had any concerns with his behavior. We do so much as a family and he keeps up and is a great kid. And now the kindergarten teacher is saying he has attention problems?!" ~ Concerned mother, whose five-year old son reports, "My mom jumps out of planes and my dad races cars!" when asked what his parents do for a living.

In many cases, attention problems seem to run in the family. A child with AD/HD is four times more likely to have a relative who also has it than children without the disorder. Researchers have found genetic markers that indicate that differences in neurotransmitters contribute to AD/HD in some families. I commonly identify attention problems in a child only to trigger a parent to reveal concerns about their own attention problems. It can be very helpful to lay out these family styles and patterns. I can also reassure parents that the attention problems their child has does not preclude future success, by simply pointing out their own successful lives.

So, if it runs in families, do we have to call this a *disorder?* Or might it be another type of normal – more of a learning and performance style? Well, that depends. If this style causes significant problems in the classroom and in other settings, making an actual diagnosis of a disorder may be fitting, along with development of a good treatment plan. I do recommend a thorough evaluation to see if the style has crossed over into something that impacts the child's quality of life.

The reason I am making such a strong point about *styles* is that that is the primary type of attention problem I see when I am evaluating. There is no medical problem or trauma - just a kid from a family that has this style in at least one parent. There is a lot of variability in these AD/HD styles, from the family of non-linear artists to the family of active daredevils. Neither type may enjoy the linear seat work of the average classroom. The profiles I see most often are:

- **Athlete.** This child plays four sports – his dad coaches two of them while working full time and renovating homes in his spare time. In elementary school, this child has trouble sitting still and particularly resists writing tasks. At home, he does not need to sit for meals because these are eaten on the run as everyone rushes off to sports practices. As he gets older, he is less physically fidgety in class, but his alertness drops the longer he has to sit still.
- **Artist.** This is the creative child, always thinking of a new way to approach things. His mother may send him off to get dressed for school in the morning, only to find

him in the basement in his underpants, playing with Legos. He may be fully dressed at school, but anything the teacher says might trigger flights of fancy as the child considers all the options. This child always has better things to do than homework.

Gifted. This child learned to read through osmosis before he entered school. Math was also a natural skill where multiplication just made sense and fractions were obvious. This child gets irritated when asked to show his work in math. The answer is obvious; there's no reason to march through those tedious steps. But by middle school (or sometimes high school or college), the demands changed. It was not about what the child was taking in, but how much he could produce. The papers had to be written, the projects had to be done. For the gifted child, all the answers were in his head, but he had no experience with the extended concentration needed to get it on paper. (See Chapter 10.5: Twice Exceptional, for more information.)

Controversy and AD/HD

There are a number of controversies in the field of Attention Deficit Disorder, especially regarding how social factors might be exaggerating the symptoms. We do have a much higher diagnosis rate in this country compared to Europe, which has much more stringent diagnostic criteria. Do we really have that many more kids who have a disorder? I have already discussed the possibility that, *at times*, it might be considered simply another learning style. Just a few additional controversies include:

- Are we over-diagnosing or under-diagnosing? If we are over-diagnosing, then this implies that we need to change the demands we place on kids so that more kids can just act their age. If we are under-diagnosing, then we are implying that we expect about 10-20 percent of the population has disordered attention. Really?
- Have we created this problem, at least in part, through higher expectations at an earlier age? Children in the U.S. are now expected to learn to read books and to count into the 100's (if not 1000) in kindergarten. That is a shift from 50 years ago when they spent kindergarten learning the alphabet, how to write their names, how to count to 20 and how to learn as a part of a group.
- Are we seeing more attention problems due to lack of activity? Children are not allowed to play outside with little supervision like in the "old days," and so do not get the needed exercise or movement that promotes good alertness. Vastly increased screen time (TV, computer games, video games, tablets) also reduces alertness for other tasks.

How much of a role do classroom management concerns play? The more crowded a classroom, the more problematic an active child is, and the less energy an overwhelmed teacher has to differentiate his needs.

I believe that cumulatively, factors like these can combine to overwhelm a child's system and skew his performance. It does not necessarily mean there is something wrong with his brain.

Research and Possibilities

AD/HD research has focused largely on dopamine function. Dopamine is a brain chemical called a neurotransmitter, which has been linked to sleep, mood, attention, and learning, among other things. Studies have shown that people with AD/HD tend to have a sluggish dopamine system. Certain parts of the frontal lobe also tend to be smaller or less active than in more neurotypical children. Finally, there can be abnormal functioning in neural pathways that regulate behavior.

Medication can certainly help if these are, in fact, the reasons that your child has deficits in his attention control. But there are always those mysterious kids that no one can seem to figure out. Recent research has begun to look more closely beyond dopamine and frontal lobe issues. Many people have examined the connection between nutrition and attention; others have begun looking at how other brain centers might contribute to AD/HD issues. One research project at Harvard is examining the effect that different kinds of trauma have on different parts of the brain, all of which might produce AD/HD symptoms, but each of which would require completely different treatment.

Furthermore, some researchers are exploring *why* a person might be having dopamine issues. Some children may not process certain nutrients that are essential to building dopa-

> **Food for Thought**
>
> Keep in mind that attention control progresses as part of the *developmental process.* A toddler should not be expected to have a long attention span. Most pediatricians will not refer a child under the age of three for evaluation of attention. Attention control and organizational capacity continue to develop well into the 20s. The frontal lobes of the brain, important for organization and attention, are the last to mature.
>
> Thus, even a child with AD/HD will often exhibit improvements in attention control over time, though their attention control may always appear immature in comparison to peers. (Of note: The youngest and therefore least mature children in a classroom are more likely to be diagnosed with AD/HD – Morrow et al, 2012.) For some kids, attention problems seem to resolve, finally, in their mid-20s when their frontal lobes mature completely *and* when they are able to pursue a career that caters to their interests.

mine; others may have global inflammation issues that would interfere with its processing. Biomedical practitioners can help identify and correct these issues.

The moral of the story is: If you are having trouble finding effective solutions, or if, for whatever reason, you're not thrilled about having your child on meds, there may be other options out there for you. Some solutions are already out there, if not well known. And hopefully, new answers will soon provide a wider range of solutions that will benefit a wider range of people.

Factors that Contribute to AD/HD-like Behavior

AD/HD is diagnosed by a checklist of symptoms, not a blood test or a brain scan. We do not know what specifically causes attention deficit disorder (and there are multiple likely causes or things that contribute). Genetics clearly play a role in many children, but there can be many reasons a child may have the symptoms of AD/HD.

While AD/HD is a neurobiological condition that can run in families, not all attention control problems are as simple as that. There are several categories of factors that can affect attention control. These factors may become cumulative, with each issue worsening attention problems. Certain conditions or situations commonly associated with AD/HD include:

- **Medical conditions.** Injuries or illness in the brain, as well as genetic disorders or neurologic conditions, will typically affect attention control. These are a range of conditions, but can all fall into the *medical* category because a physician will often diagnose, monitor, and manage the condition. These can include head injury, chromosomal abnormality (such as Fragile X Syndrome), neurological illness or insult (meningitis, tumor, stroke, prenatal alcohol/drug exposure, prenatal malnutrition, lead exposure). Treatment of the medical condition must take priority in these cases. Some of these, such as lead exposure, require medical intervention that will hopefully ameliorate other issues and improve the attention problems. Other conditions are chronic and permanent. However, identifying the underlying medical condition still helps by allowing you to research it and find treatments. I find that children whose attention problems stem from medical conditions have other issues, such as:
  - Often cannot control their attention even for high-interest tasks
  - Exhibit such poor attention control that there is a significant impact on their intelligence and ability to learn
  - Have other learning disabilities or challenges that complicate the attention problems

- **Nutritional or related biomedical factors**. You are what you eat, they say. So if a person relies heavily on sugar and caffeine, there may be some attention problems. Moreover, we are now identifying specific micronutrients that are *essential* for good attention control. Some children are found to be low in certain nutrients for unknown reasons. Making sure those nutrients get into a child in the right amounts does have an impact on attention control. This sort of nutritional work-up must be done by a specialist (nutritionist, physician), but can be quite helpful if a problem is found. Food allergies and sensitivities have also been associated with attention problems. Nutrition does not always play a role, but don't underestimate the influence these factors can have on brain chemistry and performance. (See Chapter 14: Biomedical Approaches and Chapter 15: Nutritional Approaches.)

- **Emotional issues.** Trauma can overwhelm the emotions and impair the nervous system, making it difficult for children to organize their thoughts, direct their attention, or control a nervous hypervigilance. Children with histories of abuse, neglect, or other trauma will often have poor attention control. The problems are not simply behavioral. Trauma can shift neurochemistry. Treatment must address the impact on their emotional health and nervous system, as well as the outward attention problems. (See Chapter 11: Emotional and Behavioral Issues and Chapter 13: Psychiatry and Functional Medicine Psychiatry.)

- **Situation-specific symptoms.** There can also be short term attention problems that arise from stress, illness, or injury. For example, a child may be more distracted and disorganized when parents are going through a divorce or right after an upsetting move. Some children do not sleep well when their allergies are flaring and can be more inattentive (and irritable) during the day at these times. Sleep problems, in general, can definitely affect attention and should be considered. Concussion (see Chapter 9: Concussions) can disrupt attention for several weeks or months. However, a diagnosis of AD/HD would be inappropriate in these situations as it would not be a consistent, long-term pattern.

Food for Thought: Ruling Out Other Possibilities

There is good reason for doing a thorough evaluation and not just a checklist of symptoms. Case in point: Theo. Theo's parents brought him in to me for a comprehensive evaluation, hoping to address all of his issues and avoid medication. Theo had recently turned three, which is usually a little young for a diagnosis of ADHD, but he had a handful of worrisome behaviors. In his preschool, he was so distracted and active that he could only wander the room aimlessly; at home, he could not even pay attention to things he enjoyed, and was not capable of staying seated for more than a couple of minutes at mealtimes. He was also quite clumsy, tripping over his feet and falling into the wall. His head was often bruised from these falls. Theo was usually a cheerful little guy. . . until he lost his temper. His tantrums were then so out of control that his parents were afraid he would hurt himself.

True, ADD symptoms were certainly there. But what was the deal with the odd stumbling and the severe tantrums? Upon exploration, several other risk factors emerged. Theo had been born prematurely, weighing only two pounds. He did not breathe immediately and needed oxygen support for several weeks. As he grew, the pediatrician noted that Theo's eyes were unusually wide set, which prompted the doctor to send Theo for genetics testing. He was found to have a chromosomal abnormality – a rare one for which there was little data yet, but one that could affect any number of biological and developmental systems.

When evaluated by an occupational therapist, Theo was found to have sensory processing and motor processing problems that required intensive occupational therapy. His preschool was asked to provide more intensive services and supervision to build social skills and attention. His mother began to explore nutrition more deeply in order to support optimal brain chemistry and emotional stability.

It would have been easy for the family to stop at ADD medication, but the non-attention symptoms wouldn't have budged. A year's worth of intensive treatments was beginning to see progress. Theo will have life-long challenges, but I remain impressed with the family's thoroughness and believe they are doing what is necessary to ensure the best possible outcome for their son.

~ Robin McEvoy

Dual Diagnoses:
Will the Real Culprit Please Stand Up?

This section presents another set of factors that can complicate the picture. If you've done the checklists at the beginning of the book, you may have begun to see this for yourself. Over half the children diagnosed with ADD or ADHD are also identified with other conditions, often learning disabilities. However, this is probably the least rigorously explored question in the AD/HD world. Attention Deficit Disorder is often the first (and sometimes only) culprit that is considered when a child is struggling. Whenever attention deficit is diagnosed, it is important to dig down a little more to rule out (or identify) other issues.

In these cases, you have to treat the other disorder in order to assess what attention problems remain. Sometimes, addressing the primary diagnosis will resolve attention issues altogether. At the very least, the symptoms should improve dramatically.

The most common diagnoses that coincide with AD/HD are:

- **Bipolar disorder** – Children with a mood disorder typically have attention problems, but they need a different treatment approach than children who simply have ADD without a mood component. It is critical to differentiate the two. (See Chapter 11: Emotional and Behavioral Issues and Chapter 13: Psychiatry and Functional Medicine Psychiatry.)
- **Autism** – Many children with autism also have problems with attention control. Sometimes, practitioners tend to focus on the more dramatic symptoms of autism and not consider attention control when planning treatment. (See Chapter 8: Autism Spectrum Disorders.)
- **Sensory Processing Disorder or SPD** – I believe this is a much more common contributor than is often realized. If your child is hypersensitive to a form of sensory input, he may become hypervigilant, chronically overwhelmed, jumpy, or spaced out. The kids on the other end of the sensory spectrum, who need extra sensory input, are always moving, kneeling in their chairs, crashing into people, etc. Sound familiar? SPD can take many different forms, but all of them can exhaust a child, impair focus and look a lot like ADD or ADHD. (See Chapter 7: Sensory Processing Disorder.)
- **Speech/Language Disorders or Auditory Processing Disorder (APD)** – Children who do not process verbal input well often act distracted, fail to understand instructions, and have trouble following quick or detailed conversations (so they stop paying attention). (See Chapter 5: Speech and Language Issues and Chapter 5.1: Auditory Processing Disorder.)
- **Dyslexia and other reading disorders** – It's hard to pay attention to a book when the words don't make sense. It's also hard to take notes, copy information from the board, or write essays. A reading problem can exhaust a child's attention span fairly quickly. (See Chapter 6: Dyslexia and Other Reading Disabilities.)
- **Head injury** – If your child had a concussion (or more significantly, multiple concussions), it could be contributing to ADD-like symptoms. However, keep in mind that children with ADHD are often more at risk for concussions because of impulsive, over-active behavior. (See Chapter 9: Concussions.)

Latest Research

Everyone wants to "crack" ADD. There are studies all the time revealing the "six types of ADD" or the "new ADD drugs and how they are better for the brain" or the "myth of ADD"…it goes on and on. Unfortunately, many of these theories end up not standing the test of time. But you should know that there are constant discoveries on this subject and that recent research might be relevant to you. The resources at the end of this chapter can direct you to sound information that has been vetted by professionals.

Who Can Help?

AD/HD can be a more complicated condition to treat than some other disorders in this book, depending on how you want to approach it. If your pediatrician can make the diagnosis and you are comfortable with a medication trial, then it can be pretty simple. If you're reading this book, however, there's probably more to it than that for you.

This disorder is unusual in that you will often need to see different practitioners for diagnosis and for treatment, and who you see for treatment depends entirely on the specific symptoms your child has. There is not really a category for "AD/HD specialists" – you could end up seeing a psychologist for emotional issues, a neurofeedback provider for attention control, an occupational therapist to organize his sensory systems, or practically any other specialist in this book, depending on your child's needs.

STEP ONE: GET A DIAGNOSIS

Like autism, AD/HD is diagnosed by looking at behavioral symptoms alone. No single brain scan, cognitive test, or blood test has emerged, as yet, that allows a doctor to point to a particular result and say, "See that right there? Proof positive of AD/HD!" As a result, the diagnostic process can be somewhat subjective.

Some practitioners will have you fill out a simple questionnaire. If a parent or teenager checks off enough symptoms on this single list, some doctors are content to make the diagnosis and give meds a try. A more thorough approach may yield more complex and helpful results.

Keep these factors in mind when looking for a diagnostician:

- The presence of symptoms should be confirmed *over several settings* – meaning that teachers, coaches, and other significant caregivers from a range of activities should also provide input (or at least have expressed concerns to parents).
- Other medical or psychological contributors should be ruled out, so a medical history and emotional screening should also be obtained.
- Be aware that some providers do give a "quickie" diagnosis. Be sure to seek out

a more in-depth evaluation using standardized tests or computerized tests. Find a practitioner who practices due diligence and does not just pass out diagnoses and meds after listening for five minutes, nodding and saying, "Sounds like AD/HD to me."

Methods of Diagnosis

There are a number of tools practitioners can use to determine the presence of ADD. More technologies emerge all the time, so ask any prospective practitioner which she prefers and why. I do not have a strong opinion on the best combination of specific tests; I just want to see that a practitioner used more than one of the following. The most common methods include:

- Interview with parents and, if appropriate, the child
- Medical history, including the child's social, emotional, educational, and behavioral background
- Behavior-rating questionnaires - there are many types available, varying in cost and detail; input from teachers, coaches, and other caregivers should be included (even if some of this input is simply through a parent's report or notes from school reports)
- Tests or screening to assess cognitive skills, academic skills, memory, and problem solving, which will help rule out other learning disabilities or developmental challenges (See Chapter 3: Evaluations-Who Does What.)
- Various brain imaging technologies that can reveal distinct structures, blood flow patterns, and other characteristics of the brain (this is the most recent and cutting-edge aspect of AD/HD diagnosis, so it is difficult for me to comment on the comparative efficacy of these techniques)

Who Makes the Diagnosis

Attention Deficit Disorder is a medical diagnosis, so any physician is legally qualified to make it. But not all of them do – and not all of them *should* – as it is a disorder that a practitioner should be knowledgeable about in order to correctly identify it. Always find out which methods they use to make their determination. There are three types of professionals whose experience, credentials, and expertise you can seek:

Pediatricians. This always seems like a reasonable place to start, but not all pediatricians offer an in-depth evaluation. Even if you do begin with a pediatric consult, you may want to ask for a referral to a specialist who can rule out other learning challenges or complicating factors. Some pediatricians prefer that a specialist make the diagnosis; then the pediatrician can monitor the issue.

Child psychiatrists. For more information about how child psychiatrists might approach this, see Chapter 13 on psychiatry. You should know that many psychiatrists are often only oriented toward medications for the treatment approach. If you want to explore other solutions, you will need to find a Functional Medicine psychiatrist, or get the diagnosis first and then explore some of the other possibilities presented in this chapter.

Psychologists. Neuropsychologists, developmental psychologists, and many child clinical psychologists evaluate for attention disorders. This group of practitioners tends to explore the issue in more depth. And, because they cannot prescribe medications, they usually explore a wider range of treatment approaches.

School Psychologists. Some school districts have professionals in place to evaluate and make this diagnosis. Ask the school counselor or your child's teacher.

Suggested Questions for a Prospective AD/HD Diagnostician

- What is your experience with and your approach to diagnosing Attention Deficit Disorder or Attention Deficit Disorder with hyperactivity?
- How do you approach ruling out other medical, developmental, psychological, or learning disorders that might contribute to attention problems?
- If you make this diagnosis, do you provide treatment or do you refer us to other providers?
- How does the use of stimulant medication fit into your approach to treatment?
- Do you explore issues such as nutrition, sleep, and eating habits in your assessment?

STEP TWO: GET OTHER RELEVANT EVALUATIONS

Once you have obtained a diagnosis, use the checklists at the beginning of the book to identify any other areas you may want to consider. If you decide you want to explore other avenues, read through the relevant chapters and contact those professionals. The overall picture that emerges should help guide your priorities and choices.

Step Three: Choose Your Treatment Plan

AD/HD can end up being a very complicated condition, particularly if you have other issues to sort out as well. When creating your treatment plan, you may want to refer to the section entitled, "Why Sequence Matters," which appears after the Master Checklist in Chapter 2.

Treatment Options: Standard of Care

The standard of care treatment for AD/HD is pretty straightforward:

- **Medication.** Drugs that enhance attention control are by far the most common treatment. (See Chapter 13: Psychiatric and Functional Medicine Psychiatry, for more information about the most common medications used, as well as more discussion on the pros and cons of using medication.)

- **Counseling.** Therapy, behavioral intervention, or tutoring are used to address any remaining concerns. This can include any number of resources from social skills groups (to practice not tackling friends impulsively) to a writing tutor (to help get that darn book report written). These interventions are targeted at whatever is needed, including therapy for children who become depressed and frustrated by the daily struggles of not fitting in socially or academically.

- **Lifestyle changes.** Medication and counseling attempt to change the kid by increasing attention control and shifting problematic behaviors. Sometimes though, you have to change the situation instead. If a child's attention is exhausted at the end of the day, he may need a reduced homework load or fewer extracurriculars. If an athletic child continues to be fidgety and restless in a traditional classroom, is it possible to switch schools to one that allows or requires more movement? A creative, dreamy child may need more down time where she can create and recharge rather than trying to keep up with an over-scheduled after-school agenda. Sure, we want to shift a child to be able to meet most typical demands, but by shifting the situation, we are also meeting in the middle and allowing the child to be her unique self.

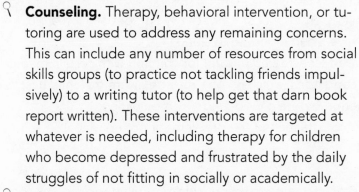

Meds as a Diagnostic Tool

Some practitioners (and many parents) think that if a child responds to a stimulant medication with increased attention, then that is in itself diagnostic of an Attention Deficit Disorder. However, the majority of the population responds to stimulant medication with increased attention whether they have attention problems or not. Bottom line: Get a thorough evaluation. A response to meds is not proof positive of Attention Deficit Disorder.

To Medicate or Not To Medicate

It's not a simple question to answer. I've seen medication make a world of difference for some kids, but I've also seen it not help that much or compound the problem because of the side effects. Many medications used for AD/HD are stimulants, but their effects on different people vary. What makes one person nicely alert may make another jumpy. Sometimes people have to experiment with medication choices and timing of doses before they find a plan that works.

Most families who see me for evaluation of Attention Deficit Disorder would prefer not to jump into medications. And just because a child meets criteria for a diagnosis of AD/HD does not mean that medication is a must. I tell parents that medication is just one tool to consider in the treatment tool box. Also, it is a *medical decision*, with health decisions that should be evaluated by a physician. Some factors to consider:

- Medication can have side effects that make them a poor choice for some children. Kids can become either overly emotional or emotionally flat, get too lethargic, exhibit tics, stop eating, or have trouble getting to sleep.
- Medication is contraindicated (considered unsafe) for children with certain medical conditions, such as heart conditions (which no one may be aware the child has). Get a thorough medical evaluation before considering any medication.
- Medication may only resolve a fraction of the problem, or not help at all in some cases.

Parents and I walk through some parameters before deciding whether even to seek an evaluation for medication:

Is there a safety issue? Does your child dart into the street or leave group situations without notifying an adult? Does he like to dare others, or be dared to do something? I had a little client once who came home from a play date with a bright blue mouth; turns out he had drunk the neighbor's chemistry set on a dare. If your child is so impulsive or hyperactive that safety is a frequent concern, then medication may be necessary, at least as a stopgap measure while you explore other options.

Is your child failing academically or socially, *and realizes it?* Is he coming home complaining that he is stupid, that everyone can do the work but him? If the child's attention problems are causing daily stress for the child, then a medication evaluation might be considered.

But what if it is not as bad as all that? OK, so your child has attention problems. But there are no safety issues, he has friends, and he's basically a happy kid. School could be better, but he is not failing. Do we need to medicate? Some tutoring support and more opportunities to move around and pursue high-interest tasks might suffice. Asking the school for an educational accommodation, such as reduced homework, might reduce conflict at home at night.

Treatment Options: Complementary and Alternative Medicine (CAM)

Considering that AD/HD is the most common diagnosis in the area of child development, most CAM providers address it. And this is helpful. I have worked with some families where at least one parent refuses to consider medication as an approach to treatment. I remind them that if their child's daily life is seriously disrupted and they are not going to try a medication trial, then they absolutely need to consider other interventions, including CAM approaches. Oftentimes CAM is a complementary approach used in conjunction with traditional approaches. However, it can also be used as an alternative to traditional medical approaches. The CAM approaches that are most commonly used and have had the most success include:

Chapter 14: Biomedical Approaches. There are medical problems, such as lead exposure, that are clearly linked to attention problems and have a medical treatment. Research continues to emerge linking attention problems with nutritional deficiencies and food sensitivities. Biomedical can be a very useful approach when trying to find the source of the attention problem.

Chapter 15: Nutritional Approaches. Even without a clear food allergy, the lack of good food can impact attention. For some children, the lack of good quality protein, whole foods, or regular meals has a huge impact on attention control skills.

Chapter 16.1: Naturopathy. A holistic approach to a child's physical and behavioral health may be able to influence attention at many levels.

Chapter 16.2: Neurofeedback/Biofeedback. This treatment uses a computerized task that measures brain wave patterns and teaches the child to access and control these patterns.

Chapter 16.3: LEAP (Learning Enhancement Acupressure Program). Because AD/HD can have such different underlying neurological causal factors, LEAP work can help organize overall neurological function.

Chapter 16.4: Chiropractic Neurology. Chiropractic neurologists are chiropractors with specialized training in neurology. They have an in-depth assessment protocol for exploring reasons for attention problems and develop an individualized treatment program from there.

Chapter 17.5: Craniosacral Therapy. Craniosacral treatment aims to promote a state of calm alertness and increase the child's overall ability to regulate his attention and emotions. This therapy helps promote overall nervous system health and may help organize underlying neurology.

Resources for More Information

Websites

www.ADDitudemag.com. This excellent website has an accessible online magazine format and an advisory board of well-respected experts in the field. It covers the standard of care approaches thoroughly, as well as any good complementary and alternative approaches. Parents and adults with AD/HD also write some excellent articles. You can order a subscription to have the actual magazine delivered to your home.

Books

There are hundreds (maybe thousands) of books geared toward the layperson wanting to know more about AD/HD. Some particularly useful ones include:

Taking Charge of ADHD: The Complete Authoritative Guide for Parents by Russell Barkley. This is a classic text that covers the traditional approach to diagnosis and treatment of ADHD and ADD.

Driven to Distraction: Recognizing and Coping with Attention Deficit Disorder from Childhood through Adulthood by Edward Hallowell, MD and John Ratey, MD. These two physicians wrote a whole series of books on the subject after this first book became so popular. Their interest stemmed from their own self-diagnoses when they were in medical school listening to a lecture on the disorder.

Spark: The Revolutionary New Science of Exercise and the Brain by John Ratey, MD. This more recent book by Dr. Ratey focuses on how movement supports alertness.

AD/HD Drug Free: Natural Alternatives and Practical Exercises to Help your Child Focus by Frank Jacobelli and Lynn A Watson. This book is full of practical suggestions and strategies that can be used to help a child better manage attention weaknesses and related behavior problems.

The Edison Gene: ADHD and the Gift of the Hunter Child by Thom Hartmann. This book reminds us that it is ok to be energetic and inquisitive, but also how our modern society can pull this style in a bad direction.

Healing the New Childhood Epidemics: Autism, ADHD, Asthma, and Allergies: The Ground-breaking Program for the 4-A Disorders by Kenneth Bock, MD with Cameron Stauth. This book explores many of the current biomedical concerns that may contribute to AD/HD.

REFERENCES

Morrow, R., J. Garland, J. Wright, M. Maclure, S. Taylor, and C. Dormuth. Influence of relative age on diagnosis and treatment of Attention-Deficit/Hyperactivity Disorder in children, *Canadian Medical Association Journal*, 184 (7) (April 2012): 755-62.

ABOUT THE AUTHOR

Robin McEvoy, PhD, is a developmental neuropsychologist and one of the editors of this book. You can find her complete bio in the back.

FIVE

Speech and Language Issues

by Lynn Anderson, MS, CCC-SLP

and Nickie Gosselin, MS, CCC-SLP

Read through all of the lists, and mark any items within your child's age range, or in his past, that are appropriate. This may give you more of a sense of the type of language challenges your child has. Some symptoms will also refer you to the Auditory Processing chapter and are noted with "APD" in parentheses.

Infancy (birth to 9 months)
- ☐ Does not respond to sounds in the room (e.g., does not startle when bell rings)
- ☐ Easily upset by unexpected noises
- ☐ Does not turn to sound of another's voice
- ☐ Does not coo or make other noises
- ☐ By 7 months of age, does not babble or make consonant sounds
- ☐ Does not take pleasure in others speaking to him
- ☐ Has frequent ear infections or history of fluid in ears

Toddler (10 months to 30 months)
- ☐ Does not respond to name
- ☐ Does not follow simple commands (give it to me, spit it out)
- ☐ Does not babble or jabber (series of speech-like sounds)
- ☐ Does not express emotions through voice (frustration, joy)
- ☐ Does not use single words by 17 months
- ☐ Does not combine words by 24 months
- ☐ Does not combine a word or phrase with a gesture (e.g., holds out cup, says "more milk")
- ☐ Covers ears in or avoids loud settings, crowds, places that might get noisy. (APD)

Preschool (30 months to 4 years)

- ☐ Only the parent can understand the child's speech
- ☐ Cannot answer simple questions (e.g., "How old are you?") (APD)
- ☐ Limited vocabulary, says under 200 words
- ☐ Does not ask "why" questions
- ☐ Does not enjoy language and talking about things
- ☐ Can't follow "if-then" instructions (e.g., "If you get your coat, we can go outside")

Elementary age (5 years to 10 years)

- ☐ Does not engage in conversation (APD)
- ☐ Only monologues about his areas of interest, does not engage others well
- ☐ Poor articulation (cannot form all speech sounds by 7)
- ☐ Speaks only in short sentences (even if they talk a lot) (APD)
- ☐ Can't tell a story or a narrative of their day
- ☐ Cannot follow directions with two or more steps (APD)
- ☐ Dysfluent speech, stutters, starts over
- ☐ Puts words in wrong order
- ☐ Cannot remember his own phone number or address
- ☐ Does not use language in play (e.g., cannot create dialogue of imaginary characters or give instructions to peers)
- ☐ Cannot learn alphabet
- ☐ Misunderstands question words (e.g., answers a "why" question with a "how" answer) (APD)
- ☐ Family history of speech or language delay

Looking back, Amy's mouth function had been a concern by the time she was six months old. Although she had nursed well enough, the transition to taking a bottle was tough. And she refused to take a spoon in her mouth, pursing her lips so tightly together you could not have flossed between them. Learning to eat was an arduous process until she was a year old, at which point she was identified with Sensory Processing Disorder. An occupational therapist worked with her to take food in her mouth, chew, and swallow, but she still could not bite through even a cracker until she was two and a half. Most worrisome of all, although she could cry and laugh, she could not make voluntary speech sounds. At the occupational thera-pist's recommendation, I took Amy to speech therapy when she was 16 months old, but her first words did not come until she was four. We used sign language to bridge the gap. Amy preferred signing to using picture cards to communicate, but it was hard to leave her with sitters or with friends, as no one else knew sign language. She spent years in speech therapy, but slowly things got better. Amy turned out to be very verbal with a great vocabulary, though articulation never became perfect. ~TC

The Basics

Oh, those first words! We can't wait to hear them…the adorable mangled baby dialect that only Mom and Dad can understand, which slowly morphs into real words. Communication connects people, and speech and language are key components of communication. Yes, gestures and facial expression play a huge role too, but words are the easiest route to meaning. They seem to emerge so easily and automatically for most children. When a child struggles, it is baffling and frustrating for both the child and parents.

Language and communication are complex, so let's break them down. First, speech and language actually refer to two different things.

- **Speech** refers to the physical ability to produce words by positioning the lips and tongue and then activating the voice. Ultimately, words should come out fluidly, but it's normal for children to display articulation weaknesses when they begin speaking.
- **Language** refers to the communicative intent of those words. To use *language* well, a child needs to understand the words said to him and to produce words that convey meaning to others. This ability has two components:
  - **Receptive abilities** (understanding of language). This refers to a child's ability to attend to and understand sounds, words, and narratives.
  - **Expressive abilities** (sharing ideas). This indicates a child's ability to communicate his wants, ideas, and feelings.

If speech or language skills are weak or disordered, they can impact academic performance in many ways. Initially, a child practices these skills only in verbal and auditory form. But by second grade, her expressive ability will need to extend to written form as well. Speech or language problems can also create emotional strain that influences a child's relationships with others, general confidence, and overall stress level. It is estimated that 15 percent of children require speech-language therapy at some point. Early intervention in this area is important, as a strong foundation in communication skills will help a child be more successful from the beginning.

There are two categories of speech/language disorders:

- **Developmental.** The child exhibited weaknesses in some type of language ability from the start, without a clear medical reason. **The focus in this chapter will be on these.**
- **Acquired.** The child has experienced a brain injury, such as stroke or head trauma, that impacts speech or language skills.

Language disorders can be quite frustrating for children who are afflicted with them. Those with expressive language weaknesses, in particular, are often a great deal more intelligent than they can demonstrate. It's all in there – they just can't get it out! This can lead to a higher overall stress level, self-esteem issues, and fear of many social and academic situations.

Speech and Language Development: The Early Years

During the first years of life, a child learns an astonishing array of new skills in every developmental area. Speech and language skills are no exception.

Children begin to develop an understanding of sounds and words far before they are able to express themselves, so a lot is happening even in the first year. In the first five years, children progress from simply turning to the sound of mom's voice to following directions with several steps, from cooing to making sophisticated little conversations in just a few years. It is an astonishing progress. At some stages, children are learning 15 new words *each and every day for months.* An adult would be hard pressed to do that.

During the elementary school years, children are using those language skills daily to learn and to demonstrate their knowledge. The classroom is a language-enriched environment. Children need both their receptive and expressive language skills for learning, reading, and writing.

- Receptive skills. Children are expected to follow directions, understand questions, and comprehend the information presented.
- Expressive skills. Children are expected to respond to questions, comment and express ideas on topic matters, and present information.

There are numerous resources for checking the general developmental speech and language milestones that occur from infancy to elementary school. The American Speech-Language-Hearing Association (www.asha.org) has an excellent breakdown of speech and language milestones. It is important to note that all children develop at their own rates, so don't automatically worry if your son isn't as "advanced" as your best friend's daughter (and yes, boys really do develop speech skills more slowly in many cases!). However, if you have concerns, you should speak with your pediatrician or contact a Speech-Language Pathologist.

A Closer Look

LET'S TALK SPEECH

Appropriate speech skills require several skills that are automatic for the typical speaker. We take these for granted and most of us are not aware of how many distinct skills go into speaking ability. For example:

- **Voice** refers to the use of both breath and vocal cords to produce sounds. When you hear a baby crying, you would think that voice is automatic. But some children can only *voice* when they are crying or laughing. They cannot produce voice voluntarily.
- **Articulation** refers to how the sounds in words are made. Once the voice is voluntary, the child learns all those intricate sounds in his language. Tongue, lip, and breath control are all critical here.
- **Fluency** refers to the rhythm of speech. Babies start practicing fluency when they babble, imitating the rhythms of speech before they have words or even all the sounds. Some children cannot organize these rhythms.

These speech processes take time to develop, but for the most part are fairly complete in children by age five (with some sounds not fully forming until the age of seven). Here are a few terms to help you understand the distinct aspects of speech:

A **speech sound disorder** is more commonly known as an articulation disorder. A child either has difficulty producing specific sounds, or she substitutes, omits, or distorts those sounds. Children who lisp or who substitute one sound for another (e.g., "torn" for "corn") fall into this category.

Children with speech sound disorders understand what is said to them (that is, they have good receptive language skills), but are difficult to understand. Their speech often becomes more unintelligible as their sentence length increases. This can be very frustrating for children because they know what they want to say, but it does not come out right. There are several types of these weaknesses that can impact speech.

- An **oral motor disorder** means that a child has poor control of mouth muscles. A child with this profile may have feeding issues along with speech issues. For example, he may not be able to grind up food well with his back teeth or chew through thicker food such as pizza crust.
- Dysarthria is a motor weakness where a child has low muscle tone. These children struggle to make precise oral movements for speech articulation, so speech may sound slurred.
- Childhood apraxia of speech indicates a breakdown between the brain and the mouth regarding how to produce and sequence the sounds in words. They usually do not have problems with mouth movements needed for other activities, such as eating.
- A fluency disorder occurs when a child has difficulty producing uninterrupted speech. Stuttering is a fluency disorder, though it is only considered a disorder if it persists into school age. It is not uncommon for younger children to go through a stuttering period. (However, prolonged periods (three or more months) of non-fluent speech in a preschool age child warrant examination by a speech-language pathologist.) Cluttering is another fluency disorder. With cluttering, a child has a rapid rate of speech, disorganized thought process, word recall weakness, and articulation errors.
- A voice disorder refers to chronic hoarseness or other signs of vocal strain. A child who has excessive yelling, growling, or even tense neck muscles can eventually damage the vocal cords. Singers and cheerleaders are also at risk for voice disorders.

Let's Talk Language

Rosie is a chatty five-year-old, popular in preschool and a leader among her peers. But her mother and teachers are concerned that she is not ready for kindergarten. She loves to be read to, but has no interest in learning letters or words herself. She has even struggled to learn colors. In testing, it quickly becomes apparent that Rosie has problems understanding language. A simple question like "how old are you?" gets the answer, "My name is Rosie." When the question is repeated, a look of irritation crosses her face and she says again, "ROSIE!!!!" Another clue emerges if you listen to her closely: For all her chattiness, her sentences are quite simple, each containing only four or five words at most. Moreover, even though she is a natural leader – being sociable, athletic, and a bit bossy – close observation reveals that she always has to be the one telling everyone what to do. She does not have the language processing skills to understand directions from others. ~LP

A child who can produce speech sounds well may still have trouble with other aspects of language. Language issues can take many forms, and often combines receptive and expressive weaknesses. This can create confusion for parents and teachers, as well as a great deal of frustration and stress for the child.

- **Receptive language disorder**. Children who have trouble understanding language may have poor vocabulary, as well as difficulty following directions, understanding questions, and following conversations and stories. They frequently have trouble with concept development, meaning that they do not necessarily connect the word *small* with the concept of size, *purple* with the concept of color, or *throw* with the concept of action word. "Throw me the small purple frog," therefore, does not have automatic meaning and can take a while to decode. It's like trying to decipher another language that you are still learning. Meaning does not flow in without effort and mistakes are easy to make.

  It's important to understand how tiring this can be for a child. Imagine having to concentrate that hard to do something that everyone else seems to do effortlessly all day long! A child struggling with language issues can become irritable, fatigued, or withdrawn after working that hard throughout the school day. There is a lot of overlap between receptive language issues and Auditory Processing Disorder (APD). See box for more information on APD.

- **Expressive language disorder.** These children may have been late talkers as toddlers. They often have difficulty with vocabulary development or recalling a known word from long-term memory. This is the "tip of the tongue" phenomenon that we all experience from time to time, but it may be so severe that it can impact overall ability to communicate.

- Children with expressive weaknesses often express themselves very simply because of difficulty with complex grammar and sentence structure. They also have trouble defining things, explaining what they mean, and describing anything in detail. When asked a question, they tend to give the simplest possible answer and may look confused, blank, or even panicky when asked to elaborate.

Receptive Language or Auditory Processing Disorder (APD)?

The difference between these two is seldom neatly delineated, as both affect a child's understanding of language. Also, the presence of one frequently complicates the other. What's the difference?

Children with receptive language disorder can hear input clearly enough, but have trouble connecting it with meaning or following complicated sentences or concepts. Their trouble lies in the part of the brain that connects language with meaning.

Children with APD do not receive signals clearly in the first place. This has nothing to do with hearing per se; that is usually fine. It's just that the signal gets garbled. Many children with APD are fine in a quiet one-on-one setting, but with any kind of competing noise – another child talking at the same time as the teacher, for example, or music coming from the next room – they lose the ability to sort through the input and just become confused. Other children cannot decipher language clearly even in quiet settings, perhaps hearing "big red ball" as "bread ball." Remember playing the telephone game? If you were the last person in line, the message you received was usually pretty far from the original. The child with APD is always the last person in line.

How do you distinguish which of these is your child's primary issue, or which issues fall into which camp? You will need to get thorough evaluations in both speech/language issues and auditory processing. A speech/language pathologist does the first; an audiologist does the second. And yes, it is worth it to do both. If you try to work on receptive language skills when your child is not even sure what was just said, you're not going to get very far.

See the next chapter on APD for more information, including details of proper evaluation and treatment methods.

PRAGMATICS: WHERE LANGUAGE AND SOCIAL SKILLS INTERSECT

Other language disorders can be even harder to put a finger on. Some children seem to have lots of language and they talk all the time, but something in the communication is off. *Language* refers to the words, the sentence structure, the information presented; *communication* is language plus social skills. Does the information the child gave fit the situation or the question? Are the non-verbal parts of the communication (the gestures, the eye contact, the tone that expresses the emotion) in place? Does the child's communication always seem somehow off-topic ("Why is he talking about action heroes when I was asking if he locked the door?").

This surpasses the mere inability to understand the question. This is now the area of *pragmatics*, which refers to the child's ability to use *social* language skills. Some children have difficulty in conversation and play with peers and adults. They may need to work on maintaining eye contact, using greetings, initiating conversation, responding to conversational questions, taking turns, expressing feelings, identifying nonverbal communication cues, and understanding others' points of view. These children may also have difficulty understanding abstract language concepts, such as expressions like "break a leg."

Pragmatics is an essential part of verbal communication. People with Autistic Spectrum Disorders sometimes have a stunning vocabulary, but weak pragmatics. Treating pragmatic disorders is a specialty in the speech/language area, but many therapists have at least some experience. (Chapter 8: Autism Spectrum Disorders, will also provide information on specialists who can support specific communication skills.)

Causes

There can be numerous causes or contributors to speech and language disorders.

- Children with hearing impairments typically have speech and language delays related to this.
- Frequent early ear infections are a marker for fluid in a baby's middle ear (the area behind the ear drums). This can distort hearing and slow language development. For some children, this leads to persistent problems with processing. Even when the fluid is cleared, these children may have lasting problems processing language. This overlaps with APD.
- Neurological injuries resulting from stroke, meningitis, or other neurological illnesses can impact speech and/or language skills.
- Speech and language delays are common in children who have other developmental diagnoses such as Down Syndrome or autism.
- Prenatal exposure to alcohol or drugs can impact speech or language development.
- Children who are not spoken to as babies will typically have delays in language development. This is a common problem for children adopted from orphanages.
- Some speech or language delays run in families.
- Sometimes, we simply do not know the cause of a child's speech or language delays.

The Impact of Speech/Language Issues

Academic Concerns

- **Expressive language weaknesses.** Any child who cannot speak easily or fluidly will have trouble participating effectively in class. Speak to her teacher if you discover issues in this area, and make sure she develops strategies to support and encourage your child appropriately. The school's speech/language specialist can help with this if necessary.
- **Receptive language weaknesses.** Obviously, if a child has trouble understanding what is said to him, he is going to have difficulty following directions or understanding lessons. Issues that may have looked minor in elementary school can become overwhelming once he starts middle school and classes shift into more and more of a pure lecture format.
- **Possible effects on reading and writing.** If language is hard to understand, then language in written form (that is, reading) may also be hard to understand. Kids who do not understand spoken language may not understand what they read either. For some children, however, it is the fleeting nature of spoken language that is the problem. For these children, reading reduces problems. Once reading is mastered, children who have trouble understanding spoken language may be able to follow written directions more easily because the language "stays put" visually, allowing for the time needed to process the concepts.

Writing is often a challenge for those with language issues. For children with expressive language weaknesses, trying to put their thoughts into written form can be challenging, if not downright torturous. They may not be able to hold on to and organize their thoughts while they are trying to write legibly, spell, and remember other writing conventions.

Some speech/language therapists also address reading and writing issues. But if you cannot find one that does, you may need to find another kind of specialist. Parents can refer to Chapter 6: Dyslexia and Other Reading Disabilities, for more information on supporting reading.

Social Concerns

- **Expressive:** Children may have trouble making friends if they cannot keep up with their peers' play, or if they say the wrong things or never have anything to say. Children with speech irregularities may be mocked or avoided.

- **Receptive:** A child may find herself at odds with her peers if she frequently misunderstands their cues and questions. Some children develop a passive persona where they quietly follow along, trying to read the visual cues. Others decide that they do better on their own, or develop only one or two close friendships with people who make them feel safe. Many avoid activities that require too much verbal processing, limiting extracurricular involvement (including sports) because they fear they will only get confused and do something wrong. Conversely, as in the story of Rosie, some children develop a coping strategy of always being the one talking. They feel safe in that role and instinctively know they can maintain some control over the situation. Others may find them "bossy," which can lead to its own consequences...but at least they are not in the difficult position of trying to make sense of what others are saying!

Emotional Concerns

Deficits in either expressive or receptive skills can affect social relationships, self-esteem, and general levels of anxiety and frustration. Issues related to expression can be easier for parents or teachers to notice because the difficulty is more obvious. It is so frustrating for a child not to be able to say what she wants to say. Tantrums are not uncommon in younger children. Older children may simply act without asking. Children with receptive weaknesses can become masters of strategic avoidance and it might take years to figure out what the problem is. They must face the constant frustration of others and may become insecure and chronically overwhelmed, sometimes believing they are "stupid" because everything is always so confusing. The constant stress of not understanding what's happening, or of being afraid to speak, can become an issue in itself. Older children who have been dealing with these issues for years may need extra support in order to gain confidence and learn new social skills.

Dual Diagnoses and Misdiagnoses

Sometimes, a weakness in communication skills may be part of a more global issue. Some common diagnoses include autism (as mentioned above), pervasive developmental disorders, non-verbal learning disability, Down Syndrome, cerebral palsy, and seizure disorders. If your child has one of these diagnoses, a speech/language specialist can still help with specific skills. However, you should be addressing her larger issues as well.

The checklists in this book should also help you identify what other conditions might be present in your child, which may be exacerbating any speech or language issues. Some common diagnoses that occur along with (and therefore complicate) these issues are:

- **Sensory Processing Disorder.** Children who are sensitive to noise (to give just one example) may not process language well in the classroom. If a child has sensory processing issues, they should be comprehensively addressed before you can focus on specific academic skills. (See Chapter 7: Sensory Processing Disorder.)
- **Food sensitivities or allergies.** There are numerous examples of children on the autistic spectrum showing a jump in language skills when certain foods are removed from their diet. (See Chapter 14: Biomedical Approaches.)
- **Reading disorders.** Some children with speech or language disorders will go on to have trouble developing reading (and writing) skills, and may need intensive support in those areas as well. (See Chapter 6: Dyslexia and Other Reading Disabilities.)

Some concerning behaviors can result from a speech or language deficit, but all people see is the behavior rather than the reason for it. This can lead them to make erroneous assumptions, unhelpful suggestions, and even misdiagnoses. For example, if a child gets anxious or angry when asked to do something that scares her (presenting to the class, reading out loud, even answering a question), teachers may be quick to tell you that she has an anxiety disorder or emotion regulation issue. Receptive language problems (or APD) can make a child look inattentive and scattered, prompting the question of whether you have had her checked for ADD. Whenever a teacher, coach, or other caregiver tells you about something your child did, make sure to do a little detective work to find out more about how and why she did it.

Who Can Help?

Speech/Language Pathologists (SLPs), also called speech-language therapists or speech language specialists, address most speech or language issues. SLPs have at least a Master's Degree in this field of study. Most states also require that a speech-language pathologist be certified or licensed and meet the requirements of the American Speech-Language-Hearing Association's Certificate of Clinical Competence.

After you discuss your child's issues with an SLP, she may suggest a formal evaluation. She may also recommend a hearing evaluation to rule out hearing impairment as a source of problems. An audiologist would explore this, and can also rule out other auditory processing concerns.

A speech/language pathologist should also be knowledgeable in more general child development, and so should be able to tell parents whether they need additional specialists, such as an occupational therapist for sensory work or a psychologist for more general cognitive, behavioral, or social concerns.

Audiologists primarily work with children who have impairments in hearing acuity, such as children with hearing loss or who are deaf. There are many audiologists who specialize in working with children who have cochlear implants. Auditory-verbal therapy may be recommended for these children. Some audiologists focus more on auditory processing issues. Chapter 5.1: Auditory Processing Disorder, addresses this in more detail.

Treatment Options: Standard of Care

If the speech pathologist identifies a speech, language, or communication weakness, she will typically want to meet with the child at least weekly to work on needed skills. The therapist will have specific strategies for building skills and will often have homework for the child to practice (with parent support) during the week. For a child with mild articulation issues, therapy may wrap up after a few months of weekly visits. For a child with severe speech or language problems, therapy may be necessary well into adolescence or beyond.

You may need to find different specialists within the field at different times. For example, an oral-motor specialist may be seen initially to support production of speech in some children, but later a "pragmatics person" may be needed to refine social language skills. Some speech/language therapists have a broad range of experience and can cover a lot of skills; others are very specific.

If your child is under three years of age, you may be able to seek an evaluation and therapy services through state-funded programs. Prior to age three, children are often provided services by a therapist who visits the home. After age three, children are still eligible for early intervention services through the school district. (See Chapter 17: Advocacy in the School System.)

Treatment at School

Once a child has entered elementary school, speech and language services may be available through the school district if the child meets certain criteria. State and local education agencies establish eligibility criteria for speech/language services in the schools and may have different interpretations as to how a speech-language impairment "adversely affects educational performance." The American Speech-Language-Hearing Association has addressed the eligibility issue and states, "If acquisition of adequate and appropriate communication skills are a part of your school's academic standards and curriculum and considered to be a basic skill necessary for all children attending school, then children with a speech or language impairment have a disorder that adversely affects educational performance." (asha.org/SLP/schools/School-Services-Frequently-Asked-Questions/#10)

Be aware that speech/language services in school are primarily focused on helping your child be successful in the school setting. They may not resolve issues completely. If your child's issues are such that he is ineligible for school services, or you suspect that his school-based therapy will not provide enough support, you may have to supplement with a private specialist. There are many SLPs who work privately and specialize in specific types of communication disorders.

Some good sources who can help you find professionals in your area include:

- Word of mouth from other parents, school officials, and doctors
- American Speech-Language-Hearing Association at www.asha.org
- Your state's speech/language/hearing organization (look up by entering the name of your state plus *speech language hearing specialists*)
- A children's hospital, if you have one in your area
- Your insurance company

Treatment Options: Complementary and Alternative Medicine (CAM)

- **Chapter 15: Nutritional Approaches.** Nutrition, as a field, is not CAM. But suggesting you consider it to help address your child's speech/language issues is not a widely accepted approach. In their book, *The Late Talker*, Marilyn Agin, Lisa Geng, and Malcolm Nicholl devote a chapter to the consideration of a deficiency of essential fatty acids as a contributor to oral motor dyspraxia. Certain micronutrients have also been linked to increasing language and social skills in children with autism. See Chapter 14: Biomedical Approaches and Chapter 15: Nutritional Approaches for more information on how dietary factors can affect brain function. Before adding any supplements to a child's diet, make sure to check with a physician or registered nutritionist.

Some therapies are calming and organizing for the whole brain, which would support all kinds of intensive therapies. The section of the book covering Complementary and Alternative Medicine covers several therapies that are considering calming and organizing. For example:

- **Chapter 7: Sensory Processing Disorder.** This chapter discusses several kinds of therapies. Specialized occupational therapy, including hippotherapy, can reduce sensory sensitivities and integrate abilities.
- **Chapter 16.3: LEAP.** If needs are severe or progress seems unusually slow, organizing the underlying neurology may help therapies be more effective.
- **Chapter 16. 5: Craniosacral Therapy.** This can help release tension in the face and jaw that may be interfering with the ability to move one's mouth. Children with oral-motor apraxia, in particular, may benefit from this. This therapy can also support the nervous system in integrating other therapies.
- **Interactive Metronome** is a computer-based treatment that is geared to helping a child synchronize different areas of the brain, with the goal of improving processing speed. Various kinds of therapists use this, and it is often used for speech/language difficulties.

A Word About Insurance

Unfortunately, insurance does not always cover speech-language therapy. Even if your insurance plan offers coverage, it may only cover certain conditions, such as speech/language problems resulting from injury to the brain or mouth. Your insurance company may use language such as "speech-language therapy is covered when the disability is due to congenital anomaly or brain injury." Developmental or academic problems are typically not considered "medical problems" and coverage is often denied.

As a consumer, it is your right to contact your insurance company and ask about the parameters surrounding coverage. Some children have language weaknesses because chronic ear infections or fluid in their ears impaired their hearing early on. This can be considered a medical problem. Some states have recently passed laws related to therapy coverage for children with a diagnosis of autism. If you live in one of these states, services should be covered until age five. Your Speech-Language Pathologist will work to identify an appropriate diagnosis code for your child and may be able to help you with insurance issues. There are many SLPs working at the national level trying to change the status quo in insurance so that more speech-language therapy is covered.

Questions for a Prospective Speech/Language Specialist

- Do you primarily work with children?
- Do you work primarily with acquired language disorders or developmental language disorders?
- Is your focus on treating speech disorders or language disorders, or do you treat both?
- Do you specialize is a particular age range? A particular area of speech or language development?
- What is your evaluation process?
- What methods of treatment do you use and why?
- What is a typical course of therapy and how are therapy sessions conducted?
- Can you tell me about insurance coverage?

Resources for More Information

Websites

www.asha.org, the American Speech-Language-Hearing Association (ASHA). This website is a comprehensive resource where you can find information and practitioners.

asha.org/SLP/schools/School-Services-Frequently-Asked-Questions/#10. This is the direct link to ASHA's information about school services.

www.interactivemetronome.com/, Interactive Metronome's website, with information on the therapy and therapists.

Books

The Late Talker: What to do if Your Child Isn't Talking Yet by Marilyn Agin, Lisa Geng, and Malcolm Nicholl. The authors give parents information to help them find the right kind of therapy and therapist, guide them in working with schools, and even give some exercises parents can use at home.

The Parents' Guide to Speech and Language Problems by Debbie Feit. This book offers both clinical research and everyday parenting solutions for children who have communication deficits.

ABOUT THE AUTHORS

Lynn Anderson, MS, CCC-SLP, has been an ASHA certified Speech Language Pathologist for over 30 years. She received both her Bachelors and Masters of Science degrees in speech pathology from Southern Methodist University in Dallas, Texas. Her experience includes public school, early intervention, home health, and private practice in Texas, Oklahoma, and Colorado. Areas of special interest include speech and language development in young children, development of early literacy skills, elementary school-age language disorders, and language-based learning differences. Lynn currently resides in Edmond, Oklahoma where she works part time for a pediatric occupational therapy and speech-language pathology clinic. She is married and has two adult children and five grandchildren.

Nickie Gosselin, MS, CCC-SLP, has been an ASHA certified Speech-Language Pathologist for over 18 years. She received her Bachelor of Arts degree in Communication Disorders from the University of Connecticut. She then received her Masters of Science in Speech-Language Pathology from Southern Connecticut State University. Nickie has worked in both public schools and private practice. She specializes in pediatric communication issues, and has special interests in the areas of childhood apraxia of speech, specific language impairments, autism, Auditory Processing Disorders, and speech sound disorders. She is happily married and the proud mother of Graham. Nickie is also a brain tumor survivor.

Auditory Processing Disorder

by Beth O'Brien, M.A., CCC-A, FAAA

Possible signs of Auditory Processing Disorder include:

- ☐ Has weak or poor listening skills, especially in noisy environments
- ☐ Frequently asks "huh?" or "what?"
- ☐ Often asks for information to be repeated
- ☐ Appears inattentive, hyperactive, distracted, or spaced out when a lot of background noise is present
- ☐ Frequently misunderstands what he hears; may respond to questions or conversations with inappropriate answers
- ☐ Has more difficulty following auditory instructions, as opposed to written or visual instructions
- ☐ Has difficulty following verbal multi-step directions
- ☐ Has difficulty remembering information that he has heard
- ☐ Appears to have weak or poor attention span when listening to speakers (paying attention does not help if a child does not understand what was said)
- ☐ Shows delayed or slow response to questions, comments, or directions, often referred to as slow processing speed
- ☐ Has poor musical skills, often noticed in rhythm and pitch
- ☐ May have struggles with reading, spelling, writing, and other language-related tasks
- ☐ Displays greater than "normal" fatigue, particularly at the end of the school day (it is exhausting to listen that hard all day)
- ☐ May be highly sensitive to, and avoid, loud sounds (may cover their ears with their hands or cry in large gatherings of people)
- ☐ Often receives teacher feedback about being spacey or daydreaming in class
- ☐ Mispronounces words even though he understands and knows the words, does not seem to register verbal corrections of those words
- ☐ Performs inconsistently from day to day, class to class, often leading teachers and others to believe that he can obviously do better when he tries

My daughter Rachel was a star student from early on, even skipping kindergarten, but there were always signs that concerned me. Long after her twin brother had mastered speech, she still mumbled incomprehensibly most of the time. Most frustratingly, sometimes she was right on target and other times she was just "absent." I couldn't figure out why she seemed smart and focused sometimes but was the total opposite a few moments later. She also had a lot of trouble understanding other people. It didn't seem to be an issue of attention or intelligence; she just couldn't seem to comprehend most of what she heard. Although she continued to do well in school, she needed extra support from teachers and seemed more and more exhausted by the effort to get through a school day. Finally, I came across information on Auditory Processing Disorder.

The audiologist we saw gave her a battery of tests and diagnosed binaural fusion difficulties – meaning that her ears did not work in sync with her brain to make aural input intelligible. During the test, for example, she had heard "housework" as "hard wood," "dollhouse" as "bow wow," and "therefore" as "air core." Background noise only made things worse. (I realize now that I have many of the same difficulties. Trying to follow a conversation in a noisy restaurant that is playing music completely blows my circuits!)

The audiologist did not provide any treatment recommendations. Instead, she gave us a list of suggested accommodations: Rachel needed to sit in the front of the classroom, to receive as much visual instruction as possible and to educate her teachers about her unique needs. I have since learned that there are treatment options, but I didn't realize that there is a huge difference in what different professionals, even within the same field, will offer. Looking back, I wish I had known more about treatments and had investigated how they might have helped her.

While she was young, I found the quieter classrooms and kept in touch with her teachers throughout the year. In high school, she had to learn to advocate for herself. She did pretty well with teachers, but was unwilling to explain her problem to peers – which meant that she got her share of people teasing her because of all the questions she asked and because she seemed so gullible. When simply understanding the words themselves is a constant struggle, interpreting the subtext (sarcasm, teasing, etc.) is nearly impossible.

Rachel is in college now, and has gotten pretty good at managing her issues. She still has some of the follow-through and disorganization problems that are typical for someone with APD, but she knows her weaknesses and usually does pretty well at staying on top of them. When she gets discouraged, I remind her that I have a lot of the same problems and look at me! She usually rolls her eyes at that point; but we both seem to be doing pretty well in life, so I'm optimistic this isn't going to hold her back. I also remind her that it's never too late! She has no interest in therapies right now, but they are out there and she could still benefit as an adult. ~E.W.

The Basics

Auditory Processing Disorder (APD) can complicate the development of speech and language skills, but it is in fact a separate disorder. APD, also known as Central Auditory Processing Disorder (CAPD), is a brain-based difficulty with understanding what is heard. *Brain-based* means that the problem is not in the child's hearing – in fact, many children with APD seem to have hyper-acute hearing and are annoyed or distracted by small sounds that most people never even notice. Just like the brain's role in speech and language difficulties, APD affects the way the brain interprets auditory input, but in a more basic way. People with speech and language deficits have trouble assigning the correct interpretation to what they hear ("I heard it, but what does it mean?"). People with APD have trouble discerning the basic components of auditory input correctly ("What did I just hear?!"). This needs to be clear before meaning is even a consideration.

Think of it this way: APD concerns the nuts and bolts of auditory input, while speech and language problems occur when you can take in the nuts and bolts but then don't know how to build anything with them.

Experts still debate the details of this disorder. This is common for learning disorders, but APD seems to be a particularly slippery one. Although both the American Speech-Language-Hearing Association and the American Academy of Audiology have published specific guidelines regarding APD, there is still inconsistency in the categorization of symptoms, methods of assessment, diagnosis, and best treatment approaches. There is also a great deal of overlap with other disorders, especially Sensory Processing Disorder, which complicates things further. However, the following guidelines will help you understand the basic difference between auditory-related challenges:

- **Hearing issues** involve simply being able to detect the presence of sound at all the different volumes and pitches that the human ear should hear. Be aware that loss of hearing across the speech frequencies of 500-2000 Hz can negatively impact a child's speech and language development.
- **Receptive language issues** (covered in the previous chapter) refer to the brain's ability to interpret, or apply meaning, to what is heard. A child may struggle to process the multiple concepts in the sentence, "Put all the red balls in the largest box." *Concepts*, in this case, refer to the idea that *red* refers to a color, *balls* indicates which object, *largest* describes size, and *in the box* gives a specific location.

APD impairs the accurate perception of what sound was actually heard in the first place. For many children with APD, the presence of other noises overwhelms their auditory systems. For example, choir practice in the next room or even having someone sharpen a pencil at the back of the classroom can render all auditory input confusing and difficult to sort out. Having performance decline in the presence of background noise is a hallmark of APD. Other children, even under the best environmental conditions, simply cannot perceive sounds accurately. A child with only APD would have no trouble understanding the *concepts* in the sentence, "put all the red balls in the largest box." Their trouble lies in the fact that they may, instead, hear "pull tall thread walls in the large stocks."

Understandably, APD and receptive language problems overlap. It's tough to interpret the meaning of what you heard when you are constantly struggling to figure out what it was, exactly, that you heard. Therefore, it can be helpful to seek out input from both a speech/language specialist and an audiologist. Fortunately, because of what we now understand as the brain's neuroplasticity (the ability for neural pathways to change), treatment and improvement are quite possible.

A Closer Look

Research continually reveals ways that auditory processing skills provide the foundation for higher order learning. Even reading, which one might imagine to be a purely visual skill, depends partially on the ability to "hear" the sounds in the words in front of you. If your child is having trouble processing auditory input, it will have far-reaching consequences on many academic and social abilities.

Infants have the ability to learn any language, because they can still hear the full range of possible linguistic sounds. After the first six to nine months, the human brain begins filtering out any sounds it has not heard, or has not heard much. For most children, this simply means that they will not be as able to recognize, say, the subtle differences between some Chinese words, in part because our language does not have the same tonal distinctions and our brains are therefore not skilled in discriminating between them.

But for children with APD, their native tongue can be just as problematic. The English alphabet has 26 letters; the language itself has 44 sounds. The brain must *map*, or learn to recognize and produce, each sound separately and distinctly in all its forms. If anything has compromised a child's ability to hear or distinguish those sounds clearly (see the Causes section), he will end up with a "mushy map" or poor sound discrimination, recognition, and production.

This is likely to affect all language development and communication skills unless it is addressed. Fortunately, there are well-researched techniques that can remap the auditory cortex.

Furthermore, language and communication skills require more than just the accurate perception of sounds. A sense of timing is crucial as well. The difference between "greenhouse" and "green house" is a subtle but important one, as is the perceived difference between a comma and a period when someone is reading aloud. If your child cannot hear that difference, then all the studying in the world will not give him a strong sense of how to use punctuation in his writing.

I once had a teenage patient who was an excellent student, but had been frustrated by deductions on his papers. It turned out he had no idea how to use commas properly because he could not hear, in the rhythm of the words, where they were supposed to go. He would simply scatter them throughout his work because he knew they were supposed to be in there somewhere.

APD also affects social interaction, other than the obvious consequences of not following conversations easily. Children with auditory processing deficits can look like they have terrible social skills. They often cannot tell the difference between the pause when someone is merely taking a breath and the pause that means he is done speaking. So they may blurt things out at blatantly inappropriate times, which understandably gets negative reactions. (Others can interpret this as a lack of impulse control, one of the many reasons APD is often misdiagnosed as ADD.) Alternatively, they might appear shy or anti-social because they feel so lost that they never speak up. Finally, the emotional content behind others' words can easily get lost. APD kids can easily miss sarcasm, irritation, or other subtext because they are still stuck on the level of basic content. This can make them seem gullible, "dense," or subtly out of step with their peers in a way that is hard to identify but easy to feel.

This disorder sometimes seems to get worse as a child ages, but often it is more related to academic and social conditions becoming more complex. Children with APD become masters at observation and compensation, watching others like a hawk for clues about what's going on because they didn't understand the teacher's directions. But as you move through the grades, there is simply a lot more talking going on. Directions get more detailed, lectures get much longer, and social conversations become much more complex. What might have kept a child a little out of step with his peers in elementary school can lead to constant exhaustion, more emotional behavior (like irritability or weepiness), and academic struggle later on.

Causes

The causes of APD are varied and often not identifiable. It frequently runs in families. When I treat children, I explain the different aspects of the disorder to parents who commonly say, "Oh, I do that too! So that's what that is!" The primary auditory portion of the brain (called the auditory cortex) has its greatest period of neurological maturation between the ages of seven and eleven, so some skills may improve because of overall brain maturation. If the symptoms are severe, however, it would still be a good idea to seek treatment rather than count on later development.

APD frequently coexists with other disorders. Current research is pointing to some ADHD as being related to sound/auditory processing. Some possible contributing factors include:

- **A history of frequent or chronic early ear infections.** During the first few years of life, a baby develops a lot of language and other skills through what he hears. If his ears are often filled with fluid or infected, he has to hear through this fluid. The sounds are muffled and distorted, so he lays down "faulty wiring" for what he hears.
- **Traumatic brain injury and some drugs (such as some used in chemotherapy).** Severe outside influences like this can cause problems in brain function, including in auditory processing.
- **Early institutionalization.** Children in institutions sometimes are not exposed to much language, which impairs their ability to process it.
- **Co-existing sensory processing issues.** Sensory Processing Disorders often appear in many forms at once, so auditory processing issues frequently coincide with other sensory issues. Overall sensory processing therapy can generate some improvement in auditory processing, even if the therapist does not focus on it. Again, however, if your child has experienced particular weakness in this area, it is best to ensure progress by seeing someone who can pinpoint and treat the issue.

Historically, Auditory Processing Disorders were not considered diagnosable until a child was seven years of age or older. Neurological maturation was not considered mature enough for a clear diagnosis. In recent years, an increasing number of pediatric audiologists are testing children at a younger age, using tests that are specifically standardized for younger neurology. As with any disorder, early intervention can substantially improve the auditory skills before it gets compounded because the later skills don't develop well or causes significant disruption in a child's life.

Assessment

APD evaluation should be done in a soundproof room with audiometric equipment. An audiologist will assess a distinct set of auditory processing skills:

- Locating the origin of a sound
- Differentiating between similar sounds (*cup* vs. *cut* vs. *cat*, for example)
- Recognizing patterns in speech, which relates to identifying emotional subtext (anger vs. sarcasm, for example)
- Following speech in the presence of background noise (testing should distinguish between different kinds of noise, such as another conversation vs. a general roar like a cafeteria)
- Understanding a speaker when he is muffled, rushed, or accented

This is only a sample list. The point is that there are several subtle skills involved. Just saying "your child has APD" is not enough information.

APD or ADD?

APD, still not a well-known disorder, is often misdiagnosed as ADD. It's easy to see why: A child with auditory processing problems often looks either distracted or spacey, responds incorrectly to what he has heard, often does not seem to have registered what people have said, and has a great deal of trouble remembering and following directions. However, if he has trouble understanding spoken language, paying better attention is not going to help. He is just not getting enough subtle cues to stay engaged. An audiologist trained in APD can help you sort out the true issues.

Who Can Help?

Diagnosis

An audiologist trained in APD should do the assessment. Only an audiologist can provide a diagnosis. Other kinds of practitioners may identify and treat it, but the evaluation should be done in a sound booth with sensitive audiometric equipment.

What to look for when seeking an evaluation:

- Start with a thorough hearing test (using audiometric equipment in a sound booth or sound-proof environment). A hearing screening at a pediatrician's office will *not* suffice; that evaluates hearing only, not the more involved components that would signify APD or receptive language issues.

◌ Look for an audiologist with expertise and experience in assessment for and treat-ment of auditory processing deficits in children. Just as there are specialty physi-cians, there are different areas of specialty in audiology. APD is becoming more and more of a specialty, so do not assume that any audiologist you find can assess appropriately.

Treatment Options: Standard of Care

Look for someone who has experience in the specific issues within APD that your child dem-onstrates. Choose a therapist who can explain to your satisfaction why he does what he does for those issues. Also, make sure that he has the following qualities:

◌ He is willing to look at the big picture and review other records – most commonly, these will be speech-language, psychological, and/or educational assessments and treatments.
◌ He takes a global view of difficulties across environments (home, school, work, etc.). Many children with auditory processing deficiencies function better in settings where they are alone with a teacher, practitioner, etc. They look fine in an individualized evaluation, but struggle in groups of people, such as the classroom, restaurants, par-ties, or even large families.

Audiologists

Some audiologists only evaluate; some are trained in treatment as well. If yours is not, get a referral to one who does or to a speech/language pathologist who is familiar with both auditory processing and receptive language needs. This is where a specific intervention plan is critical and the team of people who have evaluated your child should be working together to determine the best course of action. Because children with auditory processing difficulties will often demonstrate other challenges (reading, writing, maintaining attention, etc.) it is important to prioritize and sequence with a comprehensive eye.

Speech/language pathologists

Make sure that you find a therapist who is experienced in APD as well as the more com-mon issues. The speech pathologist should be willing to work in tandem with the audiologist and have a clear understanding of what the specific areas of deficit are and what skills should be addressed in treatment. She should also be willing to work with you and your child's school to see that everyone understands the recommended modifications for both home and school environments.

Occupational Therapists

Some OTs consider APD to be part of Sensory Processing Disorder and treat alongside other sensory issues. While this make sense, make sure to ask about specific APD training and experience. Remember that an audiologist should still make the diagnosis, as most OTs are not trained in the full protocol and do not have the proper equipment to determine which specific APD issues a child has. You might also ask the audiologist to weigh in on any treatment program your OT suggests to ensure that it addresses all issues that the assessment reveals.

SPECIFIC TREATMENTS AND SUPPORTS

There are many treatment methods available, but not much agreement on which are best for which specific symptoms. Most practitioners will cover the following main categories when helping you develop a program.

- **Intervention programs** that address each of the categories in the **Assessment** section. This is an area where there is a flood of options. New programs appear on the market all the time, many of which you can buy for yourself. A word of caution, however: Ask a professional for input, as many of these programs are not well researched. Some are not the appropriate tool for the task; even though you can hammer with a wrench, it won't be as effective as a hammer, if that is what is needed. In fact, as a professional, I often steer clear of sending people off to use the home programs, as it is crucial to allow for ongoing clinical intervention. Always ask your therapist what issues she is seeing and how, exactly, the particular program she recommends helps with those issues. Look for specificity in her answers and ask her to cite research.
- **Individualized reading programs or specific skills therapy** (in auditory memory, for example) may also help, depending on your child's specific issues. The person who does your evaluation should be able to tell you what you need.
- **Environmental modifications,** such as Assistive Listening Devices (ALDs) and personal FM systems that reduce background noise and focus sound more directly toward the listener, can help enormously. For example, the teacher can wear a microphone

that broadcasts her voice to a student's personal receiver, overriding the auditory competition that can make processing difficult. Teachers may also be able to help by doing the following:

- Providing supplemental visual materials, such as copies of board notes or power points; physical demonstrations are effective too
- Providing preferential seating (in front, with consideration of which is the dominant ear, if that is an issue and no FM is in use)
- Giving short, concise directions with defined steps
- Reducing or minimizing distractions
- Extending time requirements for processing
- Monitoring student for fatigue, checking for understanding, reviewing the material

These are just a few examples of techniques that have been successfully used in the classroom. I have heard many teachers who have tried them say that it seems to help all of their students understand the material and stay engaged.

- **Advocacy techniques will be essential.** Depending on her age, your child or you will need to educate teachers, coaches, etc. on her needs. Eventually, your child will need to learn to advocate clearly on a regular basis, such as asking the speaker to slow his rate of speech or rephrase something, or simply letting any speaker know that she may have to ask a lot of clarifying questions. While not a treatment per se, this is a skill your child will need to become comfortable with, probably for the rest of her life.

Treatment Options: Complementary and Alternative Medicine (CAM)

- **Chapter 15: Nutritional Approaches.** In their book, *The Late Talker*, Marilyn Agin, Lisa Geng, and Malcolm Nicholl devote a chapter to the consideration of a deficiency of essential fatty acids as a contributor to oral motor dyspraxia. Certain micronutrients have also been linked to increasing language and social skills in children with autism. See Chapter 14: Biomedical Approaches and Chapter 15: Nutritional Approaches for more information on how dietary factors can affect brain function. Before adding any supplements to a child's diet, make sure to check with a physician or registered nutritionist.

Some therapies are calming and organizing for the whole brain, which would support all kinds of intensive therapies. The section of the book covering Complementary and Alternative Medicine covers several therapies that are considering calming and organizing. For example:

- **Chapter 7: Sensory Processing Disorder.** Auditory processing is often part of overall sensory integration problems. Specialized occupational therapy, including hippotherapy, can reduce sensory sensitivities and integrate abilities.
- **Chapter 16.3: LEAP.** If needs are severe or progress seems unusually slow, organizing the underlying neurology may help therapies be more effective.
- **Chapter 16.4: Chiropractic Neurology.** This modality can help identify underlying issues in the brain's neurology. Addressing them can organize underlying neurology so that other therapies can be more effective.

Questions for a Prospective APD Specialist

- Do you have experience with children who have similar issues to mine?
- Are you certified by the American Speech-Language-Hearing Association and/or The American Academy of Audiology? (Keep in mind that this does not ensure experience or training in APD)
- What is your training and experience in APD?
- How do you evaluate for APD?
- Do you provided treatment in addition to assessment? (for audiologists)
- Can you refer me to qualified treatment providers in my area?
- What are the treatment approaches that you use most? Why? Is there research that supports those programs?
- What are the typical time frames for treatment?
- Do you provide strategies for the classroom?
- Do you consult with the school if needed?

Resources for More Information

Websites

Each of the following websites can help you find more information and local providers:
www.audiology.org, The American Academy of Audiology.
www.asha.org, the American Speech-Language-Hearing Association.
www.kidshealth.org, Kid's Health, with sections for parents, kids, teens, and educators.
www.ldonline.org, LD Online: The Educators' Guide to Learning Disabilities and ADHD.

BOOKS

The Woman who Changed her Brain: And Other Inspiring Stories of Pioneering Brain Transformation by Barbara Arrowsmith. The author tells the story of growing up with severe learning disabilities and how, in college, she began her journey of discovery and experimentation with brain exercises that healed her brain. Interspersed with other case histories and discoveries in brain science.

Auditory Processing Disorders: Assessment, Management, and Treatment by Donna Geffner and Deborah Ross-Swain. Geffner and Ross-Swain present a thorough, professionally-oriented resource on all facets of APD.

When the Brain Can't Hear: Unraveling the Mystery of Auditory Processing Disorder by Teri James Bellis. This is the "everything you ever wanted to know" book about APD. Goes into great detail about the symptoms and permutations of the disorder.

Like Sound Through Water: A Mother's Journey Through Auditory Processing Disorder by Karen J. Foli and Edward M. Hallowell, MD. A mother tells the story of her son's repeated misdiagnoses, struggles with APD, and journey through the difficult terrain of finding appropriate treatment.

ABOUT THE AUTHOR

Beth O'Brien, M.A., CCC-A, FAAA, is an audiologist specializing in auditory and language processing diagnostics and interventions. She has a Masters Degree in Audiology from the University of Denver and maintains her Certificate of Clinical Competence in Audiology from the American Speech-Language-Hearing Association (ASHA). She is a fellow of the American Academy of Audiology and a member of both the Educational Audiology Association and the American Academy of Private Practice in Speech Pathology and Audiology. A native Denverite, she continues to work in the Denver metro area as well as throughout Colorado and the rest of the Western Mountain Region. Beth has worked with individuals of all ages in many settings: public schools, language and learning clinics, state programs for people with developmental disabilities, and the Colorado mental health system. She provides direct clinical services including diagnostics and therapy, case management coordination, and advocacy. For over twenty-five years, she has also worked as a professional advocate for children and their parents in developing supports and policies on a national level, implementing school plans, and training school staff to increase success for children with learning challenges. Beth is a highly skilled trainer for schools, parents, and professionals who want to learn more about the neuroscience of learning and processing. She can be reached at: bobrienaud@outlook.com.

SIX

Dyslexia and Other Reading Disabilities

by Robin McEvoy, PhD

Please consider the first two items and then look through items in your child's age range and younger. Items at the end of the checklist will help you identify possible contributing factors that you can read about in other chapters.

- ☐ Family history of dyslexia or reading disability
- ☐ History of serial or chronic ear infections in infancy

Preschool:

- ☐ Has trouble understanding what rhymes (can hear that *car* and *jar* rhyme, but does not understand that *cat* and *jar* do not)
- ☐ Frequently confuses sequences of sounds in words (says "flutterby" instead of "butterfly")
- ☐ Can sing the ABC song, but cannot match the letter name to the symbol

Kindergarten through 3rd grade (or higher):

- ☐ Likes to be read to, but has little interest in learning to read
- ☐ Cannot learn to match the letter with the sound it makes
- ☐ Has trouble breaking out the individual sounds within words (e.g., cannot hear that *cat* has three sounds in it)
- ☐ Struggles to learn to blend sounds into a word (e.g., cannot take the sounds *c*, *a*, and *t* and make it into *cat*)
- ☐ Fails to learn or easily confuses simple sight words such as *at*, *to*, *in*, *on*, and *no*
- ☐ Has reading and writing skills that are far below intelligence, other academic skills, or educational experience
- ☐ Has trouble memorizing math facts, such as addition facts or multiplication facts

Higher grades:

☐ Remains slow and has to work hard at reading, does not develop it into smooth fluid skill

☐ Complains of headache or fatigue after a short period of reading

☐ Continues to be a weak speller – may be able to study and pass the spelling test, but does not remember how to spell words in other writing

☐ Struggles with writing also – writing is slow and laborious, despite good ideas and intelligence

☐ Makes frequent careless errors in reading and on tests

☐ Can understand math concepts, but math speed is very slow due to poor memory for math facts

☐ Struggles to learn foreign language

Other possibilities:

Problems with reading sometimes result more from problematic visual processing than specific reading issues. If your child exhibits any of the following behaviors, check out Chapter 7.1: Vision Disorder Issues.

☐ Frequently skips lines or words when reading aloud

☐ Experiences fatigue, eye strain, or headache when reading (young children may not be able to identify these symptoms, and may just get cranky or whiny when asked to read more than they are able)

☐ Puts book very close to (or very far away from) face when reading or cocks head to one side when reading

Difficulty with writing often accompanies difficulty with reading. If your child struggles with writing, look at Chapter 10.2: Writing Disability (Dysgraphia).

If reading skills have changed after a concussion, read Chapter 9: Concussions.

Dyslexia runs in our family. My father was dyslexic, with poor reading skills, slow reading, and very weak spelling. He was never a strong student. His sister had no academic problems and was an avid reader, but two of her five children were diagnosed with dyslexia, as were two of my siblings. Of the rest of the siblings and cousins, many of us struggle with spelling, math facts, and foreign language. I went through college an avid reader and strong student, but struggled with foreign language. In addition, I will not remember your name or phone number for some time. In the third generation, dyslexia continues to rear its ugly head. My dyslexic sister has two dyslexic daughters. However, she started reading work early and both girls are strong students despite their slower reading and related weaknesses. They both use the computer to compensate for writing and spelling issues. There are other dyslexic cousins in this generation, muddling through with extra tutoring, but making it to and through college. It has taken three generations, but we seem to understand what to do at this point. ~ KB

The Basics

Researchers estimate that 20 percent of children have some delays in reading. Because reading is so critical for academic success, this means that 20 percent of the children in any given classroom may struggle and potentially fail. However, reading disabilities are not a reflection of intelligence. Children who struggle with reading are usually perfectly bright and sometimes even gifted. This makes their struggle all the more frustrating.

Children can exhibit a reading disability for several reasons. Developmental causes include:

- **Genetics.** Dyslexia runs in families. If one parent is dyslexic, there is a 50/50 chance of any child in the family also being dyslexic.
- **Impaired auditory processing that is acquired early in life.** This can be due to serial ear infections or chronic fluid in the ears during early development. During the first year of life, a child's brain is laying down the wiring for how to distinguish the different sounds in words. Even though language skills may develop easily once hearing is improved, the ability to discern individual sounds can still be affected.
- **Impairments in visual processing.** Some children do not scan smoothly or their eyes do not team well with each other, or the brain, to track or decode the words on the page. (See Chapter 7.1: Vision Disorder Issues.)
- **Disorganization in learning.** Some children simply struggle with the process of linking the sounds with the letters and learning all the rules for reading. Poor attention control can also slow reading acquisition.
- **Impaired language processing.** Children who have weaknesses in understanding spoken language will likely also have weaknesses in reading and writing. (See Chapter 5: Speech and Language Issues.)

⚲ **Poor bi-lateral integration.** Reading is a complex task requiring coordination between both sides of the brain. One side decodes ("b-o-a-t" says "boat"); the other gives meaning to the word ("a boat is a vessel that floats on the water"). If the hemispheres do not work together smoothly or one of them does not do its job, reading slows down or screeches to a halt.

Difficulty reading can mean many things: You can have trouble recognizing the actual words; you can get through the individual words but not understand what you've just read; or you might be able to do both, but it is a slow and painful process. It is essential to get a thorough evaluation that can pinpoint the source of the problem and treat it appropriately.

Components of Reading

When discussing reading disabilities, there are several terms that come up frequently. The neurological coordination involved in effective reading is complex; there are many points where the process can break down. Many of these terms may be new to you, but it can be valuable to illustrate the number of distinct components that reading encompasses. (At the very least, this vocabulary should help you understand the report a reading specialist gives you.)

⚲ **Auditory memory** is where we store spoken or auditory information that does not have clear meaning. Meaningful verbal information, such as "Tonight you have soccer," is stored in verbal memory. However, non-meaningful information, such as "dorfina kaso," is stored in auditory memory. A child can have an excellent verbal memory, remembering all sorts of interesting facts and stories, but still struggle to remember which sounds go with which letters because her auditory memory is weak.

⚲ **Auditory sequencing** refers to the ability to remember the sequence of sounds in words. Children with poor auditory sequencing may read *saw* as *was* or say *relvant* instead of *relevant*.

⚲ **Phonology** is the study of speech sounds in a language.

Quick Tip

A simple exercise in phonological processing is to ask a person to say the word *tray* and then ask them to say the word without the *tuh* sound. A person with good phonological processing will respond "ray". A person with poor phonological processing has trouble separating the *tuh* sound from the *ruh* sound and will say "ay."

- **Phonological awareness** is the understanding that our language is made up of small, individual sounds.
- **Phonological memory** allows us to remember the sounds in the words while working with them. For example, a child with poor phonological memory might lose track of the sounds in the word *girl*, spelling *gril* instead.

Phonemic awareness enables us to hear and manipulate the individual sounds in words. For example, when the sounds in *cat* are reversed, it is pronounced *tac*.

Orthographic coding has more to do with spelling than reading, but spelling and reading are related skills. Orthographic coding is the ability to remember the sounds and sound patterns in words when writing. A child can struggle with remembering rules when writing more complex sentences. For example, a child might write "the anmole ontherite sakow" for "the animal on the right is a cow."

Clearly, there are a number of possible deficits that can cause problems in reading. It is important to find out exactly where the breakdown is occurring so that you can target remediation programs appropriately.

Dyslexia

Dyslexia is a reading disorder, but not all reading disorders are dyslexia. There is a world of confusion about what constitutes dyslexia. Due to the lack of standardization across specialties, you may come across many perspectives. For example,

Developmental optometrists often define dyslexia as a disorder of visual processing and treat with vision therapy.

The Davis Dyslexia Program uses a visual and meaning-based approach. Ron Davis developed this program after treating his own inability to read. He was not a researcher or an educator. He was simply a man who had struggled with reading problems his whole life who finally found a method that worked for him (and then developed the program for others). Davis believes that dyslexia is secondary to mental gifts in people with profoundly different learning styles. His program reflects that.

Many learning specialists simply use reading disability and dyslexia interchangeably even though they are not.

Many people think of dyslexia as writing letters backwards or flipping words around when reading. While these are often telltale symptoms, they are not, in and of themselves, evidence of dyslexia. Sometimes they simply indicate a brain that is struggling and disorganized in other ways.

So what is dyslexia? As a neuropsychologist, my thinking is guided by the current research on the brain and reading. Dyslexia is an Auditory Processing Disorder (specifically, phonological processing, which involves the understanding that there are distinct and individual sounds in words) that makes it difficult to link sounds with visual symbols. Since reading appears to be a visual task, it comes as a surprise to many that auditory processing is such an essential part of it. But it is necessary to be able to hear the sounds and understand the relationship between the sounds and the letters you are seeing on the page.

So what is a confused parent to do? I tell parents not to get too caught up in the label. Find out what a practitioner is pinpointing as the cause of the problems, not what they are calling it. What is the particular glitch that they are seeing? Can she not hear the sounds in the words? Is she struggling to visually discriminate between letters? Is reading just the tip of the iceberg for more global problems in organization and learning? Since some specialists identify any reading disorder as dyslexia (which is less than helpful), you need to get these specifics. If a practitioner can only tell you that your child is delayed in reading, seek a comprehensive evaluation to determine the true underlying mechanisms. Identifying those will drive your treatment choices.

Possible Related Academic Issues

If your child's reading difficulties are related to weaknesses in auditory or phonological skills, the following issues may also exist:

- Difficulty with spelling, related to the same poor sound/symbol relationships (spelling problems often persist even after reading is remediated)
- Slower writing speed due to the additional struggle with poor spelling (children have so much trouble trying to spell that they forget what they were trying to say)
- Difficulty memorizing multiplication tables (or even addition facts) due to the need to remember long, auditory sequences of numbers
- Difficulty learning foreign language because this also involves long auditory strings of unfamiliar, non-meaningful sounds
- Difficulty with test-taking
- Trouble remembering number series, such as phone numbers
- Trouble remembering people's names
- Difficulty with word retrieval (the child cannot find the needed word in his head)

Who Can Help?

Reading is one area where there are often different professionals who diagnose versus those who treat. Those who can help remediate dyslexia or a reading disorder can go by many names, depending on what specific issues they are addressing. Be sure to use the checklists in the beginning of this book to get an indication of what other issues might be creating or worsening your child's troubles. Common culprits include Sensory Processing Disorder, speech/language issues, or Auditory Processing Disorder. Though problems with reading are what you see, the true issue may be larger. The CAM section (Section 4) will give you other suggestions for ways to help.

Diagnosis

Many learning specialists can identify a reading weakness. These could include learning specialists, reading specialists, speech and language therapists, and others who have trained in assessment and academic remediation. However the actual *diagnosis* of dyslexia, other reading disability, or any specific learning disability can only be made when there is a cognitive evaluation to compare to the academic skills. This type of evaluation typically requires a psychologist skilled in administration of IQ tests or related cognitive assessment tests to compare to academic scores.

Determining that a child has a reading disability is fairly simple. If your child's reading is weaker than expected for her intelligence and educational level, something is off. However, specifying which type of reading issue she has, can only be done when there is a comprehensive cognitive and processing evaluation to compare to the academic skills (meaning that a child's innate intelligence is compared to her ability to complete academic tasks).

Practitioners who can diagnose a reading disability:

- ♎ A psychologist trained in assessment of learning disabilities is the most common resource for a comprehensive diagnosis.
- ♎ Some education specialists who have a Master's degree in education or special education can evaluate and diagnose.

Something to Consider

Keep in mind that bi-lateral integration issues are usually only assessed by specifically trained occupational therapists, neurological chiropractors, and LEAP practitioners. This does not constitute an official diagnosis, but if it is the root of your child's problem, you will need to address it. If your child does not seem to be progressing with reading remediation, this might be something worth checking out.

⚲ There are some specialists in auditory processing or speech and language who assess reading and plan remediation. However, for a specific breakdown of why your child has a reading disability, there has to be a cognitive assessment to compare with reading ability. This must be done by a psychologist.

⚲ Vision therapists can assess reading and any possible visual issues contributing to reading delays.

The battery of tests should explore auditory memory, phonological processing, visual processing, family history, and medical history. For a diagnosis of dyslexia, the battery typically has a subtest or subsection assessing auditory memory. The specialist should also take into account the child's overall academic experiences in case this child has had gaps in his education due to illness, injury, family moves, or other disruption.

A thorough evaluation is often the best approach, as some children will have more than one weakness. There is a high correlation between reading disabilities and other learning disabilities and attention problems.

Finding a Diagnostician

⚲ Chapter 3 outlines evaluation options and how to find evaluators experienced with your child's needs.

⚲ Your pediatrician may be able to direct you to a psychologist experienced in assessment of learning disabilities.

⚲ The Learning Disability Association of America has local chapters in many states. They often keep a list of experienced evaluators.

Questions for a Prospective Reading Disability Diagnostician:

⚲ Do you have specific training in the diagnosis of learning disabilities?

⚲ What is your approach to the diagnosis of reading disability?

⚲ Do you provide a written report with relevant scores and an interpretation of what they mean?

⚲ Do you provide recommendations for remediation, as well as for appropriate academic accommodations and modifications?

TREATMENT OPTIONS: STANDARD OF CARE

There are two main methods of intervention for students with a reading disability:

- **Remediation**. Fix it as much as possible.
- **Accommodation**. Find ways to work around the disability.

Reading remediation can be done through your child's school, but many schools do not have adequate funding to provide an individualized, sequential, and systematic intervention. Services are often done in small group formats. The special education teacher often works on key skills that the group as a whole seems to need. It is up to you to assess whether this will provide enough of the right kind of support for your child. You can ask for more intensive, individualized therapy from your school. But understand that, because of chronically limited resources, they may or may not be able to provide it.

Accommodations, however, are designed for school use. You may need to work with the school to develop an Individualized Learning Plan or similar program in order to put accommodations in place. (See the upcoming *Accommodations* section of this chapter as well as Chapter 17: Advocacy in the School System, for more information.)

Remediation

Remediation of reading, as well as related weaknesses in spelling or writing, is best done through a specialized reading program that is:

- **Individualized.** Remediation is most effective when targeted at the specific needs of the student.
- **Systematic.** There is a clear sequence of skill development with clear goals at each level.
- **Multisensory.** A multisensory reading program does not only practice sounds and reading patterns with the auditory system, as reading is often taught. Instead, it uses multiple senses to reinforce the necessary skills. For example, a child is given visual cues and motor cues to remember sounds and patterns: *b* makes the *buh* sound by popping on your lips, while *d* makes the *duh* sound by having your tongue tap on the back of your teeth. A facilitator shows this to a child in the mirror and helps him to practice the motor actions. He then has both a motor memory and a visual memory to support the weaker auditory memory.

If your child is classically dyslexic – meaning that she has weak phonological processing – you can expect that she will make slow and steady progress. If her issues are more related to disorganized learning (indicating that she does not pick up on patterns easily and needs to have them repeatedly pointed out), she will probably progress quite quickly. If her eyes are simply not working well together with the brain, you will need to do something else entirely and seek a developmental optometrist.

There are several well developed multi-sensory reading programs, such as Lindamood-Bell, Orton-Gillingham, Wilson, and Barton. Many of these programs have also developed related services to support problems with math and writing.

Accommodations

Even with good remediation, problems with reading accuracy, speed, or comprehension may persist. Your child might therefore still need accommodations and modifications in the classroom. If a child is diagnosed with a reading disability, this will need to be documented at school with an Individual Education Plan (IEP) or a 504 plan. Keep in mind that your school may be limited in what it is able to provide. Some accommodations or modifications to consider, depending on what's appropriate for your child, include the following:

- Allow the child extra time for reading (accommodation) or a reduced reading load (modification).
- Exempt him from reading aloud to the class if reading is slow and choppy, as this can be embarrassing and stressful.
- Use audiobooks to accomplish some reading assignments.
- Modify test taking. Tests are extremely challenging for many students with read-

Quick Tip

Reading is an important part of this culture and you should absolutely support your child in developing that skill. There is, however, nothing inherently better about learning from books. Especially now, with so many advances in technology, your child should be able to find the information she needs in other formats. It is your right to ask that your child be able to use them.

Appropriate non-reading activities can be as good as, or better than reading for some children. DVDs, audiotapes, and even Youtube (when monitored by parents) can be used to help weak readers get the information that their reading peers access so easily through books. These methods can also be used to support reading skills. For example, watching a video before reading a book can familiarize the student with the major characters and the plot. This may improve his ability to problem-solve text.

ing disabilities. Even if they know the answer, they may make errors in reading that cause them to perform poorly (especially if they are rushing or anxious). If a student struggles with test-taking, it may be necessary to modify the test format (e.g., fill-in-the –blank instead of multiple choice) or to re-test the student orally (have it read to them and/or have them answer orally) to ensure that his knowledge is in place.

- Give extra time for test taking, particularly longer tests such as final exams or college entrance exams.
- Give the student an outline of the lecture, beforehand, so she can follow along and take additional notes on the outline. Taking notes during lectures can be exhausting for a student with reading disorder-related spelling problems. Listening while trying to write and spell quickly can blow his circuits.
- Teachers should not penalize the student for poor spelling, outside of spelling tests.
- Let the student dictate or use voice-recognition software for at least some written assignments. This separates thinking from the more laborious act of writing.
- Teach the student to write on the computer. This will also give the student resources for checking spelling and easily editing work. Older students are often expected to complete work this way, but younger ones can benefit from developing this skill early.
- Waive foreign language requirements. Many colleges are allowing alternative studies, such as sign language, to be used in replacement.
- Look for technological supports such as Dragon-Speak (voice-recognition software) and Smartpens that record and replay a particular portion depending on where it touches the paper.

Find a Supportive Environment

Some schools may find it difficult to integrate alternative formats into their curriculum. If you have trouble getting your child the support she needs, you might consider changing schools. A smaller school, or one with a different philosophy, may be more willing and able to adjust their methods. This can be a major decision, and possibly a stressful one. But a child who feels truly supported and accepted will perform better and enjoy learning more. The adjustment could be more than worth it.

There are several excellent resources emerging for listening to books in lieu of reading them. In addition to Learningally.org (formerly known as the Library for the Blind and Reading Disabled), there is the Talking Book Library and Bookshare.org. These organizations (and others) can provide digital books where the text will appear on the computer screen while being heard orally. These resources do require a formal diagnosis of visual or reading disability in order to be accessed, but can level the playing field for students who need access to information that others get through reading.

Writing, for children with reading struggles, can be equally problematic. Especially by middle school, writing becomes a primary way that students demonstrate their understanding. But again, there is nothing magical about writing that makes it any more effective than other types of presentation. Just a few alternative ideas include:

- Watching a film on a subject and doing a project that demonstrates his knowledge
- Allowing a child to discuss or present his knowledge verbally – either in front of the class, thereby developing important public speaking skills, or one-on-one with the teacher
- Doing a hands-on science project and allowing the child to explain it to the class
- Having a scribe write for him (although this is a dramatic accommodation, I know of one young man who is now in graduate school and still using a scribe due to the degree of his learning disability)

Finding a Reading Specialist

Once you have obtained a thorough evaluation, there are many resources that can help you find the kind of help you need.

- Your pediatrician, or the person who did your evaluation, may have a list of resources for reading remediation.
- Many learning support websites, such as Ldonline.org, will discuss various multi-sensory reading programs. This will give you a list of appropriate programs when exploring local resources.
- Local learning disability chapters will also have a list of resources for reading remediation.
- There are private reading and learning clinics that have specialists trained in multi-sensory reading programs.

Questions for a Prospective Reading Specialist

- What multi-sensory reading programs do you have training and experience with?

⚲ Do you use the program systematically and sequentially, or do you tend to pick and choose which parts of the program are most relevant to the child? How do you make this decision?

⚲ Can you treat related weaknesses in spelling, writing, and math skills?

⚲ How do you decide if my child is making appropriate progress in your program?

Most reading remediation is not covered by insurance. However, if the student has a history of significant ear infections with documented disruption of hearing, remediation may fall under treatment of a medical condition. Typically, in order to be considered for insurance reimbursement, the treatment provider has to be a speech and language specialist with experience in reading remediation. (See Chapter 5: Speech and Language Issues.)

I recently evaluated a young man named Matthew for the third time. When he was in middle school, I had diagnosed dyslexia. I assessed him again late in high school to update his records, so that he could request extended time for college entrance exams. When he was 22 and seeking extended time for his GREs (he was going to graduate school, yay!), I evaluated him once again. He still had great visual-spatial and verbal skills, but very weak reading and spelling skills, despite years of remediation. He was just really dyslexic.

Matthew was smart and ambitious and had not let his dyslexia slow him down. Throughout high school and college, he had used audiotapes for much of his academic reading. I asked if it was hard to get copies of the professors' notes for his college lectures. He answered that it was actually pretty easy, given that most professors now post their lectures online. He could go online, run off the Power Point presentation of the lecture, review it in advance and take any brief notes on it during the lecture. It is heartening to see technology and the internet leveling the playing field for students in this way. ~ Robin McEvoy, developmental neuropsychologist

TREATMENT OPTIONS: COMPLEMENTARY AND ALTERNATIVE MEDICINE (CAM)

The following treatments may be helpful, in addition to directly addressing reading skills. The checklists at the beginning of the book should help you decide what else you should investigate. You can refer to the following sections to for more information.

⚲ **Chapter 7.1: Vision Disorder Issues.** Sometimes there are glitches in the visual processing system that render reading a constant struggle. A developmental optometrist can evaluate and address the various components involved in processing visual information.

Chapter 16.1: Naturopathy. A naturopath has many methods of calming a child's system. Some kids who cannot read have become habitually anxious about reading, and sometimes about school in general. Reading stress can emerge very early for children who are not progressing in reading.

Chapter 16.3: LEAP (Learning Enhancement Acupressure Program). Because reading troubles can have such different neurological roots, this work might help by identifying and addressing those roots before you proceed with reading remediation. Also, getting the areas responsible for language more functional could be very helpful (Broca's area and Wernicke's area, to be specific).

Chapter 16.4: Chiropractic Neurology. If your child seems to have poor bi-lateral integration or exhibits overall processing difficulties, this may help organize the brain and improve function in many areas.

Chapter 16.5: Craniosacral Therapy. Some kids have experienced a head injury that has impaired visual tracking or otherwise affected brain function. Cranial therapy can release compressed cranial muscles and bones and can also settle the nervous system.

Reason for Hope

Remember: Reading ability does not define success. There are famous surgeons, authors, businesspeople, actors, and highly successful people in all fields who are reading disabled or dyslexic. Many find that the challenge of working around the disability helped them to become more resourceful and resilient, and to find new paths to success. **It is important to learn to read, but not at the expense of squelching a child's joy in learning.**

> *"Why have we as a culture made the reading brain more important than all the other types of brains? Let's celebrate our talkers, builders, drawers, and connectors whether they are readers or not!"*
>
> ~ Jonathan Mooney,
> author, speaker, and education reform advocate

Resources for More Information

WEBSITES

www.learningally.org (formerly Recordings for the Blind and Dyslexic) offers an online catalog of audiobooks and audio learning resources.

www.audible.com and www.audiobooks.com have a wide selection of audiobooks for purchase.

www.bookshare.org also offers an extensive collection of books and learning materials.

www.ldonline.org/, LD Online: The Educators' Guide to Learning Disabilities and ADHD. This website has many resources for students, teachers, and parents.

Books

Overcoming Dyslexia by Sally Shaywitz. Still considered the seminal text on the subject, this book presents research about reading problems and practical techniques for overcoming them.

Learning Disabilities: From Identification to Intervention by Jack Fletcher, G. Reid Lyon, Lynn S. Fuchs, and Marcia A. Barnes. The authors offer a comprehensive resource to help practitioners classify, assess, and address a range of learning difficulties, including reading.

About the Author

Robin McEvoy, PhD, is a developmental neuropsychologist and one of the authors of this book. You can find her complete bio at the back.

A Story About SPD

Charlie's Journey

My son Charlie was never one of those kids who looked forward to going to school. He always seemed to need activity, charging around the playground and bouncing off the walls at home. Since I would rather be outside than inside sitting at a desk myself, I figured he was just like me and resigned myself to twelve years of talking him into doing his homework. Boy, did I have no idea what I was getting into.

For one thing, Charlie was a verbally precocious child. When he was a year old, he could say things like "I'd like to go to the park now, Mommy." His abilities were impressive but, as it turned out, only camouflaged his problems. He would debate with teachers when he thought the lesson was "stupid," which happened pretty much every day. I got calls from teachers complaining that he walked away from classroom activities and never stopped arguing. His precociousness was so obvious that everyone just figured he was too smart for his grade and needed more mature peers.

But other signs concerned me. I went to his kindergarten classroom to observe, and saw a child who often looked like a deer in the headlights, especially when things became noisy and confusing – which tends to happen a lot in kindergarten! Teachers got understandably frustrated when he didn't respond to verbal directions, but I knew my son better and realized he wasn't just being stubborn. The look in his eyes told me he had never even heard them. He also needed to pace when he was thinking about something, so he often just got up and started roaming around in the middle of a lesson. The more overwhelmed he became, the quicker he was to anger, sometimes pushing things over or throwing things. When things really became too much, he hid under a table crying. I think everyone was so focused on his arguing that they hadn't noticed some of these other things; they were all just part of what a pain he was. What I knew, that they didn't, was that he didn't do most of those things at home (except the arguing, of course – heaven forbid he ever stop that!). What was going on?

And he was incredibly clumsy. I didn't actually worry about this at the time, but it did turn out to be significant. Half of our Halloween pictures were of him picking up all of his candy, which he had just spilled. Again. He could trip walking across an empty room and was constantly running into doorjambs, furniture, and other kids. I just figured he was bigger than everyone else and having trouble catching up with his own body.

People told me I should put him in the next grade up, but I was hesitant. What do you do with a child who is years ahead of himself in some ways, but still two years old – a very, very, out-of-control, emotionally extreme two-year-old – in others? A young child who can throw tantrums with the verbal skills of an adult is a truly fearsome thing. It also didn't help that he was constantly making his friends mad by running into, falling over, or sitting on them without appearing to notice. The very thought of putting him with older children gave me an eye twitch.

By the end of first grade, Charlie was known for being impulsive, disruptive, and relentlessly, exhaustingly argumentative. I became something of a fixture in the principal's office. The school was focused on making him more compliant, but I had a new concern: Anxiety was beginning to be the driving force in his life. Every night, my husband and I took turns getting up to ease Charlie's intense, bizarre fears or comfort him after nightmares. He became inconsolable when he had trouble with homework (although undeniably bright, he seemed to have no tolerance for even momentary confusion on his own part) and would often end up sobbing "I'm so stupid" or "I'm going to have to find a new family because I can't do anything." The distant rumble of thunder would send him into a frenzy, to the point that if we were outside he would actually try to break car windows to get inside the car. Fireworks or even noisy movies had him crying and holding his hands over his ears.

I was lost. The school tested him, but we did not feel that it fully explained his needs. (Plus, he was less than cooperative and argued through the test, making the results very inconclusive.) We found a neuropsychologist who did a thorough assessment, found evidence of ADHD and dysgraphia (inability to write by hand) and referred us for other assessments, starting with occupational therapy for sensory integration issues.

The OT we found pretty much changed our lives. Before we even started the evaluation, she sat watching Charlie while I gave her the lowdown on what had been happening. It was, by then, a pretty long story. I concluded and she looked at me, then came out with a stream of comments that blew my mind with their accuracy.

"I'll bet he eats with his fingers, doesn't he? He probably had a lot of trouble learning to write and recognize the alphabet and numbers, but he could do it verbally, right? Does he avoid puzzles? I'll bet he hates all fine motor activities." This went on for some time. I wondered if she was psychic.

When she explained the assessment results, it all made sense. His nervous system was somehow both hyper- *and* hypo-sensitive, meaning that he literally had to run into things in order to get enough of one kind of sensory input, but was hyper-sensitive to noise and would easily get overwhelmed in an active classroom, crowded mall, etc. His proprioception was also very weak, meaning that he couldn't really tell where he was in space, with the result that he crashed or fell into things. Aha!

His nervous system, in a perpetual state of both overwhelm and needing more, was virtually never able to relax. This created anxiety and sleep issues, and made it hard for him to concentrate. His mind may have been ready to participate, but his nervous system was in a constant state of trying to find equilibrium. He needed to move to think and was very easily overwhelmed by noise. He used argumentation to control his environment, because it felt so perpetually out of control.

But that wasn't all. The dysgraphia that the neuropsychologist had told us about was enough to account for his work avoidance, but was not the only reason. A vision assessment revealed that his visual system was also very distorted. The OT had recommended we have his vision evaluated after she asked him to complete a very simple puzzle. I knew that Charlie had always hated puzzles, but had just thought that, like me, he didn't like anything requiring him to sit still for more than five minutes. But when, during the evaluation, he had been stumped by an easy five-piece puzzle, the OT had asked why he was having so much trouble.

"I'm waiting for all the lines to stop moving so I can see where this goes," my son answered. Oh boy. It's hard to read, or do any number of tasks, when every line in sight won't stop waving around. No wonder he could never finish anything.

The sensory assessment seemed to explain everything. Now we knew where the problem really started. The OT laid out a comprehensive plan for us, which was a huge relief; I hadn't had any idea where to start. We would begin OT immediately, but there were other fronts to address as well. We needed to see a naturopath and look for food allergies and deficiencies that could be keeping his brain off kilter. She also recommended a LEAP practitioner. Actually, she insisted on it, because it would "organize his underlying neurology" – whatever that meant. "His sensory problems are some of the most severe I've ever seen," she said. "If you don't see this LEAP person, it could take me ten years to shift things." I had no idea what LEAP was, but she was the first person who had a clue about what was going on, so I followed everything she said. After OT had progressed to a certain point, she said we would also have to do vision therapy, but not yet. I wanted to address everything at the same time – why not? Let's do this! But she said it would be useless until Charlie had gotten his nervous system to a certain point of functionality.

For the next few years, I felt like all we did was therapy. We began occupational therapy right away, with a rigorous program that involved three specially designed workouts a day. The OT at school had not been trained in sensory issues, so every day I went to Charlie's school at lunchtime and went through the routine. We also saw the OT weekly and got LEAP treatments twice a week. We also found a naturopath, who did some tests and then had us remove nuts, dairy, and food dyes from his diet. It was intense. I dropped work to part-time in order to get it all done.

The one thing that didn't seem to be shifting as much as we would have liked was anxiety. As you might expect, the school had recommended I look into medication, first for what they saw as ADD and then for anxiety. But as a nurse, I know the impact that strong meds can have. They can change your whole personality and affect your body in more ways than many people realize. I was also dismayed by how often I heard teachers and others with no medical background say, "That kid really needs to be on meds!" I feel that meds are prescribed much too easily, oftentimes without looking for causes or other answers. And I knew that Charlie's issues, whatever the heck they were, were much more complex than anything that would be solved by a pill. So at first I declined, determined to find the true roots of Charlie's problems.

But before we could do any more than we were already doing, Charlie's behavior became just too extreme and I found I could no longer justify not trying meds. After a long conversation with my doctor and then with my husband, I told Charlie we had something for him to consider.

"Would you mind trying a drug that might help you feel calmer?"

Charlie looked at me in wonder. "You mean I might not have to walk into classrooms and feel like I'm going to throw up? You mean I might be able to watch a movie with my friends without freaking out? You mean…" My heart broke as my son listed details I had not been aware of, revealing a world that was even more nightmarish than what I had been able to see from the outside. He ran to me, threw his arms around me and cried out, "Thanks Mom!" (To this day, I am not sure if that moment gets me a Good Mom Award or a Bad Mom Award.)

By the time he hit middle school, life was feeling a lot more manageable. The meds had played their part and his anxiety went down hugely, making life easier for all of us (especially Charlie!). Eventually, he was able to stop taking them. His sensory system had integrated enough that he could focus without slamming around the room and move around without knocking everyone over. Most interestingly, his quirky sense of humor – which had been a liability in elementary school – actually started working in his favor in middle school. As it turns out, the random, outrageous quality of most of his jokes really works for middle school boys!

We now call his elementary school years "the war years." It's not that we were at war with each other, but we all feel like it was as intense as a combat zone. Will this time of peace last? Who knows? I know the high school years can be a challenge even for the most successful kids. All I know is, it's a pleasure watching Charlie be happy. And I am really enjoying the lower drama quotient. We'll figure out whatever we may need to later.

SEVEN

Sensory Processing Disorder

by Kari Hall, MA, OTR

There are many, many ways that sensory issues manifest. No two profiles are exactly the same. The following symptoms are the most common, but this list is still, by necessity, somewhat incomplete. You can find more lists within this chapter.

Because sensory issues often coincide with AD/HD, there are markers here that indicate whether you might want to look at that chapter as well. Biomedical concerns can contribute to either a hypervigilant or sluggish system, and a concussion or mild TBI (traumatic brain injury) can disrupt sensory processing, so there are markers that might lead you to the biomedical or concussion chapters also.

In infancy and toddlerhood:

☐ Has unusual trouble going to sleep or staying asleep
☐ Resists being held (arches, cries)
☐ Overly floppy or stiff muscle tone
☐ Slow to crawl; skipped crawling; or found alternative such as scooching, rolling, or commando crawling
☐ Has trouble dressing self, feeling own body sensations
☐ Has a lot of trouble toilet training

Common childhood symptoms:

☐ Persistent trouble going to sleep or staying asleep
☐ Avoids being touched, hugged, cuddled, or seems to crave physical contact
☐ Craves or hates getting hands, face, or other body parts messy with paint, glue, sand, food, or lotion; either can't stand or doesn't notice getting messy
☐ Avoids fine motor tasks such as drawing, buttoning, snaps, attaching pop beads,

and attachable toys
- ☐ Dislikes riding equipment that moves through space (swings, teeter-totter, escalators)
- ☐ Avoids challenges to balance such as skating, bicycle riding, skiing, and balance beams
- ☐ Often covers ears to protect them from noises
- ☐ Dislikes being in noisy settings such as a crowded restaurants or parties
- ☐ Has difficulty functioning or completing tasks in a noisy environment
- ☐ Loves looking at shiny, spinning, or moving objects
- ☐ Avoids visually busy places such as stores, classrooms, and playgrounds with many children
- ☐ Covers eyes to protect them from light
- ☐ Explores by smelling non-food items such as plastic items, Play-Dough, garbage
- ☐ Craves or despises strong odors such as perfume, gasoline, cleaning products
- ☐ Has trouble transitioning from one setting or activity to another
- ☐ Has poor sense of boundaries; is always in everybody's face or space

While the following symptoms are associated with Sensory Processing Disorder, they may also be markers for other issues. The following list indicates chapters you may want to read as well.

Cross-reference guide:
SPD = Sensory Processing Disorder
ADD = Attention Problems, Chapter 4
Bio/Nutr = Biomedical Approaches, Chapter 14; Nutritional Approaches, Chapter 15
Emo/Beh = Emotional and Behavioral Factors, Chapter 11

BEHAVIOR	SPD	Emo/Beh	Bio/Nutr	ADD
Doesn't outgrow tantrumming	*	*		
Seems mentally foggy when thinking	*		*	
Seems chronically tired or low energy	*		*	
Becomes sleepy or hyperactive after meals	*		*	
Only eats "white foods" such as pastas, white bread, French fries, cereal			*	
Has excessive gas/bloating much of the time			*	

BEHAVIOR	SPD	Emo/Beh	Bio/Nutr	ADD
Has history of ear infections or sinus infections			*	
Is irritable regardless of the daily schedule	*	*	*	
Gets off-task easily	*			*
Can't sustain attention for low interest tasks	*			*
Moves from project to project without finishing things	*			*
Procrastinates	*			*
Talks excessively	*			*
Has difficulty waiting for his turn	*			*
Has history of concussion, head injury	*			
Seeks high-risk play (jumps from extreme heights, climbs tall trees, rides bike over gravel)	*			*

If your child has sensory issues that seem to have emerged after a concussion, you may want to read Chapter 9 on concussions as well.

The Basics

I cannot tell you how many families go through what Charlie and his family did in the previous story. A child displays a number of somewhat mystifying, difficult behaviors and parents are either directed towards medication or make themselves crazy trying to figure out the cause. Sensory processing issues are often the culprit, yet few practitioners recognize them or know who deals with them. The parts of the brain that do the complicated learning cannot work well if the brain's foundation is not organized and processing basic sensory input smoothly. **Therefore, if your child is experiencing difficulties in this area, you will need to address them – not just manage them, but actually remediate them – before his learning issues will resolve.**

What exactly are sensory processing issues?

We experience the world through our sensory systems: We see, feel, hear, smell, and taste our environment. Most of us never think about *how* we are doing this: Interpreting

Food for Thought

Research by the SPD Foundation (www.spdfoundation.net) indicates that **one in every 20 children** experiences symptoms of SPD that are significant enough to affect their ability to participate fully in everyday life. The percentage is higher in certain subgroups of children, such as extremely premature children and children adopted from orphanages. Most of us have occasional difficulties processing sensory information. Children with SPD have difficulties that are *chronic and which disrupt everyday life.*

the sensory data around us usually comes as naturally as learning to walk and talk. For some people, however, ordinary sensory input is either too much, too little, or too chaotic, making the world a grating and exhausting place to be.

Sensory Processing Disorder (SPD) refers to the inability of the central nervous system (CNS) to process sensory input easily. For *over-reactive, hyper-sensitive children*, this means that most sensory input is overwhelming. These children might be terrified of fireworks, melt down in a busy classroom, scream during routine hair brushing, or overreact to being touched lightly in passing. A day at school can feel like trying to concentrate in a construction site – irritating, overwhelming, nonstop "too muchness."

If you have an *under-reactive, hypo-sensitive child*, you know it: These are the children who come into my clinic and immediately barrel around slamming into everything. Their nervous systems always need more, more, more in order to function properly. At school, they probably get in trouble every other day for either being daredevils (jumping from high places, banging into walls) or playing too roughly with others.

It is easy to see why SPD gets misdiagnosed so often. The obvious symptoms can look a lot like AD/HD. Children with SPD typically have trouble staying on track, both physically and mentally. Practitioners may also diagnose hypersensitive children with anxiety disorder; the world overwhelms them and they are often in tears or afraid to try something new. Hypo-sensitive children are frequently given medication to settle them down. But none of this will get to the root…and it *is* possible to do so. Once you have, you may be surprised at how those learning problems work themselves out! (Or they should at least become much easier to address.)

A Little Science

A study out of UC San Francisco has identified a quantifiable difference between the brain structure of kids with SPD and the brain structure of those who are developing more neurotypically. Although this still does not pinpoint a cause, it does give previously lacking evidence that biological underpinnings exist. This should help bring SPD more forcefully into the world of mainstream medicine, which should, in turn, result in more physicians being trained to recognize it.

For more information on the study, see the references section at the end of this chapter.

Causes and Contributors

As with other neuro-developmental disorders like AD/HD, the exact cause of Sensory Processing Disorder remains unidentified. There is, so far, no biological "smoking gun" that can be identified by a lab test, brain scan, or other quantifiable procedure. Preliminary research indicates that it can be inherited. Many parents of children with identified sensory processing issues can relate to the challenges and sensitivities their own children are experiencing. However, sensory processing issues can also accompany other conditions like:

- Autism Spectrum Disorders/Pervasive Developmental Disorders
- Fragile X Syndrome (a chromosomal abnormality)
- Prenatal exposure to alcohol or drugs
- Extreme prematurity
- Sensory deprivation due to early life in an orphanage
- Giftedness (Some gifted children are hyper-sensitive and take in *everything*. This means that they tend to learn a lot quickly; but the flip side of this coin is that they take in *everything*! This can also make them irritable, fatigued, or overwhelmed.)
- History of head injury/concussion
- History of chronic ear or sinus infections

My mother was a fussy eater; I was a fussy eater; my sister gagged at the sight of a cut tomato; my brother chewed all his shirts. Every picture of us as children shows my brother with a wet shirt front. His daughter had to have all tags cut out of her clothes, no internal pockets, and no embroidery on her dresses. Brushing her hair each morning could only be done while she was eating her favorite breakfast in front of the television. My sister's child only eats five foods (and that is as a teenager). As an adult, I am still a picky eater based purely on textures (mixed textures in food are the worst). I also avoid really loud crowded settings. ~ D.R.

There are two or three more senses that are fundamental to our sensory world. These are core or deep senses that lay the foundation for other processing (please refer to the **Pyramid of Sensory Processing as a Foundation for Learning**, later in this chapter).

- **The Vestibular System.** This system resides in our inner ear. It helps us process the information of gravity, balance, and movement. It detects

The Five Senses

When thinking about Sensory Processing Disorder, we start by considering the seven senses. We all know the five main senses:

- **The Tactile System** – Our sense of touch - the input we get from our skin that has receptors for touch, heat, cold, and pain
- **The Olfactory System** – Our sense of smell
- **The Visual System** – What we see
- **The Auditory System** – What we hear
- **The Gustatory System** – Our sense of taste

the changes in our body position and helps to develop our muscle strength, muscle tone (the feel of our muscles at rest), bilateral coordination (both sides of our body working as a team), and motor planning. If these functions are erratic or weak, emotional security and attention will be affected as well.

The Proprioceptive System. This system processes information from muscles, ligaments, and joints. It helps us with body awareness, motor planning, and postural control. It also allows us to grade our movements, so that we can apply the right amount of force to all of our daily tasks (for example, you would squeeze a lighter object less than you would squeeze a heavy object when picking it up). It also helps with our feeling of emotional security. This is why babies often need to be swaddled and held in order to be calmed, and why deep pressure, such as you get through massage, soothes people of all ages.

Because these are foundational senses, problems with sensory integration must be addressed *first*. This means, for example, that if you have visual and auditory processing issues as well as vestibular issues, the vestibular issues must be addressed first. Vision therapy will be, at best, only partially effective if vestibular or proprioceptive issues are still at play. By the same token, if vestibular or proprioceptive issues are resolved, issues higher up in the pyramid will resolve much more quickly and easily (please refer to the Pyramid of Sensory Processing as a Foundation for Learning, later in this chapter). Learning issues typically will not resolve completely until sensory needs have been resolved. Anything involving the frontal lobe requires a solid nervous system behind it.

The Interoceptive System. Dr. Lucy Jane Miller, a leading authority in the field of sensory processing, feels it is critical to consider an *eighth* sense: the interoceptive sense. This is the system that detects internal sensations, such as hunger or the need to go to the bathroom. The internal states of hunger, heart rate, respiration, and elimination are all important to read, but some over-stimulated kids cannot read these states well. When this system is operating smoothly, it provides a foundation for proprioceptive and vestibular function.

There are many far-reaching consequences when this system is not operating well. Some children struggle with potty training; others cannot tell that fatigue or hunger is making them cranky. Some researchers believe that this system also plays a role in our ability to perceive our own sense of energy levels, well-being, and stress…and, if we extrapolate a bit further, awareness of our own and others' emotional states.

I adopted my child from China when she was nine months old. She was withdrawn and could not look anyone in the eye. For three months, I carried her everywhere, fed her in my arms, and tried to make her feel comfortable with me so she could look at me and smile at me. There was little progress. After three months, we were visiting a friend who was an occupational therapist. She watched Emma on my hip and said, "You need to swing her . . . with rotation." After this odd comment, she explained that Emma needed to be in a swing that could also rotate in circles. Feeling confused and a little desperate, I went home and had the handyman hang a swing in the living room. I put Emma in and began to swing and rotate her in circles . . . and she looked up at me. She looked in my eyes. Finally, for the first time, she looked at me for more than a glance. I called my friend and asked, "How come she can look at me when I swing her?" She replied, "Well, the vestibular system and the visual system are very closely linked." I did not really understand this, but Emma began occupational therapy the next day. ~ R.M.

Pyramid of Sensory Processing as a Foundation for Learning

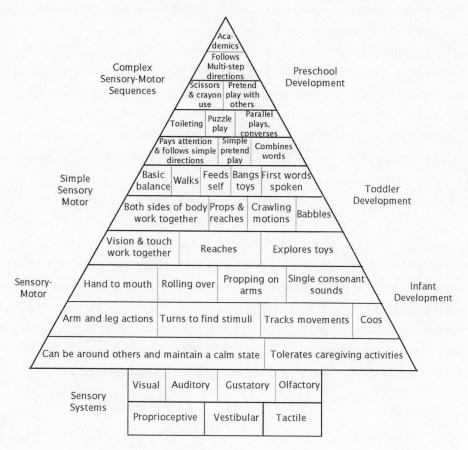

Hyper versus Hypo

Children with Sensory Processing Disorder are either *over-reactive (hyper-reactive or hyper-sensitive)* **or** *under-reactive (hypo-reactive)* to sensory input. The sensory input coming in is either too much or too little. **It is common for children to have one** or **more senses that are under-reactive and others that are over-reactive.**

Children who are hyper-sensitive often overreact to sensory input, so they tend to avoid it. A child who is sensitive to sound, for example, may find the classroom over-stimulating and fatiguing. These children usually come home from school, retreat to their rooms, and avoid interaction or after-school activities in order to get a break from noise.

A child who is over-reactive to touch may be similarly fatigued and irritated in the classroom because of the tendency to get bumped or brushed by others during the day. These children can be quite irritable when picked up from school.

Parents frequently tell me that they cannot attend concerts or birthday parties because it is simply too much for their child. Some children, because of their sensory defensiveness, are so chronically on edge that they melt down at the slightest frustration and can seem unmanageable. Others shut down in order to tune out the overwhelming input. They can seem "permanently out to lunch," in the words of one parent.

Children who are under-reactive, however, will constantly seek out more sensation and stimulation. A child who has an under-reactive proprioceptive system may often be in trouble for playing too roughly. It is difficult for these children to sit still for long periods of time; their bodies literally start moving of their own accord. As one mother lamented: "In about one minute, he's bouncing his leg. A minute later, he's tapping with his pencil. After about five minutes, he's using his desk like a jungle gym, which is usually about when he gets a time-out. I don't know how he gets any work done at all!"

Please understand: they really cannot help it. Organizing the sensory needs of the nervous system is almost as primary a developmental need as food, water, and physical safety. So when they need to move, cry, or escape altogether, it is as intense and involuntary a need in that moment as gulping air would be to a drowning man. Cultivating self-control is not the answer, and will in fact not be possible until SPD has been addressed. I have some parents who have tried systems of punishments and rewards. But this only confuses and frustrates children, as they have no power over their reactions. Medications can sometimes *look* like they are helping, but as they are not addressing the true issue at all; they are only making the behavioral symptoms appear somewhat more manageable for a time.

Hyper and Hypo Across the Senses

What exactly does SPD look like? That varies hugely. Your child's responses will depend on which senses are affected and whether they are hypo- or hyper-reactive. Remember, also, that some senses can be hyper-reactive while others are hypo, and some senses can be affected while others are not, making for truly endless series of possible combinations!

Tactile Input

The over-sensitive tactile system causes children to be on alert at all times. They don't like light or unexpected touch, which can feel irritating or be perceived as painful. They can become hyper-vigilant and distracted. The under-sensitive child is always looking for deep tactile input any way he can get it.

Over-sensitive Tactile System:

Avoids light touch, crowds

Avoids lotions or powder

Doesn't like to get wet or messy

Avoids certain food or clothing textures

Avoids grooming activities: hair, nails

Under-sensitive Tactile System:

Unaware of bruises, cuts, pain

Mouths non-food items

Seeks contact with people or things

Unaware of temperature changes

Seeks out certain textures (silk, lotion, etc.)

Olfactory Input

Smell is an old sense and hard to suppress. Some children use it as a key way of exploring the world, while others avoid situations that are noxious to them.

Over-sensitive Olfactory System:

Notices all odors

Repulsed by different food odors

Complains that perfumes stink

Under-sensitive Olfactory System:

Smells everything

Likes strong or noxious smells

Ignores unpleasant odors

Visual Input

Some children are extremely light-sensitive and aware of anything happening around them (making them highly distractible). Others are under-sensitive and can seem easily startled by what seems visually obvious.

Over-sensitive Visual System:

Excessive blinking

Bothered greatly by sunlight

Avoids eye contact

Notices all visual changes in room

Under-sensitive Visual System:

Dull eyes

Lacks awareness of objects in room

Likes to watch objects spin

Misses visual cues

Auditory Input

This is a more obvious sensitivity for those children who have it. They quickly overreact to noisy situations and can become irritable and fatigued in typical settings (such as the classroom).

Over-sensitive Auditory System:

Cries at loud or unexpected noise

Bothered by automatic flush toilets

Dislikes noise of vacuum, blender, etc.

Covers ears often

Dislikes noisy places

Under-sensitive Auditory System:

Tunes out many sounds

Ignores voices

Has difficulty following directions

Likes music and TV loud

Talks loudly

Gustatory Input

Children with sensitivities in the taste area are often described as picky eaters. Children who are under-reactive to the taste of food can be very adventurous eaters.

Over–sensitive Gustatory System:

Prefers bland foods

Strongly objects to certain foods

Often gags when eating

Has a very limited diet

Under-sensitive Gustatory System:

Loves hot/spicy foods

Seeks intense flavors

Acts like all foods taste the same

May lick or mouth non-food items,
        even after toddlerhood

Vestibular Input

The hyper-sensitive vestibular system can be intolerant or actually fearful of typical movement experiences. Hypo-reactive children are often described as the "seeker" kids. Their nervous systems are always in need of more movement input.

Over-sensitive Vestibular System:

Afraid of bike riding

Avoids climbing at playgrounds

Gets anxious when balance is taxed

Becomes car sick easily

Gets anxious when moved unexpectedly

Under-sensitive Vestibular System:

Seeks fast movement

Has difficulty sitting still

Seeks twirling

Doesn't get dizzy easily

Likes to be upside down

Proprioceptive Input

The overly sensitive proprioceptive system will do anything to avoid activities that are rough-and-tumble, while an under-reactive system will do anything to get more, more, more.

Over-sensitive Proprioceptive System:
Prefers sedentary activities
Has difficulty standing in line
Prefers light touch to deeper touch
Avoids playgrounds
Is rigid, tense, or stiff

Under-sensitive Proprioceptive System:
Puts hard pressure on pencil
Often is perceived as too rough
Likes bear hugs, leans on people
Tends to be a daredevil
Seeks falling, crashing, jumping,
        hanging, bumping

Who Can Help?

SPD is not yet in the diagnostic manuals. As a result, physicians are usually not trained to look for it. Sensory Processing Disorder can be diagnosed and treated by occupational therapists (OTs), but **not all occupational therapists are trained in SPD.** Only a specific subgroup of occupational therapists is trained to work with children who have SPD.

Diagnosis

The first part of successful treatment is a good diagnostic evaluation. Like most OTs who work with SPD, I have parents and teachers fill out a detailed questionnaire that gives me information on both the child's current behavioral patterns and past developmental milestones, as well as the child's sensory preferences in the seven senses. I also follow a commonly used protocol of standardized testing, where I observe the child through a number of tasks and note his preferences, difficulties, stamina, and anything else that demonstrates his sensory processing skills and glitches.

Common Misdiagnoses

Because SPD is not yet in the diagnostic manuals, many practitioners are not aware of it and direct parents to other resources. As previously mentioned, pediatricians frequently refer children with sensory needs to AD/HD specialists.

However, some kids whose issues are accompanied by emotional symptoms – like high anxiety or frequent angry outbursts – might be referred for a mental health assessment. I have seen far too many children medicated for attention or for anxiety when at least part (if not all) of the problem is SPD. *There are no drugs that address SPD. If that is your child's issue, he will have to do sensory integration therapy.*

TREATMENT OPTIONS: STANDARD OF CARE

Based on the results of the evaluation, your OT will develop a two-part treatment plan. This will involve the following:

- Regular sessions with an occupational therapist (once a week is standard; if the need is particularly severe, two to five times a week might be necessary for a period of time)
- Daily prescribed activities at home (these activities usually need to be done more than once a day)

As with learning to play an instrument, children need to check in with a specialist **and** practice at home on a daily basis in order to progress. Rewiring a child's nervous system is no small task!

Occupational therapists usually like to see a child at least weekly. This allows the OT to get a better understanding for how your child's nervous system is working and responding to different types of input. Activities in therapy can include jumping, swinging, heavy physical work, brushing (a specific tactile strategy), and other tasks *carefully selected and sequenced* by the therapist to meet the individual child's needs.

The *home program* consists of a *sensory diet* that has two components:

- A series of specific daily activities selected by the occupational therapist to support the child's neurological system
- Creation of an appropriate daily routine for the child. It is important that he has regular activities, outside of the OT's suggested routine, that are calming and enjoyable. It is also important to identify and avoid activities and environments that are over-stimulating and stressful. Communicating with your therapist about your child's daily life is imperative.

This daily sensory diet helps the child to perform his best and to progress. A good therapist is invaluable in finding ways to create that *just right* state of calm alertness in your child's nervous system. She should be able to help you survey the child's day, and help you to find ways to cut the stimulation and add good input in a way that matches both your child's needs and your family's lifestyle.

Your OT can also outline accommodations that your child can use to help him be more calm and focused in the classroom. Your school's occupational therapist should also have suggestions for classroom strategies, such as using an inflated cushion on his seat or seating him in the area of the classroom with the least distractions.

The home program developed by our OT did change our daily schedule. In the morning, our seven-year-old son Thomas needed at least 15 minutes of body input such as jumping on the mini-trampoline, playing in the ball pit, or bouncing down the hall on his hippity-hop ball. He also needed frequent brushing, where the skin is brushed down with a soft plastic brush. As a result, he quickly became more tolerant of the clothes laid out for him. It took extra time to get this done, but his teacher immediately commented that he was calmer and more able to pay attention in class. His teacher also followed the OT recommendations for a therapy band around the legs of his desk. Thomas pushed his feet against the band and could then stay in his seat. Also, once his teachers understood that movement was crucial to his staying calm and focused, he was never kept in from recess again. We continued with movement activities after school and homework became more tolerable, though the recommendation to reduce homework was equally important. Life is easier; Thomas is happier and feels smarter; and his father and I are much happier. ~ J.L.

Options for Treatment Settings

Traditionally, sensory therapists provide therapy in the occupational therapy room in hospitals and private child development clinics. These are large rooms that can accommodate swings, climbing walls, mini-trampolines, slides, and chutes. But therapy can also happen outside. Some therapists work in farms and in natural settings so that animals and plants can be included in the treatment. *(For more information about outdoor OT and how you can incorporate it into your child's program, take a look at our website at www.childdecoded.com ~ The Editors)* Equine-assisted therapy uses horses to organize the nervous system, strengthen physical abilities, and develop critical life skills. (See Chapter 7.2: Equine-Assisted Therapy.)

RELATED NEEDS

Social Skills

Children with SPD can struggle socially. Hypersensitive children can be anxious, prone to crying, quick to take offense or to melt down if they lose a game. They can also "check out," shutting down in a crowd or even near a particularly active group of classmates. Seeker children (the hypo-sensitive ones) are often seen as impulsive, aggressive, or out of control.

In addition to treatment for SPD, these children often benefit from social skills training to help them gain perspective and practice important skills (such as advocating for a break and using words instead of actions). Social skills groups (sometimes called *friendship groups*) can be found in child development units and clinics, with private therapists, and within many schools. (See Chapter 12: Social Skills Issues.)

Emotional

Emotional dysregulation – unusually extreme emotional reactions – is another common feature of SPD. Children can be prone to anxiety or anger due to overstimulation. Rigid and controlling behaviors are also common. For some children, their emotion regulation issues are entirely caused by SPD. For others, the problems coexist. Sensory Processing Disorder can contribute to emotion dysregulation, but it is not necessarily the sole cause. Even with fantastic sensory support, emotional control can still be difficult. Regardless of the exact relationship, the behavioral challenges that can result from sensory and emotion dysregulation will often benefit from counseling support with a strong emphasis on parenting strategies for intense and sensitive children. The chapters on Psychiatry and Emotional Issues may be good resources for additional information. (See Chapter 11: Emotional and Behavioral Issues, or Chapter 13: Psychiatry and Functional Medicine Psychiatry.)

School Supports

Children with significant Sensory Processing Disorder may struggle so much at school that the school will need to develop a specialized plan for serving the child's needs. When the educational team needs to meet to develop a formal plan, this is typically called an Individual Education Plan (IEP). There are two important considerations when sensory issues need to be addressed at school:

- Sensory Processing Disorder is often not a qualifying learning or physical disability. To receive sensory therapy at school, the child will have to be identified under a qualifying condition. Supports for SPD can then be provided as part of a secondary condition. The qualifying condition is often Attention Deficit Disorder, though it can also be anxiety or Developmental Coordination Disorder (if the child has enough motor impairment). It will be important to check with your individual school district to explore their guidelines for this.
- Parents also need to be aware that school-based services aim only to help a child be successful at school (as opposed to full remediation). School plans for sensory supports do *not* constitute a comprehensive treatment plan for resolving SPD.

If you are having trouble getting sensory supports for your child at his school, it may be necessary to check with an educational advocate about the laws in your state. (See Chapter 17: Advocacy in the School System.)

TREATMENT OPTIONS: COMPLEMENTARY AND ALTERNATIVE (CAM)

The following CAM modalities may be able to help calm the nervous system and organize neurology from a different angle.

- **Chapter 16.2: Neurofeedback/Biofeedback.** This computer-based modality can address sensory issues by teaching the brain how to calm itself.
- **Chapter 16.3: LEAP.** This helps with basic brain organization, and can open relevant neurological pathways so that therapy is more effective.
- **Chapter 16.4: Chiropractic Neurology.** This can be instrumental in "rewiring" and retraining the nervous system in a more effective way.
- **Chapter 16.5: Craniosacral Therapy.** This can work quite nicely alongside sensory integration therapy, as it supports the nervous system during a time of deep re-integration. It can also be very effective if a head injury has contributed to abnormal sensory processing.

Questions for a Prospective Occupational Therapist

- Do you specialize in pediatric or child occupational therapy?
- Do you have specific and specialized training in Sensory Processing Disorder?
- How long have you been treating Sensory Processing Disorder?
- Do you recommend a daily sensory diet for a child with sensory issues? (Author's note: We believe a home program is essential.)
- How specific are your recommendations and schedule for a daily sensory diet?
- How do you determine what would be an appropriate course of treatment for a child?
- Do you take insurance?
- After evaluation, will you be able to tell me about how long treatment will take?
- How, and how frequently, do you report on progress to parents?

Resources for More Information

Websites

www.spd4kids.com. Sensory Pathways 4 Kids, Kari Hall's private practice in Denver and Arvada, CO.

www.spdfoundation.net, the SPD Foundation. An informative website, this gives information about services, education, how to locate therapists, resources, etc.

www.childrensdisabilities.info/sensory_integration, the website for Children's Disabilities Information. You can find many resources and articles here that will give you tips on specific aspects of SPD.

www.sensory-processing-disorder.com. This website will give you information on just about every aspect of SPD you might encounter.

You can find home therapy sensory equipment at the following websites:

www.abilitations.com

www.southpawenterprises.com

www.therapyshoppe.com

Books

The Out-of-Sync Child by Carol Stock Kranowitz. This groundbreaking, informative book describes Sensory Processing Disorder and recent research in engaging, parent-friendly style.

The Out-Of-Sync Child Has Fun by Carol Stock Kranowitz. This gives many suggestions for activities for kids with Sensory Processing Disorders. It's a perfect complement to *The Out-of-Sync Child.*

Sensational Kids by Lucy Jane Miller. Dr. Miller is a world-renowned researcher who brings together a lifetime of study to teach parents and professionals about Sensory Processing Disorder.

Too Loud, Too Bright, Too Fast, Too Tight: What to do if You are Sensory Defensive in an Over-Stimulating World by Sharon Heller. This book is more geared to adults and older adolescents with SPD.

Sensory Processing Disorder Answer Book by Tara Delany. Practical answers to the top 250 questions parents ask.

Books For Children

Why Does Izzy Cover Her Ears? by Jennifer Veenendall. Meet first grader Izzy, whose behavior is often misunderstood as she tries to cope with sensory processing overload in her surroundings.

Arnie and His School Tools by Jennifer Veenendall. Arnie used to have problems at school, but using these simple strategies and tools, he is better able to cope.

References

Owen, J. P., et al. Abnormal white matter microstructure in children with sensory processing disorders. *NeuroImage: Clinical*, 2, (2013), doi:10.1016/j.nicl.2013.06.009, www.sciencedirect.com/science/article/pii/S2213158213000776.

About the Author

Kari S. Hall, MA, OTR, obtained her bachelor of arts in Occupational Therapy in 1984 from Colorado State University. She later obtained her Master's degree at Denver University in Special Education. In 1987, she became a partner at the Neuro-Developmental Center, a child development clinic offering comprehensive services for children. She developed Sensory Pathways 4 Kids for sensory processing and occupational and physical therapy support for children. You can reach Kari at the first link listed in the website section of the preceding *Resources for More Information* section.

Vision Disorder Issues

by Lynn F. Hellerstein, OD, FCOVD, FAAO

Signs that your child could benefit from vision therapy include:

- ☐ Tantrums or meltdowns when faced with certain activities that involve visual processing
- ☐ Frequent "careless" mistakes
- ☐ Sloppy handwriting, difficulty with handwriting (which might also be dysgraphia; see Chapter 10.2: Writing Disability (Dysgraphia))
- ☐ Reading avoidance or rapid fatigue
- ☐ Frequently skips lines or words while reading out loud
- ☐ Poor eye contact that does not seem related to shyness
- ☐ Visual distractibility or inattention
- ☐ Letter or sound reversals when reading out loud or writing
- ☐ Clumsiness, tendency to bump into things or people
- ☐ Difficulty remembering what has been shown
- ☐ Repeated spelling errors, different spellings of the same word

Joey was a bright second-grade student who struggled in school. He had vision and visual motor problems, and had three eye muscle surgeries for crossed eyes. He wore bifocal lenses for farsightedness and focusing problems. Joey's ophthalmologist said that he did not need more eye surgery and that his eyes were "fine" (i.e., looked straight).

Joey, however, was still frustrated. He usually understood the material covered in class, but had great difficulty completing his written work. He dreaded handwriting tasks, reporting that it "just wasn't fun." In fact, handwriting was quite difficult, almost painful for him to undertake. His handwriting was sloppy and not well spaced, as seen in the first copying sample, which was obtained as part of our assessment.

Clearly, Joey was having a difficult time. And no wonder: he hated writing and avoided any task requiring it. We discontinued the test at five minutes, even though he had not completed the sentence.

Joey came to vision therapy every week and practiced his home vision therapy activities diligently. The therapy emphasized improving his visual efficiency and visual information processing (VIP) skills. After six months of vision therapy, Joey's school experience shifted dramatically. All visual skills had improved, which improved his ability to read and write. At the end of his therapy, Joey was a happier child who no longer avoided writing.

Examine the sentence in the Post Vision Therapy sample, copied by Joey after completing his vision therapy. Note the vast improvement in his letter formation, spacing, legibility, and speed of completion. It took

Pre-Vision Therapy Copy Sample

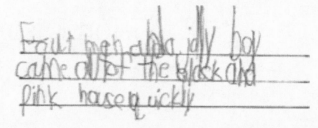

Post-Vision Therapy Copy Sample

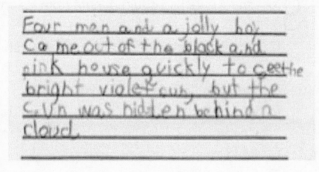

him less than four minutes to complete the sentence and did not seem to be at all the torturous task it had been just six months ago.

Joey's perception of his writing dramatically changed as well. In his words, "My writer was crammed in me and squished. Now it's gotten much bigger and I can write better." ~Lynn Hellerstein

The Basics

- **Sight** refers merely to eyesight or visual acuity. When your child passes her school's or pediatrician's eye exam and reportedly has 20/20 eyesight, it is her *sight* that is unimpaired. It does not mean that she is free from vision problems.
- **Vision** refers to processing and responding to visual information, and occurs not in the eyes but in the brain. It is quite common for a child to have 20/20 eyesight and still have problems processing visual information.

Vision is a complex process that involves communication between many different parts of the brain. If any part of your child's visual system is not functioning properly, he will have problems processing visual information. And since vision is the dominant sense used for learning and school, any difficulties in this area can represent a major obstacle to learning and successful performance.

Poor vision skills manifest in an extremely wide range of symptoms, which can confuse children, parents, and educators alike. Often, these symptoms masquerade as other learning or behavior disorders, which then turn out not to be the culprit after all, leaving everyone frustrated and no closer to an answer.

Vision and School

At a conference for teachers, another optometrist and I gave a demo. We passed out glasses containing special prisms that made the eyes turn out just a little, creating convergence insufficiency issues. This means that eyesight may be a perfect 20/20, but the eyes and brain do not quite work smoothly together for near distances. We then asked the audience to read for several minutes. The glasses did not affect the wearers' perception of the words on the page; that is, people did not experience double vision, blurriness, or any other noticeable change in their eyesight. However, after just a few minutes the effects were dramatic: people began experiencing headaches, fatigue, and an inability to remember anything they were reading. Imagine feeling like that throughout your whole school day! ~ R. Hutchins, behavioral optometrist

Most of us are not aware of how many distinct visual skills there are. The unfortunate corollary to this is that there are multiple ways your vision can be compromised. Here are some examples of common vision issues and their consequences:

- Faulty visual-motor integration often creates tremendous trouble with writing skills.
- Trouble discriminating between visual forms (that is, if your brain cannot differentiate easily between different shapes), means that you might confuse words that have similar beginnings, be unable to tell the difference between similar pictures, or even have trouble remembering the alphabet.
- Tracking disorders, where the eyes do not move smoothly along a particular trajectory, would cause you

Food for Thought

- One in four school-aged children has vision difficulties, according to Prevent Blindness America.
- 60 percent of children with learning difficulties have undiagnosed vision problems, according to the American Optometric Association.

to lose your place frequently and skip lines while reading, resulting in fatigue and low reading comprehension.

⚲ Faulty visual memory, the inability to remember what is seen, would make it quite difficult to learn any new material (even verbally presented material, since the key to remembering it lies in visualizing it).

You can see how each of these issues might be taken for other learning disorders, but attempting to remediate them without addressing the true cause would only be frustrating and, ultimately, useless. Each of these issues, and many others, are correctible with proper treatment by a qualified optometrist.

The Trouble With Diagnosing Vision Problems

I brought my eight-year-old son to a behavioral optometrist, who started him on vision exercises to address his amblyopia, or lazy eye. After just a few sessions, he reported that he could play soccer much better than before. "Why do you think that is?" asked the optometrist. "There aren't two balls any more," he replied. I was stunned to realize that he had been experiencing double vision for years. No wonder everything was so hard! Soon after beginning vision therapy, we all noticed a marked decrease in his frustrated outbursts. ~ C.S.

Most children do not complain about vision problems. They know only their own experience, and have no idea that, for example, double vision or mysteriously moving lines of text are not what everyone else sees. They just try to deal with it. Children with vision difficulties often avoid certain activities, or may act out when frustrated, mentally exhausted, or ashamed.

Unfortunately, few people, even teachers or physicians, think of vision skills as a cause for their children's difficulties. Practitioners and observers alike often jump to conclusions such as: Inattention must be ADHD. Meltdowns are probably an emotional regulation disorder. Difficulties with reading or

---

Happy Customer

The following letter was sent to my office by a patient's mother.

Kevin completed eight months of vision therapy and is no longer experiencing eye fatigue and headaches. He reports to me that the letters no longer "jump around" on the page. Words are no longer blurry. He likes to read now, and, although still behind in his grade level, he is only a few months behind rather than 1 ½ years behind.

I am a family practice physician and have realized how important developmental vision screening is for kids, not just simple vision screening. It is part of my routine now to really delve into school performance issues with my young patients to make sure they are progressing normally; otherwise they get referred to a developmental optometrist.

writing are likely to be symptoms of a learning disorder. Vision assessment is still not a very well-known option, but it could save many children a great deal of anxiety and frustration.

Who Can Help?

You will need to find a specially trained practitioner called a behavioral or developmental optometrist. These professionals are trained in holistic methods that address a range of vision and visual processing problems. You should still ask the suggested questions at the end of this chapter, as training and preferred treatment methods can vary somewhat from one practitioner to another. Explain your child's symptoms in as much detail as you can and ask each specialist how she would approach treatment.

If your eye doctor does not do a developmental vision evaluation, then you can find referral websites in the *Resources for More Information* section of this chapter.

Insurance coverage for vision therapy is highly variable depending on your insurance plan and even the region of the U.S. where you live. Check your benefits plan with your insurance provider.

Treatment Options

The most common treatment choices for vision problems are:

- Glasses (for seeing, focusing, or eye coordination)
- Patching (for amblyopia or lazy eye)
- Contact lenses
- Vision therapy (more info in next section)
- Surgery (in rare cases)
- Ergonomic recommendation and other adaptations, including sitting on certain sides of the room or close to the board (similar to adaptations made for children with hearing problems)

VISION THERAPY

Vision therapy is a treatment process used to improve vision function. It is prescribed and supervised by a developmental or behavioral optometrist. Vision therapy can involve the use of lenses, prisms, filters, patching, computer programs, and specialized 3D stereo equipment. Most vision therapy programs are provided through optometrists who are Fellows of the College of Optometrists in Vision Development (FCOVD) and Certified in Vision Development and Vision Therapy.

Vision conditions commonly treated with vision therapy include:

- Amblyopia (poorly developed vision, often called "lazy eye")
- Strabismus (misalignment of the eyes, often called "crossed" or "wall-eyed")
- Binocular disorders (inefficient eye teaming)
- Ocular motor dysfunctions (eye movement disorders)
- Accommodative dysfunctions (focusing problems)
- Visual-motor disorder
- Visual information processing/perceptual disorders

Vision therapy can take from several weeks to several months to complete, and usually involves two components:

- A home program (patients receive a packet with the materials they need) with exercises that must be done every day
- Regular appointments with the vision therapist – this may not be the optometrist, but vision therapists should always be supervised by an optometrist

---

Complementary and Alternative Treatment: Craniosacral Therapy

If vision therapy does not seem to be progressing as expected, you might consider seeing a D.O. or craniosacral practitioner to examine your child's sphenoid bone. The eye muscles attach to the sphenoid bone. So if it is jammed or not moving properly for any reason, it will impair the eye muscles' ability to respond to therapy.

You might need to explore this option if your child:

- complains of pain when he moves his eyes, even after weeks of vision therapy;
- has experienced any kind of blow to the head or face;
- was adopted and spent a lot of time lying in a crib (the head is often noticeably flat in these cases, and this can jam the cranial bones).

For more information, please see Chapter 16.5: Craniosacral Therapy.

~ The Editors

A Word on Early Detection

Fortunately, many visual disorders can be identified and addressed early on. InfantSEE®, a public health program managed by Optometry's Charity™, helps to catch vision issues in babies. The American Optometric Association (AOA) Foundation, who created InfantSEE, is designed to ensure that eye and vision care becomes an integral part of infant wellness care. Under this program, AOA optometrists provide comprehensive eye and vision assessments for infants within the first year of life, regardless of a family's income or access to insurance coverage.

Questions for a Prospective Optometrist

- Do you do *near testing* (the ability to see things held close to the face and to focus, coordinate, and track)?
- Do you give visual processing or perception testing in addition to standard assessment of vision (the typical 20/20 vision tests)?
- Do you provide vision therapy or refer to someone who does so?
- Will you be able to give me an estimate of how long therapy will take?
- How often do you check in to assess the progress of vision therapy?
- If cost is an issue for us, can we do more home therapy and have fewer appointments with the vision therapist?
- Are your services covered by insurance?

Resources for More Information

Websites

www.lynnhellerstein.com or hbvision.net. These links will take you to the websites of this chapter's author, developmental optometrist Lynn Hellerstein. You can find information about vision issues, vision therapy, and other resources.

www.covd.org. This is the website for the College of Optometrists in Vision Development (COVD), where you will find multiple resources to help you understand vision issues, their impact, treatment options, and latest research. You can also find local practitioners here.

www.infantsee.org. Here you can find information on the InfantSEE program.

www.aoa.org. The American Optometric Association (AOA) website also offers multiple educational resources regarding vision issues.

Books

See It. Say It. Do It! The Parent's & Teacher's Action Guide to Creating Successful Students & Confident Kids, by Lynn Hellerstein. This easy-to-read workbook helps readers understand and practice various vision therapy techniques in order to enhance academic and sports performance.

Jillian's Story: How Vision Therapy Changed My Daughter's Life by R & J Benoit. The Benoit family struggled for six years to find answers for their daughter. Finally, vision therapy helped her overcome learning difficulties that no one had understood before.

Eye Power: An Updated Report of Vision Therapy by A. Hoopes and S. Applebaum. This book presents a clear guide to improving many aspects of life through addressing vision issues.

About the Author

Lynn F. Hellerstein, OD, FCOVD, FAAO, optometrist, consultant, speaker, and author of the award-winning book, *See It. Say It. Do It!* has been a pioneer in vision therapy for more than 30 years. Her expertise and leadership has inspired thousands of children and adults to improve their vision and lives. Dr. Hellerstein, a Denver native, is an adjunct faculty member at five colleges of optometry and Past-President of the College of Optometrists in Vision Development.

Equine-Assisted Therapy

by Rhonda L. Roth, M.S., OTR

We adopted Kimmy when she was ten months old. She did not seem to be thrilled about it. The only way she would tolerate being carried was at arm's length, facing out. She absolutely did not want to be touched, hugged, or cuddled in any way. She was affectionate with animals and stuffed animals, but we could not touch her. Other than that, she was easy, and became a friendly, independent tomboy who excelled in sports. My husband and I respected her boundaries, and this status quo worked OK until kindergarten.

Toward the end of the year, however, Kimmy's teacher told us she was behind academically and should be retained. We were shocked. Kimmy seemed so bright. We had her evaluated by a developmental psychologist who confirmed that Kimmy was indeed bright, but also delayed in early reading skills. The doctor was also concerned about her aversion to being touched. Given that there appeared to be a sensory issue with tactile input, she felt occupational therapy with a sensory specialist would help. However, Kimmy resisted all touch, so we were temporarily stumped as to how she could receive sensory therapy. Given that she liked animals and could be physically affectionate with them, the doctor recommended hippotherapy, at least in the beginning. Later on, we might continue with more traditional sensory processing therapy. I thought Kimmy would love horses, and I was also anxious for any change in the academic situation. So off we went to a hippotherapist.

Kimmy loved it from the first minute, but the profound and immediate change was astonishing. Kimmy got down off the horse after her FIRST SESSION, came over, and HUGGED ME!! She hugged me, of her own choosing! I began to cry; it was truly life-changing in one session. Kimmy progressed quickly in reading from then on. We did work with a reading specialist, but there was no more thought of repeating kindergarten. Over the next few years, Kimmy added "strong student" and "affectionate child" to her repertoire, along with "great athlete" and "good friend." ~ K.M.

"There is just something about the horse that makes it a perfect creature for therapy."
~ Michelle LaFleur,
advanced PATH INTERNATIONAL instructor

One of the most effective recipes for therapy is to incorporate it into something that does not feel like therapy. Horseback riding is fun, exciting, and challenging enough to engage a child's full attention and emotional investment. It is also an unusual opportunity for a child to learn a new skill, forge a relationship with a beautiful and powerful creature, and exercise in a natural outdoor setting.

Advantages of Equine-Assisted Activities and Therapy

Equine-assisted activities can address a wide range of issues:

- Children with sensory integration dysfunctions benefit from the heavy work of taking care of a horse, as well as numerous other sensory experiences that are a valuable addition to any sensory diet.
- The movement of the horse naturally stimulates the brain in ways that help organize the sensory, vestibular, and speech systems.
- Social skills and speech issues can be addressed while communicating with the horse, trainer, and other riders.
- Many children who find social situations confusing or intimidating discover that communicating with a horse feels much easier and safer.
- Attention issues are quickly brought to the surface when one has to accomplish certain tasks while maintaining control of a huge animal, becoming a wonderful teaching opportunity.
- Working with animals naturally increases a child's awareness of others and the impact of his actions, building empathy and self-awareness.
- The self-esteem that comes with learning such an exhilarating new skill helps in all areas of a child's life.
- The horse is a wonderful motivational tool. Children who are resisting, or having trouble progressing in, clinic-based or school-based therapies may respond more favorably to a horse. It can be used as a primary treatment strategy, or you can use it as a complementary activity to what your child is already doing.

Resources for Equine-Assisted Activities and Therapy

There are two main organizations that you can look into: Hippotherapy and Therapeutic Horseback Riding (TR). Hippotherapy instructors are trained through the AHA, or American Hippotherapy Association. Therapeutic Riding instructors are trained through PATH International (Professional Association of Therapeutic Horsemanship International). Though you will find other organization names if you search *equine-assisted therapy*, almost all of them come under the umbrella of either the AHA or PATH International.

Therapeutic Riding versus Hippotherapy

Although there is a great deal of overlap in what these modalities can accomplish, hippotherapy and Therapeutic Riding have slightly different goals and focuses.

- **Hippotherapy** is conducted by a specially trained occupational, physical, or speech-language therapist. Therapists create a tremendous range of activities for children that can meet numerous specific therapeutic goals. In hippotherapy, the horse is used as a vehicle for therapy. The child does not actually learn horseback riding skills. You can find the location of the hippotherapy center nearest you by looking at the American Hippotherapy Association's website (see the Resources section at the end of this chapter).

- **Therapeutic Horseback Riding** aims to teach persons with disabilities to become independent riding a horse. Instructors are certified through PATH International. PATH International instructors are not therapists. They are, however, trained to recognize and accommodate special needs in their sessions. You can ask your OT, PT, or speech therapist to consult with a TR riding instructor in order to create a program that maximizes your child's therapeutic experience. Therapeutic Riding also aims to help the rider develop a relationship with the horse, by having him groom, feed, and learn about a particular animal.

Anatomy of a Session

Hippotherapy

- A hippotherapy session always involves an instructor (a specially trained therapist), a side-walker, and a horse leader. These people provide safety and the opportunity to reinforce positive social skills and speech habits.
- Hippotherapy is almost always conducted bareback. This increases the child's experience of the animal's movement, thereby increasing sensory feedback and the level of challenge to his balance and vestibular systems. Saddles and other padding may be used, depending on the child's needs.

- A therapist will typically have a child ride in many different positions, such as lying sideways on the horse, or facing backwards while holding himself up on his arms. These activities provide many benefits, including:
  - Increased range of motion and muscle tone
  - Decreased muscle spasticity
  - Increased balance and coordination
  - Increased vestibular awareness
  - Improved postural control and stability
  - Increased organization of sensory processing
- Hippotherapy also involves the use of therapeutic games, such as putting rings on a pole or shooting baskets from horseback. This reinforces the therapeutic benefits in different ways.
- Following the many complex directions in a session works with attention deficit issues, speech/language skills, auditory processing, and social skills.

Therapeutic Riding

- Therapeutic Riding typically happens in a group situation. There can be anywhere from two to six riders in a class. The presence of other riders encourages social interaction and awareness of others, both spatially and emotionally.
- Since Therapeutic Riding aims to teach horseback riding, a session involves having participants follow the commands of the instructor, thereby learning control of the horse.
- A Therapeutic Riding instructor will often incorporate games that will more specifically address your child's needs.

How to Choose If Both Are Available

While the number of centers providing therapeutic horseback riding and hippotherapy continues to grow throughout the United States, both services are not available in all areas at this time. You may be limited in your options by what the centers in your area currently offer. However, if you have the option to choose between TR and Hippotherapy, seek an evaluation with an occupational, physical, or speech therapist who is certified with AHA. This qualified specialist will be able to provide you with an evaluation of your child's needs and will be able to help you develop specific therapeutic goals. She will also be able to help you identify whether hippotherapy or therapeutic horseback riding will be the most beneficial for your child.

Some children may benefit for a period of time from hippotherapy to get more concentrated therapeutic attention, and may then be able to switch to Therapeutic Riding. They can then continue getting therapeutic benefits while learning an exciting new skill and maintaining a rewarding connection with horses.

If cost is a concern, many centers are non-profit, also known as 501(c)3, organizations and provide scholarships for families with a financial need. Be sure to check with your local center to see what types of financial aid are available. In general, hippotherapy is more expensive because of the number of specialists involved and the high level of instructor training.

Hippotherapy often requires a diagnosis and prescription from a medical professional, and may therefore be covered by insurance. Therapeutic Riding is less expensive, but since it is not technically therapy, it is not usually covered by insurance.

Questions for a Potential Therapeutic Riding Instructor or Hippotherapist

- Are you a Certified Therapeutic Riding Instructor through PATH International?
- Are you a Certified Hippotherapy Provider through American Hippotherapy Association?
- How much experience do you have with children who have issues similar to my child's?
- How are your volunteers/side walkers/horse leaders trained and supervised?
- What goals can you help my child to achieve through equine-assisted activities?
- Do you have a scholarship program for low-income families?
- Do you accept insurance or can you help me gain reimbursement from my insurance company?

Resources for More Information

Websites

www.pathintl.org, PATH International. This website offers information on Therapeutic Riding and will help you find local resources.

www.americanhippotherapyassociation.org, AHA, Inc. Here, you will find info on hippotherapy and how to find local centers and therapists.

ABOUT THE AUTHOR

Rhonda Roth, MS, OTR, graduated from Samuel Merritt University in 2007 with a Masters degree in occupational therapy. She has been a PATH International Registered level therapeutic horseback riding instructor since 2003 and completed the AHA Hippotherapy Level I training in 2010. Rhonda has worked in a variety of pediatric therapy settings over the years including schools, homes, and clinics. She owned TheraPlay of Colorado, a pediatric occupational therapy service in Colorado, for five years. She now lives in Boise, Idaho, where she does occupational therapy in schools and also owns Children in Motion, a company that offers training to early childhood educators and caregivers. You can find her at www.childreninmotionboise.wordpress.com.

A Story About Autism

Rachel's Journey

In 1996, a psychologist gave us the "good" news: Our six-and-a-half year old daughter Rachel was definitely not retarded. This came as something of a shock, since I didn't even know that was on the table. She did, however, show signs of autism. But the signs were ambivalent, and the fact that we had been living in Saudi Arabia might have accounted for some of the language deficits. So he did not feel comfortable making the final call on the diagnosis; instead, he referred us to a specialist for a full evaluation. It was possible that this was not the official prognosis. Still, it was a shocking thing to hear. Tears ran down my cheeks and I felt as if all the air had been sucked out of the room.

Ultimately, though, I was more confused than anything. I knew little about autism, other than what I had seen in the movie *Rain Man*. Rachel was nothing like the main character, Raymond, but I was pretty sure that autism was a seriously challenging diagnosis. Indeed, the doctor had painted a devastating picture: If Rachel had autism, it was very likely that she would have no friends, no job, no college, and no hope of living independently. She would never be able to read or express emotion. We would have no reason for hope.

I am so glad we didn't accept those possibilities.

Looking back, the signs of autism had been present, but we hadn't recognized them as red flags. When Rachel was only two, I had noticed that her speech was not developing as quickly as her peers'. We were living in Saudi Arabia then, but managed to find a Montessori preschool that played to her obvious visual strengths. She did quite well there, and the issue seemed to be more due to shyness than any kind of language deficit. But when, at the age of five years old, Rachel switched over to a traditional school, she began to lose what little language ability she had. By the age of six, she was seriously *echolalic* – meaning that rather than initiating speech, she just copied what others said. Our doctor said that, since we lived in a foreign country, her language abilities might develop differently. But this didn't explain why she was so dramatically behind her peers, or why she had actually begun *losing* language.

Early on, I had tried not to worry. Friends had told me that Rachel was unusually graceful and coordinated, and her visual-spatial abilities and computer skills were well ahead of her years. She had played side-by-side rather then directly with others – another autistic trait – but living in another country, with families from all over the world, had shown me how differently cultures played. She might easily have been a little confused on that front. Because of these ambiguities, and because I was struggling to care for my younger daughter Deanna, who had life-threatening asthma, I had worked to convince myself that it would be all right.

We had exhausted all of our options for treatment of Rachel's language loss and echolalia overseas, and so returned to the States when she was six, settling in Utah. After that memorable first meeting with the psychologist, we had to wait six months to get in for a full evaluation. I devoted that time to research, learning everything I could about autism. By the time the appointment came around, I knew.

My daughter was on the autism spectrum. The diagnosis confirmed it. She was almost seven.

The most difficult thing to read was that, according to the prevailing wisdom of the times, it was too late to do anything at all about it. Early intervention might have helped her, but now we were simply too late. It was hard not to despair.

As it turned out, though, moving to Utah was one of the best things we could have done. Originally, we had chosen it because of fewer asthma triggers and more pediatric equipment in emergency rooms that deal with asthma. But lo and behold, the University of Utah was one of the leading research centers for autism! So we got the speech therapy and behavioral training that all ASD (Austism Spectrum Disorder) families went through, but we were also able to participate in a number of groundbreaking studies. Through Rachel's doctor, Sally Ozonoff – who is still a leading figure in the field of autism research –we signed up for every study we could find. Many of them showed, for the first time, that kids with ASD *can* learn executive functions; you just need to break it down and present things in a certain way. It was years before the methods we learned became part of the mainstream, so we were very fortunate to find them when we did. Over time, Rachel improved her executive functions and learned social skills. It was often downright painstaking. She spent three weeks just learning how to order food in a restaurant.

Dr. Ozonoff agreed that Montessori really was the perfect approach for Rachel, relying as it did on hands-on and visual methods. In fact, it is remarkably similar to TEACCH, an autism treatment. So when we were no longer able to find Montessori schools (or other appropriate options) in Utah, we moved to Colorado and she was able to complete her elementary school education in Montessori style.

Middle school became tricky in a whole new way. Everybody feels weird or ostracized or ugly in middle school; it can be a tough time for the best of us. For Rachel, it was the advent of a painful new level of self-awareness. It was heart-rending watching her struggle to accept her differences, and her tendency toward anxiety increased. It was also a time of unprecedented conflict between her and her little sister. Deanna, whose asthma was no longer life-threatening, would get understandably tired of Rachel getting everyone's time and attention. We all endured an intense period of yelling, fighting, and hostility.

I've never been one to tell my girls what they should feel. It's not like it *works*. Rachel had times when she hated having autism, and Deanna had times when she resented having a sister on the spectrum. Our rule was: You can't be hateful, but it's OK to feel whatever you're feeling. Come and tell me about it; I can take it. This was put to the test when my mostly sweet, mellow Rachel started telling me she wanted to commit suicide. Thankfully, we knew an insightful therapist who talked to her and determined that she was not, in fact, suicidal. "Didn't you have thoughts like that in middle school?" the therapist asked me. "'Everyone hates me; I wish I were dead?' Everything is so extreme at that age. The only difference is, Rachel doesn't have the social understanding to filter what she should and shouldn't say. It's actually healthy that she's telling you, but I don't think you have anything to worry about." It was an interesting lesson for all of us. I have never regretted reaching out for help, though; when children start saying things like that, professional insight is a must! Somehow, we all emerged from that period intact, and my daughters are now good friends.

At about that time, we also began researching and pursuing CAM (Complementary and Alternative Medicine), beginning with nutrition. Nutritional approaches to autism have been part of the biomedical protocol for years, but are only now beginning to be taken seriously (sometimes) in the mainstream. Two ways Rachel benefitted from CAM are in the areas of sleep and anxiety.

For many years, Rachel's longest sleep period was 3 hours. You can imagine my sleep deprivation! Under the care of a former NASA Chief Medical Officer and functional medicine doctor, Rachel followed a supplement regimen to help with hormonal regulation and sleep. In less than a week, without having known the purpose of her supplements, she reported that she had had a full night's sleep. We were shocked and thankful. Other supplements helped reduce her constant anxiety. Little by little, life felt more manageable to Rachel. (Later on, when she was in college, she began to suffer from anxiety attacks with alarming new symptoms such as tics, hyperventilation, and heart palpitations. It turned out she had stopped taking some of her supplements and that new ones needed to be added. When she put them back in her regimen at higher doses, her symptoms disappeared. Obviously, those supplements really made a difference!)

While still in high school, Rachel also underwent supervised chelation to remove high levels of heavy metals present in her system. We used a very slow, gentle method that took two years overall. Many facets of her health improved, including aspects of endocrine function, digestion, sleep, and brain function. However, we were doing other therapies as well, including intensive nutritional approaches to support those systems, and to replace what chelation was pulling out. So even though her toxicity numbers clearly changed for the better, it is difficult for me to say which improvements resulted from these approaches, separately or collectively. I believe they all helped to rebuild Rachel's health; treatments can support each other and have dramatic cumulative effects. The Hyperbaric Oxygen Treatment, however, had very clear results: Over the course of 90 days, Rachel experienced a documented 20-point increase in verbal expression and three grade-level increase in reading comprehension. No new therapies were introduced during that time. This treatment is still controversial and does not work for everyone, but it worked wonders for Rachel and she has retained those improvements.

The whole question of why something works for one child and not for another is a perpetually thorny one, and one that I have become involved in discussing at a national level. One of the interesting results of my daughter's autism is that I experienced quite an evolution myself: I went from being an overwhelmed, isolated parent to a mom hanging onto a support group like a lifeline; then I became a community activist so that new moms facing this would have the resources and support I had found. This transitioned into co-founding the Autism Society of Boulder County (ASBC). This little organization is now over ten years old, and has provided conferences, teacher trainings, local workshops, free lecture series, and support groups. I am fascinated by the process of translating research into treatment and enjoy impacting the larger discussion however I can. There is still much to be done!

My daughter recently graduated from college, one of many things she has accomplished that we were told never to expect. She drove herself to her job and to class, and graduated with honors. It wasn't always pretty. But Rachel is a very determined young lady and very much wants to be a part of the world around her, and that is half the battle. The other half is realizing that a prognosis is someone's best guess based on what is known at the time. No one truly knows what is possible. It is up to you to test the boundaries, weigh the benefits and risks of different treatments, and help your child realize the best quality of life possible.

We have a saying in the autism community: If you have seen one child with autism, then you have seen one child with autism. No two are the same! That is true of every child of course, but it seems to get lost sometimes when you are putting treatment plans together. The truth is that there is a very long way to go in understanding the biology of autism and figuring out which treatments will benefit which members of this very uniquely affected population.

Remember that you know your children better than anyone. Play to their strengths, find physicians who are willing to partner with you and explore more than behavioral therapies, keep an eye on research, and most importantly – never give up hope!

About the Author

Theresa Wrangham is the mother and advocate of a young adult with autism, co-founded the Autism Society of Boulder County, and currently serves as an advisory board member for the US Autism & Asperger Association.

EIGHT

Autism Spectrum Disorders

by Debby Hamilton, MD, MSPH

S igns that your child could have Autism Spectrum Disorder include:

- ☐ Does not use gestures, such as pointing to something or showing something to others; if someone else points, child cannot follow that point
- ☐ Often fails to look at others when talking with them; does not make eye contact to check others' reactions (should start before 12 months)
- ☐ Does not seem to enjoy conversation (though if quite verbal will monologue to others)
- ☐ Does not seek to play with peers; prefers isolated play
- ☐ Wants to have friends but cannot develop friendships
- ☐ Prone to extreme frustrations and prolonged meltdowns well past the typical age for tantrums
- ☐ Does not seem to recognize emotions in others' faces or tone of voice
- ☐ Uses language oddly - repeats favorite phrases, mutters nonsense phrases, forms odd sentences
- ☐ Has "flat" speech with little rhythm or unusual rhythms
- ☐ Does not play make-believe or pretend, or has very immature play skills
- ☐ Does not imitate others
- ☐ Will play with toys repetitively for great lengths of time (e.g., will spin the tires on a toy truck for hours or line cars up a certain way)
- ☐ Gets obsessed with certain objects or subjects (e.g., knows everything there is to know about vacuum cleaners or backpacks)
- ☐ Requires rituals or repetition in daily living; does not adjust or adapt well to changes in routine
- ☐ Interprets instruction and other language literally (e.g., "What are you writing your essay on?" Answer: "paper")
- ☐ Exhibits repetitive motor actions, such as hand flapping, scratching, or spinning

Autism is a complex condition that affects many domains of processing and behavior. The following items are also associated with autism, but may indicate other areas to investigate more closely.

Cross-reference guide:
SP/L = Speech and Language Issues, Chapter 5
SPD = Sensory Processing Disorder, Chapter 7
Bio/Nut = Biomedical Approaches, Chapter 14; Nutrition, Chapter 15

BEHAVIOR	SP/L	SPD	Bio/Nut
By 12 months old, does not respond to their name	*		
Speech does not develop or child achieves a few words, then stops speaking	*		
Speech develops reasonably well or is advanced, but conversations are more of a monologue	*		
Often has diarrhea, constipation, or gas			*
Is a very picky eater, because of either taste or texture issues		*	*
Often seems frustrated, particularly when trying to communicate	*		
Becomes over-excited or upset in busy settings		*	
Loves swinging, spinning, or other vestibular input		*	
Seems hypersensitive to some sensory inputs (e.g., certain sounds, textures, or visual input) – sounds, in particular, can set off meltdowns		*	
Covers ears or eyes frequently		*	
Walks on toes often or has odd gait		*	

The Basics

Diagnosed cases of autism have increased dramatically. In 1995, it was estimated that one in every 3300 children had autism. In 2012, according to the Center for Disease Control, the figure was one in 88 (one in 53 for boys). Increasingly, children are descending into an abyss. Parents must find ways to reach into that abyss in order to connect with, understand, and help their children. It is a daunting, sometimes heartbreaking task. The good news is that we are finding out more and more about what creates autism and what might be done to help.

In my early training, I was taught that autism – or ASD, *Autistic Spectrum Disorder* – was a genetically determined, life-long behavioral impairment. But after my biomedical training and experience with hundreds of children on the spectrum, I have seen that autism is a complex condition wherein much can be changed.

We know more today about the inherent complexities and possibilities within this condition than we did even 10 years ago. Recent developments in research (due to advancements in such fields as epigenetics, nutrigenomics, metabolomics, and neuroscience, some of which did not even exist until recently) have revolutionized our understanding of autism and other conditions, repeatedly validating concepts that biomedically-trained doctors have used as a basis for treatment for decades.

A Closer Look

There is a saying in the autism community: "If you've met one person with autism...you've met one person with autism." While this individuality is true of all children, with or without learning or behavioral issues, it is particularly important to remember with ASD. Many people hear the diagnosis and stop seeing the person as anything other than "autistic." But your child is still a unique person, not just a compilation of symptoms, and you may need to help those around her to remember what that means.

That said, there *are* consistent core features that people with autism share. It is a spectrum diagnosis, so the severity and exact form of the symptoms can differ hugely. However, to varying extents, these are the symptoms that define the condition.

- **Communication Impairments.** Children on the spectrum have consistent issues with communicating, which can show up as any of the following:
  - Being completely nonverbal, expressing themselves through frantic hand movements and noises that caregivers must learn to interpret
  - Lacking the mechanical ability (weak or unresponsive facial muscles) to form speech sounds well, resulting in garbled words
  - Lacking the ability to modulate voice, leading to "flat" speech patterns or consistently loud speech
  - Having very limited language that often relies on reciting a few phrases or repeating others
  - Displaying sophisticated vocabulary, but limited conversation skills that lack emotional connection or responsiveness to others' participation
- **Social Impairment.** Since communication is a large part of social interaction, there is obviously a great deal of overlap between this and the previous section. In fact, because there is so much overlap, the new diagnostic criteria simply combine the two

categories into one domain: social communication. However, social skills deficits run much deeper than using the right words and knowing polite protocols. Some children with autism need to be shown, first, that interacting with others can actually be pleasant and meaningful. Other children like to talk to others, but need to be reminded to take turns in conversation and to find a shared interest. Depending on where they are starting out, they may then need to become aware of basic nonverbal cues – such as facial expressions, gestures, and posture – or be taught how to navigate more sophisticated scenarios, like finding a topic of conversation that is interesting to both parties.

Behavioral Inflexibility. This is the second major diagnostic consideration in the diagnostic manual (DSM-5). Behavioral inflexibility may range from nonstop pacing and flapping to insisting on the same routine each day for every event (with great discomfort, even tantrums, in response to changes). Also, children with autism typically do not have good "pretend play" skills and will prefer more concrete exploration for play, like lining up toys, organizing items, or staring at favorite things. They can also hyperfocus on particular and atypical areas of interest (e.g., vacuum cleaners, water towers).

The Question of Communication Skills

Parents sometimes say, "He doesn't have communication problems. He has an amazing vocabulary and talks all the time!" But remember that communication involves much more than having a lot to say. Some children, especially those with Asperger Syndrome (which is no longer a category; more on that later) are sometimes extremely bright and may have an extensive vocabulary, but their conversations are often non-reciprocal and lack emotional connection. They tend to monologue, or to "collect data and then spill it," as one parent described it – but that isn't quite communication.

Atypical Sensory Processing. If your child has autism, he almost certainly has some degree of sensory processing difficulty. The world feels overwhelming for many people with autism. They are often unusually sensitive to visual input, light touch, noise, smell, and taste. They may also crave deep pressure or vestibular input. It is no wonder they seek to be alone, often rocking, swinging, or spinning in an attempt to calm a chronically over-stimulated nervous system. This issue alone can make some of the other difficulties feel insurmountable; it's all just too much. (Read Chapter 7: Sensory Processing Disorder.)

Digestive Issues. Although research has indicated that over 70 percent of people with autism have digestive problems, I have only rarely had a patient on the spectrum who does *not* have them. Biomedically-trained physicians have long considered this to be a standard, even central, part of the overall autism profile. The exact causes, symptoms and severity differ, but the resulting neural inflammation, brain chemistry imbalance, and discomfort clearly contribute to and worsen the symptoms of autism. Research supports this and I have personally seen huge changes from addressing this aspect of a patient's health.

The Politics of Autism

Unfortunately, the subject of autism has become something of a political issue within the medical world. Many people feel that autism is one area where so-called "maverick" strains of research and treatment have outstripped conventional understanding. Biomedical practitioners and more conventional medical doctors disagree on many aspects of diagnosis and treatment. Case in point: digestive issues and their place in the list of autism criteria.

While the American Academy of Pediatrics (AAP) states clearly that digestive problems are *often seen* with autism, it will not go so far as to say that they are *part of* it. This has contributed to some conflict within the medical world. It is not unusual for parents to receive skepticism from physicians when they present the research they have done; many have even had gastroenterologists refuse to explore the issue further.

And yet research increasingly points to the significance of gut issues in ASD. Prominent Harvard researcher Martha Herbert's latest book, *The Autism Revolution*, emphasizes the extensive impact that a wide range of gut issues can have on people with autism. After decades of clinical research that have yielded impressive results, Dr. Herbert feels that this can be a central piece of the puzzle and must be addressed in any treatment plan for a person on the spectrum. Other specialists have confirmed that this approach, combined with more traditional behavioral supports, gets results. Biomedical practitioners have said this for decades. And yet, resistance to this line of thinking remains consistent.

"If my husband or I came in and said, 'I haven't had a bowel movement in two weeks and my stomach hurts so much I spend most of the day pressing my belly onto chair backs or countertops,' they'd have us in for tests by that afternoon," one mother lamented at a conference. "But it's like they hear the word *autism* and a switch flips in their heads. They immediately think 'oh, crazy autism parents' and pat you on the head and send you away – after telling you that it's all 'just autism' and you simply need to accept it. It's really frustrating."

Finding a biomedically-trained physician that you like would be an excellent option, but that is not always possible (keep in mind, though, that many biomedical doctors will work with patients long distance). Do your own research and at least find a practitioner who is willing to work with and listen to you.

The *Other* ASD Diagnoses

Prior to 2013, the following diagnoses fell under the umbrella of ASD. However, the most recent Diagnostic and Statistical Manual of Mental Disorders (DSM-5) eliminated them as sub-diagnoses, making them all answer to the same diagnosis of "Autistic Spectrum Disorder."

- **Asperger Syndrome.** This diagnosis was usually made when a child had intact language and cognitive abilities (and, in fact, are often gifted in some cognitive areas). However, they have poor nonverbal communication (such as reading gestures and facial expressions), poor emotional and social skills, and often have obsessive interests in obscure things like water towers, molecular structure, hubcaps, or vacuum cleaners.
- **Childhood Disintegrative Disorder.** This pertained to children who seem to develop normally for at least the first two years of life, then exhibit a disintegration of skills prior to 10 years of age.
- **Pervasive Developmental Disorder Not Otherwise Specified (PDD/NOS).** This was something of a catch-all category. Children who have weaknesses in social and communication skills, but do not meet full criteria for a more specific diagnosis, often fell into this classification.
- **Rett Syndrome.** After a period of seemingly normal development in infancy, the child begins to lose skills. This progresses to a severely limited state where she has no functional use of her hands (but exhibits distinctive hand wringing behaviors), displays no language skills, and has limited mobility. There are also seizures, reduced head size, and severe cognitive impairments. Rett appears almost exclusively in girls. Rather than being absorbed into ASD, this syndrome will now always be identified separately. Researchers have discovered a specific genetic mutation that leads to Rett; this clear biological cause medically distinguishes it from autism.

Now there are no sub-diagnoses. After making the diagnosis of ASD, practitioners specify the severity of the condition according to the level of support needed ("requiring support," "requiring substantial support" and "requiring very substantial support"). If an evaluator feels that your child does not fully meet the criteria for an ASD diagnosis, he may give her a number of smaller, more specific diagnoses (such as speech disorder, emotional dysregulation, social communication disorder, etc.), where formerly he might have identified one of the above. However, it is still worth it to be familiar with these terms if your child seems to fall into one of these categories. Practitioners and the autism community will probably continue to use some of these terms (particularly Asperger Syndrome) for years to come, and you can still find a great deal of valuable advice and support about them on ASD blogs and forums.

Causes and Contributors

No "autism gene" and, in fact, no single smoking gun of any kind has emerged for autism. Certain genetic syndromes (clusters of specific genetic factors) have been associated with autism, Fragile X Syndrome being the most commonly known – but even these account for only 5 to 10 percent of all autism cases.

The current consensus is that it is a combination of multiple genetic factors and environmental influences, which brings us to the concept of epigenetics. This is a relatively recent field that any current discussion of autism should include. Epigenetics refers to the interplay between the environment and genes. Basically, where we used to believe that genes determined our fate – end of story – we are now seeing that environmental factors can determine which genes get turned on and which do not. Environmental factors can include toxins, electro-magnetic frequency (EMF), food, or viruses (to name a few). Anything that negatively affects our body is stress. Stress causes chemical changes as the body tries to deal with it, and these changes impact how and whether a gene gets activated.

Autism, more dramatically than any other disorder, demonstrates the necessity of exploring this complex interaction. The important thing to understand here is that we can't change our genes, but *we can change environmental factors*, thereby impacting what manifests in the body. Research has given us increasingly precise tests that can identify which genetic differences are contributing to the chaos and how we can compensate for them.

The more we have studied autism, the more we can see that it is, in fact, an extremely complicated disorder that involves the whole body and produces a unique profile for each person. Severe biological weaknesses create unusual vulnerabilities to outside factors, and when too much stress accumulates from the interplay between them, the body can no longer handle it and flips over into symptoms of autism.

This is not to say that addressing these underlying issues will make your child's autism go away. I have seen vast improvement, and even cases where I would consider the outcome a "cure" – but even in those, mild forms of core deficits often persist. However, there is more hope than ever that you can help your child find more ease in both her body and the world. Autism simply is not a fixed state, but rather an intricate biological tapestry that we are beginning to be able to unravel (or at least impact).

Specific contributing factors include:

- **Genetics.** Research has uncovered many genetic differences – including those that impair digestion, immune function, detoxification, metabolism, and other systems – that are almost always present in people with autism. Since each of these systems encapsulates a great number of specific processes, some exploration is necessary to pinpoint the exact source of the problem. Testing in general, including genetic testing, has become increasingly sophisticated and accessible in recent years. A bio-medically-trained physician will have the tools you need to begin this exploration.
- **Brain Inflammation.** This can happen as a result of digestive weaknesses, chronic food reactions, yeast, immune problems, poor processing of emotional or physiological sources of stress…the list of inflammatory causes is quite long and includes most of the items in this section. Chronic neural inflammation can cause problems in sensory processing, cognitive ability, and emotional regulation, so identifying and addressing its causes is essential. Brain inflammation is such a significant problem that research has found that, on the whole, the brains of people with autism are larger than the brains of people without it.
- **Gut Function.** As previously mentioned, malfunctions in intestinal function can cause a cascade of problems in the brain (for more details, see Chapter 14: Biomedical Approaches and Chapter 15: Nutritional Approaches.) Poor digestion and inflammation in the gut directly impact the immune system as well. Research has revealed that people with autism are often unusually vulnerable to intestinal parasites, yeast overgrowth, and other digestive problems. The resulting inflammation creates a host of problems that, in turn, exacerbate symptoms of autism.
- **Immune Function.** Exposure to viruses (such as prenatal exposure to German measles) has long been linked to some cases of autism. In addition, intestinal bugs – bacteria and viruses – can also impact the brain and are frequent culprits in creating the overall stress on a child's system. Children with autism often have compromised immune systems, but keep in mind that this can show up in different ways: Some get sick all the time, but some never do (even when everyone else in the family is sick). This is not the boon you might think. Rather, it can indicate that the child's system is

constantly "revved" or hyper-reactive, which often leads to allergies and inflammation throughout the brain and body (which, in turn, leads to brain chemistry imbalances, learning difficulties, and erratic behavior).

Environmental Toxins. There is a great deal of speculation that the rise in rates of autism coincides with the rise in environmental toxins. Air pollution, insecticides, electro-magnetic frequency - there are many toxins to consider. The jury is still out on the exact relationship between toxins and autism, and speculation about which toxins pose the greatest risk have gotten mixed response. However, it is true that people with autism are often much less able to process toxins effectively, which impairs key systems. A biomedical or functional medicine doctor can help you assess where exactly your child's weaknesses are in this area. You can then treat by clearing out built-up toxins in the body, repairing the impaired processes when possible, and avoiding whatever stresses seem to be contributing the most.

Mitochondrial Weakness. Mitochondria provide the energy in a cell. With many of these children, various factors prevent the mitochondria from getting the energy they need for the cells to perform their functions. For example, children with chronically low muscle tone don't have enough energy going to the muscle. The brain is a high energy burner, so mitochondrial weakness can severely impair brain function. Mitochondrial weakness or disorder can wreak havoc in any number of ways. Tests can now reveal what's going on in this arena, and appropriately trained doctors can treat it.

Who Can Help?

Most families need to create a team of specialists who will help on several fronts. You will need one person to do the diagnosis and, in most cases, multiple other people to provide treatment.

Protecting the Health of Your Next Child

If you have had one child with autism and would like to do what you can to reduce risk factors in the future, my book *Preventing Autism and ADHD: Controlling Risk Factors Before, During and After Pregnancy* may help. After reviewing hundreds of published research studies and treating hundreds of children with autism, I developed a comprehensive prevention plan that covers nutrition, digestion, immune function, inflammation, hormones, and detoxification – all areas proven to contribute to the development of an autistic profile. By improving health before pregnancy, a woman can maximize her chances of having a strong, healthy child.

For Diagnosis

Appropriate treatment begins with a complete diagnosis. A psychiatrist, developmental pediatrician, neuropsychologist, or psychologist specializing in autism can make the diagnosis. This person should also be able to direct you to the most appropriate resources.

Diagnosis is based on the presence of the core features: Social-Communication weaknesses and repetitive/rigid behaviors or rituals are the key diagnostic features. Atypical sensory processing is also almost always present. Some diagnosticians will collect this information through interview and observations. Others will use specific tests developed to assess these areas from a variety of angles. From the initial diagnosis, the child should be referred for more in-depth evaluations in core areas, such as speech/language/communication, sensory processing, and academic achievement. You should also look for a biomedical practitioner who can explore biological contributors, or at least a physician who is experienced in autism.

Also, keep in mind that autism is determined by observing a *behavioral* cluster of symptoms. There is no decisive blood test or anything of that sort, so making this diagnosis involves an inherent subjectivity. If you strongly disagree with the diagnosis you are given, remember that you can always seek a second opinion.

Parents can also collect anecdotes and any evidence (including videos) that they think demonstrate your child's abilities. Help your child's diagnostician and support network to understand and see him more clearly.

The Importance of Early Identification

Exit surveys show that the vast majority of parents with children on the spectrum know that something's off by the time their children reach the age of two. They share their concerns with their pediatrician, and a high percentage of the time, the pediatrician says, "Let's wait a little longer. Children all develop at different rates." This happens particularly with boys, who do develop language and social skills later than girls.

However, there is a difference between developing a little more slowly and having the early signs of autism or related challenge, and most parents instinctively know when that line has been crossed. Trust your gut and don't be afraid to err on the side of caution. Early detection and intervention can make a huge difference. The earlier a disorder is identified – especially one as complex and potentially devastating as ASD – the earlier interventions can start.

Early intervention can be critical. If your child responds to intensive treatment, he will struggle less with health, school, friendships, and just being in the world. Behavioral interventions can help prepare him for school so that it is not such an uphill battle from the start. Giving him "training wheels" in the form of communication and behavioral support can provide the boost he needs to learn some of the same skills everyone else just picks up. So insist on a screening! It is a brief, non-intensive process, and *it is not a diagnosis*. It simply indicates whether you have reason to see a specialist or not.

Treatment Options

THE *DEFEAT AUTISM NOW* DOCTORS

Spend any time at all on parent forums in the autism community, and you will hear about "DAN doctors" – which, unfortunately, we can no longer call them because the name was copyrighted by another organization. The Autism Research Institute developed *Defeat Autism Now* protocols for biomedical training and research in the 1990s, originally intended for use exclusively with the autism community. (For more information, see Chapter 14: Biomedical Approaches.)

There has been a split within what remained of that organization. Now you will hear about the Autism Research Institute, which now focuses on current, tested behavioral therapies and educational plans, and the Medical Academy of Pediatric Special Needs (MAPS), which has continued the research, training, and protocol development from a biomedical perspective.

I would strongly recommend that, along with the behavioral therapies that any physician will tell you is necessary, you also seek out a biomedical doctor who has trained with MAPS. The science is well-researched, specialized, progressive, and gets results. If you cannot find someone in your area, functional medicine doctors have very similar underlying philosophies and tools. Naturopaths often do as well. But you should always ask about their understanding of autism, as it is definitely its own category and requires experience and specific study.

You may also be able to work long-distance with a practitioner. I have some clients that I work with over the phone. It may be helpful for a physician to meet your child at least once in the beginning, but treatment can easily be monitored from afar. If you find someone you like and trust, see what you can do to get onto her list.

THE BEHAVIORAL TREATMENTS

The following therapies are critical for building skills and smoothing out daily living. Virtually all people with autism require a combination of these approaches. With all of the following treatments, it is important to find not only a specialist, but also one who has worked with children with autism. Also, since there is such wide range of symptoms, make sure the therapy (especially if it is done in a group) addresses the specific stage your child is at.

Communication. Communication deficits are central to autism, so speech/language therapy that focuses on communication is central to treatment. Children on the spectrum may need to develop clearer speech, learn how to use words instead of melting down, and develop more appropriate use of conversational skills. Therapy must also address nonverbal communication skills – using eye contact, understanding gestures, interpreting tone of voice, and reading facial expressions. These are cues that people with autism consistently miss.

Who Does This? This therapy is typically done by a speech/language therapist. There are many who work specifically within the autism community. (See Chapter 5: Speech and Language Issues.)

Social Skills. Like communication skills, social skills vary widely from children who are completely withdrawn to children who want to interact, but do so differently than more neurotypical children. Many with autism need very basic introductions to social interaction. For instance, if a child rocks back and forth in front of the window, a parent might playfully engage him by rocking in exact synchrony. In this way, the child learns that others can share his pleasures. Other children may need help understanding how people around him feel and how he should respond in different situations.

There are a number of programs and interventions that help children connect socially by building on the child's inherent abilities and interests. Such programs include Floortime, Son-Rise Program, Relational Development Intervention (RDI), Early Start Denver Model, and Pivotal Response Treatment. The latter two also incorporate components of ABA, one of the most established protocols in the world of autism (see box). There are also social skills groups for older children with autism, which often focus on understanding social rules and building friendships.

Who Does This? There is no specific field of training for social skills therapists, so they come from several professions (e.g., psychologist, speech/language therapists, special education teachers, occupational therapists). Find a therapist who specializes in a good program, has extensive experience in autism, and works with your child's inherent strengths and preferences. For example, most children on the spectrum respond well to extremely structured, repetitive programs; but others may need a more intuitive, less linear approach. (See Chapter 12: Social Skills Issues, for more information.)

Applied Behavior Analysis

Applied Behavior Analysis (ABA) is a scientifically validated approach to breaking down and understanding behavior, and is used by many families to teach their children social and daily life skills. (It is also the only program that is consistently covered by insurance for people with autism.) ABA teaches that all behavior has meaning, so no behavior should be considered "just autism." Rather, all behavior is a form of communication from a child with limited communication skills. If you understand the meaning, you can change the behavior by helping the child learn a better way of achieving his goals. For example, a child who is banging his head and scratching his face may turn out to have a severe headache; a child who tantrums every afternoon may simply be hungry at that time.

Rob was in a preschool for children with autism. It was a good program with some strong master teachers, but there were also some younger teachers and aides still learning the ropes. One of the goals was toilet training Rob, who was nonverbal with no sign language. The plan was to take him to the bathroom every 30 minutes.

At first, this seemed to be working: Rob was having no toileting accidents. But then he began to throw tantrums about going to the toilet – not every time, just sometimes. The aides were stymied. Things had been going so well! They presented the situation to the master teacher at weekly supervision. She asked, "In the times that he has a tantrum on the way to the bathroom, when you finally get him there, does he have to pee?" The light immediately went off for the aides, "No, he doesn't have to go those times." The master teacher smiled and said, "Now we have a wonderful opportunity to teach him to communicate 'NO' instead of tantrumming."

ABA programs can be extremely intensive, approaching the child's needs from many angles. In addition to analyzing the meaning of behaviors, many ABA therapists also use Discreet Trial Teaching to break down tasks into tiny manageable chunks so the child can slowly build up a needed skill. (Little did you know that putting on a sock can be broken down into 30 small steps.) Treatment providers typically have long sessions several days a week in the home. The sessions are highly structured, in order to build skills based on the child's abilities and needs.

Sensory and Motor Therapies. Occupational therapy is critical. Sensory processing issues can overwhelm someone with an already fragile grasp of how to interact with the world around him, and motor skills deficits can make life frustrating and even more difficult.

Sensory issues can cross all sensory domains. A child can be hypersensitive in any of his senses, overreacting to noise, tactile input, smells, or sights. They may need lots of deep body input or spinning (vestibular input) to feel like they are in their bodies. Sensory overload can keep them from reading body cues for pain, hunger, or for having to go to the bathroom. Constant sensory overload creates chronic stress and a sense of overwhelm, which only make a child's day even harder.

Many people with autism also struggle with motor skills – either fine motor, gross motor, or both. They are clumsy or poorly coordinated, making everyday tasks difficult and frustrating.

Who Does This? Occupational Therapists treat Sensory Processing Disorders. Make sure to find an OT who is trained in both SPD and motor needs, as not all are. (See Chapter 7: Sensory Processing Disorder, for more information.)

Psychiatric Considerations. Psychiatric consults are a common, but not universal, part of ASD treatment. Medications can help with sleep and anxiety (common problems in autism), as well as hyperactive or aggressive behaviors. Intensive interventions using diet and supplements can also have an impact on these issues, as can sensory processing therapies.

Who Does This? If you feel that medications are necessary, a psychiatrist (or other physician with appropriate experience, such as a developmental pediatrician) can assess your child and prescribe medication based on presenting symptoms. If you would like to explore non-medication options, you can seek out a Functional Medicine psychiatrist (see Chapter 13: Psychiatry and Functional Medicine Psychiatry) or a biomedical practitioner (see Chapter 14: Biomedical Approaches). They will be able to evaluate and prescribe, but will also look for underlying causes and discuss alternative treatment plans.

Treatment Options: Complimentary and Alternative Medicine (CAM)

With the surge in autism diagnoses, there has been a corresponding surge in complementary and alternative treatments. Blogs and forums are full of advice, questions, and parent experiences. Autism conferences are awash with CAM providers discussing their programs. As happens with both conventional and alternative therapies, one parent will say a particular treatment made a world of difference for her child and the next will say it was expensive and had no clear benefits.

There are no fixed guidelines for how to sort through the options. I would suggest that parents try the following:

- Make sure that the risks and benefits are clearly explained
- Find out if there is any research that demonstrates its effectiveness (although if there isn't, that isn't necessarily a sign that it's not worth pursuing – it's just a good question to start with)
- Talk to various practitioners *who treat autism* about the therapies you are investigating
- Check out the Autism Resource Institute's parent survey, which looks at parents' experience with various therapies (which is updated regularly and is an excellent resource)
- Research with their child's particular profile in mind (Is your child verbal or non-verbal? Does he tend toward extreme tantrums or extreme withdrawal? Parents need to look for treatments that have been effective for the particular symptoms that *their* child is exhibiting.)

Keep in mind that you will still have to follow your own intuition. No two children with autism are identical; no two will predictably respond the same way to anything. Do your due diligence, solicit the opinions of knowledgeable peers and experts, and then try the things that make the most sense to you.

The ASD Community

A diagnosis of autism can be frightening and overwhelming. However, there is one silver lining: You now have access to the most active, informed, and supportive community in the world of special needs. There are multiple national organizations that keep people informed of both medical and political developments, and through which you can connect with local chapters. Autism blogs and forums are wonderful resources for information. People share and discuss many kinds of therapies, including experimental or alternative ones. Various organizations hold conferences on a regular basis, where you can hear from experts and meet other parents struggling with the same issues. Autism can be extremely challenging, but there is as much moral support as you could want!

Final Thoughts

Where autism is concerned, there is a great deal to be hopeful about these days. We have more tools than ever to determine which issues are creating symptoms, and more ways than ever to address them. I have seen remarkable progress with my patients and firmly believe that improvement is possible with any person on the spectrum.

However, the abundance of options does have a downside. The thing I have to counsel parents the most on is this: You can't do everything. And you particularly can't do everything at the same time.

As a parent myself, I completely understand the impulse to do whatever you can to help your child. But it is neither necessary nor effective to attack it from every direction. Aside from the fact that your family life and budget will suffer from trying to do too much at once, your child can only respond to so much therapy. He will probably need a certain number of foundational therapies that must happen concurrently, anyway. Don't be too eager to fill up the rest of his time trying new things! Enlist the help of an experienced professional to help you prioritize concerns. There are a lot of exciting choices available and I hope you find what's most helpful for you and your child.

Questions for Prospective Providers

Unlike many learning or developmental challenges, autism requires intervention from a team of different specialists. Given the prevalence of this disability, your pediatrician can likely also direct you to resources for diagnosis and treatment. There are clinics that specialize in treating children with Autism Spectrum Disorders that can provide a team of professionals in one place. Unless the clinic is known to specialize in treating autism, the key questions to ask of any provider are:

- Do you work with children on the autistic spectrum? How often?
- What treatment approach do you use?
- Do you use any treatment models such as ABA, FloorTime, RDI, or Pivotal Response Treatment?
- Do you use a biomedical approach in your medical assessments?

Resources for More Information

Websites

These websites will help you locate providers in your area who have experience with Autistic Spectrum Disorder:
www.autismspeaks.org. Austism Speaks

www.autisticadvocacy.org, the Austim Self-Advocacy Network (ASAN). This site was created by Scott Michael Robertson and Ari Ne'eman, both autistic adults who advocate for the recognition that differences do not always equal disability. They work closely with government and private agencies to explore the best ways to support people with autism as well as other disabilities. ASAN's motto is "Nothing about us without us."

www.autism.com, Autism Research Institute. The Institute will keep you updated with the latest research and information regarding autism.

www.generationrescue.org, Generation Rescue. Generation Rescue provides parents with information, hope, and support for their journey through autism. There's even a friendly, helpful page just for the newly diagnosed!

Books

Preventing Autism & ADHD: Controlling Risk Factors Before, During & After Pregnancy by Debby Hamilton, MD. This book helps women give their children the best chance for health from before birth.

The Autism Revolution: Whole-Body Strategies for Making Life All it Can Be by Martha Herbert, MD, PhD. Based on decades of cutting-edge research, Harvard researcher and clinician Martha Herbert presents a view of autism that brings hope and possibility to the way the condition is understood and treated.

Autism Spectrum Disorder (revised): The Complete Guide to Understanding Autism by Chantal Sicile-Kira. Newly updated as of January 2014, this book covers all aspects of the autism spectrum and includes the latest research and treatment approaches.

Diagnosis Autism: Now What? by Lawrence Kaplan, PhD. Dr. Kaplan offers ten steps that can maximize treatment outcomes, including the importance of intensive early intervention and how to find and choose effective practitioners.

Thinking in Pictures, Expanded Edition: My Life with Autism by Temple Grandin, PhD. Dr. Grandin, arguably the most famous public figure on the spectrum, illuminates what it is like to have autism.

Additional Resources

The First 100 Days Kit. This free download from the Autism Speaks website (www.autismspeaks.org) gives parents a template for the most crucial things to do in the 100 days after receiving a diagnosis of autism.

References

Buie, T., et al. Evaluation, diagnosis, and treatment of gastrointestinal disorders in individuals with ASDs: A consensus report. *Pediatrics* 125 (Suppl 1) (January 2010)

Landrigan, P. J. What causes autism: Exploring the environmental contribution. *Curr Opin Pediatric* 22 (2) (April 2010): 219-25.

Vargas, D. L., C. Nascimbene, A. W. Zimmerman, C. A. Pardo. Neurological activation and neuroinflammation in the brains of patients with autism. *Ann Neurol* 57 (1) (2005): 67-81.

Young, R. L. Parental identification of early behavioural abnormalities in children with Autistic Disorder. *Autism* 7 (2) (June 2003).

About the Author

Debby Hamilton, MD, MSPH, is the founder of Holistic Pediatric Consulting in Denver, CO. Her practice focuses on treating children with chronic diseases such as autism and ADHD and preconception counseling based on her book, *Preventing Autism and ADHD: Controlling Risk Factors Before, During & After Pregnancy*. She is board-certified in pediatrics, physician nutrition, and integrated/holistic medicine and has a Master of Science degree in Public Health (MSPH). She is on the scientific board of the Neurological Health Foundation (www.neurologicalhealth.org), a non-profit dedicated to the prevention of chronic diseases in children. In 2017, she joined Researched Nutritionals as their physician in charge of clinical research and physician education.

You can reach Dr. Hamilton at drdebby@holisticpediatric.com or www.holisticpediatric.com

NINE

Concussions

by Robin McEvoy, PhD

If any of the events in the following ***Initial Incident*** section occurred (or you suspect they did), look through the remaining lists. If you were not there right after the incident and others did not observe your child closely, you may have to make inferences based on later behavior.

Initial incident where head is hit

- ☐ Car accident in which head is either hit or experienced whiplash
- ☐ Fall off of bicycle (even if wearing helmet)
- ☐ A fall down the stairs or off playground equipment, trampoline, tree, or similarly high location
- ☐ Fall while skate/snowboarding, playing sports, or ice skating
- ☐ Sports-related injury such as fall, tackle, head-on collision, hit by a ball
- ☐ Any blow to the head that causes child to lose consciousness
- ☐ Any blow to the head that leaves child dazed

Post-injury symptoms immediately following the incident (within 12 hours of the accident)

- ☐ Pupil dilation
- ☐ Vomiting
- ☐ Ringing in ears
- ☐ Dizziness
- ☐ Confusion
- ☐ Loss of consciousness
- ☐ Vision changes (e.g., seeing stars, blurred vision)
- ☐ Headache
- ☐ Memory problems (e.g., can't remember where they are)

Post-injury symptoms that persist (length of time that the symptoms persist will depend on severity of injury; consult your physician on this)

- ☐ Headaches
- ☐ Dizziness
- ☐ Vision problems (hypersensitivity to light, visual fatigue, double vision)
- ☐ Bothered by light or noise
- ☐ Fatigue (seems more tired than usual and tires more quickly, needs more sleep than usual)
- ☐ Increased irritability
- ☐ Personality change
- ☐ Drop in school performance
- ☐ Impulsivity
- ☐ Seems to be in a fog
- ☐ Unusual or new memory problems (forgets math facts, can't remember daily schedule, can't follow multiple step directions)
- ☐ Sleeping problems (can't get to sleep, wakes at night, sleeps too much)
- ☐ Problems tolerating stress

If more than two of the immediate symptoms occurred within 12 hours after a blow to the head, then your child probably experienced a concussion. In fact, if a child experiences a blow to the head (or a hit to the body that jolts the head), plus just one of the above symptoms, it places the child at the threshold for *suspicion of a concussion*. If there were no immediate symptoms, then any perceived long-term symptoms may be due to some other issue. However, this can be hard to determine if a parent or other observant adult did not witness the injury or if a child had symptoms of headache or blurred vision but did not mention them. This is particularly common with young children who do not understand the significance of their symptoms.

The top three events leading to concussion are:

- Sports-related injuries
- Car accidents (could be whiplash related, with no actual blow to the head)
- Bicycle accidents, skate board accidents, and falls

Wesley was a 16-year-old straight-A student and star baseball player. One day, while riding home from a game in a teammate's car, Wes had not buckled his seatbelt because it was such a short distance. Unfortunately, his friend rear-ended someone at a stop sign. It wasn't fast, nor was it a particularly hard impact. But Wesley flew forward into the windshield, breaking it with his head.

The emergency room doctor examined him, determined that he did not have a skull fracture or internal bleeding, and released him. Although told that he might have a few days to a week of recovery, he hadn't been knocked out and "seemed OK" – so no one suggested seeking treatment.

Wesley's life then began to fall apart. He was always exhausted, needing to nap as soon as he got home from school. His grades dropped, and he suddenly seemed to have tremendous trouble concentrating and keeping himself organized. His behavior seemed to change, too. Formerly an enthusiastic, easy-going young man, he suddenly began arguing with his parents and getting into trouble at school.

At first, his parents figured it was all just some sort of delayed onset adolescence. "We had considered ourselves lucky to have such a sweet teenager. We figured our luck had just run out and he was going to have a surly, rebellious phase like everybody else," his mother said. Four months after the incident, however, she listened to her gut feeling that something more was wrong, and called Wesley's pediatrician. He referred Wes to me for a neuropsychological assessment, which revealed some inconsistent skills that didn't make sense in a student with no past struggles. I asked for more information about the accident and discovered that, aside from the behavioral problems, he had also been experiencing chronic headaches and neck pain, fatigue, extreme irritability, memory problems, and dizziness – all since the accident. These are all common signs of a head injury, so I convinced the family to shift their focus to post-concussive care.

To Wesley's frustration, I recommended that he stop playing baseball until the worst of his symptoms resolved. He had already been hit in the head with a ball, making for his second head injury in a few months. He insisted it hadn't been bad, but the effects of head injuries worsen exponentially the more they are compounded. The family and I also worked with school personnel to accommodate for his post-concussive symptoms, including rest breaks during the day and a more flexible schedule for completing homework. Wesley began treatment with a concussion program at the local Children's Hospital, where a physical therapist created strategies to help with pain and specialists taught him ways to ease his cognitive and organizational struggles. The family also found a craniosacral specialist, which helped with the headaches.

Despite these added supports, recovery was long and slow. This is, unfortunately, typical of head injury recovery. By graduation, he had regained enough ground to feel confident academically, but he never did get back into baseball. He now wants to be a teacher, believing that he has a unique insight into students with different kinds of learning challenges. His stu-

dent teaching in college has all been with children who struggle in different ways. Although he originally had trouble letting go of the goals he once had for himself, he now feels that he has been given the opportunity to build a life that is rewarding in ways he never could have imagined.

~Robin McEvoy, developmental neuropsychologist

Just So You Know...

All kids get a bump to the head at some point in their lives. Very few of those result in concussions, and very few concussions have lasting effects. HOWEVER: Parents and teachers should take concussions seriously, in that the child must rest completely for a few days and then reduce demands and expectations on the child for about three months. It's like strep. You have to stay in bed for a few days, allow the symptoms to abate, and then *gradually* resume activities. If you do this, you'll be fine – as good as before! But if you don't, it can become systemic and therefore extremely difficult to treat.

~ Jeanne Dise-Lewis, PhD
Associate Professor of Physical Medicine and Rehabilitation
Children's Hospital Colorado

The Basics

A concussion is the least serious, but most common, type of head injury. Also known as mild Traumatic Brain Injury (TBI), concussion is a temporary disruption in normal brain function due to a blow to the head or whiplash. Unfortunately, even mild head injuries can have devastating effects if not appropriately identified and treated. A concussion that is not given the proper care can disrupt brain activity in ways that can later appear to be learning or behavior difficulties.

Most concussions resolve with rest, good nutrition and hydration, and reduced demands. However, the Children's Hospital of Philadelphia, which has a well-developed concussion program, estimates that at least 20 percent of children with concussions experience symptoms that persist beyond one month. If your child has symptoms that have persisted even after appropriate care, you will need to seek more intensive evaluation and remediation. If, like Wesley in the opening story, a flurry of disturbing symptoms emerged after a head injury that you didn't think was serious, caregivers need to shift their awareness and focus in order to attend to concussive symptoms.

A concussion harms the brain by:

- creating bruising and inflammation of the brain tissue as a result of forceful contact with the inside of the skull;
- causing the brain to bounce and twist within the skull, stretching and damaging brain cells;
- creating a complex cascade of neurochemical reactions that disrupt brain functioning for days to weeks (or longer) after the injury.

Unfortunately, there is a great deal of confusion about what constitutes a head injury and when there is reason for concern. Here are some of the most common myths that prevent proper treatment:

- A person must lose consciousness to experience a brain injury.
- A person must hit his head in order to suffer a brain injury – and the harder the hit, the worse the injury.
- If a person reports feeling fine after a head injury, assume he is fine.
- Children heal more quickly, so you don't need to worry about them as much.
- A good helmet will prevent a concussion.
- If a person is still complaining of symptoms a month after a concussion, it is probably psychological.
- If the CT scan or MRI is normal, there is no concussion.

In fact, damage to the brain tissue or disruption of brain chemistry can result whether or not a person was knocked out. And any sudden, forceful movement of the head – as happens with whiplash – can impact the brain in a similar way, whether or not that person is wearing a helmet. Moreover, children are often not fully aware of mild symptoms, so relying on their ability to self-report is inherently suspect. And while it is true that children bounce back more quickly than adults in many situations, the Center for Disease Control has declared that "recovery [from concussion] may be slower among older adults, young children, and teens."

This chapter will *not* discuss the following:

- Strokes
- Bleeding in the brain as a result of injury
- Neurological disease (such as meningitis)
- Near-drowning

- Oxygen deprivation resulting in loss of consciousness
- Skull fractures
- Injuries resulting in coma
- Shaken baby syndrome

These types of events represent moderate to severe head injuries. Typically, a patient experiencing these conditions would have neurological and neuropsychological care as part of their treatment, and will be monitored for cognitive, emotional, or physical problems. Some of the recommendations discussed here may be useful. In general, however, these conditions fall outside the scope of this book.

Finally, you should be aware that another concussion before the first has healed completely can be exponentially harmful. Even if your child says she feels fine and seems ready to resume academics and play, you might consider waiting at least another week after that before letting her return to any activity that could result in another hit to the head. Even then, it might be a good idea to have her wear a helmet at first (despite her inevitable objections).

This chapter contains some general information on concussions so that you can better understand what may have happened to your child. However, we will focus more on how concussions can affect learning and behavior over time and what can be done about it after the fact. For an excellent resource on how to assist recovery right after a head injury, see The Children's Hospital of Philadelphia (CHOP) website for excellent information and handouts. www.chop.edu/centers-programs/concussion-care-minds-matter

Was That a Concussion?

If you know that your child experienced a head injury in the past, and are wondering if it might have played a role in any current problems she is having, start by thinking back to the time of the injury. If many of the following items occurred, there was definitely some disruption of brain function at the time. If you suspect a previous head injury, looking through this list may help you ascertain whether that was a causative factor at some point. This may guide your choices for therapy and support.

After a concussion, there are four main areas of concern. These symptoms often interact to exacerbate each other. With proper care, they should resolve.

- Physical problems:
  - Chronic headaches, neck pain, back pain
  - Dizziness

- Fatigue
- Changes in sensory processing (e.g., bothered by typical noises or bright light)

ᖳ Emotional issues:
   - Emotional lability (rapidly changing emotions) – prone to crying, irritability, angry outbursts, mood swings
   - Chronic anxiety because of discomfort (such as headaches or neck pain) or altered sensory issues (such as a ringing in the ears or aversion to bright lights or noisy places).
   - Post-Traumatic Stress Disorder – for example, anxiety about being in the car after a car accident, being afraid to ski after a skiing accident, etc.

ᖳ Cognitive symptoms:
   - Attention deficits/problems concentrating – can show up as not tracking conversations, following lectures, etc.
   - Avoidance of reading
   - Careless errors
   - Memory problems
   - Becoming overwhelmed by typical demands

ᖳ Sleep changes (good sleep is critical to recovery from concussions):
   - Trouble getting to sleep
   - Trouble staying asleep
   - Sleeping too much
   - Lethargy

Any of these can be debilitating and impact home, school, and social life. A child with chronic headaches is likely to be irritable and exhibit attention problems. A child with mood swings will be argumentative with parents and teachers, and easily upset by other children. A child who did not sleep well will be tired, irritable, and inattentive.

Keep in mind that children with certain kinds of disorders can be more accident prone, and therefore more at risk for concussions. For example, children with AD/HD are not only active, but impulsively so, making them predisposed to falls or impact-related injuries. Children who have vestibular (balance) problems or poor motor planning as part of Sensory Processing Disorder (see Chapter 7: Sensory Processing Disorder) may also be clumsy and susceptible to falls and other accidents. Do what you can to keep your child safer if he falls into one of these higher-risk groups. If he has already experienced a head injury, be aware that further injuries could be exponentially damaging. He may not like having his activities limited or having to wear a helmet for a longer period of time, but it would be very much worth it in the long run.

Post-Concussive Syndrome

Post-concussive syndrome (PCS), also known as post-concussion syndrome, refers to symptoms that persist for several weeks to several months (and sometimes indefinitely) after a mild head injury. PCS does not have a universally accepted definition in the medical field. Physicians consider this diagnosis when symptoms persist for more than three months after an injury, though it may be diagnosed if symptoms persist for more than a week or so.

Most of the literature defines post-concussive syndrome as the development of at least three of the following symptoms:

- ☐ Headache
- ☐ Dizziness
- ☐ Fatigue
- ☐ Irritability
- ☐ Impaired memory and concentration
- ☐ Insomnia
- ☐ Lowered tolerance for noise and light

If a child has persistent symptoms after a concussion, he will need an evaluation by a specialist (see *Treatment Options* later on). Many children also experience vague symptoms that they may not even think to comment on, such as more frequent mental fatigue, increasing forgetfulness, or simply an annoying sense that everything is *harder* than before. The younger the child, the less likely he will be to have the self-awareness necessary to recognize, much less verbalize, his symptoms – no matter how frustrated he may be by them.

The Tricky Part

While it is true that rest and reduced demands will suffice to heal most minor head injuries within about three weeks, there are a few components that can make the healing process a bit complicated. Everyone wants to believe he is fine after an incident, especially if it seemed minor, so it is common for people to "shake it off" and keep going. More and more, however, the recommended treatment is to start with complete cognitive rest and a slow, gradual return to both learning and physical activity. (It's the "gradual" part people seem to have trouble with.) Moreover, the cessation of headaches is not, in and of itself, a sign of complete recovery.

The brain heals slowly. Premature return to a full range of activities can delay full recovery. If the injured person *feels* ready to resume activities, it is easy to assume that the healing process is over, and overextend. A cautious return, where a child and her caretakers are watching carefully for fatigue, irritability, or other symptoms, will be more likely to ensure truly complete recuperation. If your child experienced a concussion and popped right back into action soon after, it is possible that any learning or behavior difficulties that have emerged since then stemmed from too much stress, too soon, on her brain. Think back to when the symptoms began. If they came on gradually a few weeks after the original injury, your child might not have been quite ready to dive back into her life.

Moreover, assessing the symptoms of a head injury can be inherently tricky, depending as it does on the victim's ability to report his own experience accurately. It is essentially an invisible injury (after that goose egg goes away), so it is easy for everyone involved, including the victim, to forget that he is dealing with an injury that is still healing. It is particularly difficult for younger children to self-monitor for things like lightheadedness, feeling fatigued more quickly, or increased irritability. Unless symptoms are dramatic or severe – and sometimes, even if they are – children often do not have the self-awareness to perceive symptoms that are making their lives a little harder.

Even older children and adults have trouble self-reporting accurately. Head injuries commonly lead to disrupted thinking and confusion, so people (particularly children) frequently do not recognize their own personality changes, limited stamina, or altered sensory perceptions. These issues quickly become the new normal, and they and everyone around them just try to adjust. Plus, children are constantly changing, so new behaviors are constantly cropping up anyway. Parents often assume that learning issues are emerging because school is getting harder, or that some new phase of childhood has begun, or that their teenager is just going through a particularly difficult period. It's tough to sort out. If parents are considering things after the fact, both a careful reflection and some professional support may be needed to sort out issues.

TBI and Learning/Behavior Disorders

Especially with children, it is particularly difficult to determine what learning issues are due to the head injury and what they might have developed anyway. Moreover, some problems only show up later because brain development over time was distorted by the injury. Post-concussive assessment needs to take into account the family history, other medical history, and current life events or stressors.

A brain injury of any kind will exaggerate any pre-existing learning or behavioral problems. Moreover, whatever compensations a child may have had prior to the concussion may now be seriously undermined by the injury, so the weakness will appear more pronounced. For example, a child with dyslexia may have been taught to read with the appropriate programs and was progressing well in school. After concussion, reading may become difficult again, but the causes may be related to post-concussive symptoms like headache or blurred vision.

If your child was already getting therapy for a learning or behavioral problem, don't be alarmed if he seems to stop progressing or even backslides a little after a head injury. If anything, this is probably a sign that his brain cannot respond to therapy right now. You should also get a thorough neuropsychological assessment to determine any new, concussion-related factors that might be complicating learning. Understanding the impact of a head injury should take priority for all treatment providers.

Why Identify TBI?

Why does it matter if a TBI was a contributing cause to a learning or behavior disorder? It depends very much on whom you ask. Especially if the injury occurred a long time ago, most medical doctors will consider it "a done deal" and tell you that whatever state your child's brain is now is the state it will be in forever, regardless of how it got that way. Still, there are three reasons why it could still be helpful to assert the existence of a TBI:

- **Insurance.** Many insurance companies do not offer assistance for a learning or behavior disorder, but a documented head injury represents a medical condition that could be covered. Sadly, if you did not document the injury by taking your child to the physician or a hospital at the time, this one is probably out of the question.
- **Accommodations and assistance.** Teachers, coaches, and other caregivers can sometimes be confused or skeptical about some behavior or learning disorders. A concussion and its recovery period might be easier concepts for them to understand and support, or at least, they might better appreciate your child's struggles. Your child should also learn to explain concussion and advocate for his needs as they relate to this issue. This might include being excused from physical education until a physician approves the return, permission to rest in the nurse's office if headaches occur, or reduction of homework while fatigue persists. Halstead, McAvoy et al. (in their clinical report on "Returning to Learning Following a Concussion," published in the American Academy of Pediatrics), recommend academic adjustments for the first three to four weeks. They feel that this should be sufficient for 80 to 90 percent of

the concussions. If a child needs more supports for longer, parents and the educational team should implement more formal accommodations. Dr. McAvoy notes that schools do not have to, and often don't, give formal accommodations (such as an IEP or 504 plan) for a concussion and "for milder concussions, these formalized written accommodations are not needed." However, in the rare instance that a concussion results in chronic problems, do seek formal support.

- **Appropriate therapeutic support.** If your child is seeing therapists for learning or behavior reasons, her therapist should be notified *immediately* if you suspect a TBI. Concentration, stamina, or emotional regulation issues may need to be given more space and not pushed so hard if a head injury was a causative factor. It might even be a good idea to locate a similar therapist who also has experience with TBI patients, as it is a specialty. Some CAM therapies, such as craniosacral therapists (discussed in an upcoming section), do treat post-concussive symptoms and can have a positive impact well after injury.

There are specialists who may be able to help you with TBI-related learning or behavior troubles. Western medicine-trained specialists will mostly aim to teach your child compensatory strategies, reduce physical symptoms (such as headaches), and monitor the recovery process. There are also promising alternative treatments that may help, even a long time after the original injury.

Who Can Help?

TREATMENT OPTIONS: STANDARD OF CARE

Immediately after the incident:
A physician, ER doctor, or neurologist should determine whether or not your child has a concussion, and whether he has a brain bleed or other severe condition. The primary treatment for concussion is rest, pain management, good nutrition, and reduced demands during the recovery process. Hopefully, the ER or your child's doctor will have a written handout outlining these steps.

If symptoms persist, disrupting academic progress, behavioral control, or social life, the following specialists might be able to help:

- A neuropsychologist specializing in head injury can evaluate the impact of the injury and help you develop an overall treatment plan.
- A cognitive rehabilitation specialist can help you develop cognitive strategies and other life skills that will help your child cope with the symptoms.

For persistent problems, additional consultation/treatment may need to address the following issues:

- **Pain management, such as neck pain.** Physical therapy and/or pain medication may be necessary.
- **Inability to sleep.** A sleep aide may help, though this should be done with caution as sleep aides can interfere with the brain's return to normal neurochemistry. See the next section for other suggestions.
- **Accommodations for cognitive inefficiency, such as poor memory or attention.** Persistent problems with cognition can be supported through a neuropsychological evaluation and cognitive rehabilitation therapy (CRT). CRT will work on developing coping strategies for current symptoms and ways of reducing symptoms (such as sleep strategies or hydration to reduce headaches). For long-term problems (more than three months), a child will also need some formalized accommodations at school; however, the need for an IEP for typical concussion recovery is extremely rare.
- **Stress reduction.** As previously mentioned, you'll need to make adjustments in your child's life to reduce stress however possible. Some physicians will also prescribe medication to reduce anxiety or explosive behaviors. Practitioners of alternative medicine (next section) may have other suggestions or tools for this.
- **Altered sensory processing.** If these issues did not resolve in a few days to a week, then a specialist might be consulted. Your pediatrician can help find the appropriate resources. Common sensory processing issues include:
  - Visual problems, such as light hypersensitivity, blurred vision, double vision, or convergence problems. If these are persistent issues, then a developmental optometrist may be able to provide treatment and accommodation recommendations. (See Chapter 7.1: Vision Therapy.) A craniosacral therapist may also be helpful. (See Chapter 16.5: Craniosacral Therapy.)
  - Auditory hypersensitivity or ringing in the ears. An audiologist may be able to assess and provide recommendations. (See Chapter 5.1: Auditory Processing Disorder.)

- If other sensory or motor issues emerge and do not resolve, then a neuro-logical or occupational therapy evaluation may be warranted. (See Chapter 7: Sensory Processing Disorder, but also ensure that the therapist has experience with head injuries.)

TREATMENT OPTIONS: COMPLIMENTARY AND ALTERNATIVE MEDICINE (CAM)

Editors' Note

Head injury treatment is a tricky thing that has no simple answers or guaranteed cures. Even standard-of-care cognitive retraining therapy gets inconsistent results and is somewhat controversial. We are suggesting that you consider the following approaches because we have seen so many people improve from their use. These modalities offer a range of options that at least gives some additional resources when rest and time off have not resolved the issues.

Most CAM treatments should wait until after the most acute phase of recovery is over. Even the most soothing therapy can be too much for a fragile system to integrate and could only be more fatiguing. Good nutrition and hydration, however, should start right away.

- **Chapter 15: Nutritional Approaches.** While nutrition in general is not necessarily CAM, its inclusion on a list of concussion treatments is not mainstream. Some foods and supplements support brain function, providing crucial quality input at a time when the brain needs to rebuild function. Other foods, like sugar, can actively impair reparation. This is beginning to show up in traditional Western treatments as well.
- **Chapter 16.1: Naturopathy.** This modality can help on many fronts. Naturopaths can offer homeopathy and nutritional guidance from the start, and can recommend herbs, supplements, and other lifestyle changes to continue healing and speed the reduction of inflammation in the brain.
- **Chapter 16.2: Neurofeedback/Biofeedback.** Neurofeedback is a type of biofeedback that uses computer displays of brain activity to regain control of the nervous system and bring erratic brain function back into balance. The American Academy of Pediatrics has not yet recognized neurofeedback for post-concussion treatment. Research is ongoing. (See Thornton and Carmody, 2009, May, Benson, et al 2013). However, many practitioners who use neurofeedback as a standard part of their post-concussive care regimen swear by it.

- **Chapter 16.3: LEAP (Learning Enhancement Acupressure Program).** Inflammation in (or trauma to) the brain can cause neurological pathways to shut down. Even after most symptoms seem to have receded, those pathways may not come back "online" without help. LEAP can identify the pathways that are still shut down and restore full brain function.
- **Chapter 16.4: Chiropractic Neurology.** This modality can help rebuild specific brain functions that have been compromised. This is typically done through series of small carefully planned exercises, not through chiropractic adjustments (which can be contra-indicated in some cases).
- **Chapter 16.5: Craniosacral Therapy.** This treatment can calm a chronically over-excited brain and settle the nervous system. It can also increase circulation throughout the brain, which can reduce swelling, a primary culprit in creating long-term symptoms. Gentle craniosacral adjustments are one of the few CAM treatments that may be useful during the initial recovery period.

Questions for Prospective Practitioners

If the concussion has just occurred, the initial treatment provider (your pediatrician or emergency room doctor) will typically have an information sheet and specific guidelines for immediate follow-up. Additional questions to ask might include (if not already covered):

IMMEDIATELY AFTER THE INCIDENT:

- What do you believe is the typical time for symptoms to resolve?
- What are your guidelines for returning to school and for returning to sports? How many weeks should I limit my child's regular activities (going to school, play dates, after school activities)? This might vary depending on the severity of the injury.
- What symptoms would indicate that my child needs additional treatment? (e.g., headaches, dizziness, persistent fatigue, increased difficulty with schoolwork, etc.)
- Should there be a routine follow-up and when should that be scheduled?

FOR SYMPTOMS THAT HAVE NOT RESOLVED IN THE EXPECTED TIME FRAME:

There will need to be additional consultation based on the persistent symptoms (e.g., neuropsychologist for memory problems, neurologist for headaches). Your pediatrician should be able to give you guidance on this if you are not sure where to start. Once referred to a provider, questions to ask include:

- Are you familiar with these types of symptoms secondary to concussion in a child of this age?
- Do you assess for related issues that may not be obvious (e.g. behavior that looks like an attention problem but may actually be an auditory processing problem)?
- What is your plan if issues do not resolve?

FOR CAM PROVIDERS (FOR OTHER QUESTIONS, SEE ALSO THE CHAPTERS ON SPECIFIC TREATMENTS):

- Have you had specific training in the treatment of concussion or head injury?
- What is your typical course of treatment for head injury or concussion? What is your expected course of treatment for my child?
- Will you coordinate with my other treatment providers?
- Are your certified in your line of work?
- What are contra-indications for your treatment? Are there any risks of this treatment?

Resources for More Information

WEBSITES

www.chop.edu/service/concussion-care-for-kids/returning-to-school.html# This is the Children's Hospital of Philadelphia site to support concussion recovery. They give very clear guidelines for symptoms to watch out for and specific "return to learning" guidelines.
www.cdc.gov/headsup/pdfs/providers/fact_sheet_concusstbi-a.pdf
www.cdc.gov/headsup/pdfs/youthsports/coaches_engl.pdf
www.cdc.gov/headsup/parents/ This site is about sports injuries.

BOOKS

Coping with Concussion and Mild Traumatic Brain Injury: A Guide to Living with the Challenges Associated with Post Concussion Syndrome and Brain Trauma by Diane Roberts Stoler. This resource covers a range of ages and gives strategies for understanding and coping with mild traumatic head injuries.

Concussions and Our Kids: America's Leading Expert on How to Protect Young Athletes and Keep Sports Safe by Dr. Robert Cantu and Mark Hyman. Sports-related concussions are one of the most common forms of concussions. This book gives parents the information they need to know as their child enters sports and throughout their years of playing.

Conquering Concussion:Healing TBI Symptoms with Neurofeedback and Without Drugs by Mary Lee Esty, Ph.D. and C.M. Shifflett. There are often limited recommendations for persistent post-concussive symptoms. This book lays out some alternatives to simply managing pain or headaches with medication.

References

For an excellent review of the neurochemical changes that occur in concussion, see this article: Giza, C. C., D. A. Hoyda. The neurometabolic cascade of concussion. *Journal of Athletic Training* 36 (3) (September 2001): 228–235.

Hall, R. C., M. J. Chapman. Definition, diagnosis, and forensic implications of postconcussional syndrome. *Psychosomatics* 46 (3) (May-June 2005): 195–202.

McFadden K., K. Healy, M. Dettmann, J. Kay, T. Ito, and T. Hernandez. Acupressure as a non-pharmacological intervention for traumatic head injury (TBI). *Journal of Neurotrauma* 28 (1) (January 2011): 21-34.

May, G., R. Benson, R. Balon, N. Boutros. Neurofeedback and traumatic brain injury: A literature review. *Annals of Clinical Psychiatry* 25 (4) (November 2013): 289-296.

Thornton, K. E. and D. P. Carmody. Traumatic brain injury rehabilitation: QEEG biofeedback treatment protocols. *Appl Psychophysiol Biofeedback* 34 (1) (March 2009):59-68.

About the Author

Robin McEvoy, PhD, is a developmental neuropsychologist and one of the authors of this book. You can find her complete bio at the back.

TEN

Other Learning Disabilities

by Robin McEvoy, PhD

My daughter never did grasp numbers, though she did fine in other subjects. Even as late as fourth grade, you could ask her what 7 + 8 is and you'd get a panicked look, followed by a pause, followed by a wild guess…"12?" We tried tutoring and other learning programs, but even the basics never came easily to her. It never got better, and I never knew how to help her. ~ L.H.

My son will do anything to get out of writing. When he does try to write, he becomes so agitated that he rocks, fidgets, and whines throughout. Homework is a nightmare. We took him to a clinic once where they put sensors on his head to measure brain activity during different tasks. When he wrote, we watched as, one by one, his brain centers slowed dramatically. By the end of 15 minutes, he had a pounding headache and could no longer write or even think. That was when I realized how hard writing really was for him. ~ D.C.

My daughter does not have ADD or ADHD, but is so chronically disorganized that teachers are constantly asking if I've had her tested. (I have.) She does her homework but forgets to turn it in, cannot keep track of the steps in a complex project, and loses everything. Everything. She is actually a very good student, in terms of the quality of her work, so this is extremely frustrating for both of us. She also never seems to see problems coming down the pike: If a bunch of kids are doing something they're not supposed to be doing, everyone but her will stop when the teacher shows up. She's always surprised when she gets in trouble. I didn't know how that fit in until recently, when someone finally explained "executive function disorder" to me. ~ C.S.

Both my son and my best friend's son are twice exceptional. They were both always extraordinarily sensitive and melted down constantly in crowds or loud places, which was a tough one when they were little. Both also acted like they were being tortured when asked to write, and both had trouble understanding basic social dynamics with peers, although adults have always loved them. I was so glad they had each other! They came up with amazing, creative projects (no video games for them!), understood each other's quirky sense of humor, and almost seemed to have their own language. Now that they are older teens, they are more able to bring their abilities into the world without so much struggle, but it was a long road for them. ~ C.B.

These children have one thing in common: they all have very specific, not well-known learning disabilities. This can be very frustrating to parents, who sometimes try years of therapies and supports before finally finding real answers…if they ever do. I often find that parents have tried a lot of tutoring and maybe a general learning support program or two, but to no avail because the true culprit has never been identified.

This chapter covers the main uncommon learning disabilities. Fewer specialists are trained to recognize or treat them, and there is much less in the way of quality literature or services. Only three of these (Math Disability, Writing Disability, and Motor Disability) are even in the diagnostic manual (the DSM-5) used by psychologists and psychiatrists. However, answers do exist. And, at the very least, it is helpful to know what you are dealing with so that you can help your child and her teachers understand the true issue.

- o   10.1: Math Disability (Dyscalculia)
- o   10.2: Writing Disability (Dysgraphia)
- o   10.3: Nonverbal Learning Disability (NLD)
- o   10.4: Other Motor Disability
- o   10.5: Twice Exceptional
- o   10.6: Executive Function Disorders
- o   10.7: The Complex Child

10.1 Math Disability (Dyscalculia)

People with a math disability have poor number sense. The diagnosis is simple: a child's math skills are much weaker than expected for his intelligence or academic experience. This disability can range from mild to severe and researchers are still identifying several subtypes.

A more severe math disability may be apparent from early in development, when a child struggles to master counting, quantities (e.g., more vs. less), and simple concepts of adding and subtracting. Reversing number sequences, for subtraction can be particularly difficult, but even addition facts (e.g., 8+2=10) are never obvious. They are still counting on their fingers for addition and subtraction well into middle school or beyond.

With a mild math disability, a child may muddle through early math, but then find it nearly impossible to grasp more abstract concepts in algebra or geometry. They may be able to memorize steps, but they have no true understanding of the processes they are trying to complete. These children have the basic math needed to count money and solve everyday math problems, but cannot process the more difficult concepts that are needed for high school and college graduation.

In the classroom, math disabilities are often specific to math class, whereas a reading or writing disability often interferes with many academic subjects. Math disabilities, therefore, often do not often receive the level of intervention that reading and writing disabilities do. However, in the learning disabled population, math disabilities can be as common as reading disabilities and require intensive support.

Math disabilities can continue to affect a person's life in college and beyond. You might think that a student is home free once he reaches college, since she can focus on her area of interest. But, in fact, a math disability can continue to limit her options. There are many accommodations for a reading disability – certain disabilities can even exempt a student from foreign language study – but there are few math supports. A student often cannot receive a bachelor's degree without exhibiting competence in at least algebra. It can be difficult to find a way around this, especially since science classes – which students can choose in place of math as a distribution requirement – inevitably require math skills too. (Fortunately, some colleges are now allowing a math-disabled student to substitute logic classes for math.) Even in life after academics, a math disability can limit job opportunities and impair everyday life skills, from balancing a checkbook to paying taxes to understanding timelines.

When It's Not a Math Disability

Not every problem with math is evidence of a math disability. Auditory memory weakness is another factor that can create difficulties with memorizing math facts. While meaningful auditory information is stored in verbal memory, auditory memory stores non-meaningful information, such as foreign words, individual sounds within a word, number series, and math facts.

Children with an auditory memory weakness will often struggle with early reading and spelling, but it can also show up as extreme difficulty memorizing multiplication tables and basic addition and subtraction facts. For many of these children, the move to middle school, more complex conceptual math, and the use of a calculator takes care of the problem. They can understand the concepts just fine; they just can't remember math facts. Make sure you're addressing the right issue, because the strategy will be different!

The primary interventions for math disabilities are:

- Use of manipulatives to make math a visual and kinesthetic experience. Counting with pennies and other counters can make quantities visible. There are numerous math aids marketed for this.
- Use of verbal instructions and verbal sequences for children with verbal strengths. Repetitive instructions can be memorized so that the child is eventually more independent.
- Use of the calculator. It is imperative, however, that a student understands the math concepts before relying on the calculator. Knowing to punch the ÷ sign is not the same as understanding division. However, for the student who understands the concept, the calculator will make math possible.
- As with any disability, practice, practice, practice is key. A skilled teacher or specialist can provide the best strategies and materials, but practice should occur daily and not just in math class. Counting money, cooking from recipes, sorting objects, and estimating time can all be practiced as children go through their day.

RESOURCES FOR MORE INFORMATION

WEBSITE

www.dyscalculia.org/ - This is a comprehensive site listing many books and resources to support math, numeracy skills (the math version of literacy skills), and calculation skills.

10.2: Writing Disability (Dysgraphia)

Evaluators diagnose a writing disability when a child's written work is much weaker than his intelligence or academic experience. Because writing is, neurologically speaking, one of the most complicated tasks to master, there are an extraordinary number of ways the process can get derailed. It takes years for writing habits to becoming automatic; and frankly, few of us master them with ease. But for a child who cannot get his thoughts on paper, writing can be downright torturous.

Writing necessitates a huge amount of coordination between brain centers. Think about it: Writing requires the smooth teamwork of visual and motor systems, which is already pretty complex. But, writing also requires executive function skills to organize your thoughts, time, and resources, all while keeping you on track. *Plus*, you need your working memory to remember the ideas you want to cover and how to express them. You must also recall all of the conventions of writing, from spelling and punctuation to grammar rules and clear wording. Don't forget to be original and interesting on top of all that!

Because of the number of neurodevelopmental systems involved, there are usually overlaps with other academic struggles. These are some of the learning disabilities that often co-occur with dysgraphia:

☐ Children who struggle with reading can have persistent problems with spelling. This will slow their writing and cause great problems with penmanship.

☐ Children with fine motor weaknesses can have extremely poor penmanship, which can make their writing illegible.

☐ Bright children with fine motor weaknesses can have great difficulty with writing due to the mismatch between their fast thinking and slow writing.

☐ Children with attention weaknesses can have trouble controlling their attention through the multiple demands of writing.

☐ Dysgraphia can affect math skills, if the child cannot form numbers clearly when writing or if he loses track of the columns when solving problems.

The presentation of dysgraphia changes over time. Young children show many early signs that predict writing challenges, such as:

☐ Avoidance of drawing and coloring tasks, as well as of early writing tasks

☐ A tight, awkward grip when holding a pencil, marker, or crayon (students with dysgraphia break a lot of pencil points from pushing too hard)

☐ Using a confusing mix of upper and lower case letters, poorly formed and reversed letters, and words that run together

☐ Trouble writing on lines; their letters tend to float above and below the line

Parent Perspective

If you think your child will need accommodations for the writing portion of SATs and ACTs, my advice is: Start the request process early. You will need clinical proof of dysgraphia. We had that and still got a refusal to accommodate, with a letter stating "we realize that many students struggle with handwriting because of the widespread use of computers, but..." They had no idea what dysgraphia was. We had to appeal, which took forever, and finally received permission about four days before the ACT. So do yourself a favor, have *all* your testing in order, and leave plenty of time! (Note: Documentation of both a writing disorder, and of the school accommodations necessary due to the disorder, must be in place at least 18 months in advance of your request.) ~ M. J.

Older children progress to somewhat different symptoms:

☐ Words may continue to run together and penmanship remains illegible, mixing cursive and print, upper and lower case.
☐ Spelling remains poor even as their vocabulary expands.
☐ Some words in the sentence may be omitted.
☐ Thoughts are disorganized or incomplete.
☐ Syntax, grammar, and other rules of writing are used erratically.
☐ Work quality does not reflect the student's intelligence.

Like math and reading, writing is a core academic subject. It is almost impossible to avoid writing altogether. But for the child identified with dysgraphia or a writing disability, there are a number of possible accommodations:

- Allow the child to write in either print or cursive, whichever is easier for him (for some children, cursive is easier because the letters in a word link together).
- Introduce keyboarding skills early, as typing removes the grueling task of penmanship from the list of writing demands. The computer also has spell check and allows for easier editing.
- Most writing-challenged children strenuously resist writing a first draft or making an outline before starting to write. All writing is torturous for them, so these pre-steps just feel extra taxing. It can be helpful if an adult will jot out a child's ideas for him. Writing key ideas on sticky notes allows for the ideas to then be grouped into potential paragraphs. The child can then develop his paper from there, without having to hold all his ideas mentally while struggling with writing (or typing). It also models pre-writing strategies that a child might be more willing to use when he is older.
- A child with writing disabilities will sometimes need test accommodations. Some possibilities follow:
  - If the test is about writing skill, use of a word processor may be necessary.
  - If the test is not about writing, but is assessing knowledge of history, literature, science, or other subject, the student may need to be tested orally in lieu of essay tasks or answering questions in written form. If he types well, use of a computer may suffice; but he may still require extra time because of difficulty organizing his thoughts.
  - A dysgraphic child should not be penalized for spelling errors, whether he writes by hand or types. If he writes by hand (although he should virtually

never have to), he should also not be penalized for messy handwriting.

- Some dysgraphic children have trouble coloring in the bubbles on multiple-choice tests (such as most standardized tests), and may need to be allowed to make a line through the right bubble. A few may need a scribe even for this.
- For math tests, a child may need large graph paper and instruction on how to keep numbers in columns so they do not get penalized for simply losing their place.
- Explore technological supports, as this is an area that keeps expanding. Voice-activated dictation software and recording smartpens are just two examples.

Resources for More Information

Book

Dysgraphia: Why Johnny Can't Write : A Handbook for Teachers and Parents by Diane Walton Caven. This book guides readers through the mystifying, frustrating disorder of dysgraphia.

10.3: Non-Verbal Learning Disability (NVLD or NLD)

This disability does not refer to a child being nonverbal or unable to speak. The child with NLD (the current, more commonly used acronym) typically has strong verbal skills, but is quite weak in non-verbal skills. This is typically marked by the following symptoms:

☐ Her visual-spatial skills are significantly weaker than verbal skills in cognitive testing.
☐ His gross and fine motor coordination are weak.
☐ Child has weak social skills because he fails to read nonverbal communication, such as facial expression, gestures, or voice tone. A child with NLD can be socially awkward and struggle to make friends.
☐ She struggles in several academic subjects. Academic skills affected include:
  - Reading comprehension – a child with NLD may read quite well, but may not fully process the plot line, the subtext, or the big picture.
  - Math skills – visual/spatial understanding is the underpinning of mathemat-

ics, so overall math ability can be quite weak. He will often meet criteria for a math disability, but the additional areas of weakness listed here make NLD the primary diagnosis.

- Writing – given the fine motor and visual spatial skills can be weak, a child with NLD will struggle with penmanship and often with spelling.
- Charts, graphs, and outlines – these can be hard to interpret because of visual reasoning weaknesses.

☐ She is at high risk for anxiety and depression, due to academic and social struggles. Social struggles can be particularly difficult for these children.

☐ A child with NLD may exhibit atypical sensory processing.

Because of the social struggles, children with NLD can be misdiagnosed with Asperger's Syndrome or a high functioning Autism Spectrum Disorder. Their needs can be similar in this area and there continues to be discussion about whether NLD would fall on the Autism Spectrum Disorder continuum.

Children with NLD benefit from many of following supports:

- Academic accommodations can be made according to their specific needs, for example:
  - For reading, a child may need support to see the big picture of the whole plot line, along with important cause and effect events. Children with NLD tend to miss the forest for the trees.
  - For writing, children would benefit from many of the recommendations made for dysgraphia.
  - For math, children would benefit from many of the recommendations for dyscalculia.
  - For graphs, maps, outlines, and other visual supports, children should be trained to talk their way through the visual picture, using their stronger verbal skills.
- Train the child in social skills. Children with NLD will need training in reading non-verbal cues of voice tone, facial expression, and gestures. They also need training in details of personal space, because weak visual spatial skills can make them unaware of these boundaries. They may also need training in social turn-taking.
- Teach and support organizational skills. Good organization often has a visual component, so children with NLD can be very disorganized.
- Counseling support may be needed to treat depression or anxiety. This can be particularly important during the teen years.

⚲ Explore occupational therapy or special programs to support gross motor skills, such as learning to ride a bike.

Resources for More Information

WEBSITES

www.nldontheweb.org/ This website is a thorough resource for all aspects of nonverbal learning disorder.
www.ldonline.org/article/Nonverbal_Learning_Disorders This excellent article discusses many aspect of NLD, including school modifications and accommodations.

10.4: Other Motor Disabilities

Some kids are identified with Sensory Processing Disorder (see Chapter 7). This often includes weaknesses or problems with motor skills as well. But what if there are no significant problems with sensory processing to disorganize or distract a child? There can still be motor weaknesses that cause big problems in the classroom. The DSM-5 covers the problems related to motor weaknesses under the diagnosis of Developmental Coordination Disorder. Some motor areas to consider include:

⚲ Gross motor skills - these are the large muscles in the arms and legs. They are used for all the big actions in sports and on the playground, like running, climbing, throwing, jumping. However, poor gross motor skills can also make you awkward in the classroom, bumping into people, falling off the chair, dropping your papers and books, etc.

⚲ Fine motor skills - these are the smaller muscles. We primarily think of these in relation to hand and finger movements needed for writing, drawing, using eating utensils, cutting with scissors, etc. Children with weak fine motor skills are often diagnosed with dysgraphia.

⚲ Motor planning skills (dyspraxia) – weaknesses in motor planning means the child struggles to coordinate a series of actions needed to complete a task, such as running then kicking a ball or pulling and tearing tape off of a dispenser. More complicated tasks, such as maneuvering around on a jungle gym or simply tying shoes, can feel impossible.

꜏ Motor tone- these are the muscles needed for good posture. Children with poor tone can be too stiff, but more often they are too floppy. They have trouble keeping in one spot at circle time. They slouch and tire easily for desk work. They simple do not have the core body strength needed for sitting for long periods to do desk work, but they also struggle with motor skills for sports and play.

Developmental Coordination Disorder is identified when motor skills are weak in the absence of a clear medical cause (such as cerebral palsy). These weaknesses in motor skills are treated through physical and occupational therapy, primarily the latter. School-based occupational therapy can be helpful for establishing supports for desk work (a well-fitted desk is essential, along with other supports as needed). The school occupational therapist can also consult on modifications for PE and support for social needs (a poorly coordinated child is at risk for being teased). Private occupational therapy can also be critical as this is not a weakness that disappears when the child leaves school. It is important to build skills whenever possible, as well as to develop alternative forms of play and exercise that help a child stay active and fit. Children with motor coordination disorders are at risk for obesity due to a tendency to avoid movement. There is also a high incidence of other learning challenges, such as problems with attention control or weaknesses in speech skills.

Resources for More Information

WEBSITES

www.nlm.nih.gov/medlineplus/ency/article/001533.htm. This Medline Plus site offers information about Developmental Coordination Disorder.
www.minddisorders.com/Del-Fi/Developmental-coordination-disorder.html. This site provides more information about Developmental Coordination Disorder.
www.dyspraxiausa.org/resources/. Here you can find an extensive list of helpful resources regarding dyspraxia and developmental coordination disorder.

10.5: Twice Exceptional

What parent doesn't experience a thrill when her child appears to be incredibly bright, even gifted? But that thrill can quickly disappear when that same child struggles academically or socially. With the bright or gifted child, no one ever sees it coming. However, being gifted hardly guarantees that a child will coast through school or life. In fact, the opposite tends to be true.

Twice Exceptional (otherwise known as *2e*) refers to children who have been identified with cognitive gifts, but who also struggle with some sort of learning disability or challenge (i.e., they are exceptional in two directions). While the gifted part of twice exceptional is fairly simple – the child scores in the gifted or superior range in some form of cognitive assessment – the other part of the twice exceptional label, the disability or challenge, can vary widely. Children can be gifted and also experience any of the following:

- A reading disability or dyslexia - it comes as a surprise to many when an extremely bright child who loves to be read to (and often memorizes entire passages just from having heard them) struggles with reading himself, but it is not uncommon. (See Chapter 6: Dyslexia and Other Reading Disabilities.)
- A writing disability - for some reason, many highly intelligent children do not have the fine motor dexterity to write as well as they think. For some, the discrepancy can be so severe that they qualify as dysgraphic. (See Chapter 10.2: Writing Disability (Dysgraphia).)
- A math disability - some children are gifted in verbal areas, so that reading, writing, and the verbal subjects such as history come very easily. But math is more reliant on spatial skills. If the child is weak there, he may present with a math disability. (See Chapter 10.1: Math Disability (Dyscalculia).)
- Attention Deficit Disorder - some gifted children learn so quickly that they actually do not learn to pay attention long enough to persist with longer academic tasks, such as writing papers or completing projects. They can also be inattentive in class because they already understand the material and they are bored. Some kids can then be disruptive. In this case, it can be tough to separate a brain with true ADD, from a bright kid who just needs to put more conscious effort into staying with his work. Some gifted children do have enough problems with attention to qualify for a diagnosis of Attention Deficit Disorder. Other children simply have immature attention because they have always known the answer without having to think too hard. Either way, these children would benefit from extra support learning attention skills. (See Chapter 4: Attention Problems and AD/HD.)
- Weak social skills - children with cognitive gifts can be out of sync with peers. They are interested in more complex topics and issues and some can have *very long* attention spans. This separates them from age-mates and they then have less practice with social skills. Some children have enough weaknesses in social reasoning that

they also meet criteria for Asperger's Syndrome. Make sure you understand the true source of the problem and accommodate for what is truly happening. (See Chapter 12: Social Skills Issues.)

- Sensory Processing Disorder - gifted children may be bright partly because they have hypersensitive sensory processing. Nothing gets past them, so they learn a lot quickly. However, this lack of filtering can cause them to be irritable, fatigued, and controlling. They may also socially isolate in order to get a break from overstimulation. (See Chapter 7: Sensory Processing Disorder.)
- Motor disabilities - some gifted children seem to be "all brain" and out of touch with their bodies. They can display symptoms from clumsiness to articulation disorders to handwriting weaknesses. (See Chapter 10.4: Other Motor Disabilities.)
- Autism Spectrum Disorder - there are a number of gifted children who also have autism or other weaknesses in social reasoning. Temple Grandin is the most famous example of a gifted person who also has autism. (See Chapter 8: Autism Spectrum Disorder.)

Twice exceptional children can be very challenging to educate. On one hand, they need enrichment to support their inherently high intelligence. On the other hand, they need special services to support areas of extreme weaknesses, whether in speech skills, core academics, attention, organization, or social skills.

Most schools are ill-prepared to balance out these discordant needs. Gifted children do not fit well in special education services because their cognitive abilities are far beyond students with more typical learning disabilities. Yet they struggle in regular education because their disabilities keep them from producing as well as their peers without learning disabilities. They may love the enrichment of gifted placement, but need huge accommodations for their area of disability. Twice exceptional children are at high risk for low self-esteem, frustration, anxiety, depression, tantrums, or other markers of emotional distress.

Services for 2e children need to include the following:

- Receive a comprehensive assessment (cognitive, academic, social, sensory, attention, motor skills, etc) in order to outline their unique profile of strengths and weaknesses. **Please note: Just because the child does not have a "gifted IQ" as his overall score on the IQ test does not mean he does not have gifts. It is critical to look at the individual subtests to see the child's unique profile of strengths and weaknesses.**

- Find services or activities that accentuate strengths. This could include special projects in areas of interest or after-school and summer activities that allow the child to fully explore and develop their passions and gifts.
- Seek out services or educational therapies that remediate and accommodate weaknesses. For example, gifted children who have dysgraphia can make videos about a subject instead of writing a paper. Children with reading disabilities can use audiobooks or videos to acquire information. Services have to be specific to needs and also recognize gifts.

Parents of 2e kids have to be strong advocates for their children. They play a critical role in educating teachers about their child's unique profile of strengths and weaknesses.

Resources for More Information

Website

www.2enewsletter.com/ This comprehensive newsletter covers the latest findings in research on a variety of disorders that are often found within the 2e community. It also offers parenting tips, essays from parents, and more.

Books

Twice-Exceptional Gifted Children: Understanding, Teaching, and Counseling Gifted Students by Bevery Trail, EdD. Trail provides a comprehensive overview of 2e students, as well as strategies to help them.

Different Minds: Gifted Children with AD/HD, Asperger Syndrome, and Other Learning Deficits by Diedre Lovecky, PhD. Dr. Lovecky gives professionals, teachers, and parents insight into the minds of gifted children who struggle in some ways, and suggests strategies to meet their needs and enhance their lives.

10.6: Executive Function Disorders

Executive function refers to the skills needed to organize, plan, make decisions, exercise judgment, and otherwise use all the information the brain has taken in. The term *executive* was selected to represent the brain's CEO, the chief executive officer, who runs the company using all resources well. This reference does not make much sense to children, so the issue can be described for them as the brain's *coach* who organizes the team and makes the best use of its players.

The frontal lobes of the brain are considered critical for executive function. This is the last part of the brain to mature, often not fully maturing until a person is in their mid-20s. This means that parents can hope to see improvement in their child's executive functions as she grows into young adulthood. However, some weaknesses may persist, necessitating continued structure and strategies.

Executive function disorders are often grouped with *attention* deficit disorders. But there are many types of attention problems. On the surface, Attention Deficit Disorder and *Executive Function* Disorder look very similar. Two kids may both be staring out the window instead of starting their work. Two kids may have hopelessly disorganized backpacks. Both may have forgotten to bring home the book needed for homework.

But in fact, these problems are occurring for different reasons. A simple attention deficit can be seen in the child who knows what to do next, but cannot control his attention enough to get it done. A more complex attention problem is the child who would like to keep working, but does not know what to do next. This is an executive function disorder. With Executive Function Disorder, paying attention does not help. The child may still not know what to do.

Identifying and differentiating Executive Function Disorder from a simple Attention Deficit Disorder can be difficult and requires an experienced evaluator. There are tests of executive function, which are typically performed by neuropsychologists. Some tasks involve ambiguity and require deductive reasoning and mental flexibility. Other tasks require organization, efficiency of processing, or planning.

Children with Executive Function Disorder need a lot of organizational support. Two basic areas include these:

- Provide more structure, such as:
  - Create standard routines for morning and evening time.
  - Follow a consistent daily schedule at school.
  - Provide written directions for various tasks.
  - Help student to use planners or day timers or new electronic options, which can be helpful if the child can keep track of them. (Note: planners are not always easy for kids with EF problems to use, but practice with them provides a strategy that is eventually helpful.)
  - Schedule prompts, such as a teacher or parent stopping the student as they leave school to help them consider what they need for the evening.
- Teach the child organizational strategies that can be used in many situations, for example:

- Help the child become comfortable advocating for herself with teachers. Students need to learn to ask for help or for more explanation on tasks when needed.
- Use sequencing prompts, such as "What have you gotten done?" and "What do you plan to do next?" This helps the child learn to take a step back to review what has already been done, then try to think of the next step. It can be a good mental habit.
- Practice cooking from recipes, as it helps with learning to follow complex directions. Then use the recipe format as a structure for school project, discussing the "ingredients" needed for the project and the steps in the process.
- Students can be trained to use writing rubrics for book reports and for other essays (such as a five-paragraph essay format for teens).

Resources for More Information

BOOK

Late, Lost, and Unprepared: A Parents' Guide to Helping Children with Executive Functioning by Joyce Cooper-Kahn, PhD. The title says it all; this book is a rich resource for helping children from elementary school through high school and beyond.

10.7: The Complex Child

Although any learning disability is a challenge for a child and his parents, some children are particularly hard to define. They have hugely uneven profiles in abilities, and their needs do not fall neatly into any one category (or even two or three). Although they clearly show areas of at least average ability, they have so many areas of weakness that others will assume they have global developmental delays (which, frankly, means that some people will assume they are mentally retarded).

Since their weaknesses often show up in social ability and communication skills, these children often receive a diagnosis of Autism Spectrum Disorder. However, some of these children are quite social, even if awkward to the point of seeming aggressive at times. A child with complex learning challenges needs the tireless efforts of parents and therapists. You should consider all of the following aspects of care:

- Evaluations need to be thorough, starting with good medical evaluations to rule out genetic, chromosomal, neurologic, or metabolic problems.
- OTs trained in sensory processing needs should assess all sensory systems.
- A nutritionist, naturopath, or biomedical doctor should assess nutritional and micro-nutrient needs.
- Cognitive, speech/language, and occupational therapy needs require thorough assessment and treatment planning.
- A psychiatrist who is well versed in pediatrics should attend to any medication needs.
- Families may wish to explore complementary and alternative therapies along with standard of care options.
- Educational advocacy is a must, as the complex child's needs are so unique that there is no program designed for their extremely uneven abilities. Parents will also have the most experience with the child, and so will be the best source of information about abilities, particularly strengths.

The outcome for complex children is unclear because the source of their disparate problems is unclear. Parents must move forward treating each weakness as thoroughly as possible and supporting all strengths with the hope that a future can be built on these skills.

Resources for More Information

Book

Quirky Kids: Understanding and Helping Your Child Who Doesn't Fit In – When to Worry and When Not to Worry by Perri Klass, MD and Eileen Costello, MD. The authors go beyond the advice of regular parenting books, to give parents of "quirky" children advice, insight, therapy suggestions, and even medication reviews.

And About Those Processing Disorders

Parents often call me for identification of a "processing disorder," usually because a teacher told them that's what their child has. *But there is no diagnosis of "slow processing disorder"!* When a teacher expresses this concern, it usually means, basically, that "Your child looks smart enough but the work is not getting done."

Slow processing speed simply means that work is not getting done fast enough. Is it because the child cannot control his attention? It is because her fine motor skills slow down her writing? Is her visual scanning so poor that she cannot read text with any efficiency? Are there a few small problems that ultimately add up to a big problem? This all must be sorted out in a good evaluation. (See Chapter 3: Evaluation: Who Does What?)

ABOUT THE AUTHOR

Robin McEvoy, PhD, is a developmental neuropsychologist and one of the editors of this book. You can find her complete bio in the back.

ELEVEN

Emotional and Behavioral Issues

by Carla Garrity, Ph.D, Nancy Gary, Psy.D, Robin McEvoy, Ph.D.

Your child may need support for emotional and behavioral issues if he is displaying any of the following symptoms:

☐ Expresses worry daily
☐ Anxious about many school activities (reading aloud, tests, homework)
☐ Expresses hopelessness
☐ Sudden decrease in school performance
☐ Loses interest in friends or favorite activities
☐ Change in sleep patterns

However, emotional regulation issues are tricky and can stem from many sources. All of the symptoms below can be seen in children with emotional or behavioral issues, but many indicate other challenges. If you check off a symptom that refers you to other chapters, you may want to read those as well.

Cross-reference guide:
SPD = Sensory Processing Disorder, Chapter 7
Bio/Nutr = Biomedical Approaches, Chapter 14; Nutrition, Chapter 15
ADD = Attention Problems and AD/HD, Chapter 4
LD = Indicates that the problem may be related to the presence of a hidden learning disorder

BEHAVIOR	SPD	Bio/Nutr	ADD	LD
Unable to control worrying		*		
Experiences constant restlessness	*		*	

BEHAVIOR	SPD	Bio/Nutr	ADD	LD
Feeling keyed up	*	*		
Constant muscle tension	*			
Can't get to sleep	*	*	*	
Can't stay asleep	*			
Overreactive to everyday sensations	*			
Easily triggered or set off (cries often and too easily, quickly irritated at small frustrations, gets angry often)	*	*		
Sad and uninterested in typical childhood activities		*		
Lacks motivation; appears lazy or not trying		*	*	
Has low energy and fatigue		*		
Shows difficulty concentrating			*	*
Overeats		*		
Shows very low self-esteem				*
Tantrums often beyond age four	*		*	
Gives up easily and often	*		*	
Very easily distracted when learning			*	*
Cannot calm self down	*	*	*	
Isolates self	*			
Considered a behavior problem at school	*		*	
Trouble making friends	*		*	

The Big Ones

If your child exhibits any of these behaviors, skip worrying about learning and focus heavily on mental health support. Look outside of this book for additional resources. Once these more urgent issues are addressed, then learning or developmental issues can be addressed.

- Hurts animals or people in planned way
- Sets fires
- Runs away or constantly threatens to do so

> - Extreme withdrawal from family and friends
> - Hears voices or sees things that are not there
> - Harms self by cutting or other self-abuse
> - Abuses alcohol and drugs
> - Dramatic weight loss

The Basics

Learning and mental health are often intertwined. Mental health issues like anxiety or depression can disrupt thinking skills, making learning extremely difficult. Likewise, learning disabilities can cause tremendous frustration and begin mimicking mental health problems. For example, a child with language delays might be prone to tantrums because he cannot express what he wants (see Chapter 5: Speech and Language Issues). The child with Sensory Processing Disorder can appear controlling and force the entire household to walk on eggshells. (For more information, read Chapter 7: Sensory Processing Disorder.)

Sorting out mental health from learning concerns can be a challenge. Determining which concern is primary can be tricky. Emotional and/or behavior problems can:

- Disrupt learning
- Co-exist with learning difficulties
- Develop as a result of coping with learning challenges

It Looks Like a Learning Disability, But It's Mental Health

As Dan's homeroom teacher, I was very worried about him during his first year of middle school. He was often late for class and usually did not have the supplies or books he needed. Once in class, he either clowned with friends or stared off into space. Little homework got done and he seemed consistently unmotivated and lackluster. When he was still failing all his core classes halfway through the school year, I asked the school counselor to contact his parents and explore the possibility that Dan might have Attention Deficit Disorder.

During the meeting, the counselor discovered that Dan's parents had recently separated and that his mother's new partner did not want Dan at their house. So Dan lived with his dad, who worked long hours, hardly ever cooked meals, and did not have the energy to enforce regular bedtimes or spend time with his son. Dan ate a lot of cereal and milk...hardly a diet likely to support consistent energy or learning. I checked his records and he'd had average grades throughout elementary school, with no significant behavior concerns, so clearly this was a recent phenomenon and not likely to be ADD.

We now think that Dan could be depressed and anxious, both because of the divorce and the inconsistency of his new living situation. Luckily, his parents agreed to find a therapist to support Dan through this time. They had not realized how much difficulty he was having while they went through their own stressful changes. He will be attending a support group at school for kids with divorced parents. We also signed him up for the school breakfast program, in addition to lunch. He seems to be calmer and happier, and is able to better function throughout the school day. We'll see how it affects his schoolwork! ~ L.M.

It Looks Like Mental Health, But It's a Learning Disability

We always knew Katie was precocious, active, and a little high strung. She walked at eight months of age, talked early, sang the alphabet at two, and breezed through her preschool years with no concerns. She loved drawing and being read to, although looking back, she was not interested in learning to read herself. She entered grade school with her usual enthusiasm for life, making friends and delighting teachers with her precocious style.

However, by third grade, Katie was considered a handful. Her emotions ran quite strong. She was giddy with her friends, but easily frustrated with schoolwork. She was still seen as very bright, but teachers were worried about her moods. Katie cried easily some days; other days she exploded, refusing to do work and throwing papers to the ground. We were told that all this emotional intensity was getting in the way of her learning. Her grades were barely average, but we were told it was her behavior that was the problem. The school social worker contacted us, concerned that Katie had an anxiety or mood disorder.

Horrified and frightened, we took Katie to a psychologist, who began trying to sort out what made her "blow." It was pure luck that one day, while playing school in therapy, he had Katie play the teacher and read to the students. Katie, universally viewed as bright and adept, crumbled as she struggled to read a first grade-level passage. It turns out it her behavior issues were not disrupting her learning; she actually had a learning disability, which caused her great anxiety and frustration. ~ L.B.

And then there's comorbidity.
Simply put, it's not that simple.

Comorbidity is when more than one condition, problem, or diagnosis is simultaneously present. It is typically a medical term, but can also be used in the fields of mental health and learning. It is quite common for children to have more than one diagnosis: Two-thirds of U.S. children with AD/HD have an additional disorder of either learning or behavior (Larson et. al. 2011).

This phenomenon presents parents and practitioners with quite a mess to sort through: The hot-tempered child, struggling in school and prone to tantrums, may have Attention Deficit Disorder as well as Sensory Processing Disorder. Digging deeper, the information may emerge that this child has had chronic nasal congestion and eczema for the last four years. Exploration of this may indicate sensitivity to milk products. All of these issues interact together, exacerbating each other. Treatment often starts by focusing on the most obvious symptoms, teaching the child strategies to manage his temper or prescribing medication to reduce attention problems. However, working with the dairy sensitivity first and supporting the sensory needs might reduce the severity of the temper and attention issues more completely, and without medication. See the biomedical or nutrition chapters (Chapters 14 and 15) to see why nutritional issues should almost always be addressed first.

Contributing Factors

Internal Conditions

Some children have to deal with personal challenges that create significant frustration or shame, and may be chronic enough to lead to issues with anxiety (including specific phobias such as social or test anxiety), depression, explosive anger, or extremely poor impulse control. Some examples include:

- Speech problems such as word finding or stuttering
- A visible disability such as use of hearing aids, glasses, assistance device, or wheelchair
- An invisible disability such as diabetes or migraine headaches
- A learning disability, which would also be invisible, but could still create overwhelming anxiety or frustration
- Medical difficulties such as muscular dystrophy, asthma, cerebral palsy, diabetes
- Sensory Processing Disorder can be a hidden culprit in many emotional issues. A nervous system that is never able to maintain a calm state can cause a child to be hyperactive and emotionally overreactive, or can swing in the other direction and create anxiety or a perpetually flat appearance. Equine-assisted sensory therapies (Chapter 7.2) can be especially calming because working with a horse can be soothing and requires steadiness. (See Chapter 7 on Sensory Processing Disorder – and be sure to read the story that precedes the chapter.)
- Nutritional issues are another common contributor. This can be an internal condition (food allergies, inability to process specific nutrients) or an external one (overreliance

on low nutrient foods and sugar). There is more and more research linking food allergies and specific nutrient deficiencies to mood destabilization. If a child is having a strong enough reaction to a particular food, it can look exactly like uncontrollable mood swings, angry outbursts, or depression-like lethargy, among other possibilities. Food dyes and additives, in particular, can have dramatic effects ranging from uncontrollable rages to mental fogginess. (See Chapter 14: Biomedical Approaches and Chapter 15: Nutritional Approaches.)

Outside Influences

Some children experience learning and mental health problems resulting from circumstances that can be altered, if parents become aware of them. Examples include:

- Being sleep deprived: chronic lack of good sleep can cause a child to look as if she has an attention disorder and irritability problems
- Being chronically hungry, having low blood sugar
- Being bullied at school
- Moving to a new home or school
- Issues within the family, such as:
  - High conflict in the family
  - Sibling issues (birth or adoption of a new sibling)
  - Divorce, a disruptive parenting schedule, or stepparent issues
  - Significant financial strain that causes chronic, extreme stress in the family or that disrupts regular meals or consistent housing

How Do You Know When You Have a Problem?

It's pretty subjective, isn't it? What parent hasn't had such a horrendous day with her child that she wonders if something is wrong? The line between just being sensitive and having an actual issue is a gray area that can take close monitoring at times.

We suggest you look at a combination of three things: severity, frequency, and age-appropriateness. Many young kids might have trouble in a noisy, crowded restaurant after a long week when they are depleted and tired. But if your child is over the age of three and you never even consider eating out because you know the drama level will eclipse everything else, you might have a real problem on your hands.

Most children go through a period of time when poor emotion control is normal; hence the "terrible twos" (and, some would argue, adolescence). However, when the terrible twos have stretched to the terrible *fives*, you should probably be concerned. Poor emotional control is considered a problem with emotion regulation.

For some children, the problems run deeper. Depression, anxiety, mood disorders, or other psychological diagnoses do occur in children. These disorders, and others, can emerge after a trauma or other trigger in a child's life, but they can also emerge without a clear cause.

Emotion Regulation Problems

This is a newer term, but we are hearing more and more about children who cannot regulate emotions.

Here's what you need to know:

- In emotion dysregulation, the child's response to many events is significantly stronger and harder to recover from than the typical range found at that age. They are too anxious, too angry, too fearful, too frustrated, or even too excited for what has just happened. When they experience these strong emotions, they find it difficult or impossible to calm themselves.
- Emotion regulation should not be a daily concern once the child has reached four to five years of age.
- An emotion regulation problem can appear as anxiety or a mood disorder. A mental health professional is needed to differentiate between these diagnoses. A common and clear difference is that in emotion dysregulation, the outburst is typically triggered by something external, such as missing too many spelling words, not understanding the math concept, feeling slighted by a friend, or even over-excitement from a birthday party. This differs from a mood disorder, which often has no obvious external event that triggered the mood change.
- Poorly controlled anger poses a significant problem for children. Angry children are often disliked and avoided by both children and adults.
- Children who explode or melt down at the slightest provocation can leave a parent anxiously protective, as any relatively minor outside issue can set off a strong reaction. The entire family often finds itself walking on eggshells.
- Girls with emotion dysregulation issues are more likely to exhibit anxiety and sadness. Boys tend to express more anger and aggression. However, either gender can swing either way.

- Children with emotion regulation problems often have related problems with sensory processing. Sometimes, poor emotional control is caused entirely by sensory overload. Other times, the two issues co-exist, each influencing the other. For more information, see Chapter 7: Sensory Processing Disorder.
- Emotion dysregulation is also typically seen in children with autism, due to the combined problems of communication disorders, atypical sensory processing, and poor social awareness. For more information, see Chapter 8: Autism Spectrum Disorders.
- In terms of treatment, family therapy focusing on parenting strategies can be just as necessary as any direct treatment of the child's needs.

Practitioners consider several diagnoses for children who have significant problems in emotion regulation. In addition to a mood disorder, a child could be identified with Oppositional Defiant Disorder, Intermittent Explosive Disorder, Attention Deficit Disorder, or Conduct Disorder. With the increase in problems with emotion regulation, the DSM-5 (the Diagnostic and Statistical Manual of Mental Disorders, 5th edition) has included a new diagnosis: Disruptive Mood Dysregulation Disorder. Realize that, for all of these diagnoses, a child must exhibit concerning behaviors on a daily basis for an extended period of time. These are not for occasional irritability.

Of course, it is important to place emotion regulation in perspective. A child may simply be immature and/or struggling with a recent trauma. These types of psychological difficulties will most likely subdue with time, support, comfort, and safety (although triggers derived from trauma warrant professional help). The following guidelines are just that: guidelines to help in understanding your child and gauging whether to seek consultation with a mental health specialist. (For more information on trauma, see the later section on PTSD.)

A child's mental health or behavioral issues can cause emotional issues throughout the family.

Johnny, at seven years of age, is a handful. He does not regulate his emotions at all. He explodes in anger several times a day, but his over-excitement when happy can be equally disruptive, as he gets hyperactive and tends to break things. His family walks on eggshells when he is home, and the school often calls for him to be picked up and taken home because of behavior problems. Johnny's father frequently gets angry with his mother, saying that she is not using appropriate discipline. His mother, stressed by Johnny's behavior, his father's displeasure, and the school problems,

Did You Know...

The National Institute of Mental Health estimates that 25 percent of adolescents will experience an anxiety disorder at some point during adolescence. Almost 6 percent will experience an anxiety disorder that would be considered severe.

has gained 30 pounds. His older brother stays locked in his room and will not bring friends over. Johnny's grades are dropping. His younger sister is beginning to throw longer tantrums. Family therapy may be advisable because at this point, everyone is struggling.

Specific Emotional Disorders

These children do not have pervasive problems with emotion regulation, but have so much difficulty in a key area that they meet the criteria for a diagnosis.

ANXIETY

Anxiety is a normal reaction to perceived stress, so some anxiety is just that: normal. A toddler will wail and reach for his mother when being left at daycare for the first time. Most children are nervous when going to the doctor and the nerves often skyrocket when they know they need to get a shot. These reactions are understandable. Another hallmark of a normal level of anxiety or stress is that the child is able to be comforted by a friend or trusted adult.

However, for some children, anxiety pervades their lives, keeps them from typical activities, and cannot be soothed. Some examples of anxiety disorders include the school-aged child who will not separate from a parent for play dates or the child who routinely cries in class when she does not understand the directions. This child may need outside help to learn to deal with her feelings.

Some of the behaviors exhibited by an anxious child include:

☐ Apprehension about many activities (e.g., reading aloud, taking a test)
☐ Inability to control worry and apprehension
☐ Constantly feeling keyed up, tense, worried something will go wrong
☐ Sleep problems: worrying so much that he can't fall asleep, or waking and worrying
☐ Being easily triggered or set off (this can show up as either anger or crying)
☐ Being particularly hard on himself (children may judge themselves as faulty because they do not see their peers as having similar struggles)
☐ Still having trouble separating from a parent for typical activities after five years of age

DEPRESSION

It is only in the last decade or so that depression in children became an area of serious consideration. The common perception was that children could not get depressed; but now it is understood that adolescents, children, and even infants can become depressed. Depression can result from different sources:

- **Situational depression.** This stems from an upsetting or traumatic situation in the family, in the life of a friend, or specific to the child.
- **Chemical imbalance depression.** This is the result of neurochemical transmitters in the brain being out of balance. Often, this type of depression has no obvious triggering event and seems to happen out of the blue. Commonly, there is a family history of depression. Some children with food allergies and hypersensitivities can also exhibit symptoms of depression. See more in the later section Treatment Options: Complementary and Alternative Medicine (CAM) or in the chapters discussing Biomedical Approaches (Chapter 14) or Nutritional Approaches (Chapter 15).

Distinguishing between these two types of depression is critical for treatment considerations and typically requires a professional, specifically a psychiatrist or psychologist. A psychiatrist who is well trained in psychopharmacology may help, as medications may be necessary for a chemical depression. However, a nutritionist or naturopath may also be useful.

Depression in children is suspected when a child:

- ☐ cries or is tearful often and without justifiable reason;
- ☐ quickly gets irritated or angry at small frustrations;
- ☐ seems sad, apathetic, or uninterested in activities that are typically pleasurable to a child of his/her age;
- ☐ lacks motivation, which may appear as being lazy or not trying;
- ☐ cannot sleep or sleeps too much;
- ☐ has low energy and fatigue;
- ☐ expresses hopelessness.

Post Traumatic Stress Disorder/Traumatic Reactions

Post-Traumatic Stress Disorder, or PTSD, is an anxiety disorder that can develop after a child is exposed to a terrifying or life-altering event or ordeal. In general, the child with PTSD can exhibit anxiety, weepiness, withdrawn behaviors, nightmares, poor sleep, and night fears. The reactions can range from appearing very withdrawn or depressed to looking extremely angry and mood disordered. Some children become hyperactive, inattentive, and downright reckless. When these symptoms persist for longer than one month after the event (by the new DSM-5 criteria), then the child might have PTSD.

Trauma is in the eye of the beholder. What did not appear to be traumatic to a caretaker may have been traumatic to the child.

Traumatized children may display a seemingly irrational or bizarre reaction (extreme disregulation) to something that is harmless. However, it holds significant meaning to the child.

- **Associated fears.** Something benign that was present at the time of the trauma may now be associated with the trauma. For example, a child who gets doused with his chocolate milk during a bad car accident might now have an anxiety attack whenever he smells chocolate milk.
- **Similar circumstances.** A reaction can also be triggered by a recent event that resembles a long-ago trauma. For example, a child reared in an institutional room with no windows may react negatively, even after adoption to a lovely home, to any room with no windows.

Not all traumatic events cause PTSD, but here are some events that may cause PTSD in children:

- Car accidents
- Death of a family member or friend
- Any event that badly scares the child
- Adoption or events that occurred prior to the adoption
- Witnessing violence or an accident

Who Can Help?

There is no shortage of people who can help with emotional issues. If you want to pursue medications, you will need to see a psychiatrist. Other than that, your choice is entirely a personal one. Do a little investigation and see what style of therapy sounds like something your child would respond to. Then meet some local practitioners who provide that, looking for one that seems like a good personal fit for your child.

TREATMENT OPTIONS: STANDARD OF CARE

First, make sure you understand the problem. Does it stem from a learning disability or attention problem? Are the attention problems secondary to an anxiety issue? Is your child defiant about homework because his sensory issues have exhausted him by the end of the day? A thorough evaluation can help you sort out contributing factors.

There are multiple approaches for counseling children. Your choice of therapist might determine the treatment direction. No single approach is necessarily better than another, but some are preferred for different ages, abilities, and diagnoses. Below are some examples of common therapies for children.

- **Individual Psychotherapy.** These sessions typically consist of a therapist meeting individually with the child. Therapy can be play-based or dialogue-based, or a combination of the two.
    - Play-based therapy uses toys, dolls, often a dollhouse, and art to explore themes and needs. The goal of the play is to work through feelings of sadness, aggression, or loss that emerges from the play. This is often a preferred approach for young children or those with limited language skills. Play therapy should be provided by someone trained in this modality; it is not just play!
    - Dialogue-based therapy involves talking about what is worrisome or problematic for the child. It is generally recommended for older children and adolescents. Older children or children who are very verbal may prefer this.
- **Cognitive Therapy.** Cognitive therapy focuses more on the practical aspects of changing both thinking and behavior. For instance, strategies might be given to control impulsiveness or overreactions. The feelings that cause the behaviors are directed in a more positive direction. The goal is to give the child confidence and a different focus.
- **Behavioral Therapy.** This form of therapy typically identifies specific behaviors that need to be changed. Feelings are not discounted, but the strategies are specific behavior goals. The family sets up reward systems and parents also learn how not

to engage with negative behaviors. Parents discover how to break cycles or patterns that sustain poor behaviors. Strategies are typically creative and fun, and often engage children's imagination. Some examples include:

- For the overly reactive child, the family might create a quiet place - not as punishment, but rather as a safe place to self-soothe and gain control.
- Anxious children may learn to place worry dolls into a pocket sewn into the pillowcase. The child tells a worry to each doll and the doll takes it away.
- Parents might sprinkle "fairy dust" on fears to neutralize them.
- For trauma and loss, concrete symbolic gestures such as releasing balloons with messages inside can help a child to move beyond trauma or loss. Behavioral therapy offers resources for specific disorders such as phobias, obsessive/compulsive behaviors, or attachment difficulties.

Psychopharmacology. Prescribing medications, when appropriate, is a critical adjunct for many children. This is covered in detail in Chapter 13: Psychiatry and Functional Medicine Psychiatry.

Family Therapy. This form of treatment can be focused on parents and a child together, or it may be purely parent-based. Often it is very practical and determines the issues in the household that are creating stress. Practical strategies are developed from there. The focus is on the family dynamic rather than on the individual child.

Group Therapy. Children dealing with certain stresses (e.g., a divorce in the family, a death, a disabled sibling, or sick parent) can benefit from participating in supervised groups where all children are dealing with the same issues.

Social Skills Groups. These are groups of children, close in age to each other, who practice social skills under the supervision of a therapist or counselor. For more information, see Chapter 12: Social Skills Issues.

Note from the Editors: Other Therapy Options

Shifting emotional response patterns, or taking the stress out of certain triggers, can be tricky with children. EMDR (Eye Movement Desensitization and Reprocessing) and brainspotting are two methods that can help without as much "talk talk talk." For more information on these and other forms of therapy, check out our website at www.childdecoded.com

Along with treating learning and mental health issues, children often require academic or social accommodations to ease frustrations or stress at school and other settings. Here are some simple accommodations that often help:

- Talk to teachers, other parents, coaches, and other caregivers about your child's needs. For example, if a child is very active, ensure that the adults in his life know to give him extra movement opportunities.
- Do not over-schedule some children. Hypersensitive children, for example, may not be able to handle a lot of after-school activities. Once the busy school day is ended, they may need some quiet time and a healthy snack.
- There are some standard academic modifications and accommodations that are typically made for students with specific learning disabilities, such as dyslexia. These can be considered for inclusion in an IEP or a 504 (see Chapter 17: Advocacy in the School System) and are important for reducing stress in the school day. For example, some children might not be penalized for poor spelling outside of spelling tests, or might be given more time for tests.

TREATMENT OPTIONS: COMPLEMENTARY AND ALTERNATIVE MEDICINE (CAM)

Some psychotherapy approaches address part of the puzzle, but not the entire dynamic of why a child is struggling. Many adjunctive therapies are useful and worth exploring in addition to psychotherapy. Many complementary therapies result in excellent outcomes, such as:

- **Chapter 16.1: Naturopathy.** This modality can provide insight on a number of levels, including nutrition and lifestyle changes, that can help your child maintain calm more effectively.
- **Chapter 16.2: Neurofeedback/Biofeedback.** Neurofeedback can help pinpoint and address the out of whack brainwave patterns that are resulting in emotional extremes.
- **Chapter 16.5: Craniosacral Therapy.** Craniosacral work is extremely soothing and can help bring your child's overall nervous system into a place of calm alertness and increased stability.
- **Art Therapy, Dance/Music Therapy.** The American Art Therapy Association defines art therapy as "using the creative process to help people of all ages improve their emotional well-being" with the "belief that the creative process involved in making art is healing and life enhancing."

> ## Buyer Beware:
> ## Controversial Treatments or Procedures
>
> Many therapeutic modalities are being integrated or even substituted for psychotherapy today. Some therapies are controversial and could even create harm rather than healing. For example, some of the "attachment therapies" can be as harsh as the child's extremely difficult behavior itself. In addition, some procedures or approaches are questionable. Be cautious with these:
>
> - Any therapy a child finds frightening
> - Any therapist who says therapy is guaranteed to be effective
> - Any therapist who asks for payment for an entire regime of therapy up front

Questions for a Prospective Mental Health Specialist

What professional degree do you hold and are you licensed or certified through the state?

- **Psychiatrist:** a physician who specializes in diagnosis, treatment, and the study of emotional disorders. They hold an MD degree and can prescribe medication. Psychiatrists are typically the most expensive. In this age of managed care, they mainly focus on medication evaluation and management; few do therapy. The majority are not trained in psychological testing, such as IQ testing.
- **Psychologist:** may hold a PhD, PsyD, or EdD. They specialize in assessment (including psychological testing) and treatment (such as therapy), but cannot prescribe medication.
- **Social Worker:** holds either an MSW or LCSW. Social workers help individuals and families around practical problems.
- **Licensed Professional Counselor:** a new degree that is earned after obtaining a MA in psychology, with a specialization in an area such as substance abuse or marital counseling.
- **Faith-based Counseling:** offered by most religious leaders. They are more likely to be trained in family counseling, grief and bereavement, and pre-or post-marital issues rather than specifically in child mental health.
- If you are concerned that your child may have a thought disorder or a severe

mood disorder, you may want to consider seeking help from a child psychiatrist who can prescribe medication. If you see some other kind of provider, be certain to ask if they have a referral list of psychiatrists with whom they work.

- What is your training and experience with children?
    - For a very specialized problem – such as international adoption, recent and severe trauma, infant issues, mutism, or autism – you need someone trained in that specific area. Ask how much experience they have working with similar children.
- What are your guidelines for confidentiality? The mental health field does not use volunteers because the assessments and treatments are held in confidence, but it is always a good idea to know exactly what the rules are with each practitioner.
- What are your fees and do you work with any insurance companies? Do you offer a sliding scale? If the professional is not on your insurance list of providers, ask if he or she would look through the list and identify those trained with children.
- Low-cost mental health treatment is difficult to find, but there are some resources you can check:
    - A local university with a graduate program; inquire whether there is a university-based clinic.
    - Your pediatrician; ask about providers who work pro bono.
    - Mental Health America, in your state; they often have a list of providers who will work on a sliding scale.

Resources for More Information

Websites

www.nimh.nih.gov, National Institute of Mental Health. NIMH offers a thorough website with descriptions of disorders, new research, and medication updates.
www.mentalhealthamerica.net, Mental Health America. This educational site provides resources for finding treatment, insurance information, and crisis intervention.

Books

Raising Your Spirited Child, by Mary Sheedy Kurcinka. This book offers validation, tools, and support for parenting the child who tackles life with gusto.

Raising a Moody Child: How to Cope with Depression and Bi-Polar, by Mary Fristad and Jill Goldberg Arnold. Moody children require an individualized and integrated approach in which parent, counselor, and physician coordinate. This book explains how to customize a plan.

Straight Talk about Psychological Testing for Kids, by Ellen Braaten and Gretchen Felopulos. Parents will understand psychological, cognitive, and learning evaluations as well as the meaning of the scores and descriptive language after reading this book.

Straight Talk about Your Child's Mental Health: What to do when Something Seems Wrong, by Stephen Faraone. The author explains distinctions between normal variations in mood, behavior, and thinking versus more serious signs of emotional distress that require professional consultation.

The Yale Child Study Center Guide to Understanding Your Child, by Linda Mayes and Donald Cohen. This book answers almost every question a parent might have from a solid developmental framework.

The Challenging Child by Stanley Greenspan, Greenspan Identifies five personality traits that distinguish children, ranging from the sensitive child to the very active child. He also provides tools for parenting children with diverse personality and temperament traits.

References

Larson, K., et al. Patterns of comorbidity, functioning, and service use for U.S. children with ADHD. *Pediatrics*, February 2011, doi: 10.1542/peds.2010-0165

About the Authors

Nancy Gary, Psy D, is a clinical psychologist in Denver, Colorado specializing in children and their families. She practices with a multi-disciplinary group and specializes in treating traumatized and abused children as well as children experiencing difficult divorces. In addition to her clinical practice, Dr. Gary consults with schools, mental health agencies, and non-profit organizations in designing preventative health and mental health programs for the emotional and physical well being of children.

Carla Garrity, PhD, is a child clinical psychologist who practiced with a multi-disciplinary group, supervised and taught at The University of Denver, and co-authored multiple books on children of divorce. She, along with colleagues, developed the *Bully Proofing Your School* intervention program, which provides strategies and skills for schools, parents, and children for creating safe, healthy, and inclusive school environments.

Robin McEvoy, PhD, is a developmental neuropsychologist and one of the editors of this book. You can find her complete bio in the back.

TWELVE

Social Skills Issues

by Kim Gangwish BA, AP, Robin McEvoy PhD, and Marijke Jones

Your child might need social skills support if you see these signs:

- ☐ He cannot make or keep friends – but only if depression, anxiety, or other contributing issues have already been identified and are being addressed.
- ☐ Teachers, coaches, or other parents have expressed concerns with your child's social behavior.
- ☐ He has expressed sadness about not being able to make friends or keep friends.
- ☐ She knows what she is supposed to do socially, but just can't seem to do it when it counts.
- ☐ You see your child is socially rejected frequently.

Social skills always seemed to be a mystery to my son Ian. As early as second grade, we noticed that he made friends fairly easily but never seemed to keep them for long. He had excellent verbal skills, but used them primarily to argue with his teachers, antagonize his peers, and throw some impressively articulate fits.

We worked hard to help him learn to control his anger and not throw tantrums. But when he reached second grade, I saw that Ian needed help with many other skills as well. He simply did not participate the way other children did and seemed confused and upset when others did not respond to him the way he wanted.

I coached him through every play date and put him in the school's social skills group. They talked about such basics as what happens when you ask someone to play and they say "no," how to wait your turn, and what different facial expressions might mean. It helped enormously for him to practice techniques over and over. I think he also learned much more willingly when all the lessons were not coming from me.

Then we found Melanie. Melanie, a girl in his second grade class, was like a little pocket social coach. She possessed a magical combination of social savvy, just enough bossiness to be authoritative, and an awe-inspiring amount of patience. "Wasn't that nice, the way Kyle shared his toys with everyone today?" she'd ask, sounding for all the world like a pint-sized nanny. "Ian, don't say that, it hurts my feelings. Say it like this…" she'd explain sweetly. Ian, charmed, always obeyed. I was quick to set up regular play dates for them.

In high school, social skills class was part of his IEP and was his absolute favorite subject! It helped that it was just another class in his schedule; he didn't need to be pulled out or singled out in any way. He and his peers could just be themselves there, discussing the things they struggled with and helping them all to become more self-aware in a safe environment.

I actually get a lot of compliments now, on what a nice young man I raised. I am always delighted and a little amazed. And I always think to myself, "If only you knew how much work that took!" ~ J.H.

The Basics

Good social skills are as critical for success and happiness as any academic or cognitive ability. In fact, social and emotional intelligence is a sometimes a better predictor of career success than IQ. Interactive skills are necessary to make friends, maintain a range of different kinds of relationships, work with others in school and at jobs, communicate effectively to get what you want, and basically get through life.

Social behavior is hardwired into our brains because connecting with others is a biological imperative. Many skills emerge naturally during the first years of life: looking people in the eyes, learning from others by watching their behavior, sensing who makes us feel safe and who doesn't. As we grow older, social situations become increasingly complex and our social skills must keep pace.

In fact, social behavior is an extremely complicated arena with fluid dynamics and subtle cues. Since so much of it is nonverbal, the majority of our social behavior is formed on a subconscious level. Most people are able to develop skills on their own. True, many of us could probably use a tune-up or reality check in one area or another. But the important distinction here is that most people are *neurologically capable* of self-awareness, self-control, and learning new behavior patterns.

For some children, however, social situations are a mystify-

Keep in Mind

Some children only have one or two close friends, and this may concern you, teachers, or other caregivers. However, this can be quite normal. If your child often wishes she had more friends, admits to being lonely, or seems fearful of unfamiliar people or groups, you might want to investigate further. If she seems content with her small circle, though, and those friendships seem healthy and positive, she may simply be one of those people who prefer the company of a select few.

ing world of ever-changing rules for which no one ever gave them a manual. Whether they are unable to read nonverbal cues, or their own deficits make them unable to control their own behavior, or anxiety or other issues skew the way their brains interpret the overall situation…they struggle daily with the conundrum of figuring out what is going on around them and how to respond to it.

These children are at a distinct disadvantage, no matter how intelligent they are. They struggle in sports, group projects, and games at recess, making their whole day a series of stressful challenges. If their difficulties are pronounced enough, they might even be ostracized or bullied, which can create tremendous emotional fallout.

Social skills training can help them learn what other children just seem to pick up. Having the skills broken down and rehearsed can be just what they need to fill in the gaps. In fact, sometimes children who have had this training become excellent social problem solvers, negotiators, and leaders. They may just need a little extra help to turn it around.

Social Skills and Learning/Behavior Disorders

Many learning and behavior disorders can impact a child's social abilities. For example:

- Children with Attention Deficit Disorder may interrupt a lot, lose track of the conversation or easily become impulsive and over-excited.
- Children with Autistic Spectrum Disorders can miss social cues, not know how to take turns in conversation or find topics that both people enjoy, or tantrum at parties when they get over-stimulated.
- Children with language deficits often cannot process others' speech quickly enough to be able to figure out how to participate in a game or group discussion.
- Children who are sensory seekers (a form of Sensory Processing Disorder) might tackle people when greeting them or hug everybody in sight.
- Anxious children may miss social cues or talk right over their partner without noticing. Alternatively, they may feel so paralyzed with anxiety that they find it difficult to participate in group conversations or class discussions.
- Some children lose social ground due to other disruptions in their lives. They will also benefit from training and support. For example:
  - A child who experiences a significant illness may be cut off from other children for an extended time, losing out on social practice with peers, though they may be great with adults.
  - A child who spent time in an orphanage in a developing country may have a

whole different set of social rules by which he lives.

- A child who experienced a head injury may need to practice impulse control and other more subtle social skills.

Although other treatments for specific disabilities are still necessary, all of these children might be able to develop needed skills as part of a social skills group. Just because they are unlikely to have these aptitudes develop naturally does not mean they are unable to learn them at all.

What Happens in Social Skills Groups

Keep in Mind

Merely practicing skills with a parent or with siblings will not necessarily resolve the problems. A child's family is accustomed to his communication style and will instinctively make allowances for him. He is also more comfortable with them and, while all practice helps, children need to learn to read others outside of their families. Practice with other children is critical. And the earlier, the better – by middle school, when social dynamics can become much more complicated and intense (not to mention less supervised), it is critical to have social skills in place.

Also, if your child has big problems with social skills, one six-week social skills group is not likely to be enough. Even a year-long group, combined with prompts at home and structured play dates, may only partially resolve issues in some kids. A child may need to participate in social skills groups over several years to cover the social challenges at each stage of development.

Children or teens, grouped by age or need, meet to learn about and practice specific skills. A trained therapist (or sometimes two) runs the sessions. Some groups discuss and practice general social skills; others identify specific goals for each child and help them all practice what they most need to learn. The groups allow for practice with the other kids – not just with an understanding adult.

Although this may seem contrived, children gain confidence by having the underlying dynamics and response choices spelled out for them. When they have the chance to practice different behavior options, they become more comfortable applying those lessons in real life. Presenting these kinds of strategies slowly, in a safe group and in isolation from the other considerations of life, greatly increases a child's chances of mastering social abilities.

Who Can Help?

Psychologists, social workers, licensed professional counselors, and other professionals in the mental health or educational field are possible providers of social skills groups. As always, look for a leader who has experience with the kinds of issues your child has.

You have many avenues for finding groups in your area:

- Many schools offer social skills groups (often called *friendship groups*), so you may want to start by asking at your school. If there isn't one, you can ask them to start one. This is a common program; even if they only have a few students who could benefit from it, schools are often willing to set one up. You can also ask if there are any groups or programs in the district that might be relevant.
- Depending on a child's needs or diagnosis, you might look for support groups in your area for children with similar issues (such as AD/HD, autism, anxiety, nonverbal learning disorders, and so on). Start by contacting national organizations for these issues and asking for local resources.
- Your pediatrician may be aware of psychologists, social workers, or other therapists in your area who offer social skills groups.

Questions for a Prospective Social Skills Therapist

- What is the scope of your clinical practice?
- What is your training in running social skills workshops?
- Do you have a field of expertise within your social skills work?
- What specific social skills needs are addressed in this class?
- How is the group structured? (i.e., role playing, activity-based, supervised free play, etc.)
- Do you think my child is compatible with this particular group of children? (If there are eight hyperactive boys and you have a shy little girl, it might not be the best fit.)
- How do you handle conflict in the group?

Resources for More Information

WEBSITE

www.socialthinking.com. This website offers a wide variety of resources on understanding and teaching social skills, including articles; books; products; and information on conferences, clinics, and professionals.

Books

The Unwritten Rules of Social Relationships: Decoding Social Mysteries through the Unique Perspectives of Autism by Dr. Temple Grandin and Sean Barron. Written by two people on the autism spectrum, this is a fascinating and thought-provoking account of their very different journeys in their quest to understand and display appropriate social behavior.

Diary of a Social Detective: Real-Life Tales of Mystery, Intrigue and Interpersonal Adventure by Jeffrey E. Jessum, PhD. Written as a child-friendly story, Dr. Jessum's protagonist eases children through a number of tricky (to him) social situations with heart and fun. It's an excellent guide for children struggling to understand the mysteries of social interactions.

About the Authors

Kim Gangwish, Marijke Jones and Robin McEvoy, Ph.D, *are the editors of this book. Their bios can be found in the back.*

General Resources

Each chapter lists resources that pertain to that particular topic. Here are a few books that give a nice overview of the brain, its abilities to adapt and heal, and ways parents can help their children through whole-brain approaches.

- *The Brain that Changes: Stories of Personal Triumph from the Frontiers of Brain Science* by Norman Doidge. This game-changing book introduces the concept of the brain's neuroplasticity and gives numerous stories illustrating how scientists have tapped into this remarkable feature to transform lives.
- *The Brain's Way of Healing: Remarkable Discoveries and Recoveries from the Frontiers of Neuroplasticity* by Norman Doidge. Dr. Doidge goes into more detail showing how noninvasive approaches stimulate the brain's ability to heal itself. Includes many stories from veterans; brain injury survivors; and people with chronic pain, dementia, and learning disorders.
- *The Whole-Brain Child: 12 Revolutionary Strategies to Nurture Your Child's Developing Mind,* by Daniel Siegel, MD, and Tina Payne Bryson, PhD. The authors explain some of the issues affecting young, developing brains and offer practical parenting strategies that apply this knowledge, appeal to the abilities a certain age *does* offer, and encourage appropriate brain integration.
- *No-Drama Discipline: The Whole-Brain Way to Calm the Chaos and Nurture Your Child's Developing Mind,* by Daniel Siegel, MD, and Tina Payne Bryson, PhD. Building on the principles they explained in their first book, *The Whole Brain Child,* Siegel and Bryson offer techniques and strategies for discipline that combine common sense, brain science, and a modern-day understanding of developmental stages.
- *Reset Your Child's Brain: A Four-Week Plan to End Meltdowns, Raise Grades, and Boost Social Skills by Reversing the Effects of Electronic Screen-Time,* by Victoria Dunckley, MD. Dr. Dunckley, integrative child psychiatrist and expert on technology addiction, shares the results of her research about the considerable negative effects of screen-time on children's developing nervous systems. She also lays out a practical plan for getting children off of their devices.

Section Three

DIGGING DEEP: BROADER SOLUTIONS

———◆———

WHILE EVERY CHAPTER IN THE PREVIOUS SECTION suggests specialists for that specific disorder, this section discusses strategies that could potentially affect any disorder on a more foundational level. Biomedical doctors have been around for decades, but are only now gaining visibility; their protocols are designed to identify underlying reasons for brain chemistry imbalances and other sources of poor health. Psychiatric solutions may help children who are facing any number of struggles. Like biomedicine, the Functional Medicine approach to psychiatry looks for the deeper problems that might be causing or worsening symptoms. The nutrition chapter is packed with information on how targeted nutritional approaches can make a huge difference. We urge all parents to read the chapters on biomedical approaches and nutritional approaches; the information and tips there might help the whole family.

———◆———

THIRTEEN

Psychiatry and Functional Medicine Psychiatry

by Mary Braud, MD.

Sometimes medication does the trick:

My son John attended an exclusive, academically rigorous private high school. His father had attended it and John was thrilled to be following in his dad's footsteps, but the teachers weren't seeing that. They were starting to question whether this was the best place for him. His schoolwork was mediocre at best, but the real problem was how he behaved in class: the slouch, the bored expression, the minimal participation. He was always confused about why everyone was so upset – after all, he wasn't disruptive or rude, and he did (mostly) get his work done.

He did not seem to be able to see, control, or change his behavior. I began to realize that his actions were not just due to an advanced case of adolescence, as I had assumed. We brought him in for a neuropsychological evaluation and the evaluator identified him as "ADD without hyperactivity," which explained why he seemed half asleep all the time.

We knew he had allergies, and I had read that this can create some of the behaviors we were seeing. But even our doctor's recommendation that he be tested and pursue an elimination diet could not convince John to do it. I knew he'd never follow a strict diet; it's almost impossible to impose something like that on a teenager! The doctor's next recommendation was medication.

The change was immediate. We always liked our son, of course, but now we could really enjoy him. He suddenly became so much more involved with conversations and daily activities. And when I ask him to do something like mow the lawn, I no longer have to nag, nag, nag, and then finally yell about it. He just gets up and does it! His grades and demeanor improved, the teachers stopped suggesting he find another school, and most importantly, he has seemed happier and more engaged in his own life. ~ J.N.

Sometimes, there are other solutions:

My son Alex was a handful. He had already had extensive therapy for Sensory Processing

Disorder and some reading issues, which had helped him stay focused in school and cope with the work. But it hadn't touched the mood swings. Alex would melt down completely at the slightest provocation – crying, screaming, and throwing dramatic tantrums. It was hard for everyone, especially Alex. I was frantic because he had begun to say things like, "my life is stupid and I don't want to live any more."

In desperation, I began researching possibilities. We preferred not to pursue medication first, as I had seen many families go through hell trying that route and I believed there were avenues worth exploring first. There was, to my surprise, a great deal of research linking food allergies with skewed brain chemistry. Our doctor agreed to test Alex for food allergies and sensitivities.

He tested positive for casein, a milk protein. The results, once all forms of casein were removed from his diet, were immediate and dramatic. No more tantrums. The family no longer has to walk on eggshells around him, an exercise that had become an exhausting part of our daily routine. Alex became, almost overnight, a normal, happy, well-adjusted kid. I now know many families who have had mixed results with diet adjustments like this – sometimes it takes months to see results – but for us it was truly a miracle! ~ C.C.

The Basics

For a parent, few things are as painful as watching your child suffer: seeing him so inattentive that he cannot learn and hates school; finding out that he has so little control over his emotions that he is no longer welcome in friends' houses; having him come home crying, "I hate being alive." Life feels grim and overwhelming when everything is this much of a struggle. If your child has major difficulty managing his emotions, behavior, or focus, a psychiatrist may be able to help.

Most families seek my help in order to get their child a diagnosis and prescription. The issues are usually fairly serious, such as:

- Frequent aggressive outbursts; inabiilty to control behavior
- Unusually destructive and dangerous behavior
- Self-harm
- Extreme difficulty concentrating
- Extremely impulsive behavior
- Anxiety or depression that interferes with normal learning or social behavior
- Suicidal behavior

These symptoms may reflect a chronic imbalance in brain chemistry that can be corrected through medication. Sometimes, medication will be a lifelong regimen that significantly improves the child's quality of life. Sometimes though, medication is only a short-term solution, with other factors being identified as time goes on. As we will explore in this chapter, even if medication seems to solve your child's problems in the short term, there are many things you need to be aware of to ensure that it an effective solution in the long term.

Who Can Help:
Psychiatrist versus Psychologist

Both psychologists and psychiatrists can perform diagnostic evaluations and treat with psychotherapy. However, they differ in training and the range of services that they can offer their patients.

Psychiatrists

- have a medical or osteopathic degree;
- get at least five years of training in mental health after completing medical school;
- can prescribe psychiatric medication, order and interpret laboratory tests, and order brain imaging studies.

Some psychiatrists offer ongoing therapy, but most specialize in diagnosing conditions and prescribing medications. They often work as part of a team that the family has assembled. An array of specialists may work with the child on an ongoing basis, with the psychiatrist checking in periodically to make sure that the original medication is still appropriate.

Psychologists

- hold a PhD in psychology and have passed the board exam;
- can offer diagnostic evaluations and ongoing therapy;
- are trained to recognize the need for psychiatric medications, but cannot prescribe them (except in New Mexico and Louisiana).

No matter which one you choose to examine your child, you should make sure that he or she specializes in treating children and adolescents, and has experience in the types of issues your child exhibits.

Getting a Diagnosis

PART ONE: PSYCHIATRIC EVALUATION

Doctors have different approaches, but most will do some or all of the following when trying to reach a diagnosis:

- Review records from prior assessments and past treatments from any other health-care professionals. The doctor should review details about the child's medical, psychiatric, and psychosocial history.
- Administer assessments, filled out before the evaluation, from family members, the current therapist(s), other health care professionals, and (if appropriate) the child. We usually use rating scales to assess the severity of various symptoms.
- Interview the parents. The child may be present, but this is often unrealistic. (Younger children may have difficulty sitting still while the adults talk; teens and older children don't usually like watching others discuss their problems.) The psychiatrist should gather information from parents about their current concerns, as well as details about the child's history and current functioning at home, school, and with friends. This includes information about their daily habits like sleep, energy levels, and appetite.
- Interview or have a play session with the child, if age-appropriate.

A complete evaluation may require more than one session, especially if the child is not included during the parent interview. I often find it helpful to conduct telephone interviews with other healthcare professionals who have been involved, in addition to reading their assessments.

PART TWO: FINDING THE RIGHT DIAGNOSIS

After doing an evaluation, a psychiatrist will consult the DSM, or Diagnostic and Statistical Manual of Mental Disorders, in order to make his diagnosis of your child. The DSM (in its fifth edition as of this writing) is the standard diagnostic tool used by mental health professionals worldwide to provide consistent diagnoses. This manual contains lists of symptoms, as well as descriptions of severity or duration of these symptoms, that have been organized into various categories such as diagnoses given during childhood, mood disorders, substance abuse disorders, and psychotic disorders.

Conditions whose symptoms begin in childhood include the following:

- Attention Deficit Disorder (with and without Hyperactivity)
- Autism Spectrum Disorders, including Asperger's Syndrome
- Tourette Syndrome
- Oppositional Defiant Disorder

While these diagnoses can also be applied to adults, this is done only when there is evidence the problems began earlier in life.

Mood disorders can include these diagnoses:

- Major Depression
- Dysthymia (chronic low-grade depression)
- Bipolar Disorder
- Cyclothymia (a less severe form of mood swings)

Psychotic disorders do not often appear in children, though childhood-onset schizophrenia is thought to occur in a small percentage of children.

Other diagnoses require specific assessments that are usually conducted by other specialists, including neuropsychologists. Such diagnoses include mental retardation and particular kinds of learning and processing disorders.

There are other benefits to getting a diagnosis besides the clarity it might bring. Your child may qualify for special considerations in school, including tutors, classroom accommodations, TAG (talented and gifted), or special education status. It might also be easier to explain her behavior to coaches and other caregivers, so that they might be more likely to respond with compassion rather than frustration.

Food for Thought

Some children display a combination of symptoms that defies the diagnostic categories in the DSM. (In fact, this might actually be more the norm than the exception.) For this reason, it may be most effective to consult more than one type of practitioner and have them work as a team. I often collaborate with other specialists in order to get different perspectives and to stay on top of the child's progress in other arenas.

THE TRICK TO PRESCRIBING MEDS

Here I must give a little warning about what you can expect from a psychiatrist. It's natural for parents to want clear-cut answers. Many parents come to me wanting a diagnosis and (often) medication; and they want it to solve everything. They want me to figure out the problem and address it once and for all, so that all members of the family can move on and live their lives. I completely sympathize.

However, as I tell families every week, sometimes it's just not that simple. Mental health diagnosis is an inexact science. It's not like strep throat. We can't swab your child's throat or take a blood sample, then run it through a lab and discover, beyond a shadow of a doubt, "Ah yes. Your child has X, Y, or Z." We do extremely thorough assessments – and then, much as I hate to put it this way, we make our best guess (using our education, experience, and trusty DSM as a resource; but still, it is an estimate). Sometimes we end up revisiting this step.

Then we may prescribe medication. Perhaps this is the "Hallelujah moment" you were hoping for. However, you should know that this is often just the start of our journey together. Prescribing and monitoring medication is an art. You hope that it will do what it's supposed to, liberating your child from his struggles and freeing you from worry. It may. But it may take awhile to get there.

Vigilance is crucial after prescribing a medication. There is no way to know for sure which drug, or which dosage, will get the best response. One person may respond beautifully to one med, while another feels no change at all until trying a different brand altogether. Doctors have no alternative except to keep trying until something works.

And just to make things more interesting, once we find that perfect drug and perfect dosage, both might change later on! Children and teens are particularly tricky, since their physiology is still developing and can be a little unpredictable. Some might need a fraction of the recommended dosage; others may need three times the usual amount. Moreover, since children and teens are still changing so rapidly, their brain chemistry is still shifting and we may need to make adjustments on a regular basis. Sudden negative reactions are not uncommon; in fact, that is often what alerts parents to the need for an adjustment.

There are many factors to consider, and therefore a great number of possible approaches. At times, I must prescribe more than one med at a time. Occasionally, symptoms are severe but inconclusive; then I might prescribe something merely to reduce symptoms and make life manageable. In these situations, I like to work with the family over time in order to find a more meaningful diagnosis and approach.

If the family is pursuing other forms of therapy, there may be significant changes in brain chemistry from that. I have seen major shifts from sensory integration therapy, for example; as the nervous system learns to cope with everyday sensory input, the constant anxiety the child was experiencing can finally relax. For this reason, it is important for the psychiatrist to stay on top of how concurrent therapies are going.

A final note to consider: Not all psychiatric-looking symptoms are really psychiatric territory. As in the example of PANDAS (see box), many factors might contribute to a child's condition, including ones that you never saw coming. Since I am a Functional Medicine psychiatrist (more on that later), I prefer to look closely at all possible factors and do a bit of detective work to discover the true root of the problem. If the family is open to this, we can often get more lasting, and medication-free, results.

Psychiatric or Medical?

What would you do with a child who suddenly wakes up unable to step on carpeting, or who must kiss every doorjamb ten times before passing through it? Have him treated for obsessive-compulsive disorder, right?

Maybe not. Evidence continues to emerge that Pediatric Autoimmune Neuropsychiatric Disorder Associated with Streptococcal infections (PANDAS Syndrome) can result in sudden onset of severe obsessive-compulsive behaviors. This means that if your child has had a strep infection (even if she was asymptomatic), it could have resulted in what looks like OCD. If she didn't respond to OCD meds, antibiotics may do the trick.

TAKING OTHER FACTORS INTO ACCOUNT

Keep in mind that a child whose mind works a little differently may be stressed by a number of environmental factors, and that medication can only resolve so much.

Say, for example, that you have one of those kids who thinks best while in motion, and who learns best when physically interacting with her environment. (This perfectly valid learning style is often misdiagnosed as ADHD.) But she is currently in a traditional classroom where she must sit still and absorb information in silence. You may have brought her to me for anxiety issues, and medication may help somewhat. However, she's still in the wrong classroom. There is no drug in the world that will resolve the daily stress engendered by that mismatch. She may be calmer now, but that doesn't mean she's learning. Ultimately, that fact will increase her anxiety once again, until the true issue is addressed.

Consider talking to a psychiatrist, learning specialist, or other practitioner who will help you get a complete overview of what's happening. Assess all the factors in your child's life that may be contributing to her stress level, including classroom setting, home environment, or social difficulties. It is possible that medication is only a tiny piece of your answer.

Standard of Care: A Quick Overview of Medications

The categories of medications that are prescribed to young people are essentially the same as those given to adults. Drugs for learning and behavior issues include:

- **Stimulants:** Ritalin (methylphenidate) and Adderall (dextroamphetamine), commonly used to treat Attention Deficit Disorder
- **Non-stimulant attention support medications:** Straterra
- **Alpha-adrenergic agents:** Catapress (clonidine), used to treat Attention Deficit Disorder with impulsivity and/or irritability; also used for Tourette Syndrome
- **Antidepressants:** Prozac (fluoxetine), Zoloft (sertraline), and others, used to treat mood regulation problems and anxiety
- **Antipsychotic medications:** Risperdal, Seroquel, Zyprexa, and Abilify, used for children with mood disorder or extremely disorganized thinking or behavior

NOTE: While these medications are frequently given to children, many of the medications used to treat mood or psychosis have not been studied regarding their effectiveness or safety for pediatric use.

MEDICATION CREEP AND CLIMBING DOSAGES

It is quite common for psychiatrists to adjust prescriptions at first. As previously discussed, finding the right medication(s) and dosages can be a matter of trial and error. However, if you find over time that a doctor's response to continued symptoms is always to increase the dosage, or if he has tried a number of different medications at once with minimal improvement, you may wish to get a second opinion. *Medication creep*, or combining different medications, can be especially problematic since drug combinations are rarely studied.

If your child is showing any of the following symptoms, it may be time to question his current drug regimen:

- ☐ Seems overly sedated, dull, less responsive emotionally
- ☐ Seems to need more sleep than necessary; falls asleep easily during the day
- ☐ Has more trouble concentrating or following what people say
- ☐ Just doesn't seem like himself, in a way that concerns you (this may seem vague, but it often comes down to this!)

Do Psychiatrists Always Prescribe Medications?

Usually, but not always. The majority of psychiatrists do prescribe medications based on the results of their evaluations. However, there are some psychiatrists who prefer not to prescribe medications as their primary mode of practice. Some prefer to offer ongoing therapy support, and a growing number offer a Functional Medicine approach.

Functional Medicine

Another option for treating your child is to find a psychiatrist who practices Functional Medicine, or FM. Functional Medicine is an approach to Western medicine that emphasizes the correction of underlying forces over the use of medication. Although other types of practitioners (nutritionists, nurse practitioners, etc.) can train in this model, FM doctors and psychiatrists are full-fledged physicians who have an MD degree and have then gone on to do additional FM coursework. For a more detailed discussion of the principles and practices of Functional Medicine, see the upcoming section: "The Functional Medicine Approach in Practice." Chapter 14: Biomedical Approaches and Chapter 15: Nutritional Approaches also contain information that will help you understand this model more fully.

I have been a Functional Medicine practitioner since 2006. I got into it because I was impressed with the results I saw, and because my patients were often frustrated by the side effects of medications. I sought out other options and was delighted to discover FM.

FM treatments are inherently individualized, which I have found to be the key to truly addressing underlying issues. Resolving symptoms on a deeper level can lead to greater overall health and happiness. While medication can be helpful, even life-saving, I believe that *only* suppressing symp-

Parent's Perspective

Unfortunately, both my children had learning or behavior disorders and we went the med route first. My son, who was diagnosed with ADD, said he could concentrate better but became so jittery that he refused to continue taking his medication after a few months ("Geez," he said, "It's like I always just drank eight cups of coffee!" I don't understand how being that jittery corresponds with concentrating better, but what do I know?)

My daughter was the one who really scared us, though: After treating her extreme social anxiety with some heavy-hitting meds, she became even more withdrawn, paranoid, and slightly hallucinatory. Getting her off of those drugs was slow and difficult. I know people whose children have done fine on meds, but I am extremely leery, now, of using medications for anything.

toms will ultimately result in having the underlying imbalance worsen and show up in some other way. In addition, the side effects of medications can increase over time, leading to complications that often need to be treated with more medications…leading to a cycle that will further degrade health. It is my belief that Functional Medicine represents the next shift in medicine. Quite simply, it makes sense and, in my experience, gets better results.

Functional Medicine is attracting increasing interest. Doctors of all specialties, including psychiatry, train in this approach. FM addresses chronic disease and psychiatric conditions by focusing on underlying causes rather than symptoms.

Food for Thought: Why Not Meds?

I am not anti-medication. I have seen it transform many lives. Even if someone has pursued other approaches and gotten good results, his brain chemistry can still tend to lean one way or another and may need a little help remaining stable. It is truly a miracle of modern medicine that we have the means to do this.

But, as a conscientious practitioner, I have to say that I have seen meds create problems as well. Many of my pediatric patients feel relief from the targeted symptom, but become so overwhelmed by the side effects that they ultimately decide to seek other solutions (see the *Parent's Perspective* inset).

About 40 percent of my patients currently choose medications to address their issues. About 60 percent prefer the FM approach – or at least use it in conjunction with their meds. This gives me the unique perspective of seeing, first-hand on a daily basis, the contrast between the two approaches.

I understand the relief of watching a child go from emotional chaos to calm, quiet ease. It can change what is possible for that child as well as his whole family. But is he really happy? I see a lot of ADHD kids get quieter on meds, and it is wonderful for all involved. If you look more closely, though, you will see that a lot of these children do not seem all that much happier – *nor are they learning better*. Parents often report that their children "just don't seem like themselves." They have become compliant and much easier to deal with, but is that really the most they can hope for?

In contrast, the children who work with me as I look for the true internal triggers become healthier and happier over time. I feel that I am helping them to optimize their health and cultivate lifelong vitality. When we find and correct a child's underlying imbalances, her whole system becomes stronger and she feels more fully in control of her own mind and emotions. It really is possible to address these issues in a healthy, non-medicated fashion. I see proof of this every day!

The Functional Medicine Approach in Practice

In FM, therefore, there is no standard protocol for treating conditions such as ADD, anxiety issues, or mood disorders. Each child must be assessed individually to see how *his* biological systems are interacting in a dysfunctional way. While pharmaceutical medications may be used in the short term to provide relief, the goal of an FM psychiatrist is to find the root of the problem and lead the patient into a state of sustainable, non-medicated health. I believe that, whenever it is possible to resolve a health issue without using meds, the child experiences a greater sense of clarity, well-being, and full emotional expression than he would have with medications alone.

This approach can take more time than simply prescribing a med and sending you on your way (although, as previously discussed, it is often not that straightforward). Because the human body is so complicated, it may take some time to uncover all the issues that lead to serious psychiatric symptoms. Diet changes, for example, can take a few weeks or months to show full results, although I have often seen dramatic results in a few days when a child stops consuming a major allergen. Also, clearing one layer of dysfunction may reduce some symptoms, while revealing yet another problem in another system. It is a complex process, not all of which will be apparent from the beginning.

The following sections give more detailed examples of the differences between Western medicine standard of care and FM.

AD/HD and Depression/Anxiety Disorders

Two of the most common diagnoses psychiatrists give are for AD/HD and depression/anxiety disorders. Although this book has chapters that discuss these conditions in more detail, this section examines the most common approaches psychiatrists would use to address them. The charts in this section present information on both Western standard of care and Functional Medicine approaches.

AD/HD: Western Standard of Care

We believe that the symptoms of inattention, hyperactivity, and impulsivity are due to differences in the activity of certain brain chemicals. These brain chemicals, or neurotransmitters, are called dopamine and norepinephrine. The medications used to treat AD/HD are thought to increase the activity or signaling of these chemical messengers. The first medications used were stimulants. Early versions lasted only four to six hours. Newer forms last eight to twelve hours and eliminate the need for doses during the day.

Generic Drug	Brand Name	Action
methylphenidate	Ritalin, Ritalin LA, Focalin, Focalin LA, Concerta	central nervous system stimulant
dextroamphetamine	Dexedrine, Dexedrine IR	central nervous system stimulant
mixed amphetamine salts	Adderall, Adderall XR	central nervous system stimulant
lisdexamfetamine	Vyvanse	central nervous system stimulant
atomoxetine	Strattera	selective norepinephrine reuptake inhibitors

The most common side effects of these medications are:

- Headache
- Nausea
- Stomachache
- Loss of appetite/weight loss
- Slower growth

Other possible, but less common, side effects include the following:

- A very dramatic response with respect to activity level - the child may become extremely slow, almost lethargic. This would be more likely to happen if the dose is too high, but can occur even if the dosing is within ranges that are considered safe and effective.
- Hallucinations - these can involve seeing or hearing things that are not real or feeling that something is crawling on or under the skin.
- Sudden heart arrythymia - the Food and Drug Administration uses its most strident warning, known as a *black box warning*, regarding the use of certain medications in children due to the possibility of this life-threatening side effect.

AD/HD: Functional Medicine Approach

When I have a child who is having trouble with attention and hyperactivity, I do much more than assess his performance in these areas. I also explore several biomedical areas that are known to influence attention and activity level, such as:

Just So You Know

As with side effects to medication, there are some things to be aware of when using Functional Medicine treatments:

- Heavy metal toxicity treatment can be temporarily debilitating and requires an experienced practitioner. (See box on Chelation.)
- Use of nutritional supplements should *not* be self-guided by parents.
- It is common to experience temporary worsening of behavioral symptoms or gastric distress during a die-off of yeast in the GI tract.
- Nutritional treatment can work slowly; it should therefore not be the only approach used when a patient has severe needs.

- **Nutrient deficiencies, particularly zinc, iron, magnesium, and essential fatty acids.** Chronic deficiencies in these elements have been shown to contribute to ADD symptoms. (See Oner, O; Oner, et al, 2010 or Akhondzadeh , Mohammadi et al, 2004 for examples of current research.)
- **Heavy metal overload.** Lead or mercury, for example, can contribute to a range of behavioral problems that are often not consistent across children. This can make it difficult to pinpoint the cause. (See Sciarillo, W.G., Alexander, W.G., Farrell, K.P. 1992 for an example.)
- **Sensitivities/allergies to common food.** Gluten or dairy sensitivities, for example, can wreak havoc with some people's brain chemistry. I have had many patients whose symptoms resolved after addressing this problem alone.
- **Problems with digestion, including overgrowth of undesirable bacteria and/or yeast (Candida).** Digestive problems often translate directly into brain chemistry problems. Please see Chapter 14: Biomedical Approaches and Chapter 15: Nutritional Approaches, for further discussion.
- **Low dopamine levels are associated with AD/HD symptoms.** It is possible to adjust dopamine levels without medication by using amino acids supplementation.

These assessments are done using a variety of lab tests on blood, urine, saliva, or hair samples. (For a review of the literature for CAM treatments for AD/HD, see Pellow J, Solomon EM, Barnard CN 2011)

Depression and Anxiety: Western Standard of Care

Physicians use antidepressants to treat both depression and anxiety disorders. The most common medications for children and adolescents are the selective serotonin re-uptake inhibitors (SSRIs). These medications are thought to improve symptoms by increasing the activity of the neurotransmitter serotonin, among other effects.

Generic Drug	Brand Name	Action
Fluoxetine	Prozac	SSRI
Sertraline	Zoloft	SSRI
Paroxetine	Paxil	SSRI
Fluvoxmine	Luvox	SSRI
Citalopram	Celexa	SSRI
Escitalopram	Lexapro	SSRI

Common side effects:

- Headache
- Anxiety
- Insomnia
- Nausea

Health Watch

Another serious, controversial, and fortunately rare side effect is the appearance or worsening of suicidal thoughts. The Food and Drug Administration uses its most strident warning, known as a *black box warning*, regarding the use of these medications in children, due to the possibility of this life-threatening side effect.

Depression and Anxiety: Functional Medicine Approach

Anxiety or depression in a child is a signal that the child's neurology is not in order. This may indicate inflammation in the brain. Just as the body reacts negatively to infections, toxins, or other challenges, the brain also reacts by not working as well. If I have a child exhibiting depression or anxiety, I will screen for the following imbalances:

- **Nutrient deficiencies, particularly magnesium and zinc as well as omega-3 fatty acids.** These have been shown to relate to depression and anxiety.
- **Heavy metal overload.** Lead and mercury are associated with anxiety, depression, and behavioral disorders.
- **Sensitivities/allergies to common foods.** As previously mentioned, food reactions

of any severity can disrupt brain chemistry, making a child more irritable or emotionally fragile in general, or contributing to mental fogginess.

- **Problems with digestion including overgrowth of undesirable bacteria and/or yeast (Candida).** As with AD/HD, digestive problems can directly cause complications with brain chemistry.
- **Imbalance or lack of amino acids.** These are important for neurotransmitter production, such as seratonin or dopamine. Adjusting neurotransmitters is what most depression/anxiety medications are trying to do anyway. It is quite possible to affect change in a gentler, more lasting way.

The above assessments are done using a variety of lab tests on blood, urine, saliva, or hair samples.

Who Can Help?

Finding a Psychiatrist

You can usually locate a psychiatrist by contacting your medical insurance provider and asking who is covered in your area. Shop around! Meet with different practitioners (most will do a 15-minute meet-and-greet with prospective clients). You and your child will get a sense of who you best connect with and which philosophy is most compatible with your needs.

It can also be extremely useful to discuss these issues with your child's pediatrician or family practitioner. They will likely know of psychiatrists who work with children, are in the area, and have experience with your particular concerns.

If you do not have insurance or a primary care physician, you can contact your local mental health organization. You can also ask around at your child's school or talk to parents you know from other activities. Word of mouth can be an invaluable resource.

Finding a Functional Medicine Psychiatrist

Although the number of FM practitioners is growing, there might not be one near you at this time. You can find a practitioner directory on the Functional Medicine website (see the resources section at the end of the chapter). This directory indicates the specialty of each practitioner.

For mild symptoms, an FM-trained pediatric or family doctor may be able to help you as well. Be sure to ask how much FM training he has received, as this can vary. Also ask how much experience he has with psychiatric symptoms similar to your child's. However, if your child is exhibiting severe psychiatric symptoms, it would probably be best to find a Functional Medicine practitioner who specializes in psychiatry.

If the nearest practitioner is not within easy traveling distance, it might be possible to do a one-time assessment in person and then work primarily over the telephone. Whether or not you will be able to work this way depends on the practitioner and the laws in your state.

If you want to discuss Functional Medicine with your current health practitioner, you may need to be prepared for some blank looks or even skepticism. However, FM is not so much controversial as it is not well known at this time. Rest assured that it is firmly grounded in science and Western medicine, has demonstrated consistent positive results, and that FM practitioners have gone through the same medical and psychiatric training as their more traditional counterparts.

Final Note

There are some exciting developments in pediatric psychiatry these days. Practitioners are increasingly exploring other avenues besides medication-dependent treatment. Clinics are popping up where psychiatrists work in conjunction with other kinds of practitioners to provide coordinated care. Some psychiatrists, even if not FM-trained, are exploring nutrition as a support for rebuilding brain chemistry. Others prefer to focus on therapeutic approaches that help children recognize and manage their triggers, empowering them to take control over their own lives and emotional health. In all cases, medication is a possibility if the child needs it. However, it is not seen as the only answer.

Educate yourself. Talk to the psychiatric professionals in your area. Ask them what their philosophy is and what the treatment options are. You may be pleasantly surprised by the range of possibilities that exists. And, although at first the choices may feel overwhelming, ultimately you will be better able to choose an option that works best for your child and your family.

Suggested Questions for a Potential Psychiatrist:

- What is your background and training?
- Do you commonly work with children and adolescents?
- What are the primary disorders that you treat?
- What are your approaches to evaluation and treatment?
- Do you provide therapy or do you primarily work with a medication model?
- Do you work with a team of providers outside of your scope of practice?

ᕦ Do you consider learning disabilities in your assessment process?

ᕦ Do you incorporate any Functional Medicine or integrated medicine in your approach? If not, are you open to a patient using such approaches while also working with you?

Resources for More Information

WEBSITES

www.nami.org, National Alliance on Mental Illness. This is a national advocacy group that offers a variety of resources for parents.

www.parentcenterhub.org/repository/mentalhealth/, Center for Parent Information and Resources. The center covers mental health along with a wide range of children's disabilties.

www.aacap.org, American Academy of Child and Adolescent Psychiatry (AACAP). AACAP's website gives information on child and adolescent psychiatry, fact sheets for parents and caregivers, current research, practice guidelines, and managed care information, among other things.

www.healthychildren.org/English/health-issues/conditions/emotional-problems/Pages/default.aspx, American Academy of Pediatrics (AAP). AAP has created the family-friendly site called Healthy Children, where you can find a wealth of information about emotional problems in children.

www.ffcmh.org/chapters, National Federation of Families for Children's Mental Health. The Federation, a family-run organization, offers a wealth of information, including its state and local chapters.

REFERENCES

Akhondzadeh, S., M. R. Mohammadi, M. Khademi. Zinc sulfate as an adjunct to methylphenidate for the treatment of attention deficit hyperactivity disorder in children: A double blind and randomized trial. *BMC Psychiatry* 4 (9) (2004).

Oner, O.; P. Oner, O. H. Bozkurt, E. Odabas, N. Keser, H. Karadag, M. Kizilgun. Effects of zinc and ferritin levels on parent and teacher reported symptom scores in Attention Deficit Hyperactivity Disorder. *Child Psychiatry and Human Development* 41(4) (August 2010): 441-47.

Pellow, J., E. M. Solomon, C. N. Barnard. Complementary and alternative medical therapies for children with attention-deficit/hyperactivity disorder (ADHD). *Altern Med Rev* 16 (4) (December 2011): 323-37.

Sciarillo, W. G., W. G. Alexander, K. P. Farrell. Lead exposure and child behavior. *American Journal of Public Health* 82 (10) (October 1992): 1356-60.

About the Author

Mary Braud, MD, graduated from Louisiana State University Medical School in 1989. She completed residency training in pediatrics and later in psychiatry, including a fellowship in child and adolescent psychiatry. After working at a community mental health center for several years, Dr. Braud began her private practice in Denver, Colorado. She works with children, adolescents, and adults utilizing an integrative approach combining both traditional and alternative modalities.

Dr. Braud has studied alternative mental health treatments since 2005. This includes training with the Center for Mind-Body Medicine, the Institute for Functional Medicine, and the Autism Research Institute. She was a consultant for the Riordan Clinic of Wichita, Kansas from 2007 to 2010.

You can reach Dr. Braud by contacting her office address at 2755 South Locust St, Suite 114, Denver, CO, or calling her office at 303-721-2901.

FOURTEEN

Biomedical Approaches

by Debby Hamilton, MD.

We used to call my son the Tazmanian Devil. Carlos was always bouncing off of every-thing, jiggling up and down, and picking at things. Sometimes he was extremely ir-ritable and inconsolable when things went wrong. By second grade, the school was strongly hinting that he should be assessed for AD/HD and medicated. They couldn't outright order me to do it, but his teacher found a hundred ways to insinuate that my son really needed drugs. But it didn't feel right to me; I knew other children with AD/HD and it felt different. They could settle down for short periods of time and could focus when very interested. My son was just on "vibrate" constantly, with occasional bouts of not being able to handle any-thing that tried his patience.

One day I was lamenting the situation to some friends and one of them recommended a biomedical doctor who had seen her son. I had no idea what a biomedical doctor did, but she explained the basics and, more importantly, said that this doctor had been able to identify the reasons her son had been getting sick every other week and never seemed to have any energy. Good enough for me!

The doctor took one look at Carlos' puffy face and the dark circles under his eyes and said, "Well, at the very least, I'd bet you have some food allergies going on." (After 45 min-utes of listening to Carlos fart, he was even more convinced.) After the full assessment, the doctor ordered many tests, including one for food reactions (anything from sensitivities to full-blown allergies) and one for something called methylation, which meant whether or not Carlos could break down and process certain nutrients. The tests revealed a strong intoler-ance for gluten, dairy, and eggs and an inability to methylate B vitamins. Since B vitamins, in particular, are necessary for the nervous system to develop and stay calm, he had not had ac-cess to some of the building blocks he needed to create a strong, responsive nervous system.

Interestingly, when Carlos was a baby, he had had a lot of trouble with dairy-based for-mula. After a few weeks he had stopped reacting, and I thought we were home free. Our new doctor said that his system may have learned to cope in a way, but had probably become chronically compromised in other ways.

We took him off of all gluten, dairy, and eggs and began giving him supplements with methylated (pre-broken down) B vitamins. At first Carlos resisted. We endured some epic temper tantrums for the first week, since pizza and mac and cheese were his favorite foods and the gluten-free, dairy-free options we could find tasted weird, according to Carlos (I had to agree). I had to get pretty extreme, throwing away all "illegal" food in the house so he couldn't cheat, and enlisting the help of his teachers to keep him from sneaking snacks from his friends. One day, a few weeks later, I realized that I had been sitting on the couch reading to a very quiet boy for 20 minutes – an unheard of stretch of time for him! He also began looking me in the eye more and participating in conversations in a much more coherent way. Getting him out the door in the morning was no longer an activity designed to make me lose my mind, and I stopped having to talk to his teacher every day.

We did have a few relapses. One day, Carlos got off the school bus with a very sad face. "I had some goldfish at snack time," he told me tearfully, "and then I couldn't tell myself to sit still anymore." He also reported that he was sleeping much better – "probably because I can breathe now." Apparently, he had been chronically congested at night; the lack of good sleep couldn't have helped. It was heartbreaking to see all the things I had missed. Once he himself saw the difference, the main battle was won. I became the class baker, providing safe, but still-yummy, cupcakes and treats for class events. We both had to work hard to make the shift. It's a lot to ask of a small boy, and sometimes he still slips. But in general, he hates the way the wrong foods make him feel and tries to be good. He still has a lot of energy, but no more than the average little kid. Our nightmare seems to be over! ~ M.W.

The Basics

Western medicine is still a fairly young system, and continues to develop as our understanding of the human body evolves. I feel that the biomedical approach, along with its very close cousin Functional Medicine, represent the next logical progression in medicine. Biomedical treatment is grounded in Western science and medical practices, but it goes a step further to discover and correct the causes of disease, rather than simply managing or suppressing symptoms. Biomedical care looks more deeply at how some systems in the body (especially the digestive system) affect other systems, interprets lab results a little differently in order to obtain a larger picture of what's happening in the body, and focuses on non-drug interventions whenever possible.

My interest in biomedicine began because I was interested in the DAN (Defeat Autism Now) protocols. This approach has had astonishing success with children with autism and emerged directly from biomedical research and thinking. Although it started by focusing on children with autism, the principles of this approach have proven to be equally effective with many other learning and behavior disorders as well. I felt, when I first encountered this system of health care, that my medical training had found a much more thorough outlet. Biomedicine has allowed me to help my patients in new and more comprehensive ways. After many years in private practice, my respect for this methodology has only grown.

DAN no longer exists, although on many discussion sites you will still see people referencing "DAN practitioners." An organization called the Medical Academy of Pediatric Special Needs (MAPS) now oversees the training of biomedical practitioners and the development and continuing evolution of biomedical protocols for pediatric issues. Although the website focuses quite a bit on Autism Spectrum Disorders (ASD), these protocols are effective for many types of learning and behavior problems.

A Closer Look

Biomedical practitioners have the same training as medical doctors, but look at data a little differently. Practitioners focus on **diet, nutrition, allergies, digestive problems, infection, environmental toxins, neurotransmitter levels, and metabolic problems.** Multiple studies have shown that these factors can dramatically affect behavior, mood, and learning ability. Biomedical practitioners have learned to assess all these factors and help the patient begin to heal by improving how well all the systems in the body function.

Biomedical doctors are not against medications. Pharmaceuticals can make life more manageable and enjoyable for the patient. However, we feel that a symptom, no matter how dramatic, is just an indicator of an underlying condition. Biomedicine investigates and treats the complex underlying conditions suggested by the patient's symptoms.

Biomedical practitioners typically assess the physical symptoms in the left column and how they might relate to the behavioral symptoms in the right column:

MAJOR BIOMEDICAL MARKERS

Physical	**Learning/behavior**
Gastroesophageal Reflux	Hyperactivity
Diarrhea	Poor concentration
Constipation	Spaciness
Irritable bowel syndrome	Learning disorders
Bloating	Sensory Processing Disorder
Stomachaches	Irritability
Food cravings	Emotional dysregulation
Sugar cravings	Aggressive behavior
Allergies	Anxiety
Asthma	

Skin rashes/Eczema
Acne
Fatigue
Trouble getting to sleep or staying asleep

For instance, negative reactions to milk can create obviously related symptoms like digestive discomfort and eczema. But it can also affect brain chemistry, creating symptoms such as irritability and spaciness. Removing milk from the diet might not only help the child feel better physically; it may also help her concentrate and stay calm.

Biomedical approaches have been successfully used to address symptoms of:

- Autistic Spectrum Disorders, including Asperger's Syndrome and PDD-NOS, or Pervasive Developmental Disorder-Not Otherwise Specified (See Chapter 8: Autism Spectrum Disorders.)
- Sensory Processing Disorder (See Chapter 7: Sensory Processing Disorder.)
- Attention Deficit Hyperactivity Disorder (See Chapter 4: Attention Problems and AD/HD.)
- Emotional regulation difficulties (See Chapter 11: Emotional and Behavioral Issues.)
- Other learning or developmental challenges (See Chapter 10: Other Learning Disabilities.)

Brief History

The biomedical approach was developed by physicians at the Autism Research Institute in the late 1960s. The term *biomedical approach* refers to training in the Defeat Autism Now (DAN) program. We used to believe that autism and other developmental disorders could only be treated only with behavioral therapies or psychiatric medicines. When researchers discovered that factors like infections or nutritional deficiencies could contribute to the symptoms, practitioners began examining these aspects more closely. Since there are many overlapping symptoms among disabilities, this approach has been effective in treating a broad spectrum of issues. Currently, biomedical treatment is used to help children with all types of developmental delays.

Although the idea and use of biomedical treatments have been around for decades, biomedical approaches continue to be lesser known, and sometimes controversial, for many mainstream physicians. (The use of chelation and supplements, in particular, are often viewed with skepticism by mainstream physicians.) Multiple research and clinical studies have been done to explore the effectiveness of various treatments. Due to the high interest of many parents, researchers are now trying to help mainstream physicians understand these approaches and determine which practices could be most helpful for families that want to use some of them. (Levy and Hyman, 2008).

Despite its similarity to Functional Medicine, biomedicine was developed especially for pediatric care, and is specifically designed to address children's immature, less predictable physiology.

What a Biomedical Practitioner Assesses

A thorough biomedical assessment is likely to involve various blood, urine, or saliva tests, as well as detailed questionnaires from the child and his parents, diet records, and a physical exam.

THE DIGESTIVE SYSTEM

I am still amazed at how many issues can result from problems related to the digestive system. It is usually the first thing I assess, and doing so consistently unearths valuable information. As a country, we could probably remediate an extraordinary percentage of our children's learning and behavior issues by making significant changes to our collective diet!

Researchers are finding more and more ways that digestive issues affect overall health and abilities. For one thing, 70 percent of the immune system is found in the gut, so when gut health is poor, a child is left extremely vulnerable to illness and infection. There are many more ways, however, that gut health relates directly to learning and behavior.

> ### A Little Science
>
> A whopping *70 percent* of people with ASD (Autism Spectrum Disorder) have some sort of gastrointestinal disorder. Biomedical practitioners see this as far more than a coincidence, but rather as evidence that the digestive system should be the first thing to address with children on the autism spectrum (and children with many other issues as well).
>
> Buie, T., et al. Evaluation, diagnosis and treatment of gastrointestinal disorders in individuals with ASDs: A consensus report. *Pediatrics* 125, Suppl no. 1 (2010): S1-S18.

Nutritional deficiencies and imbalances in digestive function also affect energy level, brain chemistry, mental clarity, mood regulation, and nervous system stability. There is a very close connection between the gut and the brain. In fact, there is such a tight interrelationship between the two that *neurogastroenterology*, the study of interactions between the two systems, has been a distinct field of study for almost 20 years. If your child has imbalances in his brain chemistry, it is at least possible (if not likely) that there is something needing attention in his digestive system. The converse is true also: If your child has digestive difficulties, I can almost guarantee that his brain chemistry is suffering in some way as well.

Cleaning Up Their Diet: This Might Not Be Pretty

Cleaning up a child's diet can have immediate and dramatic effects. Sometimes it's not so straightforward, and the welcome effects emerge only after a period of adjustment.

Unfortunately, like an alcoholic who cannot stop drinking, children with sensitivities to certain foods tend to crave those foods. The foods that trigger them have been acting like drugs in their bodies, making them irritable, foggy, or even violent – so you'd think they'd be happy to clean out! But they are, after all, only children. Dealing with what is basically withdrawal can be intense. (Ever try to nix your caffeine habit? It's tough!)

Young children, who cannot fully appreciate the situation, may make your life miserable until their systems are truly clear of their allergens. Older children often don't like to be told what they can or can't eat, and can be prone to cheating. And yes, I know: reorganizing your child's diet (or your whole family's) is an additional project you really didn't need!

The results are truly worth it. Get through the initial period of adjustment and it really does become part of your routine. And think of it this way: the harder it is to get them to stop eating something, the more you know you're probably on the right track!

For example: There are a number of neurotransmitters in the gut, although most people think of neurotransmitters as existing solely in the brain. There is actually more serotonin, the "calming hormone," in the digestive tract than there is in the brain (which is why stress often results in indigestion, diarrhea, etc.). Chronic stress can therefore begin to deplete the whole system of serotonin, creating a vicious cycle of mood dysregulation: stress disrupts the serotonin production in the gut, which further destabilizes the child's ability to feel calm and happy, which creates more stress. The following sections explain how the health of the digestive system (and other systems), impact overall health.

For more information on how digestion and brain function interact, see Chapter 15: Nutritional Approaches.

DIGESTIVE PROBLEMS

Problems with digestion are particularly common in struggling children, especially those on the autism spectrum. Complex children with learning or behavior issues often have poor diets, largely because their sensitive systems render them extremely picky eaters. Also, I often find multiple infections resulting from antibiotic use, leading to the loss of the good bacteria needed for digestion. Long-term imbalances like this, can lead to complications such as leaky gut syndrome or food allergies, which in turn can have significant impacts on cognitive and emotional function.

Immediate symptoms can range from gastro-esophageal reflux and vomiting to diarrhea, constipation, and bloating. Some children seem to have chronic pain that can arise from any part of their digestive system, even without other digestive symptoms. Any of these problems could disrupt brain chemistry. Looking for the cause of these symptoms is a critical piece of the biomedical approach. Treatment may involve special diets and supplements to help heal the digestive system.

Food Allergies, Intolerances, Sensitivities

Less obvious symptoms can wreak considerable havoc too. Food reactions come in many shapes and sizes and can profoundly destabilize gut and brain health. But, unless someone has an allergy that triggers an anaphylactic response (e.g., strawberries triggering immediate inflammation to the point of asphyxiation), it can be difficult to tell whether a certain food is causing problems.

A delayed food allergy or sensitivity can arise when people have problems digesting proteins in certain foods (the most common ones are gluten and the casein in milk). The body can start reacting to certain foods as if they are dangerous. It then tries to protect itself by making a protein antibody that creates widespread inflammation, disrupting normal functioning of the body and the brain. The inflammatory chemicals released during this process can also cause oxidative damage to the brain and nervous system, actually changing neurology.

This often starts a cycle that becomes more and more difficult to break: The impaired digestive system becomes more impaired and confused as the undetected triggers keep assaulting it; as a result, it becomes hyper-reactive to more foods, creating more complex digestive disorders. This leads to more inflammation throughout the system and further destabilizes the brain chemistry, and the whole system keeps getting more chaotic and compromised.

For more specific information about the different types of food reactions and the complications that can result, see Chapter 15: Nutritional Approaches.

Testing Methods

There are a number of ways to test for food allergies or reactions. Skin prick allergy tests usually measure IgE (Immunoglobulin E) antibodies (these are the severe, immediate allergies that might involve a trip to the emergency room if activated). They are also very good for detecting environmental allergens such as pollen or mold. This is how allergy specialists most often test. However, there are many different kinds of allergies, as well as responses that are not true allergies but may be disrupting your child's digestive system, immune system, and brain chemistry. IgE tests often show negative results when, in fact, your child does have a sensitivity or intolerance.

There is a wide variety of tests available to practitioners that can reveal different levels of dietary and environmental triggers. Some require you to go to a lab and have your blood taken; some need urine or saliva samples, which you can collect in the privacy of your home and mail in. There are so many testing options now, and this field changes so rapidly, that I will not attempt to present a complete list here. Ask your practitioner what testing methods she prefers and why, and make sure you are not limiting the kinds of information you will be getting.

NUTRITION

Most children in this country do not go hungry. That is extremely misleading, though. Many people still do not get adequate nutrition and our children suffer as a result.

The Standard American Diet (or SAD) consists primarily of processed foods with lots of wheat, dairy, and sugar. For all children, this diet can contribute to health problems such as obesity, cavities, and energy spikes and drops. However, the SAD can also contribute to many behavioral and emotional issues, both because of nutritional deficiencies and imbalances in brain chemistry that the SAD can exacerbate. Because of this, diet is often the first thing a biomedical doctor looks at for children with developmental issues. When changing a child's diet, a parent may be asked to some or all of these:

- Change eating patterns to include more whole foods, fruits, and vegetables
- Reduce or eliminate packaged and processed foods
- Increase organic foods
- Increase intake of water and reduce juices and sugary drinks
- Decrease sugar (this is key – please see Chapter 15 on nutrition for more info on how sugar destabilizes your system)
- Complete a trial of elimination of food dyes and preservatives
- Eliminate a food group due to food sensitivity/allergy
  (For more information on elimination and rotation diets as a way to address food reactions, see Chapter 15: Nutritional Approaches.)

Significant nutritional deficiencies often exist even in families who conscientiously avoid the SAD diet. In my practice, I always conduct a full diet analysis and almost always find dietary problems, no matter how informed their families may be. For example, I have never, ever seen anyone who gets enough vitamin D or omega-3 fatty acids, both of which are essential for brain health and mood stabilization.

Even children who have a healthy diet can have deficiencies if digestive issues prevent them from absorbing all the nutrients from their food. We all know that macronutrients such as protein are needed to grow and build tissue. Micronutrients, such as vitamins and minerals, are also needed, but might be lacking which could contribute to specific health or behavioral problems. Zinc, for example, is so critical for many enzymes involved in emotional and mental functioning that biomedical providers often learn "no zinc, no think." Vitamin B6 is critical for the formation of serotonin, the neurotransmitter that is important for calming the nervous system. Low levels of zinc and vitamin B6 lead to many emotional problems, poor stress tolerance, and learning and attention problems. Since this is easy to detect on a urine test and easy to treat with supplementation, it is something you should always test in children with emotional and developmental issues.

I usually recommend vitamin and mineral supplements, at least for a while. **Supplementation should always be done under the supervision of a qualified practitioner.** Although supplementation is not always necessary with a healthful balanced diet, recovering from a deficient diet will probably require it in order to reestablish balance. (And I must add: because of depleted soil, unhealthful agricultural practices, genetic modifications to our food supply, and other factors we have little control over, it is increasingly difficult to obtain adequate nutrition from diet alone.)

What To Do With a Picky Eater?

Some children, especially those with multiple issues, can be incredibly, scream-inducingly picky. If your child falls into this camp, and you have been feeding him McDonald's and mac and cheese because they are absolutely the only things he will put into his mouth, you are not alone. I see a lot of kids who eat like this, and they have definite health issues – including failure to grow – as a result.

There are solutions. I work with many families to revamp their diets and find creative options. (They really will eat rather than starve, I promise!) Some children have low appetites as a result of their nutritional deficiencies, and there are supplements that can address this. Also, kids with sensory issues are often picky because of the textures of certain foods, and there are occupational therapists called *feeding therapists* who work specifically with this issue. So don't despair – there are answers out there for you!

SLEEP

Sleep is one of the most crucial functions of our bodies and brains, and is essential for growth and healing. Most experts agree that children need 10 to 12 hours, depending on the age of the child. We all know what it's like not to get enough sleep: that groggy, grumpy feeling, the difficulty concentrating, the irritability. If your child has an occasional bad night, those symptoms would make life hard enough. If she has chronically poor sleep, however – whether she's lying there wide-eyed, doesn't get enough, or simply stays at the shallow end of the sleep stages – it will steadily shift her brain chemistry and degrade her general well-being. If your child is not sleeping well, it is of the utmost importance that we find and treat the cause.

The Dangers of Lyme

Lyme disease, usually contracted from a tick bite, appears much more frequently than previously believed, and can manifest with an array of alarming symptoms. Because this infection hides inside the cells, it can be quite tricky to identify. If your child has an unusual set of symptoms that no one can quite categorize, and if the approaches you have used have done little to resolve them, it may be time to look up a good Lyme specialist. Lyme disease might also be a culprit if:

- your child has a known history of tick bites;
- your child has a history of mystery symptoms, such as unexplained rash or fever;
- your child's symptoms seemed to appear suddenly;
- your child's mother has a history of the above, or has had her own chronic health problems such as fibromyalgia or chronic arthritis (Lyme disease can be passed from mother to baby).

However, even in the absence of these indicators, Lyme disease might still be present.

CANDIDA (YEAST)

A key part of digestion is the balance of the good bacteria (probiotics) that are supposed to be in the intestine and bacteria and/or yeast such as Candida that can overgrow in the intestines and cause problems. Overgrowth of Candida Albicans is a common contributor to poor digestive health. Biomedical physicians will typically evaluate for these:

◊ Yeast or fungal infections such as Candida Albicans
◊ Bad bacteria that are not supposed to be in the intestine such as Clostridium Difficile (C-Diff)

Good bacteria, such as Lacto Bacillus, are the bacteria necessary to digest food. Probiotics, and sometimes herbal supplements, are often recommended to balance digestive health. Relief is often quick when dietary irritants are eliminated and good bacteria is restored. For more information about the benefits of probiotics, please see Chapter 15: Nutritional Approaches.

Aside from the obvious benefit of eliminating the child's pain, addressing digestive problems can have profound effects on many other aspects of a child's well-being.

For example, when good bacteria and yeast are not in balance, it is called *dysbiosis*. This often leads to a condition called *leaky gut* (or *intestinal hyper-permeability*, in true medical-speak) in which the yeast has essentially eaten holes in the intestines, allowing whole proteins or unwanted bacteria into the body. These unwanted bacteria and yeast produce toxins that make children sick and cause physical, mental, and behavioral symptoms. Also, when gut dysregulation escalates because of food sensitivities, Candida can run amok, leading to digestive inflammation that prevents the absorption of nutrients.

In some children, yeast can ferment, leading to lethargy, an inability to concentrate, and/or goofy behavior similar to intoxication. Evaluation may include tests such as complete digestive stool tests and urine tests that look for markers for yeast or unwanted bacteria in the intestine. Treatment may involve special diets, medicines or herbs to treat the Candida, and probiotics to restore the good bacteria.

INFECTIONS

Intestinal infections commonly occur in children with developmental disabilities. These infections are often from yeast, such as Candida, or other types of bad bacteria. In fact, similar intestinal infections are common in people of all ages with many different chronic conditions. Chronic viral infections can also cause symptoms ranging from chronic lethargy to seizures.

I see many infections that severely impact a child's ability to learn and maintain emotional balance. Chronic Lyme is an example of an infection that can cause neurologic and emotional symptoms and can occur even in young children (Bransfield, 2008). The herpes virus can cause autistic-like behavior. Strep infections have been linked to significant behavioral issues, as well as severe obsessive compulsive behaviors (this is known as PANDAS Syndrome – see NIMH July 2010). If a child tests positive for any of these

Food for Thought: A Word About Detoxification

The subject of detox, especially for children, is somewhat controversial in medical circles. And for good reason: done improperly, it can be dangerous. Biomedical practitioners, by and large, do not support the use of fasts or over-the-counter cleanses that utilize laxatives, colonics, or even aggressive herbs. These can be far too intense for a child (or even some adults, depending on what is being cleansed from the system). Released toxins have to go somewhere before they exit the body for good, and if they are released at a rate that is faster than the system can process, they can wreak havoc in the system.

However, especially with mounting evidence indicating just how significant a role toxic load may be playing in these kinds of issues, detoxification may be the most transformational tool your practitioner has. Chelation, in particular, can bring about life-changing shifts. *Make sure you find out just how much experience your practitioner has in this area.* How does he design the program? How individualized is it? How, and how closely, does he monitor the process?

Chelation can be a powerful procedure, but it is a *medical* procedure that should be designed and monitored by a qualified, experienced professional.

types of infections, remediating them can have a dramatic impact on any behavioral or mental symptoms he has been experiencing.

REACTIONS TO ENVIRONMENTAL FACTORS

Many different types of allergies appear in children with developmental disabilities. Food allergies and sensitivities are common and don't always present with digestive symptoms. You should also address seasonal allergies such as hay fever. Some children have more problems with behavior at certain times of the year; specific allergies can be a contributing factor. Both asthma and eczema (itchy skin rash) often are caused or exacerbated by different allergies. Allergies tax the immune system, so that any underlying difficulties that the system is already fighting (food sensitivities or infections, for example) might worsen. Evaluations for allergies, avoiding allergens, and balancing the immune system are the common approaches to treat allergies and sensitivities.

ENVIRONMENTAL TOXINS

In one of his books, well-known neurologist David Perlmutter, MD, tells the story of a 10-year-old boy who was a hardworking student at the top of his class. He had started developing learning disabilities to the point where he had difficulties performing simple math such as addition. He had become discouraged and unmotivated.

It turned out that, about a year previously, this boy had started eating three to six ounces of canned tuna daily. When tested, he had double the amount of mercury in his body that the EPA (Environmental Protection Agency) considers safe. After discontinuing the mercury exposure from tuna, this boy's mental and academic function returned to normal within two years.

Just how toxic is our environment? In 2008, the World Health Organization reported that over 25 percent of global disease is related to environmental causes and that environmental-mediated disease is responsible for over 3 million deaths per year in children under the age of five.

Toxins tend to accumulate in areas of high fat, and much of the brain and nervous system consists of fatty tissue. It makes sense that with the rise of toxins, we also see a rise in disorders affecting the brain. Accumulated toxins cause inflammation in the brain, actually shifting the brain chemicals that are secreted. Toxins can also increase free radicals in the brain, which can cause micro changes in brain function - usually not to the point of being detectible by

EEG or MRI, but often enough to cause symptoms. This can be confirmed clinically by many cases where the symptoms go away when the toxic exposure is removed and the toxins are cleared.

While our bodies are designed to detoxify naturally, they were never designed to handle the sheer volume that we are bombarded with today. Toxic chemicals exist in our water, our food, and our air...not to mention cosmetics, cleaning supplies, and on and on. The table in this section shows some of the symptoms that have been linked to common substances.

We are all exposed, but children are more at risk because they are small and their nervous systems are still in the process of developing. In addition, there is a large genetic difference in people's ability to detoxify or get rid of toxins in their bodies. Therefore, certain children are more at risk for having problems with toxins than others. If a child is sensitive to a toxin, this can show up as multiple physical and behavioral problems. Evaluating for toxins is part of the biomedical approach, along with helping the body learn to detoxify well, and getting rid of harmful chemicals. Common assessment methods for toxin exposure include analysis of urine, blood, or hair samples.

The Institute of Functional Medicine shows correlations between these toxins and conditions:

ADHD	Autism	Alzheimer's	Neuro-Behavioral		Neuro-Developmental	Parkinsons
BPA	Mercury	Aluminum	Aluminum	Lead	Arsenic	Manganese
Lead		Lead	Arsenic	EMFs	Lead	Pesticides
Mercury		Mercury	Mercury	Mold	Mercury	
Phthalates			Phthalates	PCB's	PCB's	
PCB's			Solvents		Solvents	

Metabolic Problems

Metabolism is how the body uses food to make energy. Multiple chemical reactions occur during metabolism. *Biochemistry* refers to how those reactions interact with each other. Cellular metabolism is the process by which each cell makes energy. If there is a problem anywhere in these processes, it can affect energy levels, digestion, growth...basically, it can affect anything!

Everyone's metabolism and underlying biochemistry differs, sometimes dramatically - something medical science has been a bit slow to acknowledge, in my opinion. Biomedical practices treat each person's biochemistry individually; lab tests assess how well the processes are functioning and can treat problems with supplements.

NEUROTRANSMITTERS

Neurotransmitters are the chemicals in our brains that influence how we feel, learn, and think. If there's an imbalance in our neurotransmitters, there will likely be many problems in how well we function every day. It is quite common for these chemicals to be out of balance in children experiencing difficulties in learning, emotional control, and sleep. Biomedical physicians try to shift these neurotransmitters through supplementation with micronutrients, amino acids, and minerals.

Balancing these chemicals is important, but tricky. Some practitioners use urine tests to determine neurotransmitter levels, but others argue that measuring the levels of neurotransmitters in the gut does not accurately reflect the levels in the brain. So, some tests measure secondary factors, such as metabolism function, which can be an indicator of certain neurotransmitters.

Sometimes the problem is not the neurotransmitter levels, but rather the enzymes that are supposed to break them down. Some people do not have enough enzymes; some have too many or overactive enzymes. All of this must be evaluated, and there are many layers to this complex issue.

Be sure to ask your health care practitioner about the method he or she uses to evaluate neurotransmitter levels. Many practitioners now use detailed symptom questionnaires, which seem to be just as effective as, and much cheaper than lab tests.

Who Does This?

Biomedical providers can come from several different specialties. Becoming a biomedical practitioner

Don't Try This at Home

Consumer experimentation with supplements is becoming increasingly common, and not always with good results. Messing with neurotransmitters is especially risky. GABA and 5-HTP, in particular, are often recommended by health magazines and health food store employees. GABA is often given to help people stay calm and focused, while 5-HTP is often suggested for help with sleep. However, it is not advisable to take these without practitioner supervision. Some children react in the opposite manner than expected to GABA and 5-HTP, becoming nervous or hyper. Neurotransmitter function is an intricate issue involving many layers of chemistry; taking something without having been properly evaluated may skew things further.

Qualified supervision is also necessary to understand what the results indicate when a child takes any form of supplementation. Whether the outcome is positive or negative, the resulting symptoms give valuable information about what is going on. Do yourself and your child a favor and leave this one to the professionals.

involves extra, specialized training. Possible practitioners include:

- Medical doctors (MD)
- Osteopathic doctors (DO)
- Naturopathic doctors (ND)
- Clinical nutritionists/dieticians (RD)
- Chiropractors (DC)
- Nurse practitioners (NP)

Biomedical practitioners will sometimes agree to work over the phone, meaning that you do not need to find someone in your area.

Finding a Good Provider

The most important consideration is that the practitioner has the proper training and experience. The creators of the biomedical approach are from the Autism Research Institute's program called Defeat Autism Now. As previously mentioned, DAN is now defunct, but MAPS now oversees the ongoing development of protocols and training standards. Take a look at the MAPS directory to find a practitioner near you.

The MAPS website is clearly geared towards the autism community, but this approach is now used to better understand, assess, and assist children with any kind of learning, emotional, or behavioral issue. However, not all biomedical practitioners provide all types of biomedical treatment or work with multiple issues. Ask any prospective practitioner what her experience is with your child's problems.

Questions for a Prospective Biomedical Practitioner

- What training have you had in biomedical treatment?
- Are you certified by the Defeat Autism Now or MAPS program?
- How many years of experience have you had?
- Have you treated children who have the same needs as my child? What were the results?
- What kind of improvements would you aim for with my child?
- How long does treatment usually last, or how long do you think it will last in this case?
- What are the costs involved in treatment? Do you take insurance? (Many providers do not.)

Resources for More Information

Although many of the following resources focus primarily on autism, the science and protocols apply to other learning and behavior disorders as well.

WEBSITES

www.medmaps.org, Medical Academy of Pediatric Special Needs (MAPS). MAPS is the organization that trains and oversees practitioners in the biomedical approach. The website focuses mostly on autism, but the practitioners you find through it would be able to address other issues as well.

www.autism.com, Autism Research Institute. The Institute will keep you updated with the latest research and information regarding autism.

www.generationrescue.org, Generation Rescue. Generation Rescue provides parents with information, hope, and support for their journey through autism. There's even a friendly, helpful page just for the newly diagnosed!

www.devdelay.org, Developmental Delay Resources (DDR). This website does an excellent job of presenting both conventional and holistic approaches to an array of behavioral and learning issues.

www.ewg.org, Environmental Working Group. According to their website, this watchdog group examines "government data, legal documents, scientific studies, and [their] own laboratory tests to expose threats to your health and the environment, and to find solutions."

www.nimh.nih.gov/labs-at-nimh/research-areas/clinics-and-labs/pdnb/web.shtml. This is the National Institute of Mental Health information page about PANDAS Syndrome.

BOOKS

Healing the New Childhood Epidemics: Autism, ADHD, Asthma, and Allergies by Kenneth Bock, MD. Dr. Bock details the clinical approach that resulted from years of research. He discusses the deadly modern toxins, nutritional deficiencies, metabolic imbalances, genetic vulnerabilities, and assaults on the immune and gastrointestinal systems that trigger most of the symptoms of ADHD, autism, asthma, and allergies.

Nourishing Hope for Autism by Julie Matthews. Matthews, a Certified Nutrition Consultant, has put together a website, book, and plan to help parents find nutritional solutions for their children's issues.

Children with Starving Brains: A Medical Treatment Guide for Autism Spectrum Disorder by Jacquelyn McCandless, MD. Dr. McCandless presents a step-by-step guide to treating children with autism using a comprehensive biomedical approach.

REFERENCES

Levy, S. E., S. L. Hyman. Complementary and alternative medicine treatments for children with Autism Spectrum Disorders. *Child Adolesc Psychiatr Clin N Am* 17 (4) (October 2008): 803-820.

Bransfield, et al. The association between tick-borne infections, *Lyme borreliosis, and Autism Spectrum Disorders.* Med Hypotheses 70 (5) (2008): 967-74.

McGinnis, W. R., et al. Discerning the mauve factor, Parts 1 & 2. *Altern Ther Health Med* 14 (2) (March-April 2008): 40-50; 14 (3) (May-June 2008): 56-62.

ABOUT THE AUTHOR

Debby Hamilton, MD, MSPH, is the founder of Holistic Pediatric Consulting in Denver, CO. Her practice focuses on treating children with chronic diseases such as autism and ADHD and preconception counseling based on her book, *Preventing Autism and ADHD: Controlling Risk Factors Before, During & After Pregnancy*. She is board-certified in pediatrics, physician nutrition, and integrated/holistic medicine and has a Master of Science degree in Public Health (MSPH). She is on the scientific board of the Neurological Health Foundation (www.neurologicalhealth.org), a non-profit dedicated to the prevention of chronic diseases in children. In 2017, she joined Researched Nutritionals as their physician in charge of clinical research and physician education.

You can reach Dr. Hamilton at drdebby@holisticpediatric.com or www.holisticpediatric.com.

FIFTEEN

Nutritional Approaches

by Dr. Emily Chan, ND

Editors' Note

We realize that this chapter might be daunting. However, the point is not for you to commit all of this to memory or make every one of these changes. The idea is to introduce you to the complex world of nutrition and to illustrate the profound impact that nutritional changes can have on your child's learning and behavior.

Overhauling a family's eating habits can feel overwhelming. If some of this information strikes a chord with you, try a few small changes and see what happens. Or find a practitioner who can help you to identify the most important changes your child needs. We have seen firsthand how transformative proper nutrition can be, but try not to let it become another source of stress. Instead, we hope you will see it as an empowering abundance of information that can help you reclaim your family's health!

"The food you eat can be either the safest and most powerful form of medicine or the slowest form of poison" ~ Ann Wigmore

When my son Jesse was in fifth grade, he still struggled with ADD, sensory issues and anxiety. I got calls from school almost every day, asking me either to pick him up early or to come in and calm him down. Our family never went anywhere because, between the sensory problems and the anxiety, just about everything was too much for him. I was exhausted from his constant tantrums. We had tried everything for years, from sensory integration therapies to nutritional adjustments to medications, all with some improvement but a frustrating lack of real resolution.

Our naturopath began to suspect that he was not able to metabolize folic acid. We get folic acid from food and must use it to make folate, one of the building blocks for all neu-

rotransmitters. If we are not making enough folate to make those neurotransmitters, it will impair brain function and mood regulation. So we started him on a dose of metabolized folic acid, in the hopes that his body would be able to use that. Within two weeks, coaches and teachers started commenting to me about Jesse's improved calm, focus, and general ability to "just do what he's supposed to do." He didn't miraculously become The Perfect Child, but it made a clear, noticeable, and dramatic difference. I was already a believer in the power of proper, targeted nutrition...but the change in my son, as a result of this one little substance, blew my mind! ~ T.T.

The Basics

Nutrition is a core issue. It is important to address in any child, but is absolutely critical for a child with any learning or behavior difficulties. Researchers discover more every year about how deeply nutrition affects mental and emotional stability, immune function, and overall physical health.

Nutrition is a core issue. Any time nutrition is a problem, it needs to be dealt with *first* (barring any severe medical needs). No matter what your child's diagnosis is, any other therapies, modifications, or meds will very likely work better if you are not constantly fighting a dysfunctional baseline. In fact, you might be surprised to find that your child has fewer issues, or less severe ones, once you make dietary changes. I usually assess a child's diet first, and parents are often amazed at how much we can resolve on that level alone.

We all know the basic principles of nutrition: The body is like a computer. If you put in one type of signal, you get a certain result – if you put in another, you get something different. (There is a saying amongst computer programmers: GIGO, or "Garbage In, Garbage Out." Pretty much sums it up for nutrition as well.) We have all experienced, on a daily basis, how food affects our energy level and state of mind. Sugar and caffeine make us feel hyper, then crash. Big heavy meals make us sleepy. Instinctively, we all understand that *different foods affect us differently.*

In addition to the immediate impact, poor nutrition can have disastrous cumulative effects. This chapter will discuss many of the ways an unsuitable diet can affect your child's health, in subtle ways that can be difficult to spot. Significant diet change can be a lot of work, but it can yield life-changing benefits.

Important Concept #1:
The Brain-Gut Connection

Just how important is it to look at nutritional factors, if your child can barely focus for 15 minutes at a time, melts down constantly, or can't stop hitting other children? Aren't those issues a little past needing mere nutritional tweaks? Maybe not. It is entirely possible for nutrition to have a huge impact on mood, behavior, and concentration.

Neurogastroenterology – the study of the connection between the gut and the brain – has been a distinct field of study since the 1980s. Researchers are continually discovering more ways that the health and function of one affect the health and function of the other. Briefly, here are a few key points to keep in mind:

- Our emotional states are, in part, created and influenced by the neurotransmitters in our digestive tracts, making gut health an important part of emotional health.
- 95 percent of the body's serotonin – the "feel-good" neurotransmitter, and the one most targeted by anti-depression medication – is actually found in the gut. This means that digestive ailments like irritable bowel syndrome, which leaches both nourishment and necessary elements like serotonin from the system, can have a negative effect on both mood and our ability to regulate it.
- If you experience chronic emotional upheavals, it is disrupting your digestive system (think butterflies in your stomach when you're nervous. Now imagine what constant stress would do!). The converse is also true: If you have chronic digestive problems, it is affecting either your emotional state, or your brain chemistry and ability to concentrate, or both.
- It doesn't really matter where the cycle starts. Once it gets going, your digestive health, emotional volatility, and brain chemistry imbalances will all keep each other going until something breaks the cycle.

Gastro-intestinal Health and Brain Function

An elementary school child came to see me last year because she had skipped 30 days of school in the fall quarter, due to daily bellyaches and frequent respiratory infections. She had also had loose stools for the past four months. This child was fairly stressed due to family situations and also had problems in school. She tended to either fall asleep or stand up frequently during class. The teachers were concerned about her defiant behavior and low grades.

Upon evaluation, I found that her excitatory brain chemicals such as adrenaline, dopamine, and glutamate were elevated. I also found that cortisol levels were low, meaning that she had been under stress for quite a while (stress increases cortisol levels; but when stress is prolonged, adrenals become depleted and cortisol plunges). Altered cortisol levels often affects energy levels, sleep patterns, and immune function. Finally, I found that histamine was elevated. When I see on a neurotransmitter test that histamine is elevated, it tells me that the brain chemical imbalances are also related to a gastrointestinal issue; usually there is a food allergy issue contributing as well.

We worked on a diet that decreased her food sensitivities, used supplements that encouraged healthy microbial balance in her intestinal tract, and also worked to improve her gastrointestinal system, which is highly related to both the immune system and nervous system.

She no longer had bellyaches at her one-month follow-up visit, and had missed no school. In the next four months, she was only sick once (quite a feat in the middle of winter with all the bugs going around!). Her grades and general performance in school had drastically improved…merely by healing her gastrointestinal system. ~ Emily Chan, ND

I talk to parents every week who are skeptical about how much of a role diet might be playing in their child's problems. But nutrient deficiencies and food allergies can be significant contributors. Below are some symptoms that can be related to diet and digestion. If symptoms occur a few times a week, that's significant. And, although catching colds from other children once or twice a semester is normal, getting sick frequently (once a month or so) is not.

- ☐ Frequent stomachaches
- ☐ Behavioral changes after eating
- ☐ Diarrhea or constipation
- ☐ Frequent infections
- ☐ Mood changes after eating
- ☐ Allergies/Asthma
- ☐ Low appetite
- ☐ Flatulence
- ☐ Sinus problems
- ☐ Bloated abdomen
- ☐ Eczema/hives

If you see some of these symptoms, your child might have leaky gut syndrome. Leaky gut develops when the thin layer that separates the intestinal contents from the rest of the body becomes porous or permeable, allowing small, incompletely digested food bits to escape directly into the blood stream. This creates a number of problems throughout the system and can have a huge impact on brain function, which will be explained further in the section on food allergies (in both this chapter and Chapter 14: Biomedical Approaches). If you suspect a mind-gut connection in your child's behavior, you might seek nutrition, naturopathy, or functional medicine as treatment options. Leaky gut is treatable with proper diet and appropriate use of herbs and supplements.

What increases intestinal permeability?

- Frequent antibiotic use
- Not being breastfed
- Viral, bacterial, or parasitic infections
- Food allergies or sensitivities
- Chronic inflammation, which is often linked to diet
- Elevated exposure to chemicals, pesticides, or heavy metals
- Chronic emotional stress
- Poor nutrition
- Lack of probiotics
- Food introduced too early
- Frequent antibiotic or antacid use
- Family history of inflammatory bowel disease (a young child might have exhibited this by being a colicky baby)

Important Concept #2:
Biological Uniqueness

You try to feed your child a balanced diet. You've seen the food pyramid (now known as MyPlate). You know that you need calcium to build bones and iron to build blood and protein to build muscle.

However, you may not know that all nutritional "facts" are not equally true for everyone.

Biology is much more unique from one person to the next than most of us were taught. Each one of us is a giant, complex chemistry set that is remarkably easy to derail. Some children, like Jesse in the opening story, lack the ability to synthesize certain nutrients. Or, just as some people have allergies to cats and others don't, foods that don't bother one child could be disastrous to the next. If what your child is putting into his body is lacking *in the specific nutrients that **he** needs,* or is actually working against him (e.g., food sensitivities) – neither of which you would know unless you get the appropriate assessments – his diet is not working for him and it will undoubtedly show up in his mood, concentration, and behavior.

Another consequence of biological uniqueness is that there is no diet that is right for everyone. In fact, you should be wary of any practitioner who promotes a certain diet as "THE best way to eat." There is no such thing. Each person needs to find out what works best for him or her. One word of caution, however: Avoid low-fat programs with children and teenagers. No one needs bad fats (see later section on fats), but good fats are essential for growing brains.

FOOD REACTIONS: THE BREAKDOWN

"Almost 80 percent of foods on the shelves of supermarkets
today did not exist 100 years ago." ~Larry McCleary, brain surgeon

"Don't eat anything your great-grandmother wouldn't recognize as food."
~ Michael Pollan, author and food activist

I had a five-year-old patient who came to see me for OCD and behavioral issues. She would alternate between being very sweet and being argumentative, loud, and aggressive. It sometimes took hours for her parents to put her to bed because she was too hyper and restless to settle down.

Initially, I had given her some probiotics that were specific to pediatric brain support, and a nutritional supplement that was calming to the nervous system. It was somewhat of a struggle to get her to take the supplement and we did not notice much change. Later on, we decided to have her avoid gluten and dairy. She tested allergic for wheat, gluten, and dairy on an IgG food allergy test. Modifying her food choices made a huge difference in her behavior. Her mother reports that she is less hyper and her disposition is sweeter and less out of control. She still has some progress to make and working on the psychological component would be helpful. However, merely avoiding allergic foods has made a noticeable change in her behavior. ~ Emily Chan

This case reminded me of how important it is to follow the naturopathic therapeutic order: Start with lifestyle changes such as diet; then use naturopathic treatments such as nutritional supplements, then physical medicine approaches (i.e., chiropractic, craniosacral, massage, occupational therapy, etc.). Then, if need be, use very aggressive methods such as medications. Doing things the other way around might provide relief, but really it would only mask the problematic behavior. Food reactions *will* keep showing up in destructive ways, even if the most obvious symptoms are alleviated through medication.

Food Allergies/Sensitivities/Intolerances

Reactions to food can increase intestinal permeability. Basically, holes develop in the gut, and this allows undigested food particles to escape. The immune system then encounters incompletely digested food molecules, which prompts an immune response. This further triggers systemic inflammation (similar to any allergic response). The body can react in the form of respiratory allergies, joint pain, and skin issues. If there is increased inflammation triggered in the brain, your child can also have cognitive, emotional, or behavioral changes. This is why many practitioners say: "If you have a food allergy, you also have a brain allergy."

Food Allergies: Food allergies happen when the body's immune system identifies the food as an enemy. The body begins making antibodies, which usually fight invaders but now fight the offending foods. If the body makes what are known as IgE antibodies, the reaction is usually immediate and dramatic: immediate fatigue, immediate hyperactivity, swollen lips, abdominal discomfort, and respiratory symptoms. An IgE-mediated reaction is what we classically call a food allergy and is the only type of allergy that many clinicians recognize.

Food Sensitivities: If the antibodies produced are predominantly IgG antibodies, the reaction is often delayed 24 to 48 hours. This makes it more difficult to pinpoint the culprit. The symptoms are usually subtler,

Health Watch

Untreated food sensitivities tend to beget more sensitivities, because the digestive system becomes increasingly compromised and begins to react to more and more foods. Don't worry; it's not permanent. But it may take a while to heal. One teenage patient's allergy test revealed her as "reactive" (to different degrees) to over 80 foods! After a few months of avoiding all of them – which was *not* easy – the true culprits emerged. For this teen, it boiled down to four kinds of foods: Raspberries and citrus made her mouth go numb; tomatoes gave her a stomachache; and gluten gave her horrendous indigestion. Once we healed her gut with probiotics and herbs, she no longer had to avoid all the other foods. Avoiding the primary triggers allowed her symptoms to resolve, and she felt much more clear-headed and calm.
~ Nancy Rao, ND

such as poor concentration, chronic respiratory symptoms, chronic behavioral issues, and frequent illness. These non-distinct reactions, especially if chronic, make it difficult to recognize the true culprit.

Food Intolerances: Food intolerances develop when your child lacks enzymes to digest a certain type of food. A classic example is lactose intolerance, where an individual lacks the enzyme to breaks down lactose, a sugar found in dairy products. People with lactose intolerance usually will have symptoms such as abdominal pain, flatulence, diarrhea, or fatigue when consuming milk products. Children who have an intolerance usually improve when they avoid the problematic food. In mild cases, they can still eat it without reacting if they take the appropriate enzyme at the same time.

NOTE: Many pediatricians, when asked for food allergy testing, do only a skin pinprick test – accurate for environmental allergens but, in my experience, not for foods unless the person has an extreme reaction like anaphylactic shock. There is a range of more sensitive tests that show other levels of reaction. Ask for a blood IgG food allergy test that includes at least 100 foods. You can also seek out a naturopath, or a Functional Medicine or biomedical doctor, because they are more familiar with this territory. Remember that medical school does not focus heavily on nutrition.

Another problem that results from food reactions is that toxins build up from poorly digested food or excessive yeast in the gut (see Chapter 14: Biomedical Approaches, for more information). This can affect the brain, exacerbating issues like fatigue and mental fog. It can also slow down and impair many other body functions, causing a cascade of dysfunction that can result in severe disease down the road. While the body does have its own natural detoxification cycle, it is not designed to handle that volume of toxins.

How Do You Get Rid of This Gunk?

The following two diets are widely used to clear out buildup, as well as to identify and manage ongoing triggers. Other methods for clearing the system might range from using specific herbs to support and clear the gut, to various detox diets. *Always make sure that your practitioner has experience using these methods with children. Pediatric physiology is unique and requires specialized knowledge.*

Elimination Diet/Allergy Testing

The gold standard for identifying allergens is the elimination challenge test, where kids are restricted to four non-allergenic foods for two weeks, then re-introduced to one food at a time and monitored for reactions. This is a sure way to know. Many children will have a reduction of symptoms during the two-week period, so that when foods are re-introduced, re-appearance of symptoms will be even more obvious.

According to Dr. Mark Hyman MD, *New York Times*-bestselling author and chairman of the Institute for Functional Medicine, these are the telltale signs to look for when re-introducing foods. Any of the following symptoms, if they occur within even 48 hours of re-introducing a food, indicate your child probably should not be having that food (at least for a while):

- Brain fog
- Depression
- Anxiety
- Anger
- Hyperactivity
- Difficulty remembering things
- Frequent cough or respiratory congestion
- Frequent headaches
- Chronic sleep problems
- Chronic joint or muscle aches
- Chronic pain
- Fatigue
- Changes in skin (acne, eczema, rash) – skin reactions are more prevalent among young children because their detoxification systems are not well developed yet
- Changes in digestion or bowel function

Clearing Their Diet: Hard But Worth It

Clearing a child's diet of triggers can be quite a project, but it can also be life-changing. Focus on the positive rather than talking about what they *can't* have and why. Find fun new foods and be excited about them. And don't worry. You may have a rough first week as your child adjusts; but even if she is reluctant, stay strong and positive. When she is hungry enough, she will agree to eat foods that are allowed. And once she sees how much better she feels, it will make it that much easier!

Keep in mind: Some children are not resistant to a food because of the taste. It's the texture they can't stand. This is a sensory integration issue and can be addressed by a specially trained occupational therapist called a *feeding therapist*. (See Chapter 7: Sensory Processing Disorder.)

Any of these symptoms, by themselves, could be considered normal. We all feel a little foggy, anxious, or fatigued sometimes. But an elimination diet should have you feeling fairly clear-headed and calm; any symptoms that appear would stand out. For example, if something happened to make you angry, obviously that is not the food's fault. If, however, after adding in a particular food you find yourself becoming irritable and easily angered, that would warrant further inquiry.

Rotation Diet

The food rotation diet is a useful framework for incorporating *some* foods (usually those that produced only a mild reaction) back into your child's diet after a period of healing and avoidance. This dietary management works best with supervision from a nutritional practitioner. You can read more about the Rotation Diet in the book *Brain Allergies: The Psychonutrient and Magnetic Connections*. Also, some labs that run food allergy or sensitivity panels send you a customized rotation food plan along with the test results.

Most Common Offending Foods
- Wheat
- Gluten
- Corn
- Soy
- Dairy
- Sugar
- Preservatives
- Food Coloring

Important Concept #3:
The Body Adapts – But Only Up to a Point

Do you ever look around and think, how do some kids eat junk food all the time and seem to be just fine?

The key words there are *seem to be*. They are *not* fine. They may not be obese or sick all the time, but that is simply not a sustainable diet for anyone. What's happening is that they're adapting…but only in a limited way.

The body is brilliant at surviving through adaptation. If you eat junk food every day, your body will not have a huge reaction daily because that would be difficult to survive on a regular basis. The body will try to adjust to any new baseline, but not without an insidious toll on health. The price tag often shows up in concentration, mood, and behavior.

> The insidiousness of a poor diet is what makes it so dangerous. Remember the old science experiment where you put a frog into hot water, and he immediately jumps out? But a frog that is placed into lukewarm water and slowly boiled will stay in the pot until it is good and poached. A child's immediate, obvious reactions to her food may not be ringing any alarm bells, but her performance over time might be screaming that she needs change.

What Are We Eating and What Is It Doing To Us?

The SAD (Standard American Diet)

For one of the wealthiest countries on earth, we have a diet remarkably devoid of nutrients. The Standard American Diet (which refers to the way most of the population *actually* eats, not the official standards we're supposed to follow) is almost perfectly designed to create the diseases and brain chemistry imbalances that we then spend millions trying to cure. Consider its hallmarks:

- High in animal fats
- High in unhealthy or even dangerous fats, like saturated or hydrogenated fats
- Low in fiber
- High in processed foods that have unhealthy amounts of added sugar, fat, sodium, and additives
- High in sugar and highly processed flour products that act like sugar in the body
- Low in complex carbohydrates
- Low in plant-based foods

We have created a vast convenience food industry that is making us sick. So please, skip the "convenience" and stick to the periphery of the grocery store: produce, meat, dairy – you know, actual food!

Common Culprits in the SAD

There is too much to discuss on the subject of what's deficient in our collective diet for me to cover it all here. But four of the common culprits deserve special mention: sugar, gluten, chemical additives, and bad fats.

Sugar vs. Blood Sugar

Regulating your child's blood sugar is one of the easiest, most effective ways to maximize his performance and keep him healthy. Concentration and mood become much less of a struggle when you are not working against the body's constant attempts to stabilize blood sugar problems. As anyone knows who gets weak and irritable when hungry, it is difficult to perform well in a hypoglycemic state! We may not realize it, but the Standard American Diet leaves us in a hypoglycemic state several times a day. This definitely takes its toll.

The brain needs a steady supply of glucose. Yes, that does mean sugar! However, that does not mean *eating* sugar.

Most people are aware of some hazards of sugar – the cavities, the weight gain, the blood sugar spikes and crashes. But let's look a little deeper. What happens, exactly, when we eat too much on a regular basis? Keep in mind that when I say "sugar," I am also referring to bread, cereals, pasta, and other highly processed carbohydrates – even so-called healthy snacks like rice cakes. They may not be sweet, but the body converts them to sugar so quickly that they might as well be.

This is what a typical child that I see (let's call her Jenny) eats throughout the day:

Quick Tip

Want to know the easiest way to cut sugar from your child's diet? No more juice or soda! One can of soda has the same amount of sugar as two candy bars. Fruit juice, even with no added sweeteners, is basically just a less sugary drink with more vitamins. The vitamins are great, but the straight sugar is still hard on the body. You can ease your child through this transition by diluting juice with water more over time, finally switching to plain water. You can use sparkling water to make it more like soda. Most of us need much more water than we drink anyway.

- Breakfast: bagel or cereal, juice
- Lunch: ham sandwich, potato chips, apple, cookies
- Snack: goldfish crackers, fruit rollups, juice
- Dinner: lasagna, salad

Frankly, until you get to dinner, Jenny's extremely typical diet is not optimal. Breakfast is all carbs and sugar, which is not going to stay with her until lunch. In fact, after a few hours, Jenny will be in a hypoglycemic (low blood sugar) state that is literally incompatible with learning. (And for those who say they don't like to eat breakfast, not having food half an hour to an hour after rising sends the body into that same hypoglycemic state.) The body perceives this state as a stressor and secretes stress hormones like cortisol, which will make her feel more jumpy and anxious. This stress-state also diverts blood flow away from the frontal lobe – home of critical thinking – and instead towards the more survival-oriented amygdala, which can make a child react emotionally. It would be so nice if people recognized that they need to eat at this point, but in fact the sensation of hunger is not necessarily one of the symptoms of hypoglycemia. Instead, a child might feel out of sorts or just spaced out and unable to think clearly.

Lunch is not terrible, but does not have enough protein to sustain her energy through the afternoon. Also, the high sugar and carb count will send her blood sugar zooming, raising her energy (in a hyperactive kind of way) but then leading to a crash a few hours later. Her snack will do the same. Jenny's blood sugar has basically been spiking and crashing all day.

If you consider the most common snack foods and lunches, this cycle happens several times a day for far too many children, sending them on the Blood Sugar Roller Coaster all day long. The human body is not designed to operate like this. Think about it: Your body actually goes into a form of fight-or-flight survival mode. It can't be good to do that to yourself every day!

Over time, a child may appear to adapt to this type of diet, with less obvious immediate effects that might alert a teacher or parent to diet-related pitfalls. But they have not really adapted (see "Important Concept #3"). The consequences over time are fairly dire and, in my opinion, account for a much higher percentage of the problems seen in school than most people are aware. Our bodies are simply not made to process so much carbohydrate and sugar at once.

Children who follow the Standard American Diet ("all white except for the food dyes!") tend to develop a number of problems:

- They often have lower percentile growth curves or become overweight.
- Some become prone to developing diabetes later in life (rates of diabetes have sky-rocketed in the last ten years).
- In the long term, since this blood sugar roller coaster is so stressful to the body, the adrenals become chronically stressed and depleted, manifesting as lower baseline energy levels and sleep problems, and setting a child up for more complicated health problems later on.
- This sets up a vicious cycle of worsening brain chemistry imbalances that lead to either poor concentration or mood swings – or both.

Protein is a much better choice for any meal because it tends to keep blood sugar levels very stable without much fluctuation. Vegetables have a relatively neutral effect on blood sugar but contain many vitamins, minerals, and antioxidants that the brain and body need. The fiber in fruit usually slows down the speed of absorption of sugar to a rate where it is not a problem for most people.

An example of a daily meal plan that would be healthful: 2 eggs and half a slice of whole-grain toast for breakfast, one fruit for snack, organic turkey sandwich on gluten-free bread with carrot and celery sticks, nuts for snack, brown rice with chicken and salad for dinner, and a naturally sweetened fruit cobbler made with granola for dessert.

Gluten: Way Too Much of a Good Thing

As recently as 15 years ago, who talked about gluten? Now you can't get through the grocery store without seeing flags screaming "gluten free!!!" It has become the bane of many people's health and is arguably the most diagnosed food allergy, with the rate of celiac disease rising to four times higher than it was just 60 years ago, according to the Mayo Clinic (and researchers believe it is still vastly under-diagnosed). Bread has been a staple of the human diet since Biblical times. When did it become not only problematic, but, to quote Mayo Clinic gastroenterologist Joseph Murray, MD, an actual "public health issue"?

Gluten is the protein in wheat, barley, and rye. Celiac disease, far from being merely a digestive illness, is caused by an immune reaction to gluten. Celiac sufferers sometimes have digestive issues, but the symptoms may be mostly neurological in nature as well, such as brain fog and depression. There are many levels of gluten sensitivity, however, that can exist without the presence of celiac disease. Any level of reaction, if ignored over time, can lead to chronic digestive problems and a range of other health problems, as well as neurological disruption and behavioral symptoms.

So how did gluten become the enemy? The most common theories include:

- Hybridization and other recent agricultural practices have altered grains so that they are no longer what we were eating for hundreds of years. Our bodies have not had a chance to adapt to this "new" grain.
- Storage practices, especially in this country, promote the growth of a fungus that encourages the disease.
- We eat much too much of it. Bread, pasta and other wheat-based products have somehow become not just a staple, but a prominent part of each meal. Wheat is also added to a vast array of processed foods, with the result that most people overeat it without even realizing it, increasing the chance that they will develop a reaction.

Awareness has increased and doctors are much more likely to look for it now (still, research comparing bloodwork from sixty years ago clearly reveals a much smaller percentage of celiac disease than now).

Food Dyes and Other Strange and Unnatural Things

My son, at age eight, was quite reactive to chemical food dyes. He was too young to monitor his own diet, and I had trouble convincing all his caregivers that it really was crucial to avoid certain foods. One day, at a soccer game, my normally sweet-tempered little boy lost it completely, screaming furiously at his coach and refusing to come off the field as requested. I ran over to my suddenly demented son and could see that his braces were clogged all the way across with a rainbow of color. Someone had given him multicolored, sugary kids' breakfast cereal. The point was irrevocably made for all to witness: Give my kid food dye, and my sweet Dr. Jekyll becomes Mr. Hyde. ~ M.S.

Your kids may never go to bed hungry, but they also may not be getting quality nourishment. Another dubious benefit of being a wealthy, modern country is the number of things in our food that are not actually food. Super-sweet sugar substitutes like aspartame literally rewire the brain over time, make people crave sugar constantly, and can cause hyperactivity. Many food dyes can cause asthma, hyperactivity, and emotional dysregulation. A number of frequently used additives can cause symptoms ranging from hyperactivity (seeing a pattern?) to chronic gastric problems. Sodium nitrite alone has a lengthy list of possible side effects that ought to alarm anyone.

Even if your child does not exhibit sudden, dramatic responses like the child in the story, that doesn't mean you're off the hook. These chemicals do not do good things for the brain. Research increasingly shows that they can subtly shift the way the brain functions over time, in a way that can be difficult to address once those changes have become entrenched. But you don't need to come up with a whole complicated new meal plan. Just reacquaint yourself with real food!

Dietary Fat and the Brain

Did you know that the makeup of your cell membranes depends on what you ingest? And how well your cell membranes function determines, in part, how well *everything* works. Your brain talks to your body, and brain cells talk to each other, via cell-to-cell communication along nerves or neuronal tissue. If they can't talk to each other, or if the signals get slowed down, hyped up, or otherwise screwed up, you will start to see symptoms of disease or disorder.

Dietary fats play a significant role in how well these cell membranes (and other aspects of cell-to-cell communication) function. You need *good fats* to make sure they work well. *Bad fats* make the process deteriorate.

If you eat a lot of trans fats such as those found in vegetable shortening, fried foods, many forms of junk food, and arachadonic acid found in red meat, it has a number of negative effects:

- It starts an inflammatory response throughout your nervous system, which causes an increase in glutamate, an excitatory chemical in the brain. This can lead to symptoms of anxiety, hyperactivity, addictive tendencies, and inattention.
- These changes in the brain also lead to chronic excessive brain firing, which causes neuron damage and contributes to degenerative diseases like dementia, Alzheimer's, or Parkinson's disease.
- Inflammatory fats make cell membranes hard and rigid, blocking cell-to-cell communication.

Partially hydrogenated or hydrogenated oils are also extremely bad for your health. They are found mostly in processed foods, but read all labels. They are in lots of cookies, chocolate, even some peanut butter. Because of the way it's made, hydrogenated oil is toxic and its molecular structure is more like plastic than oil. These oils clog the arteries and predispose people to cardiovascular disease. They are also inflammatory fats and, like trans fats, can increase inflammation throughout both body and brain.

Good fats are essential for brain function. If you eat lots of the omega-3 fats found in fish, flax, and walnuts, your cell membranes will be nice and malleable. This allows for brain chemicals like serotonin, dopamine, and acetylcholine to communicate better with the cell, supporting positive mood, attention, and memory. Phospholipids, a fat derivative, are also a crucial component of cell membranes, and help balance stress hormone levels, decrease anxiety, improve memory, improve mood, and decrease aggression.

What Can *We Eat?*

What can you do to help your child in this arena? This chapter has covered a number of suggestions: Rediscover real food and avoid processed and fast foods, start looking at labels for chemicals and added gluten, start cutting down on sugar and processed carbs, and be aware of the fats you feed your family. A practitioner trained in nutrition can help you identify other pitfalls unique to your child, and can help you put together a diet that will help him function at his best. Here are a few specifics for you to consider as well.

Important Concept #4: Epigenetics – Cheating the Genetic Powers That Be

Some families come to me hoping for answers, but still resigned to their "fate." One mother remarked, "Almost every member of my husband's family has some kind of learning disorder. And almost all of my family is overweight. I've accepted that this is my son's genetic fate. How can changes in diet hope to shift that?"

Epigenetics means *outside the gene*, and is the study of how you can modify gene expression through environment. This is what we do with both healthy lifestyle habits and nutrition. Nutrition means giving the right ingredients to your body in order for it to function well. You can change your health outcome by making changes in your life that promote your goal. Genes do not define your destiny. Good eating habits can.

Beyond Just Food

A Word About Supplements

In this chapter, I use the word *supplements* to mean:
- Vitamins
- Minerals
- Herbs
- Probiotics
- Amino acids
- Oils (fish oils, omegas, etc.)

I have certainly had many parents who do not think supplements are necessary, and there have been many misleading reports in the media about how they don't do much good. Here's what I would like every parent to know:

- *Quality varies widely.* It's difficult for a layperson to investigate supplement purity and potency (even if it matches the claims on its own label, which many of them don't). So find a practitioner who has done her research. In my experience, I have had patients use supplements with a very similar formulation to the one I recommend because it is cheaper, but unfortunately they do not have the same effect and end up saying it does not work.

  If you take low quality supplements, you are just creating expensive urine. What is cheap and wasted is expensive. See my website in the resource section for a good selection. Popular children's chewable vitamins and all their gummy-bear-like friends do *not* pass the test!

- The body cannot synthesize many nutrients, such as essential amino acids and vitamins C and D (in fact, 90 percent of my patients do not get nearly enough vitamin D). They must be consumed. Given the information about how much less nutrition our food contains than before, and how essential these and other vitamins and minerals are to maintaining good health, doesn't it seem riskier *not* to make sure your family is getting what it needs?

- In 2008, the US had 48,700 percent more AERs (Adverse Event Reports) for correctly used prescription drugs than for supplements. (According to the FDA, an AER is anything from a concern that the drug or supplement isn't working to a serious illness that follows the consumption of said supplement.)

I have seen significant clinical benefits from using supplements in my practice. Many patients have improved when prescription drugs had either not solved their health issues or complicated them. Supplements are generally much safer, have fewer side effects, and are gentler compared to prescription drugs.

However, in my opinion the most important distinction is that therapeutic doses of herbs and supplements work in an adaptogenic fashion. This means that they can bring the body gradually into a state of balance so that it can then maintain health by itself. Prescription drugs work more forcefully, pushing biochemistry in one direction at the expense of creating imbalances elsewhere in the body. Additionally, prescription drugs often do not address the underlying cause of the problem and definitely do not help the body remember how to maintain its own health (hence, various levels of dependency tend to develop). Remember that, even if you end up using medications, you can still find ways to help your child heal so that maybe he doesn't need to continue them.

RDA: A Helpful Guide?

In a word, no.

Parents sometimes express concern that my supplement prescriptions far exceed the RDA (or the RDI or DRI, guidelines which were established later). However, these two points explain why none of these recommendations should guide your thinking:

- The RDAs (Recommended Daily Allowance) were established in 1968 to prevent diseases like scurvy. They represent the absolute minimal requirement to avoid serious disease. Optimal health requires much more…and recovering from serious disease may require even more than that.

- With our soil-depleting agricultural practices and genetically modified food sources, it's amazing anyone gets enough nutrition! It now takes *two quarts of strawberries* to provide the same amount of nutrition that used to be in *two strawberries*. In my opinion, no federally established guideline comes close to adequately taking this shift into account.

Probiotics: Not Created Equal

Here's something you should know about probiotics: Quality varies. My microbiology professor in med school ran an experiment on probiotic supplements, culturing many different brands. Of the brands she tested, only three brands matched the advertised label. All the other probiotics did not meet label claims; for example, if the bottle claimed 10 billion **Lactbaccilus acidophilus** per servings, only about 4 billion were present – indicating the product was not manufactured to be shelf stable. (She also found that some brands contained contaminants). Be sure you find a practitioner who can recommend a quality probiotic.

Omega-3 Fatty Acids: Powerhouse Supplement

Many studies show a correlation between depression and deficiency of omega-3 fatty acids. According to the journal of *Nutrition and Healthy Aging*, DHA, which is an omega-3 fatty acid, is "one of the major building structures of membrane phospholipids of the brain and absolutely necessary for neuronal function."

The *British Journal of Psychiatry* did a revealing study on prisoners. One group was fed the regular prison diet, and the other group was supplemented with omega-3 fats. The prisoners who were given omega-3 fats had a 35 percent reduction in violent crime in prison. There have also been numerous studies linking therapeutic doses of omega-3 fats with improvements in ADD or ADHD symptoms. Clinical trials have shown omega-3s to have about the same success rate as anti-depressants in reducing symptoms of depression. In my practice, I have seen patients experience huge symptom improvement from depressive mood, anxiety, and focus problems with a therapeutic dose of EPA and DHA.

Probiotics

Probiotics are supplements that increase the amount of good bacteria in your gut. With the popularity of probiotics growing, more people are becoming aware that probiotics are useful for improving immune function and gastro-intestinal health. But you may be unaware that they also have a positive effect on depression and ADHD, as evidenced by numerous studies.

How do probiotics help the brain? If there are high amounts of bad bacteria or yeast in the gut, more toxic chemicals are produced. This can cause hyper firing of the neurons in the brain, which leads to more stress in the brain and has been linked to anxiety, depression, and difficulty focusing or thinking clearly. There are strains of probiotics that have been shown to calm down this phenomenon and therefore lessen the symptoms. However, different people need different strains, and not everyone needs the most famous, *Lactobacillus acidophilus*. A Comprehensive Digestive Stool Analysis tests will help determine what's missing and what's needed.

Who Does This?

Any healthcare practitioner can train in nutrition. Providers whose training inherently focuses on it include biomedical or Functional Medicine docs, naturopaths, nutritionists, and dieticians. Anyone else would have had to go outside of his specialty. And even on that list, only the biomedical and FM docs would necessarily have studied advanced levels of individualized nutritional therapy. You wouldn't get that from someone who believes there is one best way to eat or who has only studied general health principles in order to create healthful menus for restaurants or schools. Individualized nutrition is a field that evolves quickly; research uncovers more links between nutrition, mental health, emotional control, and performance every year. General or outdated information is simply not good enough.

So always ask about training. Make sure the person you are interviewing has more than a general background or a few weekend workshops in nutrition. The questions at the end of this chapter will help you find someone with the qualifications you need.

You should also know that most primary care medical doctors are not trained in nutrition or nutritional supplements. It is a fact that medical doctors only get four hours of nutrition training – that's four actual hours, not four credit hours. So do not assume that your family doc has the knowledge you need; ask if she has done extra training in nutrition, what her philosophy is about nutrition and its impact on learning, and so on.

Questions for a Prospective Nutritional Counselor

- Do you prescribe to the idea that there is one best way to eat?
- How would you help us to figure out my child's individual nutritional needs?
- How do you think nutrition can affect learning or behavior disorders?
- Can you describe your training and philosophy about how nutrition affects health and performance?
- How do you stay up-to-date in the field of nutrition?
- As far as nutrition goes, what is your area of expertise and interest?
- What kind of testing methods do you use?
- How do you determine food allergies, sensitivities, etc.? How do you help people deal with any food reactions that are discovered?
- Do you have experience working with children who have needs similar to mine?
- Do you have experience working with children who have difficulties with textures of food due to Sensory Processing Disorder?
- What is your philosophy about food and nutrition? (This may seem a particularly wide open question, but you will probably find that anyone in this field will have a philosophy about it.)
- Do you recommend nutritional supplements to patients? How do you determine which brands to use?
- Do you work alongside a Naturopathic Doctor, Chiropractor, or Functional Medicine MD, or refer to them when needed?

Resources for More Information

Website

www.modernintegrativemedicine.com This is my website, with a list of good quality supplements and a blog article about quality control in supplements.

BOOKS

Raise a Smarter Child by Kindergarten by David Perlmutter, MD. Dr. Permmutter gives very specific information, including brands of toys that are less toxic, specific chemicals and how to avoid then, and a chapter devoted to ADHD. A fun, informative, and easy read.

The Brain Diet by Alan C. Logan, ND. This book is packed with information about the brain and includes chapters about oxidative stress, the gut-brain connection, and Japanese fusion recipes.

The Ultra Mind Solution by Mark Hyman MD. This book discusses the seven keys to wellness and outlines Dr. Hyman's program for optimal brain function.

Super Immunity for Kids, What to Feed your Children to Keep them Healthy Now and Prevent Disease in their Future by Leo Galland MD. This is a great book to have on the shelf as a practical resource, since the immune system and nervous systems are so tightly correlated.

Brain Allergies: The Psychonutrient and Magnetic Connections by William Philpott. This book explores the connection between food sensitivities and mental health, and provides information on the rotation diet.

REFERENCES

Gesch, C. B., S. M. Hammond, S. E. Hampson, A. Eves, M. J. Crowder. Influence of supplementary vitamins, minerals and essential fatty acids on the antisocial behaviour of young adult prisoners. Randomised, placebo-controlled trial. Br J *Psychiatry* 181 (July 2002): 22-8.

Harding, K. L., R. D., Judah, C. Gant. Outcome-based comparison of Ritalin versus food-supplement treated children with AD/HD. *Altern Med Rev* 8 (3) (August 2003): 319-30. Orv Hetil. 2011 Sep 11;152(37):1477-85.

Feher, J., I Kovacs, G. C. Balacco. Role of gastrointestinal inflammations in the development and treatment of depression. [Article in Hungarian] *Orv Hetil* 152 (37) (September 2011), doi: 10.1556/OH.2011.29166, www.ncbi.nlm.nih.gov/pubmed/21893478.

About the Author

Dr. Emily Chan, ND, (or Dr. Emily, as her patients call her) received her doctorate of Naturopathic Medicine from Bastyr University, and holds an undergraduate degree in biomedical sciences and music. She has interned at the Functional Medicine Research Center as well as the Emergency Department at Evergreen Hospital. She currently practices in San Diego, CA and consults around the world.

Dr. Emily specializes in chronic medical conditions that have an emotional component to them and addresses the immune/nervous system and physiological relationships in treating her patients. She frequently works with mood and behavioral issues, endocrine disorders, HPV/Dysplasia, autoimmune disease, and gastrointestinal disorders. Dr. Emily is also published in medical journals and magazines, speaks at medical conferences training doctors, and has appeared on television. You can see her health videos on her You Tube channel: Dr. Emily Chan ND. She also authors and teaches health and neuro-reprogramming courses.

You can check out more information about Dr. Emily's programs, schedule an appointment, or contact her at: www.modernintegrativemedicine.com

Section Four

COMPLEMENTARY AND
ALTERNATIVE MEDICINE
(CAM)

———— ◆ ————

THIS SECTION IS REALLY A CONTINUATION of the "Digging Deep: Broader Solutions" section. However, complementary and alternative medicine (CAM) is less well known – and certainly less well understood – than Western medicine; it seemed, therefore, to warrant its own section. Each chapter includes a brief explanation of how these modalities may help, as well as the history and fundamental philosophy. Each method has a unique view of the way human bodies, minds, and emotions function, interact, and can be accessed for healing. Please consider reading a few of these chapters to see how they may offer unique benefits to your child. We have seen such success with these methods that we would have felt remiss leaving them out.

———— ◆ ————

SIXTEEN

Introduction to CAM

You may have heard about Complimentary and Alternative Medicine, but it can feel intimidating to step into this realm. In addition, your pediatrician may not be familiar with these approaches, so it may be difficult to get accurate input. We have put together this section of the book to give you an introduction and a few ideas to get you started.

So, why do we have a whole section devoted to CAM approaches?

- If the Mayo Clinic, John Hopkins, Harvard, and other leading medical centers have integrated medicine divisions (which combine western medicine with CAM treatments), then so should we.
- CAM approaches are becoming so common that it would be remiss to exclude them.
- We love these approaches. We love having effective options to offer besides a prescription and a therapist, particularly when the prescription and therapist approach has not been effective for some children.
- Parents want a wider range of options for supporting their children. The vast majority of parents who come to us ask for more than conventional medicine can offer.

While much of the population has used some form of Complementary and Alternative medicine at some point (vitamins and other supplements count), not everyone is fully clear on exactly what CAM refers to. The first thing you should know is that in the U.S., we divide treatment options into two broad categories:

- The first category is conventional medicine with standard medical practices. For example, the standard of care for treatment of Attention Deficit/Hyperactivity Disorder is the use of medication to enhance attention control and behavior therapy for getting new skills and behaviors into a child.
- The second broad category of treatment options is CAM. These are treatments that act as a:

- *Complement* to standard medical practices, so that the treatments are used simultaneously. An example would be using medicine to increase alertness in a child with attention problems, but also changing the child's diet to increase protein while eliminating sugars and dyes.
- *Alternative* practices where the treatment is used instead of standard medical practices. For this, the family might choose to try dietary changes and increased exercise in lieu of using medication. They may even go further and have micronutrients assessed and do individualized supplementation.

We should point out that the boundaries between CAM and conventional medicine can overlap. Often, what was once CAM is now standard of care. Nutrition is a good example as it is gaining momentum not only as a support for treatment of AD/HD, but also for a myriad of health problems from heart disease to cancer. Whether a family uses non-standard approaches as a complement or as an alternative to standard medical practices, it can open up a huge range of options for treatment.

So, the good news is - there are A LOT of CAM options out there. Where there may be only a few treatment options within conventional medicine for many learning or developmental problems, there are a myriad of CAM options.

Which leads us to the bad news - there are A LOT of CAM options out there. It can be overwhelming when faced with all the options and unclear information about the efficacy of any of them. The treatment of autism would be an excellent example. With the huge increase in the number of diagnoses has come a surge of both CAM and conventional treatment options, many of them complex, intensive, and expensive. It can be extremely difficult for parents to sort through and make good decisions for *their* child.

What is covered in this section of the book is only a small subset of the CAM options out there, but these are some of the areas we have found to be particularly effective for the treatment of learning and developmental problems. Some of the modalities in this section have been around for a very long time (e.g., naturopathy) and have been getting consistent results for much longer than Western medicine has existed. Others (craniosacral, neurochiropractic, neurofeedback) are relative newcomers. But all are here because we have observed positive results and think they are worth exploration.

Advantages of CAM

Conventional medicine typically has protocols for treating anything from acne to zinc deficiency. The *protocol* is a pre-set list of steps for addressing a medical, psychological, or developmental problem. This is considered the *standard of care* for the disorder. It allows for consistency in treatment and usually reflects what the research has shown to work for most people. The standard of care is just that: standard. Everyone gets pretty much the same or similar treatment.

The advantage of Complementary and Alternative Medicine is that it is *highly individualized*. There is no standard approach. Every symptom a child has reveals something unique about her overall state. Medical history, genetics, lifestyle, diet, exercise level, stress, and a dozen other factors are used by CAM providers to evaluate the problems that are concerning parents. Having care providers look at this whole picture of your unique child is the only way of figuring out what is being revealed.

Again, Attention Deficit Disorder provides a good illustration. In conventional western medicine, the treatment for AD/HD is medication to support alertness and counseling/tutoring to reduce any behavioral, social, or academic concerns. Though the medication response may be individual and need tweaking and the other supports would also be provided according to the child's needs, that is the standard approach for every child. CAM providers do not see AD/HD as simply needing medication and therapy. In just about any CAM treatment, your child with AD/HD will be evaluated to explore the unique underlying reasons that AD/HD is present. For example:

- A nutritionist may find that one child with AD/HD lacks essential fatty acids, but that the next child is not getting nearly enough protein. A third child may be hypersensitive to sugars, food dyes, or a particular food. The treatment would be directed by these individual factors.
- A LEAP Practitioner may find that one child with AD/HD does not have good communication between the two hemispheres of the brain, where another child has immature reflexes indicating weaknesses in brainstem function.
- In neurofeedback, the evaluator may find that one child has slow wave patterns in the language center of the brain making him look inattentive, while the next child has a brain wave pattern indicating poor coordination between different parts of the brain.

Guidelines for Navigating CAM

The basic tenets of CAM require that the provider do the following:
- Treat the whole person (for example, a provider treating a child who appears to be autistic would not just ask about behavioral symptoms; they would also ask about

physical symptoms, sleep patterns, food preferences, and personality styles)
- Be highly individualized
- Look to treat underlying causes of the disorder, not just eliminate the symptoms
- Support natural healing processes

At least, this is what CAM providers *should* do. But some providers in CAM are not much different from some providers in conventional medicine. They provide a singular treatment (their protocol) and try to use it to treat a broad symptom category. Not every child with AD/HD can be successfully treated with dietary changes just as not every child with AD/HD will be successfully treated with a prescription for Ritalin. In both conventional medicine and in CAM, you as a parent must feel informed enough to determine whether the care she is receiving is right for her needs. But while conventional medicine has some standards of care, CAM is a broad field without clear guidelines in some areas (which is why we list some of the following basic guidelines).

For the parent venturing into CAM for the first time, it can feel intimidating. How do you vet each approach and try to pick the one that could be beneficial to your child? Some questions to help you feel more comfortable with your pursuit are:

- Think about how you found out about the CAM provider. Who referred you to this person? This could be anyone from a physician to a friend, but you have to trust their knowledge level of the CAM and trust that they understand *your* child's needs.
- Check for certification and/or licensure. Does this CAM provider have certification by a national organization that has set standards for treatment in this area? Chiropractors, nutritionists, and hippotherapists are just a few examples of CAM providers who can seek certification. If there is no certification available for your CAM provider, go back to the first question above.
- Educate yourself about the approach you are pursuing. Ask yourself, "Do I have an understanding of what is being done by this provider and why it is being done?" As much as a parent would like someone to wave a magic wand and make her child better, no treatment will be magical. But people new to CAM (and anxious to see change) may be hoping for a magically quick response. Educating yourself will help you be realistic. All therapies will need some time to work.
- A good provider is collaborative. Be wary of any providers (CAM or conventional) who says that their treatment is the only treatment for the issue and that they are the only ones who can provide the treatment.
- You as a parent can ensure your child receives integrated medicine. Communicate

with your primary care doctor, so he or she is aware of any CAM treatments you are pursuing for your child. Do the same with any CAM provider, so he or she is aware of any conventional treatments your child is receiving. **This is important to ensure that one care approach does not conflict with another. For example, some supplements can alter the effects of some medications.**

- Ask the treatment provider about the expected length of treatment, as well as the expected number of sessions before any changes start to appear. Be wary of any provider who would like all services paid for in advance and cannot offer any sense of outcome for your particular child.

- And finally, remember, CAM is not a silver bullet. Just as not all children respond to medication the same way, not all children will respond to any one CAM approach the same way. What worked great for the neighbor's child, may not work as well for yours. It is a frustrating reality of any approach. Do your research, then approach things with an open but realistic mind.

As we said in the beginning, we love CAM approaches. They have given us options for our clients when western medical approaches have not worked (or have not worked well enough). As more families are trying to explore new options, we hope the following short chapters give them not only information, but also the confidence to pursue something new.

Naturopathy

by Hadi Ali, ND

A 10-year-old boy came to my office with a diagnosis of ADD. The parents did not want to jump into treating him with Ritalin because they favor natural approaches to health. They wondered if there might be any contributing factors we could address. His symptoms included an inability to focus, difficulty managing stress, and getting over-stimulated easily.

Watching the boy in my office, I noticed an interesting pattern. His parents had cut all the tags out of his clothes, because the sensation on his skin drove him crazy. Every time I put my hand on his back or his head, he squirmed or shrugged away from my touch. His parents confirmed that he was uncomfortable with physical contact, and that unavoidable touch (like in crowds) made him hyperactive and upset. Upon further inquiry, his parents informed me that they had not been out to a restaurant with their child since infancy, because the background noise in crowded places would over stimulate him to the point of emotional breakdowns.

This child looked like he had been misdiagnosed as ADD, when he really had something more like Sensory Processing Disorder. However, as a naturopath, I am always looking to see what may be the underlying cause of symptoms. Since his symptom picture looked largely neurological, as Sensory Processing Disorder does, I wanted to rule out both Lyme disease and Celiac disease (gluten allergy). Lyme disease is far more common than previously believed, and can mimic a range of behavioral and learning issues. Celiac is primarily a disease of the nervous system, although it is often thought of as mainly a digestive disorder. The fallout from Celiac disease affects the central nervous system and can look like ADD, ADHD, multiple sclerosis, sensory integration disorder, and Lou Gehrig's Disease (ALS).

The Lyme tests came back negative, but the tests for Celiac disease came back positive. I helped the family remove all gluten-containing foods from his diet, healed his gastrointestinal tract with herbs and supplements, supported his nervous system and blood/brain barrier with natural medicines, and waited for his system to respond. Over the course of four months, his constant nervous system agitation abated. His sensitivity to clothing and tolerance for noise normalized, and his focus and ability to manage stress improved. He was left with an intoler-

ance to touch and an aversion to crowds, for which I recommended occupational therapy to help with any remaining symptoms of sensory integration problems.

Sam, another 10-year-old came, into my office at about the same time, exhibiting symptoms of ADHD. Upon interviewing the parents, I found that a very different profile emerged. Both parents worked, and their schedules varied from week to week. This made it difficult for them to maintain a regular home routine. Sam did not observe a consistent bedtime, and usually got less sleep than I would recommend for a boy his age. I often find that sleep deprivation, if chronic, causes a lot more problems than mere sleepiness.

He also ate a lot of soda, junk food, and "white food" – processed white flour and sugar – because it was easier. As a result, he experienced insulin spikes and crashes all day. This taxed his adrenals, which were trying to maintain even blood sugar, which in turn led to a weaker immune system and inflammatory cascades as a result of the overworked adrenals, which in turn led to tremendous nervous system agitation from all the inflammatory byproducts in the body. Rather than recommend further testing for AD/HD, I ordered lab tests that would assess fasting glucose and salivary cortisol levels throughout the day. The results were revealing: Sam was, adrenally speaking, a "total puddle."

I worked with the family to educate them about the importance of a regular home routine and making sure Sam got enough sleep. We also discussed the absolute necessity of a good diet. We worked to heal his very tired adrenals and his irritated digestive tract, focusing on basic dietary issues. I recommended supplements for gut and adrenal support, then helped them shift Sam's diet: the whole family increased good proteins, vegetables, and fruits, and switched from soda to water. Over the next several months, Sam gradually became a much happier, more focused child. ~ Hadi Ali, ND

The Basics

Naturopathic doctors, or NDs, are trained in the same subjects as traditional Western doctors, qualifying them to act as family practitioners. An ND learns different diagnostic techniques and then treats with different tools from most medical doctors. While I respect many aspects of Western medicine and acknowledge that it has revolutionized features of health care, I feel that naturopathy offers a more complex understanding of healing and a broader range of effective but non-medication-oriented solutions.

Part of the power of naturopathy stems from its emphasis on exploring what makes each patient unique, how his issues emerge from a distinctive overall picture, and how treatment, therefore, must be individualized to suit his particular situation. When a child walks into my office, I don't think, "OK, this is an ADHD case." I don't want to determine merely what set of symptoms is sitting in front of me. My goal is to get to know the child, so that the symptoms can be put in the perspective of the whole person. I think, "Who is this person, and what has happened to create these symptoms *right now*?"

Naturopathic medicine is built on the philosophy of *Vis Medicatrix Naturae,* or *the healing power of nature*. Naturopathic doctors help patients restore health by removing obstacles (such as harmful eating or lifestyle habits) and by gently supporting and stimulating the body's inherent healing capacity. Today's naturopathic physician easily blends modern and indigenous diagnostic and therapeutic procedures to create a comprehensive health care plan.

Naturopathy evolved into a distinct profession in Germany in the mid-1800s. Dr. Benedict Lust (MD) brought naturopathy to America in 1896, when he established the first naturopathic college in New Jersey. As a result of political and social shifts, naturopathy took a backseat to Western medicine in the U.S. for much of the 20th century.

However, it has re-emerged in the last 30 years for a number of reasons. There has been increasing consumer demand to find "new" solutions to the healthcare crisis. The resurgence of naturopathic medicine has also reflected growing interest in preventive healthcare, non-toxic medicines, and respect for the body's inherent ability to heal itself, given the proper support. While Western medications definitely have their benefits, they typically mask rather than resolve symptoms, and can have negative side effects. Naturopaths prefer to try less invasive approaches at first, giving the body a chance to reestablish its own balance.

Parent's Perspective

We started using a naturopath because my daughter Jessie kept getting sick once she started school. Her pediatrician told me this was normal, but I felt there must be more to it. A neighbor told me about her naturopath and I thought, "Why not?"

The naturopath took one look at Jessie's shiny red cheeks and said, "You have a food allergy here." Tests confirmed a dairy sensitivity. The ND also discussed other dietary changes that made a huge difference in Jessie's overall health. And when she did get sick, I was amazed at how thorough the ND's examination was. She asked about everything from what temperature foods Jesse craved to what color the phlegm was, then prescribed herbs, vitamins, and foods to address those particular symptoms. I had no idea there were different kinds of colds!

Now we have two main doctors: our pediatrician, who does Jesse's yearly checkups and prescribes antibiotics or other drugs as needed; and Dr. Nancy, whose thorough approach has helped Jessie through the everyday maladies that come up throughout childhood. (We live in a state that does not license NDs to

> *prescribe, work with certain labs, or be covered by insurance, so it is necessary to keep our MD as well.) I feel much more empowered as a parent when she's sick, since I now have so many more tools than just fluids and rest. And Jessie seems to recover much faster with more targeted remedies. ~ R. F.*

Principles of Naturopathic Medicine

Naturopathic doctors can differ hugely in their approaches, but there are a few principles that provide the foundation for any practice. These ideas guide an ND's choices no matter what tools he may use.

First, do no harm. For a naturopath, that means following these guidelines:

- Avoid the harmful suppression of symptoms. Symptoms are like the check engine warning light in your car: You can do something that just makes the light go away, but then you haven't done anything to find out why it went off in the first place. That problem isn't going to get better by itself. Using medications only takes care of that surface level, and will probably force the imbalance to show up in some other way.
- Use the least amount of force necessary to diagnose and treat disease: Start with the least invasive method and working toward more forceful ones. Don't use a sledge-hammer when a nudge will do. This helps prevent side effects and gives the body a chance to mobilize its own defenses.
- Use techniques and methods that reduce the risk of dangerous side effects.

Let nature heal. One of the primary beliefs of naturopathy is that the body wants to heal itself and is always striving in that direction. We try to support the body's innate healing capacity by removing anything that is blocking health, such as a sugar-laden diet or an exhausting schedule. We also may prescribe herbs, foods, or supplements to support a person's return to health. But basically, naturopaths believe that the body fares better with minor prompts in the right direction, rather than the overpowering approach that drugs tend to be. There is a difference between healing and just making a visible symptom go away. (Obviously, sometimes this is an ideal and extreme measures are needed right away.)

Identify and treat causes. Naturopathic physicians believe that, unless the root causes are addressed, issues probably will return, worsen, or be re-routed to show up elsewhere in the body. Therefore, we prefer not simply to suppress symptoms unless they are severe.

For example, if a patient has problems with acid reflux, some kinds of practitioners might give a prescription that eases acid reflux along with standard warnings about fried or spicy foods. A naturopath will examine the patient's diet carefully and will help identify triggers that might be more subtle.

Treat the whole person. This involves doing a thorough assessment and getting to know your child, not just his symptoms. My intake, therefore, not only covers the issues that parents and teachers want me to resolve, but also encompasses the child's diet, social life, emotional tendencies, daily routine, likes and dislikes, physical environment, and family life. A detailed intake is a hallmark of naturopathy, and forms the basis for any treatment plan.

Doctor as teacher: educate your patient. Naturopaths believe that the more engaged a patient is in her healing process, the better the result will be. I like to give my patients the tools and understanding to take responsibility for their own health. This is much more than a pretty-sounding concept. Studies consistently show that when people feel informed and empowered, they are more likely to heal quickly than if they are simply told what to do.

Prevention. Any practitioner has this as a goal, but most of us only see patients when something is already wrong. However, I believe that most naturopaths have a different standard of health they are trying to maintain. Health is not just a lack of symptoms. The ultimate goal of a naturopath is not simply to have a patient be asymptomatic. Symptoms indicate illness, but there is a lot of territory between illness and optimal health. We want to see full health and vitality: enough energy to do whatever you want (within reason), healthy emotional range, creative engagement with the world, and excitement about the future…not just better numbers on his adrenal tests and more regular bowel movements.

Just So You Know

One concrete way that naturopaths differ from medical docs is in how they read lab tests. Western medicine tends to be pathology-oriented; doctors look for disease. If a test marker falls outside of certain parameters, you're in trouble; if it doesn't, you're fine. This is changing with the advent of Functional Medicine and the biomedical approach – see chapters 13 and 14, respectively – but by and large, this is how medical doctors are trained to read lab tests in the U.S.

Naturopaths play more in the grey areas. We look for overall patterns: a low normal marker in one test, combined with a high normal marker in another, for example, may not indicate a particular disease, but may reveal a worrisome trend that is worth addressing. I believe there is a great deal that can be done before you are actually sick, and lab results are one way I determine what's going on, whether or not the numbers are officially pathological.

The Making of a Naturopath

Naturopaths go through a similar training to medical doctors in the Western tradition:

- First, we must complete the same undergraduate coursework as premedical students.
- We then attend a four-year accredited Naturopathic Medical School. Students also undergo hands-on clinical training, treating patients under the supervision of other licensed doctors.
- Finally, we must pass the full set of national board exams, at which point we receive a doctoral level degree in Naturopathic medicine.
- Most NDs then go on to do additional coursework in specialties of their choice.

NDs are trained to be primary health care providers, and in some states (see box) are listed as such by insurance companies. Naturopathic physicians treat all medical conditions, providing comprehensive individual and family healthcare. All NDs are trained to recognize the need for prescription drugs, but in states where they are not licensed they are not legally allowed to prescribe (and in any case, they emphasize the use of natural medicines). Minor surgery, such as removing cysts or suturing superficial wounds, is also within the scope of naturopathic physicians. Naturopaths typically leave drugs and surgery as the last options in treatment (except in cases of acute crisis).

Choosing a Naturopath: Shop Around!

You should interview a range of practitioners no matter what you're looking for, but with naturopaths this is particularly important. There are probably as many differences between naturopaths as there are naturopaths. Our basic training may be the same, but after that, people often get continuing education from a wide variety of sources. No two end up with the same final list of skills or favorite tools. One might prefer acupuncture and Chinese herbs; another might rely mostly on nutrition and supplements; a third may use a more Functional Medicine approach.

Tools of the Trade

Naturopaths are trained in a wide variety of techniques, but these almost always form the basis of any naturopath's bag of tricks:

- **Clinical Nutrition** - A cornerstone of naturopathic practice is that food is the best medicine. Many medical conditions can be treated effectively with the addition or removal of specific foods along with the targeted use of nutritional supplements.

- **Botanical Medicine** - Botanical medicine has long been an integral part of traditional, indigenous medicine. These plant-based medicines have been in use for thousands of years, long before the advent of synthetic drugs. Many plant substances are safe and potent medicines. They have low toxicity and lack the tendency to accumulate in the body, but should be used only under the supervision of an experienced practitioner.

- **Homeopathic Medicine** - Homeopathic medicine is based on the principle of *like cures like*. It works on an electromagnetic level, gently stimulating the body's inherent healing capacity.

- **Oriental Medicine** - Many naturopathic physicians employ oriental medicine: Chinese herbs, nutrition, and acupuncture. Acupuncture involves the insertion of fine needles through the skin at precise locations, in an effort to both move and balance energy (qi) in the body, resulting in the restoration of the body's inherent healing capacity.

The Oriental approach to health and healing is completely outside of the Western paradigm, and it is outside the scope of this book to explain this whole paradigm.

Food for Thought: To Prescribe or Not to Prescribe

Be sure to find out what scope of practice is permitted in your state, as it varies. Naturopaths all learn to prescribe medications, order and read lab tests, and perform minor surgery. However, due to political pressures, they are not licensed to do so in some places.

As a matter of fact, even if the law allows it where you live, I am not sure I would recommend that you have a naturopath prescribe meds for you or your child. Prescribing pharmaceuticals is simply not a main focus of our training (unless a practitioner has done extra training in that area). We may know when the "big guns" need to be brought in, but we do not spend the majority of our time prescribing drugs. You may want more experienced practitioners – people who have to stay up-to-date on new drugs and their side effects, etc. – making that call. When I suspect that medications are in order, even temporarily, I refer patients to other practitioners to make sure that someone thoroughly trained in pharmacology is taking a look at the situation too.

However, the following website provides a solid tip-of-the-iceberg explanation: tki-health-om.blogspot.com/2011/11/chinese-herbology-explained.html

Lifestyle Counseling and Modification - Mental attitudes and emotional states can influence, or even cause, physical illness. Counseling, nutritional balancing, stress management, hypnotherapy, biofeedback, family counseling, and other therapies are often useful for addressing or easing root causes. A naturopath can either perform these therapies or refer a client out as needed.

Naturopathy and Learning or Behavior Disorders

This section offers a brief overview of the areas a naturopath assesses when addressing learning or behavior issues. Naturopaths, biomedical doctors, and functional medicine doctors look at the same areas in roughly the same ways, so please see chapters 13, 14, and 15 for more detailed information about psychiatry/functional medicine, biomedical approaches, and nutrition. ~ the editors

Even if a naturopath is specially trained in learning or behavior issues, his approach will probably still encompass the elements already described in this chapter. When dealing with a child who has these types of problems, most naturopaths pay particular attention to the following areas:

Foundational issues. As was the case with Sam in the opening stories, foundation is key. Is a child getting proper nutrition, sleep, exercise? How is his family dynamic, health and developmental history, and general health? It is not unusual in our busy society for families to lose track of these foundational issues and need a re-set in one or more areas.

Immune system function. If your child seems sickly – that is, prone to catching every cold that passes through – or has chronic symptoms like rashes even if everything else seems fine, I will typically review immune function. Immune system weakness is often related to digestive issues and can impact learning and emotional stability dramatically.

Digestive issues. These can disrupt many other systems in the body, and can have a huge impact on brain chemistry. Inflammation in the digestive system, resulting from a number of possible sources, disturbs smooth functioning of the blood-brain barrier and can wreak havoc on a child's ability to think clearly or be emotionally stable.

Toxic overload. This is an equally important area of focus, particularly if your child shows unusual sensitivities emotionally, cognitively, or physically. Just as different people have allergic reactions to different substances, there is a huge range of reactions to everyday toxic sources such as electromagnetic fields, mercury in fillings, and certain food dyes.

Chronic toxic buildup can have a profound effect on a child's ability to function properly. Cognitive symptoms can include mental fogginess, disorganization, memory problems, or simply "odd" thinking. Behavioral symptoms can include aggressiveness or withdrawal.

Physical symptoms can range from headaches to skin problems. Despite Western medicine's frequent assertion that detoxification is unnecessary, people do have varying abilities to detoxify naturally and your child might need extra help performing this important task. Identifying problems in this territory can transform severe issues.

Food for Thought:
Detox and Chelation

Some practitioners, especially naturopaths and others who profess to use holistic healthcare approaches, promote aggressive detoxification methods as the answer to all health problems. Some base their whole practices on it. But beware, please: it is not a matter of simply eating vegetables, drinking hot lemon water, and clearing out all the bad stuff. (In fact, some research shows that without animal protein, detoxification does not happen correctly.)

A good detox program requires the proper herbs, amino acids, and foods to support all the detoxification pathways involved in Phase I and II of liver detoxification. If this is not done, your tissues will release all sorts of toxins and free radicals...but they will not be safely processed out of the body. A badly done cleanse basically helps you stockpile still-reactive toxins in your system and do even more damage.

It is outside the scope of this book to go more into detail than that, but at least make sure any practitioner proposing a detox program knows what the previous paragraph means. Detoxification of any sort is a medical procedure that can have potentially dangerous side effects if not set up and monitored properly, especially with children. If any practitioner offers to include detoxification in his treatment plan, ask about his experience and approach.

As for chelation, my advice would be: please don't. Unless your child has experienced an overt, acute exposure to a heavy metal such as mercury, there is too much we don't know to justify messing around with this one. Some people develop antibodies to heavy metals, so that squeezing them out of the tissues would be a huge disruption to the system (and there is currently no way to test for this contingency). But recent research also reveals some alarming indicators that when you try to mobilize heavy metals out of the system, they may just be relocating to the brain, where they will do much more damage than the peripheral tissue they were in before. There isn't even evidence that they're doing much damage, hiding out in cells throughout the body. I can't believe that's a *positive* thing, but trying to clear them out may well do more harm than good. Do your homework, ask a lot of questions, and please proceed with caution.

Questions for a Prospective Naturopath

- What is your background—where did you train, are you licensed or certified?
- What kind of professional development/continuing education have you done since your schooling? Do you have a specialty you like to focus on?
- What is the scope of practice for naturopathy in this state?
- Can you tell me about your success in treating patients with a condition similar to my child's?
- When might you refer patients to conventional health care professionals?
- What is your philosophy concerning medications, and when and how might you prescribe or refer us to someone who can? Will you continue working with us if we opt for medications but would like to continue using your approach also?
- What treatment approaches do you use the most in your practice?
- Do you have a network of other professionals that you like to work with? If not, do you mind working with other types of practitioners?
- Do you order blood work or other diagnostic tests? Do you interpret lab work parameters the same way as mainstream medical doctors? (If not, please explain.)
- How long do you spend with each patient for an initial visit? For a follow-up visit? How easy is it to get an appointment in an emergency? Are you available for phone consultations, if we just have a few questions?

Resources for More Information

Websites

www.naturopathic.org. This website provides a great deal of information on naturopathic practices, including health tips and up-to-date research. There is also a page that will help you find practitioners in your area.

tki-health-om.blogspot.com/2011/11/chinese-herbology-explained.html, TKI Health. This is a good overview of Chinese herbology.

Books

Nature Doctors: Pioneers in Natural Medicine by F. Kirchfeld and W. Boyle. The authors give a thorough description of the history and practices of naturopathy through accounts of its colorful founders' life stories.

Herbs in the Treatment of Children by J. Scott and T. Barlow. Not just a list of herbs and their applications, this guide will also help you understand some of the deeper patterns of various illnesses and how herbs can lead a child back into a state of health.

Natural Medicine Instructions for Patients by L. Pizzorno, J. Pizzorno, Jr., and M. Murray. This book gives clear guidelines on naturopathic approaches to specific conditions.

ABOUT THE AUTHOR

Hadi Ali, ND, studied naturopathic medicine at Bastyr University and University of Bridgeport College of Naturopathic Medicine. He later completed post-graduate studies in Craniosacral Therapy with The Milne Institute; Thai Massage, Acupuncture Injection Therapy, and Mesotherapy at the Miami School of Medicine; Systemic Family Constellation Therapy with Dr. Dietrich Klinghardt; Psychosynthesis Therapy; and Field Acupuncture for Traumatic Events. Hadi has degrees in Philosophy and English from Tufts University and a Masters in acupuncture from the Institute of Taoist Education and Acupuncture, where he is currently on the faculty teaching acupuncture and nutrition. He is also the Medical Director at the Integrative Medicine Foundation in New York City, a non-profit organization focusing on the research and development of traditional medicine in sub-Saharan Africa. He lives and works in Boulder, Colorado with his wife and children.

Neurofeedback/Biofeedback

by Steve Rondeau, ND

NOTE: Neurofeedback is known by several names, including biofeedback, neurotherapy, brain biofeedback, EEG biofeedback, and EEG training. There are also several types of neurofeedback machines and protocols, such as LENS, LORRETA, and HEG, to name a very few. Although it is outside the scope of this chapter to discuss the differences, I will address the general features that I believe are most helpful for children with learning or behavior problems.

N orman, a 16-year-old boy, came to me for help with his aggressive behavior and outbursts. His behavior was threatening enough that the police were called regularly, to everyone's distress including his own. After being adopted at an early age, he had been diagnosed with autism, intermittent explosive disorder, and anxiety issues. His family had tried many avenues: Norman was on three different medications and referred to them as "his friends" because of how intensely fearful he became without them. He had also had years of behavioral therapies and dietary interventions, and had participated in a few medical trials. However, the turmoil at home and calls to the police continued. Norman's psychiatrist referred the family to me for neurofeedback. Desperate to find answers, they agreed.

The brainwave readings we collected did not surprise me. Norman displayed an array of conflicting brain wave patterns that explained his struggles perfectly. They were, however, a tricky combination to address. The patterns in his frontal lobes reflected his inattentiveness and cognitive difficulties. This by itself would have been helped by AD/HD medications. But he also had slowing and abnormal patterns in other parts of his brain that, when combined with the first findings, often creates high levels of frustration and angry outbursts – and would be exacerbated by AD/HD meds. Other patterns explained his severe sensory integration and spatial-orientation deficits. Still others accounted for his difficulty regulating his emotional states and behavior.

Medicating this combination of factors is complicated at best. It is almost impossible to address one pattern without aggravating another. The mix of drugs they had settled on seemed to be helping because Norman was basically sedated most of the time, but the problems persisted anyway because the underlying maelstrom of battling brain wave patterns remained untouched.

We had to proceed in a way that addressed both the under- and over-arousal patterns in his brain, without destabilizing him further. Norman eventually completed 40 sessions of neurofeedback over the next year. He went from weekly arrests, to monthly, to not having the police called at all! His mother now refers to him as a "rock star" with "great behavior, no aggression, no irritability, and only positive moods." He is currently stabilized on only one medication and will probably return to behavioral therapies, as he is in a much better position to be able to respond to them. ~ Steve Rondeau, ND

The Basics

If I suggested to you that playing video games or watching movies would help your child overcome learning or behavior problems, you might think I was off my rocker. But with neurofeedback, that is exactly where many families are finding answers. Neurofeedback targets specific problematic brain wave patterns, using specialized software – often in the form of video games or movies – to retrain these patterns. This treatment modality aims for three broad goals:

- It exercises and builds a state of focus, by showing the patient's brain how to get to a calm, alert, productive mental state.
- It can help the brain work more *harmoniously*, meaning how smoothly different brain sections work with each other. Many activities, such as writing by hand or understanding social dynamics, require the coordination of several brain centers; but sometimes they have trouble communicating with each other.
- It also increases *brain flexibility*, meaning how quickly and easily a person can shift between brain states. A child using neurofeedback for emotional dysregulation issues, for example, might gradually become less and less upset by frustration, as well as learn to come back from that frustration more smoothly and in less time. Flexibility issues can also affect impulsivity, attention, and behavior.

A Little Neuroscience

The neurons in your brain communicate through electrical changes. These electrical changes can be seen as brain waves on an EEG (electroencephalogram) and are measured in cycles per second (Hertz – Hz for short). They can also be referred to as frequencies. The lower the Hertz or frequency, the slower the brain activity. There are four major categories of brain waves that reflect certain Hertz ranges:

- Delta waves (below 4 Hz) occur during deep sleep.
- Theta waves (4-7 Hz) occur in lighter sleep, deep relaxation, or meditation.
- Alpha waves (8-13 Hz) occur when we are relaxed and calm. This is a good state for learning.
- Beta waves (10-38 Hz) occur when we are actively thinking and problem solving.

The human brain is remarkably malleable. While we used to believe that a person's neural responses were hard-wired at a young age, we now know that environment, events, injury, or training can shift even adults' brain function dramatically. This ability of the brain to change the way it responds is called *neuroplasticity* and without it, no cognitive or behavioral therapy would work. Neurofeedback looks past symptoms at the underlying brain wave patterns themselves, and directly engages the brain's own ability to learn how to shift them. While this can be helpful for any learning or behavioral issue, it is particularly valuable for two reasons:

- **Addressing the whole picture.** Human beings do not operate according to textbooks. Categorizing symptoms can be slippery. I often see children who have ADHD, for example, but who also have other symptoms that do not fit the ADHD profile. Sometimes a dual diagnosis makes sense, but sometimes those other symptoms are just there and no one quite knows what to do with them. With neurofeedback, I don't have to worry about the diagnosis or which labels fit or don't fit. I can look at the overall patterns in your child's brain waves and address those directly.
- **Adding more information to the medication game.** By the same token, meds can address one symptom but worsen another. I see many families whose children are on multiple meds in order to both address the problem and counteract the side effects of the meds for that problem. The qEEG (a specific type of EEG) can give

insight to which meds might be most effective and which might be problematic. It can also lessen or even eliminate the need for meds in the first place.

I use neurofeedback for a wide variety of conditions and have seen it make a huge difference for many different cognitive or emotional issues. However, most research has examined its use for:

- AD/HD
- Seizure disorders
- PTSD
- Emotional dysregulation, including anxiety, depression, and anger issues
- Autism
- Addictions

There is a growing body of evidence that neurofeedback is an effective tool for resolving many childhood behavioral and learning disorders. Families seek it out to avoid medications, to supplement current medications with additional treatment, to enhance other therapies, and to find a way to help a child that is confounding everyone.

Brief History

Neurofeedback emerged from research that started in the 1960s, involving cats, sleep, and EEGs. Researchers wanted to see if they could teach the cats how to produce a specific EEG frequency at will. If the cat produced a half second of the researchers' desired frequency, they were given a reward of milk. Over time the cats learned how to produce the frequency at will. These exciting results were published in 1967. Dr. Sterman, the lead researcher, was fascinated by these unexpected findings and continued to observe the effects of brain wave training when he moved on to somewhat related research for NASA (that is, it was related in that it used some of the same cats, which yielded similarly interesting results – the simple act of monitoring the cats' brains, in a way that gave feedback, improved their overall function). Sterman began looking into the effect of neurofeedback on people, and in 1972, published findings discussing the effectiveness of neurofeedback in helping humans suppress epileptic seizures.

From there, various lines of research emerged demonstrating that people's brain waves could change using this approach. Participants in those early studies consistently reported increased feelings of calm and focus. In the decades since then, many specific neurofeedback protocols and machines have been developed that help people learn to control and maintain more optimum emotional, behavioral, cognitive, and attention states.

Despite decades of published research, neurofeedback is still not a widely known option, or widely accepted in the medical world. Because psychiatrists, pediatricians, and family doctors like myself are not usually trained in medical school about neurofeedback, they are often reluctant to recommend this therapy unless they have had personal experiences themselves. I can assure you that neurofeedback is a well-researched science. It is not a guaranteed solution – nothing is – but its positive affects have been well documented. (See References at the end of this chapter.)

For many families, waiting for science to catch up to what is currently working is not an option. Using the guidelines outlined in this chapter can help you make an informed decision as to how to pursue neurofeedback therapy for your child.

A Closer Look

The brain has a remarkable capacity to change itself, given proper feedback and support. Neurofeedback rewards desired electrical activity and inhibits troublesome activity by giving the brain direct, immediate feedback. The brain then has the choice to take this information in and alter its course, or not. This treatment does not force new pathways to be forged. It simply gives the brain information about what it is doing, so that it can make different choices. While this premise may seem almost underwhelmingly simple, I have seen hundreds of children change their experience through this approach.

Most neurofeedback protocols begin with a qEEG reading (a specific type of EEG, or electroencephalography). This non-invasive method, otherwise known as brain mapping, measures the electrical activity in a given region of the brain. After identifying a child's unique qEEG pattern, clinicians are able to identify problem areas and retrain the abnormal patterns in a given region.

The retraining process happens in slightly different ways, depending on the specific neurofeedback protocol the practitioner uses. Many use a video game that your child would basically control with his brain. The game acts as a mirror, showing his brainwaves on a screen. The electrical activity in his brain then determines what happens in the game. Self-regulation is the key, as the brain begins to learn more healthy patterns of functioning in order to get better results in the game. Some methods use movies, which operate more smoothly the more in control your child is of his brain activity.

Brain function and dysfunction is highly individual. No two brains operate quite the same way. However, there are several consistent patterns in the qEEG of children with certain diagnoses that have allowed for the development of consistent treatment programs.

- The most common patterns are excessive slow wave activity relating to *hypo function* in one area of the brain. For example, slowing in the language centers of the brain often results in language delays or speech disorders. *Hyper function*, where the activity is too fast, often relates to AD/HD and anxiety issues.

- Other brain patterns are related to how well different parts of the brain work together. The brain should run like a well-oiled machine. But some children's brains do not, resulting in disorganization, inattention, emotionality, and other challenges. (A child can have an excellent memory for dates or events, for example, but be unable to perform simple tasks such as shoe tying or addition.) When the brain works unevenly, it is measurable on the qEEG and we can address it with neurofeedback.

- In the last few years, I have begun to see more and more dysregulated kids – children with a combination of several diagnoses, including AD/HD, depression, oppositional defiant disorder, Autistic Spectrum Disorder, anxiety, or bipolar disorder. QEEG readings on these children reveal combinations of brain patterns: some too slow, others too fast. These children can be a challenge to work with, as there is so much going on. They are particularly tricky to medicate, as one med might help the ADD but worsen the anxiety, for example (more on medication in the next section). However, the qEEG identifies these combination patterns and treatment can then address the core underlying brain abnormalities.

- Head injury, a condition that is well-known for being difficult to treat if it does not heal on its own, responds quite well to neurofeedback. Once any remaining neural inflammation has been addressed (see Chapter 9 on concussion; naturopathic doctors and some other kinds of physicians also use products that are specifically designed to deal with this), neurofeedback can identify and correct the erratic brain wave patterns that can result from a concussion.

As with any treatment, not all children respond to neurofeedback. The non-response rate is somewhere in the 5 to 10 percent range, which could possibly be attributed to various other reasons such as trauma or biological metabolic abnormalities.

It is also true that some people need periodic tuneups, but this should not be a common occurrence. I consider these the most common reasons for needing additional treatment a year or more after brain waves have stabilized:

- Very complex, extreme patterns such as the ones in the opening story – these may need to be nudged back in the right direction every few years or so, but you should not need to go through the whole sequence again.

⚲ Unaddressed underlying factors – low-key food allergies or intolerances, as well as many kinds of ongoing digestive disturbances, can wreak havoc on brain function. Ongoing environmental stressors, ongoing or unresolved trauma, medication changes, or significant head injuries can similarly derail brain wave patterns.

⚲ Provider inexperience – If a practitioner considers it normal for many of his patients to need repeated treatments over the years, you might want to try someone else. I consider it highly unusual to have to redo this work.

Neurofeedback and Medication

Many families bring their children to me because they would rather avoid meds if possible. Others are happy with their medication results, but feel that their children could perform even better if they got more support. Some have become uncomfortable with the number of meds their child has accumulated and would like to lessen the need for so many (this often happens with the dysregulated kids I mentioned earlier; they are often put on a cocktail of many different meds). I have seen neurofeedback be successful with all of these cases, though many of the more complicated or severely impaired children do need to continue their other therapies.

The Process

Step 1: Evaluation

Some practitioners may have a separate first session just to talk with you (especially if you request that), but many will combine that with the initial qEEG reading. During the interview portion of the evaluation, the provider will go through your child's academic, behavioral, and medical history, including any medications she is taking. Although he will also ask about any diagnoses your child has been given, it doesn't really matter; he will see what he needs to in the qEEG.

After the interview, your child will have an EEG recording done of her brain wave patterns. This is a completely painless process that can take anywhere from 20 minutes to an hour. Typically, a number of electrodes will be attached to your child's head, which record her brain waves and give the provider a thorough picture of what her predominant brain patterns are and how well (or poorly) the different parts of her brain are working together.

Using the qEEG as a guide, the practitioner then creates an individualized treatment plan

⚮

"Why Isn't Anything Happening?"

The most common complaint I hear is that the patient does not notice changes. While neurofeedback – like any treatment – does not work for everyone, the truth is that very gradual changes can be hard to spot without using sensitive assessment tools. Children, in particular, are looking for relief from their inability to focus, or the tantrums they can't control, or the overwhelming anxiety they feel during tests – whatever symptoms are making their lives miserable. When those don't just go away, they say they don't feel any different.

But self-awareness is a lot to ask of a child, especially one who is struggling every day. It may be up to you, the observant parent, to notice the increments. Your son was able to sit still for five minutes longer while going over spelling words. Or your daughter melted down just a bit less dramatically, or calmed herself down a little more quickly, when she lost a board game. Perhaps the morning crunch to get out of the house went a teeny bit more smoothly. Sometimes, the first changes don't even happen in the area of the symptoms you want to address (some children find they can fall asleep more easily, for example). Once your child starts to feel the changes and understands better how to work the neurofeedback program, changes should accelerate. Be patient, and adjust your radar to look for the little things. All little things.

that will address your child's specific issues. This can be easily adjusted as you go along, depending on how your child is responding.

STEP 2: TREATMENT

This is the easy part, but it is also time-consuming. Treatment itself is non-stressful and often fun for the child, but rewiring the brain takes consistent training and commitment. A typical course of treatment can last from 20 to 50 sessions, sometimes more. Many providers suggest that you get sessions at least once a week, if not two or three times. Sessions typically take about half an hour (younger children may only be able to handle 15-minute sessions).

Your child will come into the office, have the electrodes placed on her head and will then use whatever program has been selected – movie, video game, music, whatever. It's that simple.

STEP 3: MONITORING PROGRESS

Methods here vary hugely. Some providers will just have you write down the five most problematic behaviors or symptoms that you are trying to address. You then observe any changes in those specific behaviors over time. Progress may seem subtle or slow at first, but it is by nature a gradual process. Look for baby steps. Be excited when you see them. Brain function does not change dramatically overnight.

Other methods include re-doing the qEEG at regular intervals, or assessing your child's abilities through a type of standardized test that seems relevant to her issues. I would caution you to be wary of elaborate, high-tech sounding re-evaluation tools. There's nothing wrong with them, but they can be expensive and are not always necessary. As long as you start with a qEEG reading and are seeing concrete improvements, that is what's important.

However, if neurofeedback is covered by your insurance carrier (yes, it does happen!), you should find out what they need. Some companies require certain types of progress documentation. This can sometimes come into play for school services as well.

Finding a Practitioner

Finding a provider who has worked with children who have similar issues to your child is important. This ensures that the practitioner:

- has the ability to relate to a child with special needs;
- can help with medication decisions as symptoms change or reduce;
- can recognize when things are not progressing as they should.

Background and training within the field can vary greatly, as anyone can train in neurofeedback. If you can find a physician, psychologist, or someone with mental health experience, that can be valuable since the provider is then more likely to have an understanding of the neurochemistry and pathophysiology involved with certain conditions. This would make him more qualified to assist with medication decisions and other consultation services. These types of professionals are also more likely to be able to bill insurance. Not all providers can.

However, not all communities have a range of choices and there are many types of experienced practitioners out there. The following information can also help in your search:

- The Biofeedback Certification International Alliance (BCIA), which is the governing body and credential agency that oversees neurofeedback, has a website listing all of the providers who are certified in your area (www.bcia.org). If a provider is BCIA certified, it demonstrates that he has overseen a set number of neurofeedback sessions, has been educated in the fundamentals, was mentored by someone experienced in the field, and passed a board exam while maintaining yearly continuing education requirements.
- It is also advisable to find an individual who is licensed in his area of speciality, such as a licensed physician, or a licensed therapist, in addition to their BCIA certification.

This ensures that he is maintaining a minimum standard of continuing education in his field, as well as providing a governing body to which he reports.

When considering whether neurofeedback is good for your child, there are several things to take into account.

- **Age of your child** – Typically, children over five are best able to sit through the sessions, depending on their capacity for compliance. Although neurofeedback will work with younger children, this requires a special office setting and collection of skills not all therapists can provide.
- **Location of therapist** - This may seem obvious, but typically sessions are performed one to three times per week and commuting can become a big factor if you need to do 30 or more sessions.
- **Other medical issues** – Some may need to be addressed prior to starting therapy. For example, visual acuity should corrected, hearing should be tested, and other medical explanations for behavior and developmental challenges should be explored. Personally, I prefer that patients have their nutritional status assessed as well.

Questions for a Prospective Neurofeedback or Biofeedback Therapist

- Are you certified with Biofeedback Certification International Alliance?
- How long have you practiced neurofeedback?
- What types of learning challenges and needs have you worked with the most? What were the outcomes?
- How do you determine if this is an appropriate therapy for my child?
- Do you have a cut-off point at which you can determine that this approach is not working for my child?
- At what point can you give an estimate of how many sessions may be necessary and how often these should occur?
- Is it possible to obtain insurance coverage for this treatment with you?

Resources for More Information

Website

www.bcia.org, Biofeedback Certification International Alliance. This website not only lists providers in your area, but gives information on many topics related to biofeedback.

Books

Symphony in the Brain: The Evolution of the New Brain Wave Biofeedback by Jim Robbins. This book takes you through the history, applications, and growing use of neurofeedback, using case studies and scientific research.

Getting Rid of Ritalin: How Neurofeedback can Successfully Treat Attention Deficit Disorder Without Drugs by Robert W. Hill and Eduardo Castro. This book discusses the use of neurofeedback for AD/HD specifically, and also addresses the importance of nutrition, elimination of toxins, and other relevant subjects for addressing ADD.

ADD: The 20 Hour Solution by Mark Steinberg and Siegfried Othmer. The authors explain how and why neurofeedback addresses and corrects the underlying cause of AD/HD. They also discuss some of how the brain works and other elements of effective treatment.

References

Arns, M, S. de Ridder, U. Strehl, M. Breteler, A. Coenen. Efficacy of neurofeedback treatment in ADHD: The effects on inattention, impulsivity and hyperactivity: a meta-analysis. *Clinical EEG Neurosciences* 40 (3) (July 2009): 180-9. This is a compilation of a number of studies of Neurofeedback to determine the effectiveness for treatment of ADHD.

Monastra, V. J. Electroencephalographic biofeedback (neurotherapy) as a treatment for Attention Deficit Hyperactivity Disorder: Rationale and empirical foundation. *Child and Adolescent Psychiatric Clinics of North America* 14 (1) (January 2005): 55-82, vi.

Lofthouse, N, L. E. Arnold, S. Hersch, E. Hurt, R. DeBeus. A review of neurofeedback treatment for pediatric ADHD. *Journal of Attention Disorders* 16 (5) (July 2012).

Thornton, K. E., D. P. Carmody. Traumatic brain injury rehabilitation: QEEG biofeedback treatment protocols. *Appl Psychophysiol Biofeedback* 34 (1) (March 2009): 59-68.

Steiner, N. J., E. C. Frenette, K. M. Rene, R. T. Brennan, and E. C. Perrin. In-school neurofeedback training for ADHD: Sustained improvements from a randomized control trial.

Pediatrics 133(3) (March 2014).

There are also many relevant articles, nicely outlined by subject and condition, at www.isnr. org/resources/comprehensive-bibliography.cfm.

About the Author

Steve Rondeau, ND, is a doctor of naturopathic medicine who attended medical school and internship training in Arizona and received his doctorate degree at Southwest College of Naturopathic Medicine. He then did specialty training in developmental disorders in Utah, focusing on treating pediatric neurodevelopmental disorders with a combination of conventional medication and alternative therapies.

Dr. Rondeau believes that our nation's children are highly over-medicated and that there are safe and effective therapies that blend the best of conventional western medicine with natural therapies. In his current practice, he utilizes traditional naturopathic approaches such as nutrition and herbal medicine as well as hyperbaric oxygen therapy and neurofeedback. He also serves on the medical advisory board of the PANDAS Resource Network, is BCIA-EEG certified in EEG biofeedback or neurofeedback and has trained with the ARI or Autism Research Institute (formerly DAN!, or Defeat Autism Now) and MAPS (Medical Academy of Pediatric Special Needs). Dr. Rondeau works as part of a collaborative team at the Wholeness Center in Fort Collins, CO, a collaborative health center that uses a blend of western, eastern, and alternative techniques to provide cutting-edge health care for the whole family.

You can find more information about Dr. Rondeau at www.wholeness.com. You can contact Dr. Rondeau at: 2620 E. Prospect Road, Suite 190, Fort Collins, CO 80628 , 970-221-1106

LEAP (Learning Enhancement Acupressure Program)

by Kim Gangwish, BA, AP

By the time my daughter Charlotte was four years old, she had already had more than her share of struggles. She had a severe speech delay, so communicating was a constant challenge and frustration for her. Identified with sensory integration issues, she also ran around constantly, climbing things, burrowing into people, and crashing into walls. She never seemed to follow her preschool teacher's instructions, wandering off constantly or causing some kind of ruckus. A paraeducator was necessary in order to help her manage the activities, control her behavior, and stay on task. Transitions were especially tough: she melted down when it was time to go home, time to leave home, time to go outside, time to come back inside…life was intense and difficult for Charlotte.

We had taken her to early childhood services. The people there could not diagnose but said that they believed her to be "profoundly autistic." I never did believe that. Despite her inability to speak, she connected just fine at home, engaged her younger siblings in play, made wonderful eye contact, and displayed a wonderful capacity for imaginative play…not characteristics that matched the profile of autism. But when she was over stimulated and frustrated at not being able to say what she needed, she did throw tantrums, shut down, and stop responding to others. In other words, she looked exactly like a child on the autism spectrum. Occupational therapy and speech/language therapy had had no observable impact on her behavior or abilities.

Then, to my intense relief, we found a LEAP practitioner and things began to change. Although she warned us that it might take time to see improvements, her behavior altered noticeably after just two treatments. All of a sudden, Charlotte was trying to verbally communicate about everything. It was amazing! Whereas before she would gesture or repeat one (barely discernible) word over and over, she was suddenly able to use two and three word sentences. She was proud of her success and we all celebrated.

Probably because of her increased ability to communicate, her tantrums lessened immediately. Her teachers in school started talking about removing her paraeducator because she *didn't seem to need them anymore. Her focus increased and she took part in classroom activities of her own accord. She communicated more with peers, which enabled her to become a part of the group. She was happier, calmer, and more easily directed when an issue did arise.*

We still had to address her sensory issues, so the LEAP therapist referred us to a new occupational therapist. The OT was blown away by the speed of her progress. Our LEAP practitioner explained that once the relevant neural pathways were clear and available – which is what LEAP does – other therapies could progress more quickly and easily.

We attribute most of Charlotte's improvements to LEAP. Her behavior improved markedly when she began LEAP treatments, whereas all other therapy had stressed her out and sometimes made her behavior worse. Since LEAP, we've seen only minimal backsliding in her progress. It is real and it is permanent. ~ S.L.

The Basics

LEAP, or Learning Enhancement Acupressure Program, is an effective method of helping to rectify learning, sensory, and behavior disorders. Using a complex acupressure-based protocol, practitioners can identify which specific neurological pathways are blocked or disorganized and then restore correct flow of information through the brain.

Along with being an effective modality on its own, this approach can also help to augment other therapies by helping to shorten the duration or increase their effectiveness. Over the last 18 years, I have cultivated quite a network of therapists that I work in tandem with; our work complements each other nicely, allowing the child to progress more quickly. As the underlying neurology becomes more integrated, processing in general becomes more efficient and the brain is more available to learn and process sensory information.

Brief History

LEAP is the brainchild of Dr. Charles Krebs, PhD. In the 1980s, Dr. Krebs was in a diving accident that nearly took his life. The extensive damage initially rendered him a quadriplegic. Unwilling to accept this fate, he began to explore a number of therapies, including modalities in both Western and Eastern medicine. A friend then brought him to a kinesiologist, who worked to restore some of the connection between the brain and the muscles in his lower body. Within an hour and a half, the kinesiologist had restored a remarkable amount of function. Dr. Krebs found that he could walk – not particularly well, but it was far more than anyone had predicted.

This astonished and intrigued Krebs. As a lifelong scientist, who also taught anatomy and physiology at the university level, he wanted to find out how this was possible. He expanded his studies to include everything he could find about brain function and neurology. As a result of his research and his own experiences of recovery, and with the help and feedback of physicians, clinical psychologists, neurologists, and many other kinds of health professionals, he spent years developing the protocol now known as LEAP.

As our understanding of neurology continues to develop, so does this work. Dr. Krebs is involved in research projects all over the world so that he is always on the cutting edge of the rapidly evolving field of brain science. Krebs now teaches all over Europe, Australia, and the U.S., and has established ongoing LEAP training programs in several countries.

A Closer Look at the Brain

The human brain is designed to learn. Our very survival depends upon certain kinds of learning; our search for pleasure, satisfaction, and meaning keep us exploring and learning throughout life. It is a natural function that a healthy brain thrives upon. Why, then, do some brains have so much trouble with certain functions, or with learning in general?

When you consider the staggering complexity of the brain, it's a wonder that anyone's brain works smoothly. Timing and synchronization are everything. All input must follow certain pathways in a particular, precise sequence. Moreover, every single thing the brain does fires both sides and involves several brain centers. Every activated pathway must coordinate with the others so that all information gets to the right places in proper synchronized order.

Take reading, for example. "When a person reads a story, the right hemisphere may play a special role in decoding visual information, maintaining an integrated story structure, appreciating humor and emotional content, deriving meaning from past associations and understanding metaphor. At the same time, the left hemisphere plays a special role in understanding syntax, translating written words into their phonetic representations and deriving meaning from complex relationships among word concepts and syntax." (Levy, J. Right brain, left brain: fact and fiction. *Psychology Today* 19 (5) (May 1985): 38-45.)

The human brain is masterful at finding ways to make up for compromised function. In a way, brain function operates like water flowing down a hill: if the most direct route is not available, it will take the next direct, and then the next, and so on. But there is a limit to how compromised function can become. Past a certain point, brain function goes from being a precisely orchestrated symphony to a chaotic cacophony that just feels confusing, frustrating, and overwhelming. The main factors that impair neurological function are:

- **Biological factors.** This can include nutritional imbalances that affect brain chemistry, and food sensitivities or toxic environmental input that cause inflammation in the brain. There is no point in battling upstream against unaddressed neural inflammation or a brain that lacks the specific nutrients it needs. Mitochondrial dysfunction (mitochondria provide the energy that the cells need in order to function) can also fail to generate enough fuel for the brain to operate. Researchers and practitioners are also finding a growing number of children whose brain function responds poorly to electromagnetic fields (EMFs) and other environmental factors. Even something as simple as hydration can impact neurological function.

- **Emotional stress.** Strong emotional strain or overwhelm can cause certain pathways to close down. Specific triggers can cause specific kinds of problems, such as test anxiety. A high level of chronic stress, such as difficulties at home or bullying at school, can cause general overwhelm that makes all processing more difficult. While this would not cause a learning disorder per se, it could worsen it or make it very difficult to resolve because the brain is basically "offline." The point here is that if your child is experiencing strong emotional states, either in general or directly related to learning, you will have to address those as well or the brain will simply not be available for learning or therapy. A calm brain functions, learns, and repatterns much more effectively than a stressed one.

- **Structural damage.** This can be the result of events in utero, stroke, head injury, or abuse.

We can call any of these *stress*. Stress, in this context, does not mean the emotional distress we usually associate with the word. Rather, it refers to anything that places more of a burden on the system than it can handle. Stress can impair function at any point in the neurological sequence. The following list describes a general overview of where a LEAP practitioner would check to pinpoint the source of the problem:

- **The nuclei.** There are basically two different types of tissue that make up the brain: white matter and grey matter. The grey matter consists of *nuclei*, centers that have particular processing functions. You've probably heard of the thalamus, amygdale, or hippocampus, which process sensory input, regulate emotions, and encode memory, respectively. These are just a few examples of the nuclei in the brain, each of which has specific processing functions. All of these must work in concert to process information and sensory input smoothly.

- **Neural pathways.** This refers to the neural connections in the brain – the white matter – which transmit information to the nuclei, up to the cortex, and down the spinal column. Unimpeded connectivity in the brain is essential for all of our functions. When processing is slow, uneven, or unsynchronized, we see sensory processing problems, emotional instability, or difficulty learning (among other possibilities).

- **Corpus callosum.** This is the main connective pathway in the brain. Comprised of an estimated 200 million fibers, it enables communication between the right and left hemispheres of the brain. Proper corpus callosum function is so essential to almost every function, that I check it in each patient I treat, and commonly find it in need of help. When this is impaired, a "traffic jam" in the brain results, and processing becomes extremely inefficient and slow.

These provide the foundation of subconscious processing, what we are referring to here as *underlying neurology*. After information has been through these areas, it then gets sent to the cerebral cortex, which continues the task of processing information. The frontal lobes, which are located in the front of the skull, are where we do most of our higher order functions such as thinking, reasoning, planning, etc. LEAP is one of the few modalities that can distinguish whether an issue is originating in, for example, the underlying neurology or the frontal lobes. Many therapies and academic tutoring techniques try to work with frontal lobe function, but it is an uphill battle if the underlying neurology is disorganized.

A practitioner must also know which other pathways to check besides the obvious ones. There are specific neurological pathways that contribute to the skill of reading, for example. But other pathway impairments could be contributing to a reading disorder, such as those of visual, vestibular, or auditory processing. Certain speech centers of the brain, if compromised, can also impact the ability to read.

Moreover, there are lifestyle considerations to explore as well, such as nutrition and either chronic or situational emotional stresses (test anxiety would be an example of a situational anxiety trigger). Lifestyle and daily routine also play a role. Whether the child has a stable, supportive home life, enough sleep, and a steady routine that feels calming can have a deep impact on brain function.

As you can see, what looks like a specific learning disorder on the outside can have any number of possible origins. If you take 20 children who have AD/HD, for example, it is entirely possible for each of those 20 to have an entirely unique neurological profile. For this reason, something like LEAP, that can identify the particular underlying problem, is an excellent way to help children with complex learning or behavior disorders.

A Closer Look at LEAP

LEAP uses a combination of applied kinesiology, acupressure, and a detailed understanding of neurology to pinpoint, first, where the neurological function becomes disorganized. Then, the practitioner utilizes acupressure techniques to relieve the stress that is causing function to lose its integration at those points. This allows the brain to reorganize its previously convoluted function into the most direct path once again.

The work involves the following components:

- **Applied kinesiology.** This is a natural health care system which uses gentle muscle monitoring to evaluate many functions of the body in the structural, chemical, neurological, and biochemical realms. Kinesiological muscle monitoring does not assess strength, but tests the integrity of the many factors that determine its response when called upon to contract. The muscle testing enables analysis that detects minor functional imbalances.
- **Acupressure.** This is a technique derived from China, designed to increase blood flow and restore body functions, including in the brain. The human body, it is believed, encloses an ongoing flow of bioenergy sometimes known as *chi*. This energy flows along specific pathways called *meridians*, and controls the functioning of all of the organs. Along the meridians are a large number of controlling nerve endings, or *acupoints*, which act as valves for the flow of chi. Proper stimulation of these points restores balance to, in this case, the brain.
- **LEAP protocol.** Dr. Krebs developed a complex protocol that combines kinesiology and acupressure in a complex, precise sequence in order to assess and remove blocks that inhibit learning, memory, and sensory processing.

Practitioners detect stress or dysfunction in mental processing by monitoring muscle response in conjunction with the activation of specific acupoints, either singularly or in combination. The assessment gives the therapist feedback on how the client's brain is processing information.

The therapist then utilizes gentle acupressure techniques to help release blockage in the brain's energy flows and better integrate the two hemispheres. As soon as the stress that caused the shutdown resolves, those neurological pathways come back online and are available for learning. LEAP protocols can effectively repattern the way the brain is able to process.

What Does a Session Look Like?

I like to work with a child once a week if possible. A session can last anywhere from half an hour for little ones to an hour and a half, or more if the person is from out of town and we need to get as much work done as possible within a short amount of time. It can be hard for children to lie still for a long period of time, so I offer toys, audiobooks, or movies to make it a fun and relaxed atmosphere.

First, I evaluate the foundational components of how the brain is processing information (or isn't). I assess the corpus callosum to see if bilateral communication is integrated and effective. I also examine visual, auditory, and vestibular processing, since they are crucial to learning. I then look at specific functions such as speech/language processing, memory, etc. I also ask clients to do certain tasks such as marching in place, quick visual tasks, or reciting a few numbers in a particular sequence (otherwise known as digit span) to get a baseline of neurological function. The results show me where I need to explore further. Based on the child's presenting neurology, I then follow LEAP protocol to remove the stress that is causing the blocks for learning, sensory, or behavioral issues. Sometimes I also give homework, simple tasks to do once or twice a day, to support the development of certain connections in the brain.

I prefer to work closely with parents, other caregivers, and other therapists so that we have a sense of the child's overall performance. Working as part of a team gives any practitioner a broader understanding of the child's needs and overall progress. This allows for all the needs to be efficiently and effectively addressed.

LEAP and Other Therapies

As an occupational therapist, I work with many children with sensory processing needs. My goal is to help the client in the most efficient and effective manner possible. To this end, I am happy to have access to a local LEAP practitioner. We have shared many clients and I have found it to be an effective way to progress through therapy more quickly. After she works with them, the neurological pathways I have been trying to access and coordinate are "online" and available. What I have seen time and time again is the speed at which their systems organize after LEAP work. ~ Amy Rogge, OTD, occupational therapist

I have consistently received feedback from other therapists that LEAP helps other therapies progress dramatically faster. Many therapies aim to stimulate a certain pathway repeatedly. Vision therapy, for example, consists of a number of exercises that activate particular vision-related pathways. Often, however, the relevant pathways may not be open in the first place. The first several repetitions of an exercise, often performed over weeks or even months, serve mostly to "wake up" the relevant pathways and start to organize the system. Once the pathway is available, it does need to be exercised so that the brain develops a consistent pattern of processing correctly. This is why repetition is helpful.

However, when the underlying neurology is very disorganized, repeating a certain function over and over is usually not enough to wake up and organize all the relevant pathways. In these cases, children will only get frustrated from repeating the same exercise for weeks or months without perceivable progress.

This is where LEAP can help. By organizing the underlying neurology, therapies such as occupational therapy for sensory issues or vision therapy often proceed more rapidly. This spares a child the exasperation of feeling like he's banging his head against a wall for little or no return. The resulting feeling that "I just can't do this" can create a great deal of emotional resistance and low self-esteem, and the child may just resign himself to not being able to learn this skill. This additional emotional stress will further shut down access to learning centers, making the brain generally less able to take in the therapeutic intervention. It's a self-defeating cycle that can make the whole enterprise an increasingly uphill battle.

Moreover, sometimes there is more to it than simply waking up a particular brain connection. In fact, for many children the problem is much more complicated than that; the problem lies deeper. If underlying neurology – such as the brain stem or connective pathways between the left and right hemispheres – is not functioning smoothly, it will be very difficult to address higher order frontal lobe functions (such as specific academic skills).

Who Does This?

Most practitioners have previous experience in the field of health care. Practitioners are expected to complete an intensive two-year training that covers detailed neurology and physiology, as well as the LEAP protocol. Students must complete an extensive oral, practical, and written exam.

Questions for a Prospective LEAP Therapist

- Have you been certified and are you up to date in your certification?
- How long was your training? (Should have been at least a couple of years; there are similar approaches that have much shorter trainings)

ℜ   Have you worked with children who have issues similar to mine?
ℜ   Do you consider diet and other lifestyle factors?
ℜ   Are you comfortable working and communicating with a team?

Resources for More Information

Book

A Revolutionary Way of Thinking: From a Near-Fatal Accident to a New Science of Healing by Dr. Charles Krebs. This book chronicles Dr. Krebs' journey from a life-threatening accident to developing his groundbreaking LEAP work.

References

Levy, J. Right brain, left brain: fact and fiction. *Psychology Today* 19 (5) (May 1985): 38-45.

About the Author

Kim Gangwish, BA, AP, Ms. Gangwish is one of the editors of this book. You can find her complete bio in the back.

Chiropractic Neurology

by Michael Pierce, DC, DACNB, FACFN

A mother came to me, seeking consultation for her 12-year-old daughter Melanie. Melanie seemed slow in school, with poor grades; she was also easily distracted and clumsy. After the physical exam, I asked the mother if Melanie tended to bump into things more on her left side. Her mother was amazed (as this was true) and asked how I could tell. During the exam, I had seen that this child did not perceive even light touch on the left side of her body. This was most likely due to dysfunction within the parietal lobe on the right side of her brain, which controls the ability to sense spatial relationships and sensory information on the left side of her body.

I find that dysfunctions are often concentrated in one side of the brain or the other, and that observable symptoms such as those Melanie exhibited affect other right-brain functions as well. Also, impairments in one side of the brain frequently limit full development of function on the other side. In Melanie's case, her abilities to learn new information and to maintain focus were compromised.

I developed a series of carefully sequenced exercises to build proper function on the right side of her brain. I also had her do 12 sessions of Interactive Metronome, a computer-based series of tasks designed to build coordination between brain and body. In addition, I did some gentle chiropractic adjustments to her left side in order to stimulate the right side of her brain. Within four weeks, she had dramatically improved her awareness on her left side, reflecting improved function in her right parietal lobe. By the next semester in school, her grades had improved to average, with even some above-average scores. ~Paul Austin, chiropractic neurologist

The Basics

Like the field of medicine, the chiropractic profession has a neurology specialty that focuses on the diagnosis and treatment of nervous system disorders. Like traditional chiropractors, these professionals are trained to use spinal manipulation techniques to support overall health. However, unlike other chiropractors, they are extensively trained to evaluate and address neurological imbalances in minute detail. This specialty is known as either *chiropractic neurology* or *functional neurology.*

Medical neurologists and neurosurgeons are the best for medication, surgery, and acute brain injury, while chiropractic neurologists offer rehabilitation for chronic brain and nervous system conditions. There are many natural methods that lie outside the realm of pharmacology, but that can also be combined with medication when necessary.

If a child is exhibiting atypical behavior or development, it is important to rule out some form of neurological disease (such as seizure disorder). If there is no neurological disease associated with the child's behavior or development, then there is an imbalance in how the brain is processing. Chiropractic neurologists treat children with atypical development of all sorts. Many specialize in the treatment of children with some of the following:

- Neurodevelopmental disorders such as Autism Spectrum Disorders, Tourette's syndrome, or Attention Deficit Disorder
- Learning disabilities, such as dyslexia or dysgraphia
- Neurological injury such as concussion or traumatic brain injury

The brain is *neuroplastic.* This means it can change with proper therapy or healing. The chiropractic neurologist will determine what parts of the brain are not working well and develop a plan to correct the imbalance. Correct stimulation of nerve cells through specific exercises has been demonstrated to build neuronal pathways. The treatment plan consists of customized tasks that exercise specific parts of the brain. It's like occupational therapy for the brain. You do these exercises to organize the brain and allow all the parts to work cohesively.

Chiropractic neurology has an extremely thorough protocol that:

A Little Science

Perhaps the most famous of the profession is Dr. Ted Carrick, of the PBS special *Waking up the Brain: Amazing Adjustments.* This thirty-minute program introduces the viewer to two patients that were helped by his work. He discusses his approach, including coma recovery for some patients. His website can be accessed through www.carrickinstitute.com.

- identifies exactly where the origin of the problem is in brain activity;
- develops a treatment plan to correct these glitches through precise activation of

targeted neural connections;
- modifies and fine tunes the exercises on a regular basis (such as weekly) to gently build a balanced brain that functions optimally.

The common denominator here is that neurological function has been compromised. Determining the origin of that dysfunction – "ground zero," if you will – is how this specialty works. Chiropractic neurological care can help whenever there are enough live neurons available to form new connections with each other. If we can get those neurons to talk to each other again (or sometimes for the first time), it can remediate a wide range of disorders. Children with any number of developmental or behavioral challenges may finally develop faster, cope better in school, improve their grades and social interactions, and improve their everyday coordination or sports performance.

Functional chiropractic care does not resolve disorders that are the result of neurological degeneration, such as Niemann-Picks Disease or Tay-Sachs Disease. However, it can sometimes be helpful as a palliative treatment in those cases.

Brief History and Practitioner Training

Functional neurology, or chiropractic neurology, evolved as a non-drug, nonsurgical alternative to addressing neurological dysfunction. The discipline of chiropractic neurology evolved out of the idea that there was much to offer patients beyond medications, surgery, and referrals for physical therapy.

The chiropractic neurology specialty, like medical specialties, requires a rigorous course of post-doctoral study with written and practical testing to pass the board exams. A chiropractic neurologist is a licensed chiropractor who has completed an additional 3-year course of study in neurology, including coursework and residency-based clinical training, and has passed a comprehensive certification examination administered by the American Chiropractic Neurology Board. There are currently only about 600 board-certified chiropractic neurologists in the world.

Can I Just See a Regular Chiropractor?

Chiropractors are trained to maintain the health of the spine. As the brain's pathway to the rest of the body, the spine allows for transmission of information in both directions. In particular, spinal asymmetry is directly related to brain asymmetry; thus, treatment of the spine can absolutely affect brain function. Given this, it is understandable that many chiropractors feel that basic spinal adjustments can be used to treat learning or attention problems. Some chiropractors also incorporate nutrition and other types of wellness assessments into their work, and see huge shifts in their patients' wellness and function.

I personally believe in the power of chiropractic care as an important part of improving health and *general* brain function. But spinal adjustments, even accompanied by other types of support, cannot possibly treat neurological dysfunction with the precision or depth that a chiropractic neurologist can. Functional neurology training, while it does build on basic chiropractic skills, goes so far into assessing and addressing specific neurological circuits, that it often seems to me to be a separate field entirely. If you are looking into chiropractic care because of a learning or behavior disorder, I believe you would be best served to find a chiropractic neurologist. Chiropractors can help you enhance existing abilities and perhaps ease some symptoms a bit, but I do not believe the training prepares them to rebuild the circuitry in the way that is needed to affect deeper, substantial changes.

~ Paul Austin, chiropractic neurologist

What Chiropractic Neurology Targets

We think of chiropractic treatment as adjustments to the neck and spine, and chiropractic neurologists are certainly qualified to treat in this way. But we have a range of other tools as well, and look at a completely different set of criteria when evaluating a patient. We typically assess someone in the following areas:

- **Brain Circuits.** This refers to the process of mapping the brain and evaluating how its circuits are functioning. We assess a patient's "electrical system" through a series of physical and sensory tasks that reflect functioning in the deep parts of the brain (such as the brain stem). If some circuits are immature and not firing well, their dysfunction will affect the rest of the system and manifest outwardly as learning and behavior difficulties.

- **Metabolic Functions.** Practitioners assess nutrition, diet, and metabolism to evaluate the chemistry part of the program. This is done through lab work and interviews about the child's diet and digestive characteristics. Problems here will require diet changes or supplementation, or both. NOTE: Although functional neurology training covers the importance of metabolic issues, it does not go into deep detail. Not all chiropractic neurologists assess this area to the same degree or depth. Ask any potential practitioner how he deals with this, and if you want more in-depth attention than he offers in this area, look for biomedical or naturopathic care.

It is not uncommon to find issues in both domains, necessitating treatments in both areas. In the fields of psychology and learning disabilities, many children receive a diagnosis that seems to cover most of what's going on, but it is common for miscellaneous symptoms to escape categorization. This is frustrating for everyone involved, but does make sense: There is much we still do not understand about the human brain, and disorders do not come in neat packages where everything is out of balance in a predictable, orderly way. A chiropractic neurologist may not give a traditional diagnosis as seen in the DSM-5 (Diagnostic and Statistical Manual of Mental Disorders, the diagnostic guide used in the United States), but will develop a treatment plan to remediate the problems seen in either brain circuitry or metabolic domains, no matter what diagnosis a patient has received in the past.

At the Evaluation

When you take your child to a functional neurologist, expect a range of thorough examinations:

Interview

The chiropractor will take a complete history of your child, including family history, history of the presenting symptoms, surgical and drug history, hospitalizations, social history, mental health history, review of the body systems, and other relevant information. I have found that 90 percent of a diagnosis comes from a thorough patient history interview.

The Importance of Little Things

A subtle difference in "normal" may be a significant finding in chiropractic neurology. For example, if the right eye responds to light slightly differently from the left eye, the chiropractic neurologist will see this as a marker for problems in brain stem function, a deep area of the brain that lays the foundation for the rest of the brain's functioning.

BRAIN CIRCUITS

The functional neurology practitioner will typically have your child perform an in-depth series of physical tests, including many reflexes and motor skills. Results indicate how different parts of the brain are functioning, and show me where the brain or brain stem is weak or less developed.

Sometimes we are lucky and a patient's neurodevelopmental disorder presents as a simple right-brain or left-brain imbalance. For example, obsessive or repetitive thoughts and behaviors reflect disorders in the left side of the brain, whereas stiff language and poor communication skills are usually more due to weakness in the right brain. If a parent reports issues that indicate weaknesses in both right and left brains, I usually suspect that a deeper part of the brain is not working correctly. I then explore for issues that start deeper in the brain, such as the brain stem or cerebellum.

Parents will see their kids watch moving checkers, listen to sounds, perform balance tests, have their lung expansion measured, have their pupil responses assessed, and even have their soft palate response checked. Some doctors will use high tech computer tests for balance, eye movements, and blood flow, and may order brain imaging for particular measurements.

METABOLIC ISSUES

For remediation of metabolic issues, I assess the body's biochemistry by exploring such things as:

- Blood sugar
- Micronutrients
- Food sensitivities
- Cholesterol

Practitioners who address metabolic issues usually assess them through various laboratory tests that analyze blood and urine. Think of the body's biochemistry as a soup circulating in the blood. The state of this soup fluctuates constantly (within a certain range, which differs from one person to the next) and affects every physical, mental, and emotional function. Our understanding of normal ranges within this soup is shifting and there is still much we do not understand about it. However, I will say that chiropractic neurologists do not interpret lab tests in quite the same way as medical doctors, whose parameters are restricted to pathology. Like naturopaths, biomedical doctors, and functional medicine doctors, we tend to look for patterns throughout tests rather than at whether individual numbers are pathologically high or low. We also aim for a narrower, more functional range that reflects the presence of optimum health rather than the absence of extreme disease.

In order to be thorough, functional neurologists usually check for food sensitivities by using both IgE and IgG tests. IgE is the traditional test for a true allergy, one that causes an immediate and sometimes life-threatening histamine response. IgG tests for antibodies in the blood, indicating a reaction to a particular food. The reaction is often delayed, causes inflammation in the brain, and can trigger headaches, nausea, stomach aches, fatigue, foggyheadedness, hyperactivity, irritability, or tantrums. Some chiropractic neurologists also look for IgA, another kind of antibody that indicates the body is having trouble with a particular food. (See Chapter 15 on Nutrition for more information about different kinds of food reactions.)

Additional Tests (If Necessary)

Chiropractic neurologists sometimes use many of the same diagnostic methods as medical neurologists, such as MRI, CT scans, and electroencephalography (EEG). A thorough history and assessment help me determine if any of these measures are needed.

Treatment

Brain Circuits

For remediation of the brain circuits, I develop a very particular series of exercises. **The sequence of rehabilitation always follows the sequence seen in early infant development, because the chain of development in the brain stem must follow a certain order.** Exercises start with eye movements, the baby's first skill to control. They then proceed to trunk movement, then to the periphery of the body. The exercises given are VERY specific and often quite simple, but must be done the prescribed number of times in a day. Rewiring a nervous system is

The Goldilocks Affect

My concept of the Goldilocks Range emerged from research in the early 1970's that identified "cellular immediate early gene response (CIEGR)." When nerve cells are *precisely* activated or fed *specific* vital nutrients, they begin the process of starting to repair themselves within nanoseconds. Likewise, if they are given detrimental signals or toxic foods, this triggers a cascade of destructive processes within nanoseconds. Exercises and nutrition must be just right. Too much stimulation of neurons can damage or kill them, but too little will fail to help. Chiropractic neurologists study how to measure and aim activation to precise brain areas in order to maximize repair.

quite an undertaking!

Each treatment protocol is individualized to the child's unique needs. The regimen is also gentle. Neurons respond better to gentle, regular stimuli and less well to a blast of activity once a day. Patients require frequent, often hourly sessions, and more important, each set may last only seconds, not minutes. This idea is new and strange for a lot of people.

I think of the exercises as being in the "Goldilocks Range" – not too hot, not too cold, but just right (see inset). I will monitor the child's response to each exercise and adjust each week to track and continue improvement.

When the brain is dramatically out of balance, the initial exercises can seem so trivial that a parent might wonder HOW these could be effective. People with good brain functioning can tolerate all types of stimuli and activities, but when the brain is not functioning properly, that child cannot tolerate even simple activities. Therefore the exercises are graded to the tolerance level of the child's brain. Exercises must be carefully prescribed so they do not overwhelm the system. Too much input will not lead to progress.

> ### Just So You Know
>
> Do chiropractic neurologists do traditional chiropractic adjustments? Naturally, we are trained in chiropractic adjustments and can do this if it seems to be the appropriate course of treatment. However, we are also trained to determine who might be overwhelmed by an adjustment. For more complex disorders, specific exercises in small increments are the only way to help a compromised brain heal. For others, dietary changes are the only way to reduce inflammation in the brain.

Metabolic Issues

When we detect a food allergy or sensitivity, I recommend that families eliminate the offending foods. Although restricted diets can be a pain, the positive behavioral or learning outcome can be dramatic.

When Should Parents Seek Out a Functional Neurologist?

Functional neurology may be an option when parents would like to pursue alternatives to medication for their child's attention or behavioral problems. This approach can also be an adjunct to medication to further support good functioning. Other factors that lead families toward chiropractic neurology include these:

- The child has an unclear category of learning disability
- The child has a clear diagnosis, but is making slow progress in more traditional therapies
- The child is not progressing or has ceased to progress with her prescribed therapies
- The child has some developmental delays and has retained infant reflexes
- Medication side effects in the current treatment are too problematic
- Parents have explored all metabolic and genetic lab tests with no clear diagnosis for their child's behavior or learning problems

Chiropractic neurologists use natural methods and techniques that have very little risk. Exercises can range from simple light exposure, eye movements, touch therapies, joint movements, exposure to certain sounds, or balance exercises. The exercises can feel trivial as they appear so simple, but the goal is to stabilize function deep in the brain.

How Long Does Treatment Take?

With consistent treatment, I expect to double the firing rate of useful synapses in the affected area every seven to fourteen days. Several weeks of care should give us a sense of the final prognosis. A practitioner may be able to give you an estimate before that, but until you start working together and he can observe your child's response time, it will only be an estimate. Having all areas of the brain function optimally is the goal of care. I have many patients who begin care in the summer, when there is more time, and then it is usually easier to integrate school and activities around the established routine.

Just So You Know

Parents should understand that this type of care can be an intensive undertaking. Exercises must be done several times a day, which, especially for younger children, is probably going to need to involve you! The exercises are, by and large, extremely simple and will not take long, but *must be done the prescribed number of times a day to have an effect.* Any suggested dietary changes are also mandatory. Save yourself some frustration and decide now whether you and your family will be able to adjust accordingly. This work has tremendous capacity for transforming your child's experience, but it will require investment and commitment on your part.

Minor head injuries (mTBI) can be fairly straightforward and might resolve in a few months. More pronounced developmental disorders or severe head injuries could take years.

Finding a Practitioner

Board-certified chiropractic neurologists from all over the globe can be found on www.acnb. org, in the doctor locator tab. The post-doctoral training programs endorsed by the American Chiropractic Association are found here as well.

There are also resources in your community who may be able to refer families to functional neurological care. Some possibilities for useful contacts include:

- Local chiropractors who treat children with autism or related disorders
- Other providers of bodywork, such as physical therapists or massage therapists
- Behavioral optometrists
- Biological dentists (a specialty that emerged from concern about mercury in dental fillings)
- Health food stores (some track local integrated medicine and holistic health care providers)

Questions for a Prospective Chiropractic Neurologist

- Do you include metabolic assessment as well as brain circuitry? How do you assess these and can you give examples of how you usually treat? Do you take blood, stool, urine, or saliva labs into consideration? (Like almost all CAM treatments, there is variation from one practitioner to another. This chapter outlines the chiropractic neurological standard of care, but you should ask any practitioner for details just in case.)
- How many children with my child's diagnosis or symptoms have you treated in your career?
- What is your success rate? How do you define success?
- What factors do you find interfere with success?
- Is there anything you try to avoid in a patient?
- Is there any risk involved in this treatment modality?
- Can you show me a sample treatment plan you have followed with a child?
- How many times a week will we need to come in? (This will probably change; you should ask about this as well). How much will be involved at home?
- Can you give me names of families who have worked with you and given permission for communication?

Resources for More Information

WEBSITES

www.acnb.org, the American Chiropractic Neurology Board. This site has a doctor locator to find board certified neurologists all over the world.

www.novapublishers.com, Nova Science Publishers. This site is the home of a peer-reviewed, indexed scientific journal in functional neurology, rehabilitation, and ergonomics.

www.carrickinstitute.org is the website for doctors who want to take Dr. Carrick's many programs of study.

www.pbs.org/bodyandsoul/209/carrick.htm. Here, you can learn about the PBS segment about Dr. Carrick, called *Waking Up the Brain: Amazing Adjustments,* from the *Body and Soul program.*

BOOKS

Why Isn't My Brain Working? by Datis Kharrazian. This book explains how the brain is affected by issues like blood sugar, allergies, sex hormones, and especially neurotransmitters like dopamine and serotonin. He describes how to support functional neurology with blood tests and nutrition.

My Stroke of Insight: A Brain Scientist's Personal Journey by Jill Bolte Taylor. Dr. Taylor, a neuroscientist, explains her own stroke experience and recovery from a right-brain, left-brain perspective.

ABOUT THE AUTHOR

Michael Pierce, DC, DACNB, FACFN, attended the University of Wisconsin-Stevens Point and Palmer College of Chiropractic in Iowa. His parents started him on the path of rational alternative medicine at age seven. Having completed his post-doctorate in neurology from the Carrick Institute for Graduate Studies, he became a diplomate of the American Chiropractic Neurology Board and is a fellow of the American College of Functional Neurology. He was an adjunct professor of clinical science for Northwestern Health Sciences University in Minnesota. He had continuing education courses approved by the National Certification Board for Therapeutic Massage and Bodywork and the American Massage Therapy Association. He is on faculty for several massage schools, nutritionist programs, and culinary schools. He is also the CEO of a Healthcare nonprofit.

You can reach Dr. Pierce at www.brainplanners.com

16.5

Craniosacral Therapy (CST)

by Claire Dolby DO, RCST

Addie was born in Russia and spent her first 15 months swaddled tightly, lying on her back in a crib. When we adopted her, she was not able to sit up and could barely hold her head up. She had had no opportunities. Once we were home, she seemed to blossom quickly, gaining strength and skills in rapid succession over the next year. We thought it was an amazing recovery, but Addie still struggled in some areas. She was emotional, quick to melt down, and very clumsy. As she grew to school age, teachers were always concerned about her attention span. She was basically happy, but struggles were starting to intensify and we worried about things getting to be too much in the future.

Through another adoptive parent, we heard about a therapist doing craniosacral work. This mother had found the treatment to be hugely beneficial for her child. I had never heard of it, but Addie needed help and her pediatrician was suggesting medication and I did not want to start there. So we decided to give it a try.

After his assessment, the therapist felt that Addie's long months lying on her back had caused problems with the flow of cerebrospinal fluid up and down her spine and through her brain; he said that that proper flow of this fluid was critical for proper brain and body function. From the outside, the treatment itself almost seemed non-existent. Addie lay comfortably on a table playing with a toy and chatting with me, while the therapist lightly placed his hands on her head and her lower spine. He would hold any position from several seconds to a few minutes. After the first session, he said he had released a lot of traumatic charge that had been held in her nervous system and that Addie might fall asleep after the treatment. I almost snorted. Addie had dozed off in the car on the way over; there was no way she was falling asleep again before bedtime. But she was asleep in the car within five minutes of leaving. More importantly, after a few sessions, Addie seemed more relaxed, more attentive, less easily stressed. Teachers commented on her improvement. I did not yet fully understand this therapy, but I was so relieved that Addie was feeling better and doing better. Talk of medication ceased. ~K.M.

The Basics

Craniosacral therapy treats the nervous system in order to resolve dysfunction throughout the body and brain. The Central Nervous System (or CNS) is the master regulator and organizer of almost all of our systems or movements – whether automatic or voluntary – and provides the basis for our behavior and responses to the world. Problems in basic nervous system health can manifest as anything from illness to depression to learning or behavior disorders. There are many approaches to treating these issues (just read this book), but craniosacral therapy (CST) attempts to directly change the core patterning of the CNS.

Children often respond very quickly to CST, as any dysfunctional patterns have not had years to become entrenched and to develop further complications. There are two main aspects of CST that have proven to be very effective.

- **Restoring cranial movement.** According to craniosacral practitioners and osteopaths, the bones of the skull and the membrane system within the cranium have subtle, articulated movements in a healthy child. However, events ranging from head injuries to birth complications can alter or restrict this essential rhythm. These restrictions can create a host of problems such as headaches, dizziness, visual problems, balance issues, and more. With gentle, manual corrections, a CST practitioner is able to free up these restrictions in the bones and membranes and thus return the system to normal function.
- **Resetting the Central Nervous System.** As children grow, their nervous systems create layer upon layer of increasingly sophisticated patterns. We can see this

Practitioner Perspective

My practice is comprised almost entirely of children with learning and behavior disorders. Many of them do other therapies besides mine, with vision therapy being one of the most common. I sometimes find a child whose vision therapy just hasn't been progressing past a certain point, or perhaps never got any traction on the issue at all. When I hear this, I refer to a craniosacral therapist to assess the status of the sphenoid and related cranial bones. Some of the eye muscles attach to the sphenoid bone and when its movement is restricted, the eye muscles and ocular nerves are impaired as well. When this happens, vision therapy, in my experience, doesn't have a chance until that is addressed. I send kids off for a session or three, and vision therapy usually progresses much more effectively. (If it doesn't, there are other avenues we can explore, but this often does the trick.)
~ Kim Gangwish, LEAP Therapist

in their ability to handle progressively more complex tasks. Social interactions and emotional self-regulation, two things we expect our children to just pick up as they go along, are actually very complicated and demanding skills. They can easily lag or develop difficulties if some of the foundational nervous system patterns did not develop fully. Craniosacral work can help the CNS reset core patterns. This can be a huge relief to a child who has no idea why he acts or feels the way he does and just wants to be able to stop.

Often, I find that children are quite aware of their patterned responses (so-called "bad habits" like impulsive responses or meltdowns) and are longing to change them. I frequently hear statements such as "I don't want to get angry so often, but I don't know how not to" or "I wish I didn't start crying whenever I take a test, but I can't help it." Children often know how they want to respond; they just can't get there. This conscious awareness helps: CST resets the nervous system so that they can create new response patterns. This translates into change on a behavioral level.

Brief History and Practitioner Training

Originally, Cranial Osteopathy was a specialty within the larger field of osteopathic medicine. It began to emerge on its own in the early 1970s. Today there are at least five major schools of Craniosacral Therapy. An education in CST means mastering the art of very light but perceptive touch. The therapist learns to lightly place her hands on the skull, spine, or other area and detect subtle rhythms, such as in the flow of cerebrospinal fluid or the position of certain bones. This can involve multiple layers of perception of bone, muscle, and fluids.

Training protocols can vary enormously, from weekend workshops to full two-year trainings. Most shorter trainings involve basic calming techniques, while the more thorough ones teach extensive methods of detecting specific disorders and how to treat them.

I recommend you seek practitioners with substantial training and years of experience, because the cultivation of this super-sensitive touch takes intensive, long-term schooling with proper supervision. Working with nervous system disorders is tricky and requires extensive knowledge of neurology, trauma, embryology, anatomy, birth dynamics, and different nervous system states. There are therapists who take a quick course in order to be able to integrate a specific technique into the other forms of physical, occupational, or massage therapy. However, a comprehensive approach to a child's developmental issues requires an experienced and thoroughly trained therapist.

A Closer Look at the Nervous System

In order to have even an introductory discussion of CST, you'll need to understand some basics of the nervous system. This is an extremely brief, simplified discussion that will help you understand the principles of this work.

Cerebrospinal fluid (CSF). This fluid bathes and nourishes the brain and spinal cord. By assessing CSF flow through the spine and brain, a therapist can identify areas that need to be treated. This is one of the primary diagnostic tools of a CST practitioner.

Cranial bones and membranes. These work together in an articulated, complex interaction. When they are out of sync with each other or their movement is impaired or distorted, it will negatively influence some aspect of brain function, depending on the location, nature, and severity of the restriction.

Sympathetic and parasympathetic nervous systems. These are two of the primary aspects of the human nervous system, and essential to understanding CST. The sympathetic mode is the working nervous system for daily living. A healthy sympathetic system can differentiate between a friendly conversation, a demanding mental task, and a low-level threat. It will gear up for each with an appropriate level of resource, from calm attention to concentrated focus to full-on danger readiness.

At the extreme end of this range is the stress response, "fight, flight, or freeze." (Conventional wisdom used to be that this was the primary feature of the sympathetic nervous system, but it is in fact only one component.) Theoretically, this should only kick in when muggers attack or when a child is caught under a car, but the reality is that most of us have developed fight/flight/freeze-based response patterns to many seemingly innocuous situations. I believe that stress-related sympathetic responses often worsen the learning and behavior disorders I treat. The improvement I see when I readjust children's

Just So You Know

The Central Nervous System is exceptionally complex and has been difficult to study in depth until recently. This field is one of the fastest-evolving areas of research in modern science; witness the spate of books and media attention about all the breakthroughs in brain science. It's a difficult field to stay up-to-date in, so don't be surprised or discouraged if other types of care providers are skeptical of CST. If you're curious about the science, you can check out the work of Stephen Porges, PhD, Allan Schore, PhD, and Peter Levine, PhD, all of whom have websites online. Their groundbreaking work in developmental neuroscience, trauma, and its effect on the nervous system, along with new discoveries about how the CNS works, has guided and informed the evolution of craniosacral work. This work supports many central concepts in CST that used to be considered soft science.

nervous systems to react in a calmer, more organized way supports this.

Parasympathetic is our rest and relaxation mode, and is much slower. We are in parasympathetic when we sleep, rest, or digest. It is essential to healing and maintaining health that we access this mode on a regular basis. If you have sleep problems, eat on the run a lot, or are constantly stressed to the point that you have trouble relaxing, then chances are you're not healing either. Like the sympathetic, parasympathetic has a stress response as well – manifesting as a collapsed, shut down, spaced-out state where any response is difficult.

Social nervous system. There is a third branch to the CNS, a more recent concept that revolutionizes the way we understand the nervous system. Stephen Porges, PhD, has done a great deal of work that indicates the presence of the Social Nervous System. This aspect is present only in the most sophisticated creatures, those with extended developmental stages and complex social structures.

Unlike most other creatures, human beings take many years to develop self-reliance and are helpless, and then dependent, until they reach a certain point. Social bonding, therefore, is a biological imperative that ensures that their needs get met. They *must* get appropriate care, affection, bonding, and mirroring in order to develop a healthy and functional nervous system on all levels.

Early problems in this area, ranging from inattentive or very anxious parenting to being in an institution where care and stimulation is simply lacking, can impair this aspect of the nervous system from the start. Later traumas such as the death of a loved one (especially a parent), abuse, or even severe ostracization from peers can also compromise the social nervous system. All bonding can then become fraught with feelings of danger and uncertainty, and since bonding is such a basic biological need, the sympathetic and parasympathetic aspects of the CNS begin to function from a place of chronic stress too. When that much of the nervous system is operating in a compromised state, it is no surprise that problems might arise in the form of learning or behavior disorders. The brain simply does not have the foundation it needs for optimal function.

I would recommend that you seek a practitioner who has extensive instruction and clinical experience in the social nervous system. So many of these complex children have damage in this area, and it is a tricky one to rebuild. A compromised social nervous system will often mimic trauma states in either the sympathetic or parasympathetic systems – but the clinical response should be completely different. Rebuilding a healthy social nervous system can be done, but it involves a delicate balance of addressing the right sequence of parasympathetic and sympathetic issues first, then restoring social bonding function through a combination of craniosacral work and teaching the patient to reengage the social system slowly and with support. It can be transformative work, but it takes time and a high level of expertise.

Changing nervous system patterns. One of the core functions of the nervous system is to lay down patterns that are more and more complex. When a child learns to catch a ball, for example, he first learns by catching a ball thrown very slowly. After a while, he can build on that skill by catching a ball thrown at high speed, then catch it while he himself is running, then do all that while calculating where to throw it next.

But what if, for whatever reason, he never got past catching it slowly? Maybe his hand-eye coordination just wasn't developed enough yet; maybe he was hit by a ball and now fears it. For whatever reason, it was too much too soon. His reaction is not a smooth development of a new skill; it is chaos and confusion *on a neurological level*. If he is pressed to try to develop the other skills while he is still struggling with the first, his confusion will only increase. Once those neurons are firing in that disorganized pattern, the rest of those skills are going to be hard to build.

Both patterns are self-perpetuating – either he responds to similar tasks eagerly and calmly, or with tension and anxiety. I see this with all sorts of disorders in children: they had trouble reading in the beginning, and by the time they come to me they have developed serious, complex disorders in that area. Or they started school a bit too young and felt anxious and lost; by third grade, their anxiety has completely overtaken them and made learning next to impossible. Trying to build complexity on a dysfunctional foundation often leads to disorder and greater struggle later on.

Sometimes, working only on a conscious level (as with verbal-only therapies) or only on the problematic symptoms (such as with a reading tutor) may get limited results or be more difficult than it needs to be. CST provides a way to interrupt the nervous system, break it out of the quick pace of the sympathetic (and the even quicker pace of the *stressed* sympathetic), and access change on a level much deeper than emotion or cognition. Once a practitioner creates a pause by accessing and supporting the parasympathetic mode, disruptive patterns are much easier to shift. The nervous system has space to relax and create new patterns. It may still be necessary to do the reading therapy or occupational therapy to work out the details, but the CNS is ready.

What Happens During a Session

Intake

Different practitioners will evaluate patients differently; there is no standard protocol. But most will start with some sort of intake focused on external events that might have impacted the development of the nervous system, such as:

- Nature of the birth process – were drugs or surgery involved? Was it a particularly long or difficult labor? As the first event of one's life, it can set up patterns in the nervous system or constrictions in the cranium that can subtly persist throughout life.
- Early childhood developmental milestones – at what point did this child crawl, walk, talk, etc? Did she make these transitions easily and smoothly?
- Traumas and accidents – this can encompass both emotional and physical incidents.
- Response to school from the beginning – how did he feel about school and about his ability to learn?
- Overall state of the mother's nervous system, especially during pregnancy – the child's CNS is basically a mirror for the mother's, during infancy and often later.

We can never say for sure how any event has influenced the nervous system. A child's baseline state of health, determined by a complex combination of factors from diet to the emotional health of the family, can influence whether her CNS resets in a healthy way or begins to develop unhealthy response patterns. Most practitioners find it helpful to get an overall picture of how the child has developed so far and what influences have played a part. However, they will usually hold off on drawing conclusions until they have actually worked directly with a child's nervous system. Even then, nothing is certain about how each piece contributed to the child's overall response patterns. It is still important to be aware of all the factors that might have played a role.

Most craniosacral practitioners are also adept at observation. Everything a child does reflects the state of his CNS. By watching a child, a therapist can gain a lot of information about the general state of the nervous system. Therapists watch such behaviors as:

- Baseline state – calm, agitated, fearful?
- Eye contact – can the child make or maintain it?
- Breathing patterns – what are they at resting and when responding to different stimuli?
- Speech patterns – is the child's speech rushed, slurred? Does she use complete sentences or fragments (appropriate to her age)? Does she convey complete and organized thoughts? Can she express herself the way she wants to or does she seem frustrated?
- Movement patterns – smooth, jerky, erratic?
- Attention – can she sustain attention to a task or is she constantly interrupting herself and starting new things?
- How does she come into relationship with a new person (i.e., the therapist)?

The intake represents the "outside in" part. The "inside out" part begins when the child lies on the table and the practitioner directly assesses the CNS. This part doesn't look like much. (I have had observers compare it to watching grass grow). Generally, a patient lies on his back with the practitioner's hands touching his head, though she might also hold his sacrum or feet. Very little movement is visible.

With gentle movements of the hands, the practitioner tests the responses at the deep levels of the nervous system. The practitioner knows how the CNS is responding because she has felt it directly. This gives information about how exactly the system is resisting relaxation, how it is responding in a dysfunctional way (i.e., when it stops responding fluidly, does it go into overwhelm and shutdown, confusion and anxiety, fight or flight?), and how it needs support or redirection. Practitioners learn to distinguish between many types of dysfunction, such as whether it results from strain in the membranous tissues, imbalance in the cerebrospinal fluid, or cranial bones that are stuck in restrictive movement patterns. The therapist then guides the CNS into a parasympathetic state, which permits a therapist to release restrictive patterns.

Cranial Work and Specific Issues

CST can address both specific issues and the overall state of nervous system health. It can also help other therapies to be more effective. Here are some issues it can be particularly helpful with:

- **Closed-head injuries.** If a child did not receive proper care after a head trauma, ramifications can persist. If there was an internal brain bleed, neural tissue can become damaged and even necrotic. In the absence of a bleed, chronic inflammation can still impair neural function. Cranial therapists can help by intensifying the flow of cerebrospinal fluid to the injured areas, which may help to heal the tissue by easing inflammation and giving the tissue extra nourishment. It also helps by supporting other parts of the brain in taking over the functions of the impaired areas. I have seen many cases of near-full recovery when medical doctors had given up hope.

- **Impaired visual system.** Various events can distort the cranial bones. If the sphenoid bone cannot move properly, it may affect the visual system since many eye muscles connect to the sphenoid. If your child complains of headaches after a period of reading or other prolonged visual activity, or pain when he moves his eyes, or if vision therapy doesn't progress past a certain point, it may be worth having some-one check on the state of the cranial bones.

- **Complications from dental work.** I have seen probably hundreds of children who complain of headaches and trouble sleeping after getting orthodontic work. Braces frequently create tremendous strain on the cranial bones, transferring distortion and compression throughout the skull and generating pain and a range of possible other difficulties. I find that regular cranial work throughout the course of orthodontia can not only avoid some of the pain and complications, but may also speed up the whole orthodontic process. Even aggressive dental work like getting a tooth pulled can impact the cranial system, so this does not just apply to braces.

- **AD/HD and SPD.** I don't imagine many modalities would put these disorders into the same category, but from my perspective, they are both symptoms of extremely disorganized nervous systems. ADD can certainly have other contributing factors (and I often recommend that families address diet), but in both cases, I find that a child's nervous system has developed similarly chaotic response patterns and must be strengthened, calmed, and organized in similar ways.

Finding a Practitioner

In general, I would say that seeking these criteria should help you find a good practitioner:

- 700-1000 hours of training
- A minimum of two years of experience (thorough training should provide the basis of any practice, but it takes time to develop the sensitivity and skill to work with the subtle levels of the nervous system)
- Experience working with the issues your child is experiencing
- Successful outcomes (this is one modality where I would suggest asking for client references)

Questions for a Prospective Craniosacral Therapist

- How much training have you had in CST? If you integrate it into other therapeutic modalities, please tell me about how and when you do that.
- Have you worked with children who have similar issues to mine? Was there anything tricky about working with those cases? What were your outcomes and how long did it take you to get to that point?

- At what point will you be able to give me an estimate of how many sessions this may take?
- Are you familiar with the work of Peter Levine on trauma? (While not all practitioners need to have studied all the relevant work that has informed CST, they should at least understand the basic effect of trauma on the nervous system.)
- Do you take insurance; what are your fees; do you take payment plans or give discounts?
- How do you think CST can help my child?

Resources for More Information

WEBSITES

stephenporges.com/. This is the website for Dr. Stephen Porges, and contains articles about how a person's neurology is affected by their sense of safety, and other topics.

www.allanschore.com/, is Dr. Allan Schore's website. Dr. Schore has written extensively about emotional regulation and neurology.

www.traumahealing.org/peter-a-levine-phd.php. This page of the Somatic Experiencing Trauma Institute is about Dr. Peter Levine and his work on trauma and neurology.

BOOKS

Why Love Matters by Sue Gerhardt. This book explains why love is essential to brain and nervous system development. It presents the latest findings in neuroscience, psychiatry, and biochemistry in a very accessible way.

Parenting from the Inside Out by Daniel J. Siegel, MD, and Mary Hartzell. The authors, experts in the field of child development and child psychiatry, explain how early experiences shape brain development, using findings in neurobiology and attachment research.

Craniosacral Therapy for Babies and Small Children by Etienne and Neeto Peirsman. The authors explain in detail how craniosacral work with young children can impact their development. Written more for practitioners, this book can nevertheless help parents understand what a CST therapist is doing, what kind of impact it can have, and what babies need in order to remain healthy on a nervous system level.

ABOUT THE AUTHOR

Claire Dolby DO, RCST, qualified as an osteopath in 1984 and a craniosacral therapist in 1987. Since then, she has established an international teaching career focused mainly on family work and early development. She has been a senior tutor at the Karuna Institute, an international training and retreat center in Devon, England, for 25 years, and has been closely involved in developing the current course curriculum. Her passion for the work is communicated clearly through her teaching. Her other interests include singing, meditation, and walking. She lives and practices in the U.K.

Section Five

MOVING FORWARD

———◆———

NOW THAT YOU ARE LOADED UP with more information than you may have ever wanted, we would like to offer you some last food for thought to help you make sense of it all. The Care Management chapter presents a valuable range of tips for how to organize and manage your priorities and information throughout this often difficult journey. The Advocacy in the School System chapter discusses ways to work more effectively with the school, and offers further resources to help you find your way through that confusing process. The final chapter reminds you to take a breath and remember, in the midst of the flurry of activity you may be beginning, that inside all the issues is a child that still needs your connection and support even more than therapy…and sometimes support may mean ditching the expectation that your child will go through school and life the way most kids do.

———◆———

SEVENTEEN

Advocacy in the School System

by Anna Stewart, Parent, Family Advocate

Editors' Note:

If you've read all the chapters indicated by your checklist results, your head is probably swimming with new insights into your child and new options to investigate. But one of the reasons you're doing all this is so that your child can be in school without so much suffering, right? Schools can and do give students the supports they need to learn. Teachers want to see their students succeed. However, the public school system is also bound by laws and policies that can be difficult for parents to navigate. The guidelines may not be very parent-friendly, but you and your child do have rights. This chapter will help you understand the systems you will need to work within to get your child what he needs.

"Your son has ADHD. He needs an IEP," your new psychiatrist tells you. So you take your marching orders and tell his classroom teacher at pick up. You think you have done your part – you have a diagnosis and a treatment plan. Now it is the school that needs to step it up and provide your smart but distracted child with the services and supports he needs to be successful. After all, isn't that what public education is supposed to do?

Do public schools have to provide ALL students an education? Yes. But the difference between how the federal government defines the role of public education and how we as parents define it, is often like speaking two different languages while trying to have a conversation.

Public schools are required to provide a Free and Appropriate Education (FAPE). In more understandable terms, all they have to do is ensure students access to curriculum and that is good enough. For example, the boy recently diagnosed with ADHD has difficulty getting his work completed during class so his teacher expects him to do it at home. Evenings are a nightmare in his house, as it takes him (and his mom) two to three hours a night to complete an hour's worth of homework. If his grades are average (C is considered average) then the school may say that he is "accessing his education." The boy and his parents have something else to say and it may include a lot of worry – not only about his academic struggles, but also regarding his growing dislike of school and his feelings of being a failure.

Before you throw up your hands and homeschool (which is always an option), there are structures and systems in place to provide supports for students in public school. Let's walk through the three systems that are part of every state and every school district, as dictated by federal laws. States and districts can broaden federal laws, but they cannot narrow them. There are differences in interpretation and implementation, which doesn't help, but knowing some of your rights can go a long way towards securing the supports and services your child may need to truly access his education.

There are three avenues for support. The options intersect and overlap, so it is not a continuum but a range of school supports. We will go over each one:

1. **Response to Intervention** (RtI) gives struggling students direct interventions to help them catch up to peers. Direct means explicit instructions tailored to the student's weak areas (often only in literacy).
2. **Section 504 Plan** gives students with identified learning or health needs an equal playing field by providing accommodations.
3. **Special Education Services** give students who qualify as having a disability, services and accommodations through an Individualized Education Plan (IEP).

Option 1: Response to Intervention (RtI)

RtI was developed as a response to too many kids not being given quality literacy instruction and falling behind, then being tossed into Special Education to be fixed. Instead, in 2004, when the Individuals with Disabilities Education Act (IDEA) came up for reauthorization, the lawmakers added RtI, which was designed to provide direct instruction by using research-based literacy programs to help children who are struggling to read and write. Other than assessments used to determine baseline and progress, no additional tests or evaluations are required for students to get help. The idea is that if a student is behind for whatever reason, the school staff should be trying something different than what the other students are doing. It could be a reading program or help with completing schoolwork or a new way to learn the spelling words.

RtI is not a program, but rather a guideline – so each state, and then each district, can decide how to implement it in schools. This makes it potentially very difficult for parents to get their minds wrapped around it. The feds designed it for supporting students with literacy and some states have included any student who is struggling with any issue, including inappropriate behaviors.

GETTING SUPPORT THROUGH RtI

Many students are getting support through RtI without their parents' knowledge, because the classroom is set up with lots of ways to learn to read. Or your child may be working on reading in the morning with the rest of the class, and again for 30 minutes in the afternoon with a small group of students. Since it does not require parental agreement for assessments (if they are given to all students, then parents do not have to provide consent), and there are no disability labels and it doesn't necessarily involve special education staff, it can look just like good teaching (and it should!).

The specific interventions (such as a different reading program) should be based on data that shows that a student is not at grade level in any of the five main areas of literacy (phonetics, phonemic awareness, vocabulary, fluency, and comprehension). Then targeted instruction should be provided, and it should include a way to monitor the student's progress to be sure the intervention is working. It can also address math skills, attention issues, or behaviors, depending on the district interpretation of the law. RtI is not one program – it's an approach to helping a student catch up with his or her classmates.

Though RtI is mostly used in the elementary grades, it can be used in middle and high school as well. For instance, a student who seems to be falling further behind in math skills may be placed in a math clinic class to get some one-on-one instruction along with taking the regular math class.

If you feel your child is not reading at grade level, then the first step is to set up a private time to talk to the classroom teacher. Do not ask during after-school pickup. This is a private discussion.

- Start with thanking the teacher for her time and work with your child.
- Briefly state you have some concerns about your child's literacy level.
- Ask the teacher what she thinks.
- Clarify how she is measuring your child's progress.
- Discuss next steps (include writing up an RtI plan).
- Follow up with a short email summarizing what you agreed upon.

An RtI plan should include:

1. Data showing student's current academic level as compared to peers
2. Intervention decided upon by teachers and parents, which should include how often and how long (such as daily for 30 minutes)
3. Tool to monitor progress
4. Timeline to monitor progress (usually six - eight weeks)
5. Date to meet and discuss intervention's effectiveness

A good elementary school teacher often provides such a great learning environment that it is hard to document exactly what she/he does to accommodate each student's needs. If you are seeing progress in your child's learning, you may not want to ask the teacher to write it all down. You want to team up with the teacher and support what is working. The exceptions to this are in these situations:

1. In the last year of elementary school if your student is still behind academically (this is important in order to prepare for middle school)
2. If you have documentation of a disability that impacts your child's ability to learn

This leads us to the next option:

Option 2: Section 504 Plan

A 504 Plan comes out of the Americans with Disabilities Act and is not directly connected to education laws. It is a law that says that people with a disability need access to buildings, education, and their community in order to level the playing field. In public school, it can give a student with physical, medical, or educational disabilities the right to accommodations so they can access the building and education.

Accommodations are objects, strategies, tools, and systems that allow people to access what others in that environment are accessing. In a classroom, it does not change the content of what a child is learning or the expectation to complete as much schoolwork as every other student in the class. But it does provide some formal tools and ways to make school easier.

The law lists 22 services that must be available in regular education classrooms for Section 504 eligible students. These are among the most common:

- Repeating and simplifying instructions about in-class assignments (check for understanding)
- Changing test delivery (such as allowing oral exams)

- Using computer-assisted instruction
- Tailoring homework assignments (such as shorter assignments)
- Providing lecture or assignment notes

GETTING SUPPORT THROUGH A 504

As with all federal laws, states and school districts interpret things a bit differently. Some districts require parents to provide medical proof of a disability diagnosis given within the last three years. If you have decided to pursue a private diagnosis and want your child to receive accommodations, then the following components can speed up the process:

1. Proof of disability such as a letter from a psychiatrist or doctor
2. Data that you gather, demonstrating how the disability impacts your child – this can include:

- Log of homework issues (how much time, reaction, completion)
- Work samples (especially if it shows contrast between first drafts and final projects)
- Email or notes from conversations with teachers along with notes from parent-teacher conferences

A child can have both an RtI plan and a 504 plan. RtI can provide direct instruction. The 504 provides accommodations. The next option, qualifying for special education services, includes both direct instruction and accommodations – but only to students who meet the state's definitions of disability. Let's walk through the IEP process and you will see how it is (and is not) connected to RtI and/or 504 plans. Stay with me here, it is confusing.

Option 3: Special Education and Individualized Education Plans

IDEA (which also includes the RtI model) was created in 1975 to allow all school age children and teens the right to access an education regardless of their disability. The law covers all kinds of disabilities, including ADHD, autism, cerebral palsy, and Down syndrome.

It is important to understand this, when discussing special needs services: A diagnosis does not equal services. It is the *impact* of the disability that affects services.

Many medical professionals equate giving a child a disability diagnosis with the expectation of also getting an IEP. But it doesn't work that way. For instance, most kids who have ADHD do not have an IEP. Hopefully, they do have a 504 that is actually used!

Each state has an Education Department that defines the disability categories they use and the qualifying criteria. If you think an IEP is the right support for your child, check out your state's requirements. It can help to work backwards from the criteria as you gather your evidence and diagnoses.

There are two approaches to qualifying for a learning disability. The first is an old model commonly referred to as a *discrepancy model*. If a school team suspects a learning disability, they give the child both an IQ test and an academic skills test. If the difference between the two falls into their criteria, then the child qualifies. This model is no longer considered best practice and is partly why the federal lawmakers added RtI to IDEA. It's the old "wait to fail" system, which both fails to provide support in a timely manner and also labels many kids with a learning disability that is not accurate.

The newer approach requires a *body of evidence* to make a determination. That evidence can include any or all of the following:

- Academic testing
- Classroom work examples
- Teacher observation
- Testing/assessments done by non-school professionals
- IQ test, neither required nor usually given

Schools are required to assess a child if the team suspects a disability. However, they are only required to assess within the area of concern. So if they think it is an attention issue, they don't have to test for math abilities. Schools can provide educational identifications of conditions like AD/HD and autism, though that is not equal to a medical diagnosis.

If your school is using the body of evidence model, much of their evidence may be gathered through the RtI process. Unfortunately, many school principals and general education teachers are not aware of the distinction in the law that says:

- Parents can formally request, *at any time*, that their child be evaluated to see if they are eligible for special education services. This must be done in writing.
- A school cannot say they won't do this until they try RtI.

I am going to say that in another way, as it is complex. At any time, a parent can make a formal written request to have their child evaluated for special education services. In this request, they need to state why they think their child may qualify, such as "my daughter is reading two years behind her peers, can't spell the grade-level, 'no excuse' words and rarely knows what she is supposed to do when trying to do her homework. She is also complaining of stomach aches every school night and is saying things like she is stupid." And the school then has 15 days to respond with a yes or a no. If they say no, they have to provide a written answer of why they do not suspect a disability.

And if they say yes, then they will ask parents to sign a form giving the school permission to evaluate in certain areas. The school does not have to provide a comprehensive battery of assessments, only those that they believe are related to the suspected disability. From the day the parents sign the form, the school has six weeks to complete the evaluations, write up their reports, and give the parents a chance to read the report before a formal eligibility meeting is held. If the child does have a disability, then the team writes an Individual Education Plan (IEP). Accommodations are part of the IEP and have their own section in the paperwork.

If the student is not eligible for special education services, but now the team knows more about the student, they could develop a 504 plan and/or a more targeted RtI plan.

Got all that?

Special education is meant to help students with disabilities. But is wrapped up in so much daunting jargon, with so many policies and procedures, that it can make your head spin. School teams have to do a lot of work to get a student set up with an IEP, and they often delay that in lots of subtle and not-so subtle ways that keep putting parents off. That's why it is important to know that you do have a right to ask for your child to be tested for special education services.

Once an IEP is developed, then the school's job is to help your child make reasonable academic progress. One of the main reasons that parents feel they have to fight for their child is because the public school's level of good enough is nowhere near a parent's level of what is good enough. If your child is dyslexic and cannot spell well, it is not the school's job to make him a great speller or even an average one. As long as he spells better than he did the year before, his gains may be considered reasonable academic progress.

The school has to give your child access to an education. As parents, you want to give your child what they need to become happy, healthy, and well-educated adults. That may mean that you will need to need to augment public school resources with private therapies, supports, and opportunities. You can also seek out a private school that specializes in your child's needs, or is more willing or able to accommodate him.

Some students also require modifications in addition to accommodations. A modification is when a change is made to the content or material to give a student access to it. An example would be to have a student write a simple paragraph while the peers are writing a five-paragraph persuasive essay. Most students with AD/HD or learning disabilities only need accommodations and do not receive modifications.

Private schools are not required to qualify or implement IEPs or RtI plans. But a private school can offer things a public school can't, such as small classes, lots of individual instruction, and diverse educational models. There are schools designed for students with learning disabilities, autism, and twice-exceptional (having both a disability and being gifted) students.

One More Option: Independent Educational Evaluations (IEE)

If you feel that the evaluations used to develop the IEP do not accurately reflect your child's needs or abilities, you can request an IEE. This is an evaluation done by a specialist outside of the district. If the district agrees to do this, they cover the cost. (Parents can, of course, have private evaluations done at any time, and can choose whether or not to share it with the school.) Getting an IEE is uncommon, but can provide detailed information about your child that may give a more comprehensive understanding of who he is as a learner. This might be a good time to bring in an educational advocate (see upcoming section) to help you through the process, as it is complex.

Tips From the Trenches: Advice From Other Parents

- **ASK:** Don't expect that school staff will tell you about supports and services. Keep asking questions like:
  - How can we help John to improve his writing?
  - What else could we try?
  - Are there any school or district resources we could ask about?
  - Who else could I talk to about my concerns?
  - What other programs, technology, supports, or schools are available?
- **ENGAGE**
  - Volunteer in the classroom, the library, or for events. Become a familiar and trusted face.
  - Join the PTA or other parent-school organization.
  - Show your appreciation to the classroom teacher or other staff with notes and goodies, or nominate them for education awards.
  - Join the local and/or state Special Education Advisory Committee.
  - Join the local group for learning disabilities, AD/HD, or autism.
- **RESEARCH**
  - Know your state criteria for school support by spending time on the state Department of Education website. They usually have parent advisors on staff as well.
  - Understand your child's disability or area of concern so you know the jargon and the best strategies and accommodations to support them.

- Seek out private therapists, tutors, activities, and professionals that may be able to help your child – not only with academics, but also with self-esteem, emotional control, and social skills.

♀ **PREPARE**

- Keep logs at home of struggles and concerns such as how long homework actually takes and anxiety issues around school, such as sleeping, stomach aches, crying, and worry.
- Have any private practitioners (doctor, therapist, psychiatrist, tutor, etc.) provide written reports prior to progress/IEP/504 meetings.
- You may need to go into the classroom and help the other students understand, accept, and embrace your child. If you are already volunteering in the class, you will be able to see what is needed.

When to Engage an Educational Advocate

Sometimes schools, despite having caring educators, are just not providing the appropriate, regular, or targeted support your child needs. You may be worried about your child's attitude towards school and towards himself. Parents have the right to engage an educational advocate if they feel stymied with a school team or with the plan that was put in place. It does create two sides when you go in with an advocate, so it's best if parents can find a way to work with the school team and set up appropriate supports for the student without one. However, an advocate can also be a huge resource and relief if you are extremely frustrated or just lost in the process. Not only are they familiar with the process and all possible options, they can also explain the IEP process and the full range of your rights and options to you.

How to find an Educational Advocate

♀ Many local learning disability groups can refer parents to advocates.

♀ Throughout the country there are local ARC chapters. They have free advocates that usually only work with youth that have developmental disabilities, but it's worth a call to see if they will accept cases with milder needs.

♀ COPRA is a national organization of educational advocates and lawyers.

♀ Children and Adults with Attention Deficit Disorders has an online advocacy manual at www.chadd.org/advocacy/chadd-advocacy-manual.aspx.

♀ Wrightslaw has yellow pages with resource and advocates listed by state along with other resources (www.yellowpagesforkids.com).

Questions for a Potential Advocate

- What is your educational background and training in advocacy?
- How long have you been an advocate?
- Have you worked with my school district before? What were your experiences?
- Have you advocated for children with needs similar to my child's?
- When asking about rates, make sure to ask about the charges for phone calls, travel time if necessary, attending meetings, and any other specific services that may not be straightforward.

Resources for More Information

Websites

nichcy.org/laws/, the website of the National Dissemination Center for Children with Disabilities. This website covers a wide range of education, special education, and legal topics relevant to various disabilities, including learning disabilities.

www.Wrightslaw.com. Peter Wright is an educational lawyer who himself experienced learning disabilities in school. He and his wife, Pamela, developed this extensive site that covers everything from how to write a letter requesting services to how to find an advocate. It is relevant to parents, teachers, advocates, and attorneys, providing up-to-date information about special education law.

www.yellowpagesforkids.com, a section of Wrightslaw, with resources listed by state.

www.copaa.org, the Council of Parent Attorneys and Advocates, which is for parents, education attorneys, and advocates. It has a national list of all members that is searchable by state.

www.chadd.org. The Children and Adults with Attention Deficit/Hyperactivity Disorder national website has extensive resources, including local support groups and a manual on advocacy.

www.ed.gov. The United States Department of Education website has it all - reports, policy, and research, along with info for teachers and families for all levels of education.

ABOUT THE AUTHOR

Anna Stewart, Family Advocate, is a parent, school and community liaison for her school district as well as a writer, speaker, facilitator, and single mother of three unique teens. She is passionate about helping families learn to advocate WITH their children and teens and supporting those with disabilities. Anna is the author of *School Support for Students with AD/HD*, and is currently the Kids with Special Needs Guide at www.ESME.net, and a contributor to www.empoweringparents.com. Recently, she was featured on Canadian Public Radio in a segment called Neuron Therapy. You can search her articles at: www.empoweringparents.com/?s=anna+stewart or visit her Facebook page at: www.facebook.com/ParentADHDAdvisor.

EIGHTEEN

Care Management:
Organize, Prioritize, Lead

by Gail Haun, RN, MS, CCM

At four years of age, Dylan had extreme Sensory Processing Disorder and still could not speak at all. When over-stimulated, he looked quite autistic. He could gesture some and made great eye contact, and his parents were thankful that he could usually indicate what he wanted and that he was loving and protective towards his little sister. But this speech delay was frightening and they were throwing everything they had at it.

Dylan had three different speech therapists - one at school, one as part of an occupational therapy program, and another who worked with him privately. He had two occupational therapists to remediate his sensory processing issues. A chiropractor was adjusting Dylan and trying to help the family explore a gluten-free, casein-free diet. They were also consulting with a naturopath. An ABA therapist came to the home twice a week to teach Dylan important routines and help him build better communication skills. A LEAP acupressure specialist was trying to reset neurology through that modality.

On paper, it looked like the family had a thorough program in place, but problems were starting to emerge. Dylan hated the sessions that combined the Occupational and Speech therapies. It was unclear why, but he really hated them. Could there be any progress when he cried through every session? Running from one therapy to another was taking up every spare minute (and every spare dime – they were now borrowing money from relatives), and the whole family was feeling exhausted and frazzled. The marriage was strained as both parents questioned their choices at different times. Every therapist was giving it his best shot, but no one was talking to anyone else. Were some therapies working at cross purposes? And, worst of all, Dylan was burning out. He was increasingly irritable and fussy whenever they got in the car...and it seemed as if they were always getting in the car.

The family met with me, seeking a better understanding (and possibly a singular diagnosis) to help put a structure to these therapies. Would a diagnosis help direct the choices they made? I worked with the family to pare down to the essential and most useful therapies. I recommended some lab work to determine if there was clear evidence for eliminating foods *and which foods those should be. They enrolled Dylan in a private preschool for children with special needs. All occupational and speech therapy would be provided there five days a week and therapists were in constant contact with each other. Chiropractic visits were cut back, but the family became more exacting with the foods he was allowed. They had more mental energy to keep track of this and to convince grandparents to follow the plan. LEAP acupressure was kept bi-monthly as it was not very often and seemed to be clearly beneficial. They began hippotherapy and Dylan loved it. Finally, he was happy to get back in the car and they began to see slow, but steady, progress. The family felt they finally had a clear manageable plan that was comprehensive enough to meet Dylan's needs. ~ Robin McEvoy, neuropsychologist*

The Basics

Having a child with multiple issues affects the whole family. As a care manager, I see many families who, in an effort to ensure their child's progress, start throwing in therapies and treatments based on every article or piece of advice they see. Every therapist may say his work is critical, so parents have a hard time knowing what to pare down. Anxiety can lead a parent to rush from one place to another, afraid of missing the most critical component of her child's care. It can be challenging to keep things streamlined, but still effective.

Your child may need multiple therapists – speech, occupational, learning specialist, nutritionist, psychiatrist, etc. Who decides what is necessary and then coordinates care? In the medical field, care managers do this job. In schools, there are often special education case managers who coordinate the Special Education aspects. Care managers are responsible for coordinating the larger picture, organizing care so that treatments and medications do not work against each other or the sum total of treatment at any given time is not too much for the child to handle. She also keeps everyone talking to each other, in order to ensure the most effective coordinated care possible.

However, care management is not nearly so standard in the field of child development. Who gets the job of coordinating complex care needs? Parents, of course. I acknowledge that this can be confusing and stressful job. But there are many resources that can help a parent access care, find support, and build the skills necessary find their way through this process.

This chapter will give you a template for moving forward in a way that will maximize results while lowering your child's stress level, lessening the impact on your family and wallet, and keeping you sane.

Start with the Big Picture

The first part of any plan is what you are probably doing right now. Find out as much as you can about what's happening for your child. You will need a complete diagnosis (see Chapter 3: Evaluations) and possibly some other types of assessments, such as sensory or biomedical. Use the checklists in this book to help you determine which evaluations seem pertinent. Do further research on your child's issues.

Once you know *what* you're addressing, figure out *how*. Examine the treatment options in this book, follow leads that your diagnostician gives you, obtain referrals from other parents, choose and meet a range of practitioners, see who you feel comfortable with, and make sure you understand what they do. Talk to your child's school and, if necessary, begin the process of arranging alternate learning plans, classroom modifications, and school-based therapies. (See Chapter 17: Advocacy in the School System.)

What Are You Coordinating?

Make sure you know all the pieces of your child's puzzle. This list summarizes how many pieces might possibly be in the treatment puzzle at any given time.

- Medical
  - Pediatrician
  - Specialist physician provider (ENT, neurology, cardiology, GI, Functional medicine)
  - Psychiatrist
  - Pharmacist*
  - Care manager (nurse or social worker)
- Behavioral/Social
  - Applied behavior therapist
  - Psychologist
  - Other counselors/therapists
- School resources
  - Special education teacher
  - Primary teacher
  - Speech/language therapist
  - Occupational therapist
  - Social worker
  - School psychologist

- Principal
- School nurse
- Paraprofessionals working with your child
- Private therapists
  - Occupational therapist
  - Speech/language therapist
  - Learning specialists and tutors
  - Social skills therapists or groups
  - Dietician or nutritionist
- Complimentary and alternative care providers
  - Acupressurist
  - Chiropractor
  - Naturopath
  - Massage therapist
  - Craniosacral therapist
  - Vision therapist

Pharmacist as Resource
Most people think of pharmacists as people who just hand out your meds at the drug store, but in fact they can be a wonderful resource – especially if it is difficult for you to make a separate appointment with your doctor just for a conversation. If your child seems to have accumulated a number of prescriptions (I often see this with kids with AD/HD in particular), and you want to make sure there are no contraindications, you might try talking to your pharmacist. They have extensive training in drug content and interaction, and can provide you with thorough, up-to-date information. Make an appointment and take advantage of this local, free resource.

Assembling Your Team

Keep the following considerations in mind when choosing practitioners:

- First and foremost, find someone your child responds to positively. Assuming that all of your candidates are qualified, choose the one that your child will look forward to seeing (and that you, too, can deal with for the next indeterminate amount of time).
- Consider which practitioners might be your "go-to sounding boards." Yours is always the final say, but that doesn't mean you can't have support and resources. One or two members of your team should be able to help you sort through your choices and brainstorm when problems come up.
- You should be able to ask questions of any provider. Especially if you are care managing a complex situation involving many practitioners, you will need to ask more in-depth, comprehensive questions to support complete treatment. Make sure that

all specialists are open to this.

- To this end, find out *how* each specialist prefers to keep you informed. They may save a few minutes at the end of each session for discussion or be willing to set up regular phone check-ins. On occasion, you may need to make a separate appointment for more in-depth discussions.
- Can your team work together? Some therapists are very open to collaboration and appreciate the work of the other disciplines. Some people are more singular providers and prefer to work independently. This can be fine, but if a provider thinks that he is the definitive one-stop shop for a child with significant needs, you should probably move on.
- You can also ask your team of providers to meet with each other. This can be particularly helpful at school meetings, when developing goals that cross settings. In particular, services in speech/language, occupational therapy, and behavior therapy often work better when all therapists have consulted with each other.
- Your team members may not be able to provide this service by physically traveling to a meeting, but many families keep everyone in the loop through group emails or online conferences. Be aware that you will probably need to pay them for their time.
- Don't hesitate to let go of a member of the team who isn't working out. I spend much of my time helping families find physicians or therapists who have more appropriate backgrounds, or who are simply more willing to listen and respect the family's needs. It's true that changing practitioners creates a whole other item on the to do list, but you will ultimately be better served by someone who communicates with you, has better rapport with your child, or whose treatment plan is more likely to be effective.

> ### Consolidate, Consolidate, Consolidate!
>
> If you feel you have accumulated a number of practitioners, reevaluate to see where you could consolidate. For example, if you have been seeing a naturopath, added a nutritionist, and are still seeing your pediatrician, a functional medicine doctor may be able to perform all of those roles. Or perhaps you could put some therapies on hold until after SPD has been addressed, since your child's nervous system will probably respond better after his nervous system has been strengthened anyway.
>
> However, some conditions may require you to see many practitioners at once in order to progress. In fact, certain conditions might not resolve if you take the philosophy of "one thing at a time." Consult with your team to see who understands the overall picture best and can help you determine priorities. Save yourself money and time by keeping your team as lean as possible, and always make sure you are not targeting too many areas at once.

Your Job Description

These tools and practices will help you keep your child's treatment plan going smoothly:

- **Keep good records.** Have an expandable file or 3-ring binder that has a section for each specialty. Keep practitioners' reports here, as well as your own notes. Other possible sections: bloodwork and medical tests, IEP information, diet changes and observed results, goals, and other potential therapies. (Also: Never give away your last copy of a report.)
- **Keep a brief overview, no more than two pages, of your child's history and treatment plans.** Most new practitioners will need some version of this. Briefly list your child's challenges, along with all past and current treatments in chronological order. Include the names and contact information of all practitioners.
- **Communicate, communicate, communicate.** You are the hub of this wheel. Communicate any progress or setbacks to all therapists. Keep a notebook to help you remember what you want to communicate. E-mail lends itself well to this.
- **Report across therapies.** If a child speaks more during occupational therapy, let the speech therapist know. If a child got red cheeks and had a tantrum after eating a highly dyed food, let *all* therapists know, particularly those who give food treats.

- ♀ **Monitor progress carefully.** Ask all practitioners for a few specific things you should be watching in your child. If your child does not seem to be responding, be vocal about it…but also be willing to be patient if the therapist says it is normal for substantive change to take a while.
- ♀ **Be realistic.** Consider what is realistic for your time, finances, and family life. Every time you are considering adding a new therapy, re-check the larger picture. Is there so much overlap that you could cut out something else? Is your child now so stressed trying to keep up with therapies and school that it's counterproductive? Although some challenges require simultaneous therapies, perhaps there is something you could cut, or at least cut back on, for now. Stay in touch with your team when trying to make these decisions.

Therapy Fatigue: What to Do When You Want to Quit

There can come a point when the strain (financial, emotional, time) on the family seems too much and you want to say, "We are done. She is who she is and we have to accept that." When everyone has therapy fatigue, it may be fine to take some time off and just be a family. Enjoy the summer. Pick things up in the fall (or vice versa). A therapy break can be enlightening for parents to see how the child progresses without therapies. Some children hold onto their learning curve; others will slowly lose ground. Some seem to benefit from the lack of pressure and "being fixed" all the time.

But for some of these complex kids, therapy is often a lifetime process. You will probably need to get back in there after the break. If your child plans to be college bound, you will have to maintain a long-term vision and see it all the way through – working with learning or vocational specialists by early high school in order to position your child for future success. Even professional athletes schedule in times when they don't train. Breaks may be necessary in order for your child to reach her ultimate goals.

Sometimes, *you* may be the one who needs the break more than your child. Honor that too! Caregiver strain is real. Make sure you plan in breaks for yourself so that you can continue to work effectively for your child. Plan regular weekend breaks for yourself if you can. In the summer, you can find summer camps appropriate for your child. Look into Easter Seals, which runs several camps for children with specific disabilities and sometimes offers reduced prices for those in need.

And Remember . . .

Your child has natural gifts and talents. Look for them and nurture them. Day after day, therapy is directed at building up the weaknesses. But parents and therapists should also routinely acknowledge and praise strengths, so that children also learn to appreciate and recognize their own gifts. Your child has already had to contend with challenges that most people never face. Persistence through those challenges often builds resilience, confidence, and valuable perspective.

My son had years of struggle, therapy, isolation, and more struggle before life finally started to come together for him. Years later, during his sophomore year in high school, I was worried about some difficult peer dynamics that were happening for him. Something I said one day showed him how concerned I was that he might withdraw again or revisit some of the dark places he'd inhabited when things were really rough. He looked at me with this sweet smile and said, "It's OK, Mom. After what I've been through, this is nothing." I realized then how much he had learned from his experiences – and that, much to my surprise and tremendous relief, he was actually out on the other side of it all. He is now in college, and seems to be one of those kids to whom people turn for kindness and support. He knows what it is to suffer, doubt, feel lonely and "weird"…he is incredibly compassionate and wise for one of his age. It didn't come without a price, but I think it is now one of his greatest strengths. ~ M.J.

Finding a Care Manager

There are some situations where you may be able to employ a professional care manager. For example, you would be lucky to find a clinic or private school that will address all or most of your needs in one place. You will then have built-in coordination. Professional care managers include:

- Nurses in the role of care managers within your insurance company - They can assist parents in identifying insurance benefits, as well as referral to various therapies and resources (even if they are not covered by insurance). These professionals provide support for complex or severe conditions or disabilities (e.g., autism).
- Providers in some child development clinics, particularly those within hospitals - This may be a physician, nurse, or other specialist who is assigned to support parents who need comprehensive services.

○ Educational consultants - Some educational advocates have the experience to help parents connect with and manage the school resources. Some also have the background to weigh in on private therapies. (See Chapter 17 on Advocacy in the School System, to find out more about these professionals.)

The Parent as Care Manager

When you, the parent, are the only care manager, there are certain advantages. You are at every appointment (or at least the most critical ones, if you share the role with another parent or a nanny). You see the impact of any individual therapy, good or bad. From your direct observations, you can tell if a therapy or a therapist is a good fit for your child and whether the therapy seems to be progressing. Most of all, you know your child better than anyone else and can assess his level of well-being, happiness, and stress.

Care Management Questions to Ask of Your Team Members

Here are some suggested questions to help you find the right practitioner for your child. Some are fairly open-ended, in order to elicit a broader range of answers. Other questions will reveal their usefulness when you talk to more than one practitioner, as their answers will vary by content and attitude. No matter how impressed you are by a person's credentials, try to look for one who answers your questions patiently, thoroughly, and respectfully. You and your child deserve to work with someone who will work cooperatively with both you and any other team members you assemble.

○ What do you charge for attendance at a team meeting?
○ Do you typically communicate with other practitioners/school when working with a child?
○ Do you have a team of people you typically work with that we could utilize for our child's care?
○ What releases do you require in order to speak with other providers?

ABOUT THE AUTHOR

Gail Haun, RN, MS, CCM, has served as a Director of Nursing in acute care hospitals. She went on to study the field of professional and personal life coaching to assist people to create and live the life of their dreams, with an emphasis on health and wellness. For the past six years, she has worked in one of the largest health care insurance companies as a certified nurse care manager. In this role she has served thousands of people across the country.

Don't Lose Sight of Your Child

by Marijke Jones

My whole life, I felt like I was being shuttled along this highway that everybody thought I needed to go down. It's like everyone thinks we all have to head down Route 5 to get to…wherever. So they do everything to make sure you get down flipping Route 5 somehow. But there are so many other ways to go! I didn't see a reason to even show up for my education – or my life, for that matter – until I found a whole other route that made sense to me. ~ K.H., age 22

We hope you've gotten ideas and hope from these chapters. You should now be armed with a better idea of what your child's issues might be, what resources are available, and how to navigate the whole *school* thing. We have tried to give you the tools to help you figure out your particular child's map, or at least the next few steps of it.

Now that you're loaded up on data, we'd like to come back around to the real reason for all of this: your child, and his or her needs as a *human being*, not just a learner.

Each of us who created this book has been there. We know what it's like, being parents of these kids. We get so busy trying to find answers that it takes up all our time and all the space in our heads. It's awful seeing our children suffer, so we knock ourselves out trying to figure out what the problem is and how to approach it. We line up assessments, therapies, tutoring, doctors, and more therapies. We buy books and do research online until one in the morning. Our families turn their lives inside out trying to make *something* work.

And sometimes, we get so caught up that we forget to check whether the child we are trying so hard to help is still in there somewhere. Is he invested in *any* of this? Is it even what he wants – getting "repaired" enough to be able to participate in a particular environment in a particular way? Is there somewhere in his life where he can come back to just being himself? Is he ever happy?

That seems so basic, but we know how easy it is to forget.

Raising these kids is hard, no question. It's a strange balancing act. On one hand, you have to steer the ship as hard as you can, keeping track of everything, figuring out the next step. Feeling like you're the one responsible for keeping this weird, uncharted journey on course only adds to the urgency. But you also need to check, sometimes, to ensure the ship is still heading for the right destination. Sometimes, you'll need to let go of your death grip on the wheel and rethink what the right destination really is. This might mean making a small adjustment; it might mean reconsidering your whole perspective. This can be scary. Believe me, we get it.

Note that we're not saying you should only do the things your child enjoys. Sometimes, everyone just has to do things that are not fun, in order to progress. But if they're not progressing – if it's starting to feel like you're making them bash their heads against the same brick wall, and the only change you see is their plummeting motivation – it might be time to take a step back.

Ultimately, the most necessary ingredient for success is this: your child needs to *want* to show up and participate in life, for his own reasons and in his own way. And he needs you to help him figure out what that even means, whether it involves finding a school where he can thrive, letting him follow his hobby more intensively, letting go of a normal-looking path altogether…they're all options. Be willing to take a deep breath, let it all go, really *look* at your child and ask: "Hey, are you OK in there? What do you need?" This could make the difference between a seriously shut down child and one who is ready to give it all one more try.

We'd like to leave you with a few last stories and perspectives. They demonstrate the power of children finding their own unique paths, as well as what all of this well-meaning effort can sometimes feel like to the child. Keep an eye out for the similarities in these stories; we see these themes all the time.

Many of these kids have similar needs. For one thing, they need the right environment for *them*, a place where they do not constantly feel like they are fish out of water and doing everything wrong. Feeling every day as if you are on the wrong planet simply is not an effective way to prepare for life. What are your child's strengths; what does he need in order to thrive? Can you find those elements somewhere? It may be worth a little investigation – and there are more and more options available besides private school.

Inspiring relationships, particularly with teachers or mentors (i.e., someone other than you, the parent), can also have a huge impact. Struggling kids need to connect with someone who makes them want to move forward, and who shows them that there is a way for them to be in the world, even if it isn't the way everyone else does it. These kids so often feel alone. Showing them that there are people out there who will be able to see and appreciate them can work wonders. Everyone needs to feel special and seen.

And finally, they need to see a reason for it all. They need some larger purpose for doing schoolwork and therapies and activities. It needs to mean something to *them*. Explaining why *you* think something is important, or telling them "this is just what you have to do," is not going to be enough over time. They need to have some skin in the game too. It's hard work, being fixed all the time. Just like the rest of us, they need a reason – their own reason – to keep showing up for it.

The good news is: The human spirit is pretty darn resilient. People inherently want to be fulfilled. Finding purpose can be a potent energizing force. It's still important to find answers and diagnosticians and good therapists. But remember to keep coming back to your child, too. Look your child in the eye and let him know you're there and will listen. Like most of us who have gone through this, you may have some trouble setting aside your own agenda and entering your child's world. But if you do, you may well be surprised and delighted at who you find.

Don't ask me what my diagnoses were, or what doctors I saw, or what grade I was in when I did what therapies. My mom would know. All I remember is being dragged around from doctor to doctor and getting a whole lot of therapy I didn't understand and getting pulled out of class for special ed stuff. It's kind of a blur.

I know that I wasn't talking at all by the time I was a year old. My older sisters spoke for me, so it took my mom a while to realize that I actually couldn't talk. I remember lots and lots of flash cards with a special ed teacher in kindergarten, because I was having so much trouble reading. I vividly remember struggling to read, to express myself in words, and to work with numbers. And I know that at some point in middle school, someone determined that I had APD, Auditory Processing Disorder. It was one of many labels I heard over the years, and the one that people decided was the "right" one.

As far as I was concerned, it was no more meaningful or helpful than any of the other

And Don't Forget about Play!

Remember also that *all* children need down time, unstructured play time, and time in nature. In fact, there has even been discussion amongst child development experts that we are increasing the rates of ADD-like symptoms and other problems by working so hard to get our children "ahead."

In American culture, we have tended to forget the importance of play, but it is critical for development of so many skills. Groundbreaking educator Maria Montessori claimed that "play is the work of the child." Play involves thinking, creating, sequencing, solving problems, resolving conflicts, and more. Yes, you can do all those things with math or school projects, but play is fun, open-ended, and often a more realistic approach to life than the more sterile classroom. Being able to play by oneself or with others is a critical life skill, and knowing how to have fun is a crucial part of life!

labels had been. For one thing, no one ever explained anything to me. Doctors and thera-pists talked to my mom, throwing around big words I didn't understand and telling her which therapies or skill development practices or whatever that I should do next. I did what I was asked to do, but never understood why. I'm sure it helped, but I never really felt like it made a difference. I felt too stupid to be in advanced classes, but was smarter than others in the special needs classes, so I was always bored and frustrated and confused.

In my whole therapy/special needs career, I had exactly one therapist who talked to me like I was a person and told me to believe in myself. She explained things in terms that made sense, connected and joked with me, and told me what she saw as my strengths. She made me feel special, not dumb. It made such a difference to have someone actually see me for me, not just as a collection of learning disorders. I am still in touch with her.

By high school, though, I had just kind of given up. I had tried really hard to get it right, and I was tired of trying and getting nowhere. By high school, the only thing I lived for was dance. I was happiest when I was moving; in dance class, I was alive, powerful, focused. When I performed, I felt proud and confident. My mom made me stop for awhile so I could concentrate on school more, and it was just a disaster. I fell apart and partied and got into trouble.

Then I did this 15-day backpacking trip with an outdoor education organization and it changed my life. For the first time, I felt like I understood what it meant to want to learn and that it could actually be fun. For those 15 days, I felt alive. Because we were outside and mov-ing, and because the things we were talking about were right in front of us, the lessons actu-ally made sense to me. My mom picked me up and was shocked. Usually when she asked me how my day was I'd say as little as possible – what was there to say? "I felt stupid again"? But this time I was passionate, joyful, and so excited about what I'd just done. I didn't shut up the whole way home. I knew I'd found something important. Before, I'd had no idea why I would ever go to college. Then I found this amazing world of outdoor education and I couldn't wait to get going!

I just graduated from college, with a major in – yes – outdoor education. Experiential edu-cation is definitely where it's at. I work with kids and adults with disabilities, and I see them happy and expressive in a way they didn't know they could be. I relate to how tired they are of not knowing why they are doing what they are doing. I understand how stressed they are, trying to fit in and jump through everybody else's hoops that don't even make sense to them. I get such joy helping them connect to life in a whole different way.

When I look back, it's kind of sad. I don't see a stupid girl so much as a confused one that no one really knew how to help. I'm so glad I found something that I'm excited about and good at. And when I have kids, they are definitely going to some awesome school where you can be outside and learn in a way that makes sense. It's just not necessary to suffer that much.

I think everyone has something they can do well and some way to learn that works. You just have to find it. ~ K.H., age 22

I grew up being told that success and happiness meant you made great grades, went to college, got an advanced degree, and landed a professional job. Then you had a family and made sure your kids were more successful than yourself. My kids threw all of it out the window. All of it. Grades, they said, don't reflect what they know, only what the teacher wants you to know. Success, they said, has nothing to do with achievement in school. Happiness, they said, was the opposite of what school asks of them daily. A lot of teenagers talk like this and I admit I was slow to take them seriously. I was gradually warming up to the idea of releasing my visions of elite college and instead – maybe – letting them attend state college. The kids, on the other hand, were talking about quitting high school altogether and striking out on their own. My goals and their goals were as different as a trip to the corner store is from a flight to Mars.

It took a long time for me to let go of my own very narrow concept of the paths that lead to success, and to accept that what success looks like for my kids will be vastly different from my own experiences and beliefs. The letting go was painful and terrifying. The hardest part was overcoming my fear about their future, ranging from "what if they don't go to college" to "what if they can't support themselves" and "what if they become homeless, or drug addicted or...?". When I started to see the world from my kids' points of view, I began to accept that their path, their vision of success and happiness, was galaxies away from mine, but just as meaningful and true. That was when our relationship changed, and I truly became an advocate for my kids.

Both of my sons are passionate about the performing arts. My older son finished high school early by taking a GED exam; he then moved to the West Coast to perform and work. My younger son chose to homeschool, following our school district's online program; he graduated at 16 and will attend a circus arts school. They are happier and more excited about life than I have ever seen them. Both of them are forging brand new pathways to destinations I can't even imagine. ~ Y.E., mother of two sons, aged 19 and 16

When I was a kid, I always had intense focus. I was quiet and I would find projects to work on in depth, for long stretches of time. I heard the word perfectionist a lot. Sometimes this fixation with certain projects meant running out of time for other things. In school, I struggled with the emphasis on quantity of work, and I often had trouble speaking up, especially in groups. Beginning in high school, my reservedness escalated into a bout of social anxiety that

left me unable to leave my own house for a little over a year.

A lot of people in my life spent a lot of time trying to convince me to do the things I couldn't do, as though the only reason I wasn't doing them was because I didn't feel like they were worth the bother. This happened when I was working "too slowly" and missing assignments, and it happened later when I started finding myself unable to face social situations.

I constantly had parents and teachers trying to explain to me all the reasons why I should do something (work faster, or go somewhere). Especially with the social anxiety, my family would tell me how much they wanted me to go, how much less fun they'd have without me, how much people would miss me if I didn't attend this or that. These tactics never made me any more able to do the things I struggled with. They just made me feel bad about it.

The more reasons I was given to work faster, the more it seemed like my perfectionism was a devastating weakness that would haunt me all my life. When I couldn't make it out the door to school or family functions, people would tell me how sad it made them, seeming to think it would coax me out of the house. The issue is that I never needed convincing. And piling on reasons only ever added weight.

The anxiety was something I was always going to have to deal with, but the depression wasn't a problem until people started laying on the guilt.

I did try medication for a while, but it didn't seem to make a difference. Getting off of it was a month and a half of hell for me and the whole family, though. Yay, meds.

I spent years listening to all the people who wanted to help – telling me that, not only was I more broken than I ever realized, but that it was hurting the people I loved. It told me that I should feel ashamed and I should feel guilty. And I did.

In spite of all the best intentions, finding constructive ways to be supportive and encouraging was something that took time and communication. Luckily, my family was willing to listen and make adjustments, and they have played a huge part in helping me successfully navigate my education and my life. ~ E.H., 21 years old

P.S. This young woman has just graduated from a college in London, UK, where she has spent many a break traveling around Europe. She has overcome obstacles (including not only leaving home, but leaving the country!) that would have been unthinkable for her only a few years ago. Since beginning college overseas, she has also spent a summer living and working in LA. Everything about the experience - having to react spontaneously to new opportunities, relocating, networking, and navigating chaotic work situations - challenged her, but she found her incentive to hang in there. No particular therapy or program helped her turn herself around. What she needed more than anything was time and a chance to work through her challenges in her own way.

These stories also illustrate something that can be all too easy to forget: your child will build her future on her strengths and passions, not her weaknesses. It is easy to focus on all the things you are trying to fix, especially since figuring that part out takes so much time and energy. But helping her recognize and cultivate her strengths is just as important. Not only will that help her be more invested in all the therapies; it is an essential part of her identity, her self-esteem, and the life she will eventually build for herself.

About the Editors

Kim Gangwish has been practicing in the fields of mental health and applied physiology for the last 18 years. Ms. Gangwish specializes in a form of acupressure that focuses on neurological integration, called LEAP (Learning Enhancement Acupressure Program). She works with both children and adults who have learning or sensory issues, or mild traumatic head injuries. Her passion for educating caregivers has led her to present at international health conferences, educational programs for school districts, and parent and adoption support organizations, where she emphasizes the importance of exploring underlying causal factors that contribute to learning and sensory issues. Being an adoptive mother herself, Ms. Gangwish is very active in the adoption community. She has written an ongoing column in Adoption Today magazine and founded a non-profit organization that supports adopted children and their families through an integrated team of therapeutic professionals. Ms. Gangwish runs her practice, The Life Enrichment Center, in both Louisville and Denver, Colorado. Kim is also the founder and CTO (Chief Technology Officer) of a biomedical company, Genovus Biotechnologies Inc., which is developing a peripheral neurostimulation device to help people with degenerative neuromuscular diseases. She lives in Louisville with her two sons and many animals. You can read more about her and her work at www.neural-integration.com.

Dr. Robin McEvoy is a developmental neuropsychologist practicing in Denver, Colorado. She evaluates and diagnoses a wide range of learning disabilities and learning needs in children, adolescents, and adults. She then works with the family to develop a treatment plan to remediate weaknesses and accentuate strengths. In addition to her private practice, Dr. McEvoy is an assistant professor at the University of Colorado Health Sciences Center. Although evaluation is the heart of her work, Dr. McEvoy also loves the educational process - speaking to parents, schools, or other health professionals about learning, development, and parenting in this new age where many learning and developmental challenges are more frequent.

Dr. McEvoy and her daughter, Tessa, have published a children's book, *Buddy: A Story for Dyslexia*. This book has a lovely endorsement from Dr. Sally Shaywitz, a leading authority in the field. Proceeds from the book are being used to fund reading remediation for low income children. You can find the book at www.learningmoxie.com.

You can read more about Robin McEvoy at her website www.robinmcevoy.com. She blogs about learning and learning challenges at www.learningmoxie.com. You can follow her on Facebook at www.facebook.com/DrRobinMcEvoy or on Twitter at twitter.com/RobinMcEvoy. She will try to be fascinating.

Marijke Jones got her BA from Cornell University, and finally settled down in Colorado after living in Japan and traveling throughout Asia and other parts of the world. She has been a copy and developmental editor for over ten years and has worked on a number of manuscripts, McGraw-Hill textbooks, website content, and other miscellaneous projects during that time. She has also published essays, mostly about her experiences raising, homeschooling, and trying to figure out her twice exceptional son. Ms. Jones is passionate about helping families with struggling children find answers and peace of mind. She believes that for each thing a child can't do, there is something amazing that he can do. A former therapist who specialized in trauma, she also believes that monitoring children's emotional and mental health is every bit as important as remediating their learning issues. She lives with her incredibly patient husband in Louisville, Colorado, where she enjoys the beautiful Rocky Mountains and all they have to offer. Occasionally, her two adult children come home from college or Europe or wherever they have been having more adventures than she has.